ACCELERATED FRENCH

Design, story line and Name Game
by

COLIN ROSE

Translation and Activations
by

MICHÈLE BATE
Department of French Studies, Reading University

and

ARTHUR MILLER
Oxford High School, Oxford

Front cover photograph R Lockyer/Image Bank ©
Memory Maps by Mick Davis
Line Illustrations by
Artset Graphics Ltd., Chesham, Bucks.,
Recorded by Post Sounds Studios Ltd.,
2/7 Springbridge Mews, London W5
Fretless Ltd., 27-37 Broadwick Street, London W1

Origination by Print Origination Southern Ltd.,
MM House, Sebastopol Road,
Aldershot, Hants.

Printed in Great Britain by Ashford Colour Press, Gosport, Hants.

©Accelerated Learning Systems Limited 1986

Accelerated Learning is a trade mark of Accelerated Learning Systems Limited

First Published in Great Britain 1986
Second Edition April 1989

Reprinted September 1989
Second Reprint December 1989
Third Reprint March 1990
Fourth Reprint October 1990
Fifth Reprint October 1991
Sixth Reprint May 1992
Seventh Reprint November 1992
Eighth Reprint November 1993
Ninth Reprint March 1996
Tenth Reprint March 1998
Eleventh Reprint March 2002

ISBN 0 905553 23 3

WELCOME TO

ACCELERATED FRENCH

There are a lot of new ideas in the Accelerated Learning Language Courses - so it 's a good idea to read THE SECRETS OF LEARNING A LANGUAGE first. It will explain what is in the course and why. It may seem like a lot of reading before you actually start learning your new language but the better you understand how to learn languages, the faster you will acquire this one!

Do:

1. Make a conscious effort to relax before each session.

2. Try out Section One of the Physical Learning Video,
   which follows.

3. Complete Act One.

4. Read through Part One of the Name Game.

5. Move on to Act Two - even if you haven't mastered Act One.
   It's more interesting and productive to finish and then repeat
   the whole course than to repeat each Act over and over until
   you know it perfectly.

   Above all enjoy yourself - then the learning happens automatically!

Colin Rose
Course Designer

INTRODUCTION

Hello. Let me tell you something about your French course. It has been prepared on the principles of Accelerated Learning to enable you to gain a rapid and enjoyable introduction to French. When you have finished the twelve units, you will be able to understand and use French well enough for everyday travel, business and social situations.

Each unit contains a story and an exploitation section. We call the story sections 'Acts' because the course is contructed like a drama — with the characters using everyday language in practical situations, just as you will eventually need to do. You will hear each Act read in several different ways. The readings have been planned so that you will become completely involved in the learning process and also so that learning will be easy and enjoyable. The exploitation material will help you practise and activate the language contained in each Act.

Throughout the course, you will study the important scenes in dialogue form. You will learn to handle simple situations that you are likely to experience in France. This will be done in easy stages, first by listening to the story, then by repeating some simple phrases in the pronunciation exercises and the dialogues, and finally by speaking for yourself on occasions like the ones you've met earlier in the unit. You will also find explanations of the grammatical structures you've been practising.

The story takes place mostly in Paris, a city well-known for its romantic atmosphere in the Spring, particularly in the small colourful streets on the left bank on the river Seine. But you will also visit the Château of the Fontainbleau and picnic in the nearby forest loved by French painters, before catching the plane to Geneva for the surprise ending.

The story begins with our young hero, Philip West, arriving in Paris. He has been asked to deliver a package to a certain Monsieur Dubois. He calls at M. Dubois' house, meets the beautiful Jacqueline, M. Dubois' niece, and hands over the package to her. Jacqueline asks Philip to come back to meet her uncle the next day and Philip goes off to spend the night in a nearby hotel where Jacqueline has already booked a room for him.

Read the English text of the first Act. You will subconsciously begin to pick up some of the French in your peripheral vision. Now switch on the tape until you are familiar with the English text. You can relax and follow either French or English in your book and listen for the intonation and rhythm of the French language.

So off you go! **Bonne chance!** Good luck!

THE FRENCH LANGUAGE NAME GAME

Almost everybody likes games and puzzles. As part of your Accelerated Learning Course let us introduce you to a fascinating game. It is a game with a very valuable payoff.

At the end of the **Name Game** you will be able to see the meaning of a worthwhile proportion of the entire French language without consciously trying to learn a single word!!! Just treat the language like a fascinating but easily soluble puzzle. But first let us give you three very simple and apparently unrelated puzzles:-

1.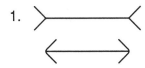

Q.   Which horizontal line is the longer?

A.   They are both the same. Sometimes things only look different superficially.

2.   2 6 10 14 18

Q.   What is the next figure in the sequence?

A.   22. Because there is a principle involved. Once you know the principle you can work out hundreds of similar puzzles. Working out the <u>principle</u> is always more efficient in time and effort than learning thousands of individual facts.

3.   BOOK — FILM

Q.   Can you change **BOOK** into **FILM** by just changing one letter at a time? Each new word must make sense.

A.
<u>BOOK</u>
TOOK
TOOL
TOLL
TILL
FILL
<u>FILM</u>

The principle involved is that quite small individual changes can add up over time to a big change. And that is what happens to languages over the centuries.

The purpose of these little games is to show that after you have played even once, you can solve any similar puzzle in the future because you know the principle involved.

Well, you can play just such puzzle games with the French language.

The central point to realise is that the French language was not invented word by word on a random basis. It has evolved over the last 2,000 years in quite a logical way — just as English has evolved.

And here is the good news:-

A large portion of English and French have evolved from the same language. The original single language was Latin. So in a real sense English and French are like dialects of each other. The fact that they do not always look alike at first sight is partly because even our own language has changed substantially over time, and partly because English actually has two roots — the Indo-Germanic and, of course, Old French which itself descended from Latin. This double origin accounts for the fact that English is a very rich language — there are very often two words in English that essentially mean the same.

The 'posh' word will descend from Latin, via Old French, which was for centuries the language of the Court and of diplomacy. The more basic word will have come from Germanic .

An example would be 'aspire' and 'hope'. The French for 'to hope' is **espérer**, the German is **hoffen** where the **f** sound in German has been modified over the years to a 'p' sound in English.

Now, as you would expect, over the 1,500 year period in which the two dialects, French and English, developed, these two words, to aspire and **espérer**, are certainly not the same — but you can obviously see the association and the most important single principle of Accelerated Learning is association. When you associate two items together — one that is new, one that you already know — you have formed the basis of strong memory.

Incidentally, as you might have begun to suspect, the French for 'accelerate', (a 'posh' word in English), is **accélérer** and the French for 'association' is indeed **association**. The second most important aspect of Accelerated Learning is that it is easier to learn one basic principle that can apply to hundreds of future situations, than tediously learn each new individual example.

So the **French Name Game** we shall play is this. We will first give you a French sentence. Then the English translation. Your task is to puzzle out, (sometimes with a clue, sometimes without), the principle involved. Then we will give you some examples of how the principle works in practice.

We believe if you read through the **French Name Game** before you start the full taped course you will benefit a lot. And we really do mean just read it through and play the game. It is absolutely <u>NOT</u> necessary to solemnly try to learn any of the principles at all.

Then, perhaps after Act Four, you should read through the **French Name Game** again. It will mean even more to you then. After that you should keep this name game section near you and when you get to a new word that really looks different — try to see what principles are involved and, therefore, try to form an association with a familiar English word.

Once you have seen the association — then you have created the basis of a firm memory in your long-term memory store.

In this simple and undemanding way, you will not only learn a lot of French but gain a fascinating insight in how it evolved.

<u>CAUTION</u>   This **Name Game** is an optional extra and a fun way of acquiring information and familiarity with written French that we think is valuable. If at any stage you feel you would prefer to leave it, to get 'stuck into' the recorded course, please do so.

<u>French</u>	<u>English</u>

A. **Le professeur est intelligent.**   The professor is intelligent.
      La duchesse est élégante.   The duchess is elegant.

<u>Principles</u>

These little sentences have a surprising amount of information packed in them for you.

(a)   **Le** is, as I am sure you know, a way of saying 'the'. So is **la**. In common with almost every European Language, other than English, French has masculine and feminine words, i.e. gender. It is surprising how fast you begin to relate which is which — but remember our main aim is to <u>communicate</u> and, saying **le** occasionally when you should say **la**, is hardly a major problem when you are just starting French.

(b)   **est** = is. From this you will see that the English and the French make up sentences in a very similar way.

<u>Principle 1</u>

(c)   Intelligent is an identical word in English and French. **Professeur** and **duchesse** are almost identical to the English.

So the first major principle is one to give you a fabulous start — there are literally thousands of French words that are identical in English, and thousands more that are almost identical (in fact the French for identical is . . .**identique**!).

Here, to give you a fast start, are just a few:-

<u>identical</u>	<u>nearly identical</u>
le document	**chocolat**
le fruit	**mariage**
le train	**riche**
le plan	**agréable**
l'idiot	**la visite**
le kilomètre	**la différence**
pardon	**salade**
la fascination	**valide**
la fatigue	**idiome**
la table	**arriver**
bizarre	**réserver**
le service	**le fantôme**
la gratitude	**personne**
gratis	**identité**
la tenure	**passeport**
le tennis	**entrer (enter)**
le café	**la toilette**
la place	**extraordinaire**
la queue	**famille**

normal	gratuit
minute	payer
le chèque	heure (hour)
le vase	fleur (flower)
	tulipes
	les tomates
	la banque
	musique
	oncle

IMPORTANT   As we have pointed out English and French can be said to be a little like distant dialects of each other, so whilst the words may <u>be</u> identical — they are not necessarily, or even often, pronounced the same. However, this section of the Accelerated Learning Course is designed to get you familiar with the <u>sight</u> of French, and let you actually see how the language has evolved by treating it as an interesting game.

In the Accelerated Language Course proper you will have plenty of opportunity to hear and absorb the distinctive rhythm and 'music' of the French language.

Still other words are identical because they actually <u>are</u> French words which we have borrowed — in the same way as the French have borrowed from English e.g . **le weekend** and **le marketing**.

Here is a further list of French words you probably didn't know you knew!

attaché	au revoir	abattoir	avalanche	abandon
bureau	barrage	brochure	brunette	buffet
camouflage	coquette	croissant	coiffure	chic
dépôt	débris	délicat	délicatesse	démarcation
escargot	endurable	endurance	ensemble	ennui
famé	familial	farce	fatal	gourmet
gastronome	général	hémisphère	hésitation	incarnation
inexplorable	inepte	hôtel	jaguar	jade
jamboree	jasmin	kilo	kaléidoscope	kiosque
mirage	maisonette	mousse	marquis	motel
nuance	nitrate	nimbus	nomination	noblesse
nonchalant	nonpareille	nihilisme	prétention	paquet
préjudice	précis	profil	profit	routine
raconteur	risque	restaurant	rendez-vous	silhouette
soufflé	salvation	terrasse	tirade	tolérant
terrible	terminal	thérapie	torrent	tourist
valise	vassal	western	warrant	lauréat
latent	uniforme	ultra	union	valet

B. **L'auteur a un téléphone.**
The author has a telephone.

Now, this deceptively simple little sentence is absolutely jam-packed with information to enable you to see behind the apparent differences between French and English and into their common origins.

Can you deduce the principles involved?

Principle 2

1. The **l'** is only a shorthand way of **le auteur** — as we often say he's or it's for he is/it is. So you would say **l'hôtel** and **l'express**.

2. **Auteur** is an interesting word. If you analyse it you might conclude correctly that:-

    (a) The French do not have a 'th' sound in the language. (Those very few words that do contain 'th'— like **théâtre** are pronounced tay a̲ tre.)

        So it is:

thé	tea (pronounced tay)
théorie	theory (pronounced tayoree)
autre	other
autorité	authority

    (b) **eur** is associated directly with the English '-or/-er' endings which denote a 'doer'.

        So it is:

vendeur	seller or vendor
directeur	director
professeur	professor
instructeur	instructor
chanteur	singer or cantor
compositeur	song-writer
artilleur	gunner

(c) Whereas **le** and **la** mean 'the', the French for 'a' or 'one' is **un** or **une**.

(d) **Téléphone** indicates that there are many words that are the same or nearly the same in English and French except for the French practice of using accents. You will learn the effect of these accents later. Meanwhile here is a list of the sort of words we mean:-

opéra	opera
pêche	peach
théologie	theology
théâtre	theatre
vanité	vanity
conservé	preserved
l'hôtel	the hotel
pâté	pate

The last two words are interesting. They contain an ∧ accent (which is called a circumflex). This accent very often shows that long ago there was an 's' after the vowel containing the ∧ accent.
Let us see:

La ville a une fête.
The town has a fete.

Can you deduce the associate word for **fête**? It is feast.
Try the principle of ∧ = missing 's' on the following words:-

la bête noire	literally black beast
l'hôtel	hostel
l'hôte	the host
pâté	paste
cloîtres	cloisters
forêt	forest
mât	mast
maître	master
intérêt	interest
honnête	honest
crête	crest
hôpital	hospital
arrêter	to arrest
île	isle

C.   **Le matelot quitte la barque après le voyage.**
     The sailor leaves the ship after the journey.
     <u>Principle 3</u>

     A lot of French words are recognisable and translatable if you remember to look for an
     <u>association</u> with either a posher word or a more specialist word.

     So we certainly understand that **quitter** means 'leave' but in English 'to quit' is used in a
     rather specialist sense. Similarly 'voyage' is really now restricted to a sea journey — but is
     generally used in French for any journey.

     See if you can find the meaning of the following using this principle:-
     Play the game by covering up the right-hand column.

		<u>Associate Word</u>
en retard	late	retard
fumer	to smoke	fume
le domaine	home	domain
désirer	to wish/want	desire
regarder	to look	regard
appellations	names	appellate
grossir	to grow larger	gross
pouvoir	to be able	power
lever	to raise	levitate/lever
tout	all	total
secours	help	succour
gagner	to win	gain
pied	foot	pedicure
savoir	to know	savvy
règle	rule	regulation
semblant	appearance	semblance
sembler	to appear	resemble
sucre	sugar	sucrose
médecin	doctor	medical man

D.   **Il a une raison claire d'employer le mécanicien.**
     He has a clear reason to employ the mechanic.

     Clair comme le jour.
     As clear as daylight.

     Here is another sentence jam-full of principles to speed you into French.

     Let us look at **claire** and **raison**.

Principle 4

As could be expected from languages that are effectively distant dialects of each other, vowel sounds do change over the centuries.

The principle does not end with the gradual transformation of **ai** into 'ea'. You will find many others. Here is a fascinating list of 'mutilated' vowel sounds that will make literally thousands of French words recognisable to you at first sight.

(1) | **raison** | reason | **faible** | feeble/weak |
| **saison** | season | **aigle** | eagle |
| **plaisir** | pleasure | | |

Conclusion: **ai** can become 'ea' or **ai** can become 'ee'

(2) | **beauté** | beauty | **cri** | cry |
nécessité	necessity	**emploi**	employment
facilité	facility	**tranquillité**	tranquility
qualité	quality	**liberté**	liberty
spécialité	speciality	**anxiété**	anxiety
parti	party	**joie**	joy

Conclusion: **é** can become 'y' or **i** can become 'y'

(3) | **mouvement** | movement | **coûter** | to cost |
| **gouvernement** | government | **pouding** | pudding |
| **ouverture** | overture | **pouls** | pulse |

Conclusion: **ou** can become 'o' or **ou** can become 'u'

(4) | **abondance** | abundance | **nombre** | number |
encontrer	encounter	**annonce**	announcement
profond	profound, deep	**plonger**	dive, i.e. plunge
compte	count	**oncle**	uncle

Conclusion: **o** can change to 'ou' or **o** can change to 'u'

(5) | **nécessaire** | necessary | **sommaire** | summary |
| **littéraire** | literary | | |

Conclusion: **aire** = ary

| (6) | **victoire** | victory | **gloire** | glory |
| | **histoire** | history | **laboratoire** | laboratory |

Conclusion: **oire** = ory

(7)	**naturel**	natural	**marchandise**	merchandise
	actuel	actual	**marchand**	merchant
	officiel	official	**marmelade**	marmalade
	artificiel	artificial	**embûche**	ambush
	par	by (originally per!)		

Conclusion: **e** can be 'a' but also **a** can be 'e'!!

(8)	**en**	in	**chimique**	chemical
	entre	between (inter)	**chimie**	chemistry
	permettre	permit		

Conclusion: **e** can be 'i' . . . but also **i** can be 'e'

| (9) | **seul** | only (sole) | **langueur** | langour |
| | **heure** | hour | **fleur** | flower |

Conclusion: **eu** = o or 'ow' sound

This has been such a long section you have probably forgotten the original sentence!

The other point you probably noticed is that the order of words **raison claire** was strange to the English ear. It is because the French want to stress the main object of attention first and then let the descriptive word follow it. You probably already instinctively know this from phrases like:

le coq d'or   (the cockerel of gold)   i.e. the golden cockerel
le moulin rouge   (the windmill red)   i.e. the red windmill

Actually it is more logical because, although we say 'she has a black cat', the cat is the most important idea in our minds — the fact that the cat is black is of secondary importance. You will see the word order in action when you start the Accelerated French Course proper.

Incidentally the French for 'a black cat' is **un chat noir.**

If you are getting into the spirit of this French Name Game you will be asking whether there is a principle that **ch** in French can be 'c' in English?

There is!

So:

charpentier	carpenter	**chandelier**	candlestick
chat	cat	**chaton**	catkin
chanter	to sing (as in cantor or cantata)		

E.   **Les émeraudes sont précieuses.**
The emeralds are precious.

Again we have a sentence with two helpful principles built into it.

<u>Principle 5</u>

To put something into the plural in French you normally add an 's'.

So it is:

Les maisons sont grandes.
The houses are large.

Les tables sont noires.
The tables are black.

Les jupes sont propres.
The skirts are clean.

An **x** in French can associate very precisely with 'c' in English as the following sentence should show.

Le prix de la chemise est cher.
The price of the shirt is dear.

Just as:
prix	price
choix	choice
voix	voice
paix	peace (remember **raison** = reason)

A final **eux** can also indicate not a plural but the direct equivalent of the English 'ous' or 'ish'.

You will have little difficulty, therefore, in recognising:

sérieux	serious
amoureux	amorous
envieux	envious
rigoureux	rigorous
merveilleux	marvellous
douloureux	grievous
malicieux	mischievous
vigoureux	vigorous
spiritueux	spirituous

Principle 6

Quite a lot of French words with **u** in them can be recognised if you know that this sound has sometimes to be transmuted into 'l' in English.

saumon	salmon
paume	palm
baume	balm
cruauté	cruelty
aussi	also
faucon	falcon
chaudron	caldron
émeraudes	emeralds

INTERLUDE

You will, of course, be familiar with the French word **château**. You also know it means castle. If you take the last few principles you will see a fascinating example how English has developed from old French.

ch	**ât**	**eau**
↓	↓	↓
c	ast	le

i.e.   **ch** has hardened into 'c'
      ^ indicates an 's' that has dropped out
      eau can be 'el' or 'le'.

In a real way we are seeing <u>into</u> the structure of the French language.

What animal do you think is **un chameau?**

If you said camel you are doing <u>really</u> well.

F.   **La peinture de la Joconde est un objet d'art.**
       The painting of the Mona Lisa is a work (object) of art.

     <u>Principle 7</u>

     The fact that **objet** means object does indicate that a number of French words have lost the 'c' that still exists in English before 't'.

     So it is:

objet	object
sujet	subject
rejeter	reject
en effet	in effect

     <u>Special Case</u>

     There is another important way in which you can see an immediate association between English and French.

     We are used to the specialist word **conduit** meaning a link. It fairly obviously relates to conduct. Well the missing 'c' in French suddenly makes all sorts of French words understandable.

So:

fait	fact
parfait	perfect
produit	product

N.B. Because the Name Game teaches you to <u>think</u> about your French language and see into it, the principle above can even help with two words that apparently have little association:

lait   milk

The link is **lact** — the basis of lactate. Again, if you look for a possible 'posher' word you may find an association that helps you remember.

<u>And association is the basis of Accelerated Learning</u>

Now we have introduced the subject of looking for a possible posh association, how about this sentence:

G.   **Je pense qu'elle porte une valise.**
I think that she carries a briefcase.

<u>Principle 8</u>

You can remember a lot of French words if you relate them to another associated but more 'latinised', i.e. posher, English word. See if you can guess the posh associate from the following list:

penser	to think	pensive
respirer	to breathe	respiration
donner	to give	donate
dormir	to sleep	dormitory/dormant
voir	to see	voyeur
porter	to carry	porter
dent	tooth	dental
visage	face	envisage
mort	death	mortal
libre	free	liberty
secours	help	succour
gagner	win	gain
hiver	winter	hibernate
fin	end	final

Here is an idea for a game of your own. Why not take the Glossary at the back of the Accelerated Learning Course and for just 10 minutes a day go through it seeing if you can figure out an English associate word from each new French word. It's fun.

H. **Ils sont charmants.**
They are charming.

Principle 9

The French equivalent of the frequent English ending -ing is **ant.**

So it is:

durant	during
menaçant	menacing
résultant	resulting
répondant	responding
flagrant	glaring
finissant	finishing

Finissant has another principle built into it. If you knew that **pousser** means 'push' and **finir** means 'finish' you may correctly conclude that **ss** in French is sometimes represented as 'sh' or 'th' in English.

The **ant** ending can also be used in a direct association with the English '-ent' as in:

résidant	resident
plaisant	pleasant
maintenant	at present. i.e. now or maintaining the current status

I. **L'école est grande.**
The school is large.

Principle 10

If you look at the words **école** and school they have little <u>immediate</u> similarity. But if we were to find that **épice** is the French for spice then a linguistic trend is becoming clear.

There are quite a few words in French that start with **e** where the English is 's'.

So it is:

épouse	spouse
épier	to spy (we still say espy)
épine	spine
écrire	to write (scribble is the link)
étrangler	to strangle
étranger	stranger
esprit	spirit
état	state

J. **La guerre — c'est horrifique!**
    War — it's horrific!

Principle 11

The easy principle of the two main areas exemplified is contained in the word **horrifique**.

The French equivalent of the English adjectives that end in 'ic' or 'ical' is **ique**.

So it is:

gymnastique	gymnastic
linguistique	linguistic
pratique	practical
publique	public
politique	political
électrique	electric or electrical
critique	critical
magnifique	magnific
fantastique	fantastic
comique	comical

Principle 12

At first sight there seems little association between **guerre** and 'war'. But there is. If you know that the French for wise was **guise** I think you would figure it out.

There are a few words where the French **g** has been transmuted into an English 'w' so **guêpe** is wasp and **guichet** is wicket.

Here are two more sentences packed with useful principles.

La chambre est dérangée.
The room is disordered.

Les voitures sont garées devant sa porte.
The cars are parked outside his door.

Principle 13

We have seen that **le** = 'the' and **la** also = 'the'. The difference is that you use **le** for masculine nouns, **la** for feminine nouns. If 'the' refers to several things (in the plural) then you must use **les**. The same principle extends to his or hers.

Consequently there are three ways of saying 'his'. **Son, sa** and **ses** depending on whether the word that follows is masculine, feminine or plural. So you would say **son père** (his father) but **sa femme** (his wife) and **ses enfants** (his children).

Now compare the words **sont garées** with the words **est dérangée** in the first sentence. The extra **e** in both cases indicates that **chambre** and **voitures** are feminine. The **s** in **garées** refers to the plural of the feminine **voiture**.

Now please remember you are not trying to learn any of this. You are simply reading it and absorbing it. You will assimilate this key grammar point automatically as we go through the stories in the book. However, if you have understood it — congratulations. It is just about as complicated as we will ever get.

Principle 14

By the way, you have now already indirectly seen the way the French put things in the past tense. So the verb is **déranger** — to disorder or disarrange. To say I have disordered is **j'ai dérangé.** In the same way 'I look' is **je regarde** and 'I have looked' is **j'ai regardé** or 'I speak' is **je parle** and 'I have spoken' is **j'ai parlé.** So **é** is the equivalent of 'ed' in English.

<u>Principle 15</u>

The final principle is simple enough, **arranger** is 'to arrange', **déranger** is 'to disturb' or 'to disarrange'.

You can often make opposites by using the prefix **dé**. In this way **dé** in French corresponds to 'de' or 'un' or 'dis' in English, hence:-

débander	to disband	**défavorable**	unfavourable
dégoûter	to disgust	**débarquer**	to disembark
débloquer	to release/free	**déloyauté**	disloyalty
débobiner	to unwind	**déplaire**	to displease
déboiser	to deforest	**dérouler**	to unroll
déboucher	to clear (unstop)	**désaccord**	disagreed
débourser	to disburse	**déboutonner**	to unbutton
décaisser	to unpack/uncase	**désagréable**	disagreeable
décamper	to decamp	**désapprouver**	to disapprove
déchaîner	to unchain	**désavouer**	to disavow
décharger	to unload	**dévoiler**	to unveil
décoller	to unstick	**désenchanter**	to disenchant
déshabiller	to undress	**décolorer**	to discolour
désillusionner	to disillusion	**décourager**	to discourage
découvrir	to uncover	**désobliger**	to disoblige
décrier	to decry	**désordonner**	to disorder
défaire	to demolish	**dévaluer**	to devaluate
(**faire** is to make)			

Well enough of the principles, we are now almost ready to start the Accelerated Learning Course proper. What we hope the **Name Game** has done, is to stimulate you to <u>think about</u> French, and see the fun to be had in treating it as a linguistic game. Don't read it passively — if you <u>actively</u> get involved you will learn FAST. How good are you at these linguistic games? Well, the following short section should tell!

Can You Figure Out The Association?

You know that a key to Accelerated Learning is associations. The stronger the associations the more vivid the memory and the easier it is to learn. If you figure the associations out for yourself you will have created the strongest possible memory link.

Here are some teasers. Find the linguistic link and you will help yourself see your way into the very heart of how French relates to English.

Play the game by covering up the English translation.

French	English	Linguistic Link
pauvre	poor	poverty/pauper
étoile	star	stellar
sang	blood	sanguine
jour	day	journal
travail	work	old English travail
plein	full	plenary (is a full assembly)
réver	to dream	reverie
trouver	to find	trove (treasure)
coucher	to sleep	couch (something to sleep on)
briller	to shine	brilliant

and now a tough one . . . . . .

pêcheur	fisherman	pescatorial, (i.e. pertaining to fish)

Remember ^ = missing 's'
and **ch** can be 'c'

As we have suggested before, why not go through the glossary at the back of the Accelerated French book every now and again and try to figure out if there is an association in a new word — there obviously isn't always!

Finally, here is a sentence which contains a fascinating example of how French and English verbs can develop in very similar ways.

Je prends un gâteau.
I take a cake.

We have seen that **prendre** means 'to take'. From the basic French verb has developed **entreprendre** meaning to undertake (a task). The French (and then English) in turn have derived the word 'entrepreneur' — someone who undertakes something.

In a similar way **apprendre** means 'to learn' or 'to take on', **comprendre** means 'to comprehend' or 'understand' — or again take on.

To say 'I have taken' is **j'ai pris**. Yes, I know you would logically have expected **j'ai prendé** but French has some irregular verbs as well as English! So just as it is 'I have taken' or 'I took' <u>not</u> 'I have taked' — so **j'ai pris** is correct.

The important point, though, is that this past tense enabled you to see other fascinating associations such as:-

l'entreprise	something undertaken
la surprise	something overtaken (by events)
compris	complete or taken with

WHAT DO WHEN THERE IS NO LINGUISTIC ASSOCIATION

Despite the fact that the Name Game section of the Accelerated Learning Course will make a signficant proportion of French words understandable to you from the beginning, there will clearly still be many words that simply do not have an English association. And we know that if there are no associations, it takes a lot more effort to create a lasting memory, i.e. to learn.

Now the whole point of the unique techniques built into Accelerated Learning is to maximise the chance of strong associations being formed quickly and easily in your mind. Hence the novel memory maps to create visual associations and thus memory. Hence the unique use of Baroque music to create sound/emotional associations and thus memory. Hence the emphasis on gesturing and acting out the scenes to create physical associations. Hence the use of games to involve you. Indeed involvement is the most powerful learning tool of all.

Despite this unique combination of memory aids, there will realistically still be words that are not easy to lock into your long term memory store.

When this happens take a tip from a professional memory man. Create your own 'mnemonic dictionary'. (Mnemonic merely means a memory aid and is described in full in the ACCELERATED LEARNING book.)

Creating a mnemonic dictionary is simple but it does require a little imagination. However, it is fun and we guarantee it works. Here's what to do.

Take the new French word and find a strong visual image to associate with it. The image should deliberately be as odd, comic, or bizarre (even vulgar!) as possible. If there is a rhyming association so much the better.

Let's take a look at a few examples of what you might do, taken from the lessons you are about to start on.

MNEMONIC DICTIONARY

Poisson — Fish

The prime principle of Accelerated Learning is the power of association — operating a memory link between the new and the already familiar.

So you might say to yourself:

'An old **poisson** can be poison.'

or better still:

Un poisson agé — c'est le poison.

An old fish — its poison.

How did I know the French for 'old' or 'poison'. Well old = **agé** is in the first lesson and I looked up poison in a dictionary. Learning a language is an exciting and <u>active</u> voyage of discovery and now I have learned two words instead of one.

Never mind that the sentence is extremely simple — you didn't begin your native language with sophisticated sentences. Getting started, with the simplest possible sentences, is the fun way to successful communication.

Of course, the artistically minded might be inspired to make a very visual link:

La Clé — The Key

Imagine having 'feet of clay' but using **la clé** to unlock (release) them! So in your mind's eye you would visualise holding a key between your toes.

Maintenant — Now

This is really an easy one — 'I am maintaining my mnenomic dictionary **maintenant** (now.').

Invest some of your own creativity in an association and you have created the basis of strong memory.

Le Monde — The World

How do you visualise the world — as a globe held up by Atlas? Was he 'fond of **le monde**'? You remember things that rhyme, that are comical (or vulgar!) or bizarre and especially that are visual.

Vite — Fast

The dictionary definition is fast or quick. But you could also say fleet. With what we have learned already I could visualise:

les pieds vites — fleet feet!

It is not our intention to give lots of examples here because a thousand different people will have a thousand different ways of making up their own 'mnemonic dictionaries'.

The point is to have fun and invest a bit of yourself in the ideas.

One last example. I was thinking of some French words that just 'look' awkward at first sight. An example would be **peut-être** — perhaps. But if you tried for the linguistic association first you will find a great example of how language does not evolve randomly, there is usually some logic behind it. Thus **peut-être** actually breaks down into:

peut — may

être — be

Neat isn't it?

POSITIVE THOUGHTS TO LEARN A LANGUAGE

We have chosen these sentences for you to learn.
Learn each Positive Thought (they are sometimes called affirmations)
and repeat them over and over to yourself. You are not only learning
your new language - you are helping to program your mind to become
a confident language learner!

1	French is interesting to learn	**Il est intéressant d'apprendre le français**
2	I am delighted at how much I understand	**Je suis content que je comprenne autant de français**
3	I can speak more and more	**Je peux parler de plus en plus**
4	I enjoy listening to the cassettes	**J'aime écouter les cassettes**
5	I am confident when I speak French	**J'ai confiance en moi quand je parle français**
6	I notice satisfying progress every week	**Chaque semaine je remarque un progrès satisfaisant**
7	Learning is easy	**Apprendre, c'est facile**
8	I like to read French	**J'aime lire le français**
9	I am proud that I am becoming a good French speaker	**Je suis fier de devenir quelqu' un qui parle très bien le français**
10	I tell myself I can, and I can	**Je me dis que je peux, et je peux**
11	I have faith in myself and my skills	**J'ai confiance en moi et mes compétences**
12	I have an ever-increasing vocabulary	**Mon vocabulaire est toujours en train d'augmenter**
13	I enjoy remembering French	**J'aime fixer le français dans ma mémoire**
14	I can quickly use my French	**Je peux vite utiliser mon français**

ACT I | ACTE 1
Scene I | Scène I

Philip arrives in Paris (Monday). | **Philip arrive à Paris (Lundi).**

Philip looks at the house. | **Philip regarde la maison.**
It is big and beautiful. | **Elle est grande et belle.**
Philip goes up to the front door. | **Philip s'approche de la porte d'entrée.**
He rings the bell and waits. | **Il sonne et attend.**
An old lady opens the door. | **Une dame âgée ouvre la porte.**

Mme Brossetout: What do you want, young man? | **Qu'est-ce que vous voulez jeune homme?**
Philip: Hello. | **Bonjour madame.**
Is this Mr Dubois' house? | **C'est ici la maison de Monsieur Dubois?**
Mme Brossetout: Yes it is. | **Oui, c'est ici.**
Philip: I have an appointment with Mr Dubois. | **J'ai rendez-vous avec Monsieur Dubois.**
Mme Brossetout: Who shall I say it is, please? | **C'est de la part de qui, s'il vous plaît?**
Philip: Mr West. | **Monsieur West.**
Mme Brossetout: Ah yes, Mr West. Please come in. | **Ah oui, Monsieur West. Entrez, s'il vous plaît.**
Philip: Thank you. | **Merci madame.**

Philip goes into the house. | **Philip entre dans la maison.**
Madame Brossetout calls Mademoiselle Dubois. | **Madame Brossetout appelle Mademoiselle Dubois.**

Mlle Dubois: Who is it? | **Qui est-ce?**
Mme Brossetout: It's Mr West. | **C'est Monsieur West.**

Scene 2 | Scène 2

Mademoiselle Dubois comes down the stairs. | **Mademoiselle Dubois descend l'escalier.**
She is tall and beautiful. | **Elle est grande et belle.**
She has blue eyes and black hair. | **Elle a les yeux bleus et les cheveux noirs.**
She smiles to Philip. | **Elle regarde Philip avec un sourire.**

Mlle Dubois:	Hello. Can I help you?	**Bonjour, monsieur. Vous désirez?**
Philip:	Hello. I've come from England and I've brought a package for Mr Dubois.	**Bonjour mademoiselle. J'arrive d'Angleterre et j'apporte un paquet pour Monsieur Dubois.**
Mlle Dubois:	What's your name?	**Comment vous appelez-vous?**
Philip:	My name's Philip West.	**Je m'appelle Philip West.**
Mlle Dubois:	Have you some means of identification? It is important.	**Vous avez une pièce d'identité? C'est important.**

Philip gives the young woman his passport.	**Philip donne son passeport à la jeune femme.**

Philip:	Here's my passport.	**Tenez, voilà mon passeport.**
Mlle Dubois:	All right, your name's Philip West and you're English.	**D'accord, vous vous appelez Philip West et vous êtes anglais.**
Philip:	Yes, that's right. I'm a student. I'm twenty three years old and I live in London.	**Oui, c'est ça. Je suis étudiant. J'ai vingt-trois ans et j'habite Londres.**
Mlle Dubois:	Good. I'm pleased to see you. Welcome to Paris. I'm Jacqueline Dubois. The package is for my uncle, Mr Anatole Dubois.	**Bien, je suis contente de vous voir. Bienvenue à Paris. Je suis Jacqueline Dubois. Le paquet est pour mon oncle, Monsieur Anatole Dubois.**
Philip:	Fine. Here's the package.	**Bon - tenez, voilà le paquet.**
Mlle Dubois:	Thank you very much.	**Merci bien.**
Philip:	Is that all?	**C'est tout?**

Mlle Dubois:	No. My uncle is coming back to Paris this evening. Come to the house tomorrow morning at ten. A room has been reserved for you for the night at the Hotel d'Angleterre, rue Bonaparte. It's a small hotel but it's comfortable.	**Non, mon oncle rentre à Paris ce soir. Venez à la maison demain matin à dix heures. Vous avez une chambre réservée pour la nuit à l'Hôtel d'Angleterre, rue Bonaparte. C'est un petit hôtel mais il est confortable.**
Philip:	Is it far?	**C'est loin?**
Mlle Dubois:	No. It's two hundred metres away. You go out of the house, you turn right and the rue Bonaparte is on the left.	**Non, c'est à deux cents mètres. Vous sortez de la maison, vous tournez à droite et la rue Bonaparte est à gauche.**

Je m'appelle Philip West.

Philip:	Thanks very much.	**Merci beaucoup.**
	Goodbye.	**Au revoir mademoiselle.**
Mlle Dubois:	Goodbye.	**Au revoir monsieur.**
	See you tomorrow.	**A demain.**

Scene 3   **Scène 3**

	Philip arrives at the hotel.	**Philip arrive à l'hôtel.**
	Mme Marat, the hotel-owner,	**Madame Marat, la patronne,**
	is at the reception desk.	**est à la réception.**

Mme Marat:	Good evening, sir.	**Bonsoir monsieur.**
	Can I help you?	**Vous désirez?**
Philip:	Good evening.	**Bonsoir madame.**
	Have you a room reserved	**Vous avez une chambre réservée**
	for Mr West?	**pour Monsieur West?**
Mme Marat:	Sorry? What name is it?	**Pardon? C'est à quel nom?**
Philip:	Mr West.	**Monsieur West.**
Mme Marat:	Is it a single room	**C'est une chambre pour une**
	or a double?	**personne ou pour**
		deux personnes?
Philip:	A single.	**Pour une personne.**
Mme Marat:	Ah yes, here we are.	**Ah oui, voilà.**
	You have room	**Vous avez la chambre**
	number seven.	**numéro sept.**
	It's a room with a	**C'est une chambre avec**
	bathroom.	**salle de bains.**
Philip:	Very good.	**Très bien.**
	Which floor is it on?	**C'est à quel étage?**

Mme Marat:	It's on the first floor.	**C'est au premier étage.**
	Here's the key.	**Voici la clé.**
Philip:	Thank you.	**Merci madame.**
Mme Marat:	Good night, sir.	**Bonne nuit monsieur.**
Philip:	Good night.	**Bonne nuit madame.**

SEPT
7
°Hôtel d'Angleterre

	Philip goes upstairs.	**Philip monte l'escalier.**
	He finds room	**Il trouve la chambre**
	number seven.	**numéro sept.**
	He opens the door and goes in.	**Il ouvre la porte et entre.**
	The room is nice	**La chambre est agréable**
	and quiet.	**et calme.**
	The bed is comfortable.	**Le lit est confortable.**
	Philip is tired but	**Philip est fatigué mais**
	happy.	**content.**

	'What an incredible day!'	**'Quelle journée extraordinaire!'**
	he thinks.	**pense-t-il.**

3

ACTE 1 (i)

Philip regarde la maison.

Philip s'approche de la porte d'entrée.

Il sonne et attend.

Une dame âgée ouvre la porte.

Philip entre dans la maison.

Qu'est-ce que vous voulez, jeune homme?

ACTE 1 (ii)

Mademoiselle Dubois descend l'escalier.

Elle regard Philip avec un sourire.

Bonjour, monsieur. Vous désirez?

Je m'appelle Philip West.

J'arrive d'Angleterre et j'apporte un paquet pour Monsieur Dubois.

Je suis étudiant J'ai 23 ans J'habite Londres

PHILIP WEST PASSEPORT

Tenez, voilà mon passeport.

Le paquet est pour mon oncle.

Venez à la maison demain matin à dix heures.

Vouz avez une chambre réservée pour la nuit à l'Hotel d'Angleterre.

C'est un petit hôtel mais il est confortable.

C'est loin?

Vous tournez à droite.

et la rue Bonaparte est à gauche.

RUE BONAPARTE

Philip arrive à l'hôtel.

7

Part Two : Pronunciation and Intonation
Section Deux : Prononciation et Intonation

a)   Making a statement in French:

Je suis angl*ais.*

b)   Asking questions:

Vous êtes angl*ais?*

Some examples:

1.   **C'est la maison de Monsieur Dubois?**
      Oui, c'est la maison de Monsieur Dubois.

2.   **Vous avez une chambre?**
      Oui, j'ai une chambre.

3.   **Vous êtes Philip West?**
      Oui, je suis Philip West.

4.   **Vous êtes anglais?**
      Oui, je suis anglais.

c)   The sound **a** as in Jacqueline:

1.   **Je m'appelle Jacqueline.**

2.   **J'habite Paris.**

3.   **Quatre rue Bonaparte.**

4.   **J'apporte un paquet.**

5.   **Vous avez un passeport?**

6.   **J'arrive à Paris.**

C'est la maison de Monsieur Dubois?

8

d)   The sound **oi** as in **Dubois**:

I.   **Monsieur Dubois.**

2.   **Voici la clé.**

3.   **J'ai vingt-trois ans.**

4.   **Elle a les cheveux noirs.**

5.   **Je suis contente de vous voir.**

6.   **Bonsoir mademoiselle.**

e)   Listen to the difference between these English and French words which
are very similar:

Paris / **Paris**   packet / **paquet**   passport / **passeport**
comfortable / **confortable**

Comptines:

I.   **Am stram gram**
Pic et pic et colégram
Bour et bour et ratatam
Am stram gram.

2.   **Dans la cour de chez Dubois**
Il y a sept oies:
Une oie, deux oies, trois oies,
quatre oies, cinq oies, six oies,
C'est toi!

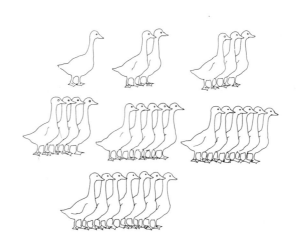

9

Part Three Section Trois
Functional Dialogues Dialogues Fonctionnels

I.

Philip arrives at
5 rue Madame in Paris.

**Philip arrive au
5 rue Madame à Paris.
Mme Brossetout = Mme B.**

Mme B:	What do you want?	**Qu'est-ce que vous voulez jeune homme?**
Philip:	Hello. Is this Mr Dubois' house?	**Bonjour madame. C'est ici la maison de Monsieur Dubois?**
Mme B:	Yes it is.	**Oui, c'est ici.**
Philip:	I have an appointment with Mr Dubois.	**J'ai rendez-vous avec Monsieur Dubois.**
Mme B:	Who shall I say it is, please?	**C'est de la part de qui, s'il vous plaît?**
Philip:	Mr West.	**De la part de Monsieur West.**
Mme B:	Ah yes, Mr West. Please come in.	**Ah oui. Monsieur West. Entrez, s'il vous plaît.**
Philip:	Thank you.	**Merci madame.**

2.

Philip introduces himself
to Mademoiselle Dubois.

**Philip se présente
à Mademoiselle Dubois.**

Mlle Dubois = Mlle D.

Mlle D:	Hello. Can I help you?	**Bonjour monsieur. Vous désirez?**
Philip:	Hello, I've brought a package for Mr Dubois.	**Bonjour mademoiselle. J'apporte un paquet pour Monsieur Dubois.**
Mlle D:	What's your name?	**Comment vous appelez-vous?**
Philip:	My name's Philip West.	**Je m'appelle Philip West.**
Mlle D:	Have you some means of identification?	**Vous avez une pièce d'identité?**
Philip:	Here's my passport.	**Tenez, voilà mon passeport.**
Mlle D:	All right, your name's Philip West and you're English.	**D'accord, vous vous appelez Philip West et vous êtes anglais.**
Philip:	Yes, that's right. I'm a student. I'm twenty-three years old and I live in London.	**Oui, c'est ça. Je suis étudiant. J'ai vingt-trois ans et j'habite Londres.**
Mlle D:	Good. I'm pleased to see you. Welcome to Paris.	**Bien, je suis contente de vous voir. Bienvenue à Paris.**

3.

	Philip is phoning a friend in London. He talks about Jacqueline.	**Philip téléphone à une amie à Londres. Il parle de Jacqueline. Une Amie = Une A.**

Une A:	Does she live in Paris?	**Elle habite Paris?**
Philip:	Yes, she lives in a big house.	**Oui, elle habite une grande maison.**
Une A:	Beautiful?	**Elle est belle?**
Philip:	The house?	**La maison?**
Une A:	No, Jacqueline.	**Non, Jacqueline.**
Philip:	Oh yes! She's got blue eyes and black hair.	**Oh! oui. Elle a les yeux bleus et les cheveux noirs.**
Une A:	Is she young?	**Elle est jeune?**
Philip:	Yes, she's twenty-two.	**Oui, elle a vingt-deux ans.**

4.

	Jacqueline is booking a room at the hotel for Philip West. **Jacqueline = J.**	**Jacqueline réserve une chambre à l'hôtel pour Philip West. Réceptionniste = R.**

J:	Hello.	**Bonjour monsieur.**
R:	Hello. Can I help you?	**Bonjour mademoiselle. Vous désirez?**
J:	Have you got a room for one night, please?	**Vous avez une chambre pour une nuit, s'il vous plaît?**
R:	Yes. A single or a double room?	**Oui. Une chambre pour une ou deux personnes?**
J:	A single room, please.	**Une chambre pour une personne, s'il vous plaît.**
R:	What's the name, please?	**C'est à quel nom, s'il vous plaît?**
J:	It's for Mr Philip West.	**C'est pour Monsieur Philip West.**
R:	I've got room seven on the first floor.	**J'ai la chambre numéro sept au premier étage.**
J:	Good. Thank you.	**Bien, merci.**

5.

	Philip arrives at the hotel.	**Philip arrive à l'hôtel. Mme Marat = Mme M.**

Mme M:	Good evening, sir. Can I help you?	**Bonsoir monsieur. Vous désirez?**
Philip:	Good evening. Have you a room reserved for Mr West?	**Bonsoir madame. Vous avez une chambre réservée pour Monsieur West?**
Mme M:	Sorry? What's the name?	**Pardon? c'est à quel nom?**
Philip:	Mr West.	**Monsieur West.**

Mme M:	Ah yes. Here we are.	**Ah oui, voilà.**
	You have room seven.	**Vous avez la chambre numéro sept.**
	It's a room with	**C'est une chambre avec**
	a bathroom.	**salle de bains.**
Philip:	Good.	**Très bien.**
	Which floor is it on?	**C'est à quel étage?**
Mme M:	It's on the first floor.	**C'est au premier étage.**
	Here's the key.	**Voici la clé.**
Philip:	Thank you.	**Merci madame.**
Mme M:	Goodnight, sir.	**Bonne nuit monsieur.**
Philip:	Goodnight.	**Bonne nuit madame.**

Part Four : Personalised Dialogues
Section Quatre : Dialogues

a) You are visiting Madame Dupont for the first time. An old lady has answered the door-bell.

Dame:	**Qu'est-ce que vous voulez?**
Vous:	(Say hello and ask if this is Mme Dupont's house.)
Dame:	**Oui, c'est ici.**
Vous:	(Say you have an appointment with Madame Dupont.)
Dame:	**C'est de la part de qui?**
Vous:	(Give your own name.)
Dame:	**Ah oui. Entrez, s'il vous plaît.**
Vous:	(Say thank you.)

b) You are introducing yourself to Madame Dupont who is expecting you but who has never seen you before.

Mme Dupont:	**Comment vous appelez-vous?**
Vous:	(Say your name.)
Mme Dupont:	**Vous arrivez de Londres?**
Vous:	(Say which town you have come from.)
Mme Dupont:	**Vous avez une pièce d'identité?**
Vous:	(Give her your passport and point out your name and nationality.)
Mme Dupont:	**Vous êtes étudiant/e?**
Vous:	(Say yes and add how old you are.)
Mme Dupont:	**Bien. Je suis contente de vous voir. Bienvenue à Paris.**
Vous:	(Say thank you.)

c) You are talking to a friend about Jacqueline.

Amie:	**Elle est anglaise?**
Vous:	(Say no, she is French.)
Amie:	**Elle habite Londres?**
Vous:	(Say no, she lives in Paris.)
Amie:	**Elle est belle?**
Vous:	(Say yes and describe the colour of her eyes and hair.)
Amie:	**Elle est jeune?**
Vous:	(Say how old she is.)

d) Booking a room at an hotel.

Hôtelière:	**Bonjour. Vous désirez?**
Vous:	(Say hello and ask if she has a room for one night.)
Hôtelière:	**Une chambre pour une ou deux personnes?**
Vous:	(Say a single room.)
Hôtelière:	**C'est à quel nom?**
Vous:	(Give your name.)
Hôtelière:	**J'ai la chambre numéro quinze.**
Vous:	(Say thank you and goodbye.)

e)   Checking in at the hotel.

Hôtelière:	**Bonsoir. Qu'est-ce que vous désirez?**
Vous:	(Say good evening and ask if she has a room booked in your name.)
Hôtelière:	**Pardon? C'est à quel nom?**
Vous:	(Repeat your name.)
Hôtelière:	**Ah oui. Vous avez la chambre numéro quinze.**
Vous:	(Ask which floor it is on.)
Hôtelière:	**C'est au premier étage.**
	Voici la clé.
Vous:	(Say thank you and goodnight.)

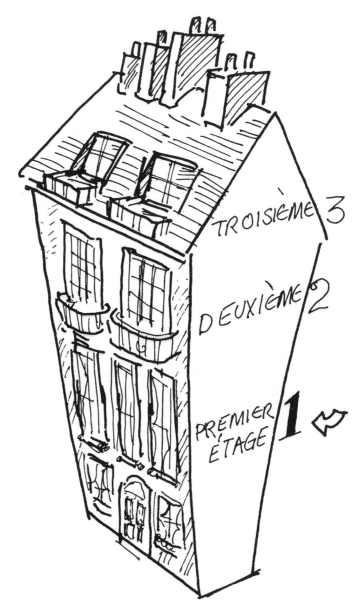

C'est au premier étage.

Part Five : Grammar
Section Cinq : Grammaire

To make specific rules and important points easier to remember they have been put into a rhyme or 'jingle'.

I. **LE** or **LA** or **L'** — The

REMEMBER: In French as everyone expects,
gender is often linked to sex.

So you say **Le jeune homme** because he is male and
you say **La jeune femme** because she is female.

However, many words do not have an obvious gender. In which case you just have to absorb the gender by listening to the lesson.

So you say le **paquet** and la **porte**.

When the French word has **l'** in front of it, it can be masculine as in **l'hôtel** and **l'escalier,** or feminine as in **l'heure** and **l'entrée.**

2. **UN** or **UNE** — A or An

You have seen **le** is the masculine form of 'the' and **la** is the feminine form. So how do you say 'a' or 'an' in French?

REMEMBER: **Un** goes with **le** — it's masculine you know.
Une goes with **la** the feminine to show.

e.g. **le jeune homme** and **un jeune homme**
le paquet and **un paquet**

la jeune femme and **une jeune femme**
la porte and **une porte**

3. **IL** or **ELLE** — He, She or It

We have seen it is:

le paquet	—	the packet
un paquet	—	a packet
la femme	—	the woman
une femme	—	a woman

So how do you say he, she or it?

REMEMBER:
Il (it or he) from **le** descends
elle (it or she) on **la** depends.

e.g.
un jeune homme arrive
le jeune homme est anglais
il s'appelle Philip

and

une jeune femme arrive
la jeune femme est française
elle s'appelle Jacqueline

4.   ADJECTIVES

In French the ending of the adjective needs to agree with the noun. If the noun is masculine, you just use the adjective as you've learnt it e.g. **content**, **grand**, **petit**.

If it is a feminine noun normally you add an **e** to the adjective.

REMEMBER:
All adjectives it's plain to see
with nouns (and pronouns) must agree
and the sign for feminine is **e**.

So   **Philip est content**
but   **Jacqueline est contente**
or   **il est grand**
but   **elle est grande**

NOTE: Sometimes you can both see and hear the added **e** as in:

grand — grande, anglais — anglaise

Sometimes the **e** is added silently

bleu — bleue, noir — noire

Some other words have the **e** already

jeune, calme, agréable

You will see how the endings change if you look at the word cards — the masculine version of each adjective is coloured blue — the feminine is pink with the **e** added.

Philip est content

16

5.   **A** or **AU** — To, At or In

In French the word **à** is very useful. It can mean 'to' or 'in' or 'at'. That's how you use it with a feminine noun or with **l'**.

e.g.   **à la maison** or **à l'hôtel.**

However with a masculine noun there is a simple rule.

REMEMBER: When **le** precedes the noun you know
                                  you don't say **à le,** you say **au.**

e.g.   **au café**   (le café)
                       au cinéma   (le cinéma)

6.   VERBS

In French, just as in English, you can have a different form of a verb depending upon whether you are saying 'I' 'you' 'he' etc.

So in English you say 'I do', 'you do' but 'he does'.

French is simple enough and you'll see that verbs end in **er** or **ir** or **re**. If you look at the Grammar Tables at the back of the book you will find all the various forms of these verbs.

e.g.   **donner** (to give)   or **ouvrir** (to open)   or **attendre** (to wait)

If the verb ends in **er** you say:

je donne
il donne
elle donne
vous donnez

In other words you drop the **r** for **je** and **il** and **elle**
but in the case of **vous** you add **z**. *

* This symbol means that fuller details can be found in the Grammar Tables.

Most verbs are regular but, as in English, some verbs have no real rule, but you will absorb them as you go along.

So 'to be' is:

je suis
il est
elle est
vous êtes

and 'to have' is:

j'ai
il a
elle a
vous avez

If you think back to your first lesson, you will find you already know all this.

REMEMBER: **je suis Monsieur West**
il est confortable

elle est grande et belle
vous êtes anglais

j'ai rendez-vous avec Monsieur Dubois
elle a les yeux bleus
vous avez la chambre numéro sept.

Part Six : Key Phrases
Section Six : Expressions Utiles

In every language a comparatively few words or phrases allow you to generate a great deal of everyday communication and help you build up useful language really quickly.

Some words and phrases can be used again and again in a variety of situations. We'll call them 'Key-Phrases'. Here are a few from Act 1:

I.   **QU'EST-CE QUE . . .?**

If you want to ask 'what' somebody wants or is looking for, and so on, use this phrase at the beginning of the sentence, like this:

Qu'est-ce que vous voulez?	—	What do you want?
Qu'est-ce que vous désirez?	—	What do you want?
Qu'est-ce que Philip donne à Jacqueline?	—	What does Philip give to Jacqueline?

2.   **A . . .**

You've seen that **à** can mean 'to', 'at' or 'in'. You can also use this word when you are arranging to meet somebody later on, like this:

A demain	—	See you tomorrow
A ce soir	—	See you this evening
A dix heures	—	See you at ten o'clock

3.   **C'EST . . .**

Sometimes we use 'It's . . .' at the beginning of a sentence in English, without referring to a specific object, for example, 'It's important'. In French, we use **C'est . . .** in the same way, like this:

C'est important	—	It's important
C'est ici	—	It's here

See if you can find some other examples in Act 1.

4.   **VOICI . . .**

If you are handing something over to somebody or introducing one person to another, you would begin with **Voici . . .**, here is, this is:

Voici la clé	—	Here's the key
Voici mon oncle	—	This is my uncle

Part Seven : Games
Section Sept : Jeux

1. Using the word cards, can you make up the French versions of these English sentences. Now, write down each sentence which you have composed and check the correct answer at the back of the book.

   When you have completed this activity, see how many more sentences you can make up on your own in five minutes, using the word cards only.

   1. Philip looks at the house.
   2. The house is big and beautiful.
   3. He goes up to the door and rings the bell.
   4. An old lady opens the door.
   5. Is this Mr. Dubois' house?
   6. Philip goes into the house.
   7. Philip gives the passport to Jacqueline.
   8. I live in London.
   9. My name's Jacqueline Dubois.
   10. The package is for M. Dubois.
   11. M. Dubois is coming back to Paris this evening.
   12. It's a small hotel but it's comfortable.
   13. Philip arrives at the hotel.
   14. You have a room reserved for Mr. West.
   15. Madame Marat gives the key to Philip.
   16. He goes upstairs and finds the room.
   17. The room is nice and quiet.
   18. He is tired but happy.

2. Using the cards, can you now make up one long sentence to summarise the story in Act 1? When you have done this, compare your sentence with the one on the answer page at the back of the book.

3. Fill in the spaces with adjectives in French corresponding to the clues. if you get the right answers the letters in the outlined column will give another adjective to be found in the text.

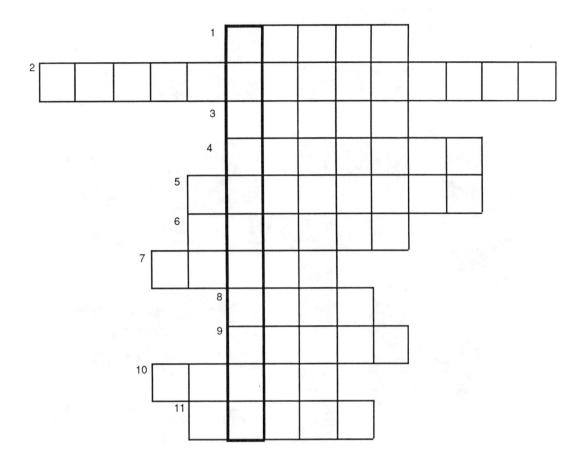

1. **La chambre est _ _ _ _ _.**

2. **Quelle journée _ _ _ _ _ _ _ _ _ _ _ _ _ _!**

3. **Jacqueline a les cheveux _ _ _ _ _.**

4. **Philip est _ _ _ _ _ _ _ mais content.**

5. **Jacqueline est _ _ _ _ _ _ _ _ de voir Philip.**

6. **Philip entre dans une _ _ _ _ _ _ maison.**

7. **L'hôtel est _ _ _ _ _ et très confortable.**

8. **Une dame _ _ _ _ ouvre la porte.**

9. **Jacqueline a les yeux _ _ _ _ _.**

10. **La maison est grande et _ _ _ _ _.**

11. **Une _ _ _ _ _ femme descend l'escalier.**

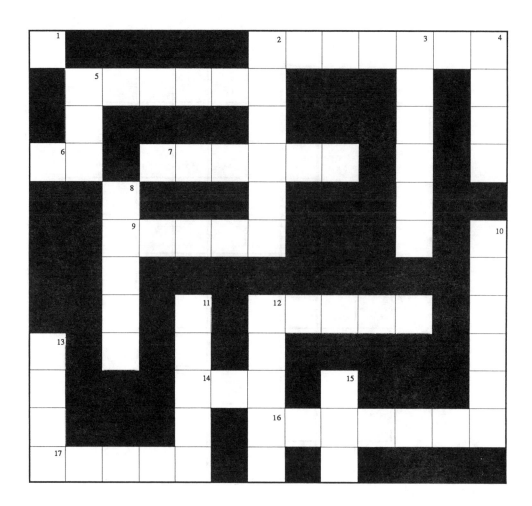

4.

Across

1. Elle ... les yeux bleus.
2. Philip ... un paquet.
5. To come in (infinitive)
6. Elle est grande ... belle.
7. J' ... Londres.
9. Philip ... dans la maison.
12. ... beaucoup.
14. No = ?
16. Vous ... à droite.
17. Philip ... et attend.

Down

2. Philip ... d'Angleterre.
3. M.Dubois ... à Paris ce soir.
4. Vous ... Monsieur West?
5. Jacqueline ... belle.
8. ... à la maison demain.
10. Vous ... de la maison.
11. Philip ... son passeport à Jacqueline.
12. Philip ... l'escalier.
13. Je ... Philip West.
15. Yes = ?

5. **Vrai ou Faux** (True or False)

1. La maison est grande et belle.
2. Une jeune femme ouvre la porte.
3. C'est la maison de Monsieur Dubois.
4. Une dame âgée descend l'escalier.
5. Jacqueline a les cheveux bleus et les yeux noirs.
6. Monsieur Anatole Dubois rentre à Paris ce soir.
7. Philip a une chambre réservée pour quatre nuits.
8. L'hôtel Bonaparte est dans la rue d'Angleterre.
9. L'hôtel est petit mais confortable.
10. Philip monte l'escalier.
11. Philip trouve la chambre numéro trois.
12. La chambre est agréable et calme.
13. Philip est français.
14. Jacqueline est anglaise.

	Vrai	Faux
1.		
2.		
3.		
4.		
5.		
6.		
7.		
8.		
9.		
10.		
11.		
12.		
13.		
14.		

The answers are at the back of the book.

BONUS

1.   You may have to fill in a form like this at an hotel:
     So get in some pratice now!

FICHE
D'ÉTRANGER

Chambre

n° _____

HOTEL DE LA CLOCHE

14, Place Darcy
21000 DIJON

Écrire en majuscules (In block letters).

NOM _____
(Name)

Prénom _____
(Christian name)

Date de naissance _____
(Date of birth)

Lieu de naissance _____
(Place of birth)

Domicile habituel _____
(Permanent address)

_____

Profession _____
(Occupation)

Nationalité
(Nationality)

Passeport n° _____ délivré le _____
(Passport n°)   (Issued the)

à _____ par _____
(at)   (by)

Date d'entrée à l'hôtel _____
(Date of arrival in hotel)

Date probable de sortie _____
(Probable date of departure)

Signature _____

Nombre d'enfants de moins de 15 ans
accompagnant le voyageur _____
(Accompaying children under 15)

ACT 2 ACTE 2
Scene I Scène I

Next morning at the Hotel (Tuesday morning).	**Le lendemain matin à l'hôtel (Mardi matin).**
Philip wakes up next morning. He has slept well. He rubs his eyes.	**Philip se réveille le lendemain matin. Il a passé une bonne nuit. Il se frotte les yeux.**
'Where am I?' he thinks.	**'Où suis-je?' pense-t-il.**
He looks around the room. There is a table, two white chairs and on the floor a blue carpet. He is warm under the covers. The pillow-case and sheets are white and clean.	**Il regarde la chambre. Il y a une table, deux chaises blanches et par terre un tapis bleu. Il a chaud sous les couvertures. La taie d'oreiller et les draps sont blancs et propres.**
'Ah yes. I'm in the Hotel d'Angleterre in Paris,' he says to himself.	**'Ah! oui, je suis à l'Hôtel d'Angleterre à Paris,' se dit-il.**
He hears noises in the street.	**Il entend des bruits dans la rue.**
'What time is it?' wonders Philip.	**'Quelle heure est-il?' se demande Philip.**
He looks at his watch. It is eight o'clock. He gets up and goes to the window.	**Il regarde sa montre. Il est huit heures. Il se lève et va à la fenêtre.**
'What's the weather like today?' he wonders.	**'Quel temps fait-il aujourd'hui?' se demande-t-il.**

Il tire les rideaux

He pulls back the curtains and opens the window. It is not raining, it is sunny but it is windy.	**Il tire les rideaux et ouvre la fenêtre. Il ne pleut pas, il fait du soleil mais il y a du vent.**

'Great,' exclaims Philip, 'the weather is going to be nice.'	'Chouette! Il va faire beau,' s'exclame Philip.
Philip goes to the table and opens his suitcase. He takes out his toothbrush, toothpaste, soap, razor and comb. He goes into the bathroom and switches on the light.	Il se dirige vers la table et ouvre sa valise. Il sort sa brosse à dents, son dentifrice, son savon, son rasoir et son peigne. Il va à la salle de bains et il allume la lumière.
The bathroom is very clean. There is a bath and a toilet but there isn't a shower. And there are beautiful, big towels.	La salle de bains est très propre. Il y a une baignoire et des toilettes mais il n'y a pas de douche. Les serviettes sont grandes et belles.
Philip shaves and washes his hair. The water is nice and hot.	Philip se rase et se lave les cheveux. L'eau est bien chaude.
He thinks about the package and Mr. Dubois. It's a funny business but after all, it is exciting. Mr. Dubois is paying and I'm having a free holiday.	Il pense au paquet et à Monsieur Dubois. C'est bizarre mais après tout, c'est passionnant. C'est Monsieur Dubois qui paie et moi, j'ai des vacances gratuites.

Philip se rase

Philip gets dressed quickly and goes downstairs to the dining-room to have breakfast.	Philip s'habille vite et descend à la salle à manger pour prendre son petit déjeuner.
Scene 2	Scène 2
Philip comes into the dining-room. He sits down at a table. The waitress comes up and smiles.	Philip entre dans la salle à manger. il s'assied à une table. La serveuse s'approche et sourit.
She has fair hair and green eyes. She is wearing a black skirt and a pretty, white blouse.	Elle a les cheveux blonds et les yeux verts. Elle porte une jupe noire et un joli corsage blanc.

26

Waitress:	Good morning, sir.	**Bonjour, monsieur.**
Philip:	Good morning.	**Bonjour, mademoiselle.**
Waitress:	What will you have for breakfast?	**Qu'est-'ce que vous allez prendre pour le petit déjeuner?**
	Coffee? Tea? Chocolate?	**Du café? du thé? du chocolat?**
Philip:	I'll have a coffee, please.	**Je vais prendre un café, s'il vous plaît.**
Waitress:	Black or white?	**Un café noir ou un café au lait?**
Philip:	Black, please.	**Un café noir, s'il vous plaît.**
Waitress:	Would you like some croissants?	**Voulez-vous des croissants?**
Philip:	Yes. I'd like two croissants.	**Oui. Je veux bien deux croissants.**

The waitress goes to the kitchen. Five minutes later, she brings his breakfast. **La serveuse va à la cuisine et cinq minutes plus tard elle apporte le petit déjeuner.**

Waitress: I'm sorry. There are no more croissants but there's fresh bread, butter and jam. **Je suis désolée, il n'y a plus de croissants mais il y a du pain frais, du beurre et de la confiture.**

Philip is hungry and thirsty. He eats three slices of bread and drinks his coffee with sugar. **Philip a faim et il a soif. Il mange trois tartines et il boit son café avec du sucre.**

'Lovely!' he thinks. **'C'est délicieux.' se dit-il.**

Ten minutes later, the waitress comes up to Philip. **Dix minutes plus tard, la serveuse s'approche de Philip.**

Waitress: Would you like some more coffee? **Voulez-vous encore du café?**
Philip: Yes please. **Oui, s'il vous plaît.**

She pours some coffee into Philip's cup. **Elle verse du café dans la tasse de Philip.**

Voulez-vous encore du café?

Waitress: Where do you live? **Où est-ce que vous habitez?**
Philip: I live in England, in London. **J'habite en Angleterre, à Londres.**
Do you know London? **Connaissez-vous Londres?**

27

Waitress:	Unfortunately, no. Do you know Paris?	**Non, malheureusement. Est-ce que vous connaissez Paris?**
Philip:	No, this is my first visit.	**Non, c'est ma première visite.**
Waitress:	You speak French very well.	**Mais vous parlez très bien français.**
Philip:	I can understand if you speak slowly but I don't speak it very well. What about you? Do you speak English?	**Non, je comprends si vous parlez lentement mais je ne parle pas très bien. Et vous, est-ce que vous parlez anglais?**
Waitress:	No. I speak Spanish well and I can understand Italian quite well.	**Non monsieur. Je parle bien espagnol et je comprends assez bien l'italien.**
Philip:	Maybe you're Spanish?	**Vous êtes espagnole peut-être?**
Waitress:	No. I'm French but I often go to Spain and Italy.	**Non, je suis française mais je vais souvent en Espagne et en Italie.**
Philip:	You are lucky.	**Vous avez de la chance.**
Waitress:	Yes. Have a nice day.	**Oui. Bonne journée monsieur.**
Philip:	Thank you.	**Merci mademoiselle.**

Non, c'est ma première visite.

Scene 3   **Scène 3**

	Philip gets up and goes out of the dining-room. He looks at his watch. It is half-past nine. In half an hour he is going to meet Jacqueline. He walks across the foyer and finds Mme. Marat near the front door.	**Philip se lève et quitte la salle à manger. Il regarde sa montre. Il est neuf heures et demie. Dans une demi-heure il va rencontrer Jacqueline. Il traverse le hall de l'hôtel et trouve Madame Marat près de la porte d'entrée.**
Mme Marat:	Good morning. How are you?	**Bonjour monsieur. Comment allez-vous?**
Philip:	Fine thanks.	**Très bien merci.**
Mme Marat:	Did you sleep well?	**Avez-vous bien dormi?**
Philip:	Yes thanks. The room is very quiet. The weather is nice today, isn't it?	**Oui, merci. La chambre est très calme. Il fait beau aujourd'hui, n'est-ce pas?**
Mme Marat:	Yes, but according to the weather forecast it's going to rain or snow this afternoon.	**Oui, mais d'après la météo, cet après-midi hélas, il va pleuvoir ou neiger.**

Philip:	But isn't the weather always fine in Paris in the Spring?	**Mais il ne fait pas toujours beau à Paris au printemps?**
Mme Marat:	No. Unfortunately it often rains.	**Non, il pleut souvent malheureusement.**
Philip:	Oh well, it's just like in England. Good-bye.	**Alors, c'est comme en Angleterre. Au revoir, madame.**
Mme Marat:	Good-bye and have a nice day.	**Au revoir, monsieur et bonne journée.**

Il pleut souvent malheureusement.

ACTE 2 (i)

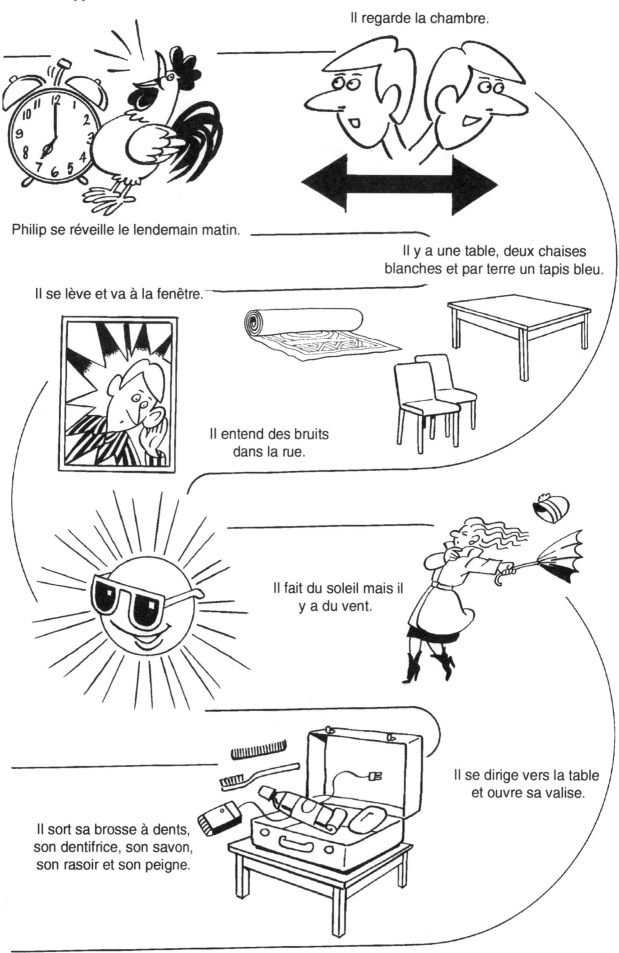

Il regarde la chambre.

Philip se réveille le lendemain matin.

Il y a une table, deux chaises blanches et par terre un tapis bleu.

Il se lève et va à la fenêtre.

Il entend des bruits dans la rue.

Il fait du soleil mais il y a du vent.

Il se dirige vers la table et ouvre sa valise.

Il sort sa brosse à dents, son dentifrice, son savon, son rasoir et son peigne.

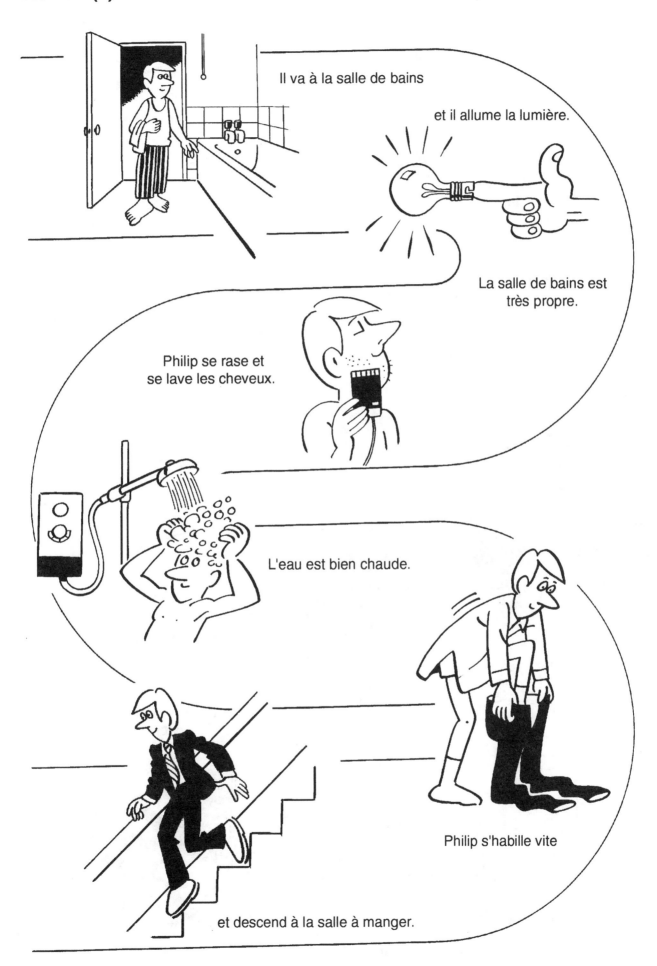

Il va à la salle de bains

et il allume la lumière.

La salle de bains est très propre.

Philip se rase et se lave les cheveux.

L'eau est bien chaude.

Philip s'habille vite

et descend à la salle à manger.

ACTE 2 (iii)

Il s'assied à une table.

Bonjour, monsieur.

La serveuse s'approche et sourit.

Je vais prendre un café, s'il vous plaît.

Il boit son café avec du sucre.

Mais il y a du pain frais.

Voulez-vous encore du café?

Où est-ce que vous habitez?

J'habite en Angleterre, à Londres.

Est-ce que vous connaissez Paris?

ENGLAND

EUROPE

Part Two : Pronunciation and Intonation
Section Deux : Prononciation et Intonation

Asking a question:

a)   Without a question word:

        Some examples:

           I.   **Voulez-vous des croissants?**

           2.   **Voulez-vous encore du café?**

           3.   **Connaissez-vous Londres?**

b)   With a question word:

        Some examples:

           I.   **Où suis-je?**

           2.   **Comment allez-vous?**

           3.   **Quelle heure est-il?**

           4.   **Où est-ce que vous habitez?**

           5.   **Quel temps fait-il?**

c)   With **Est-ce que** or **Qu'est-ce que**:

        Some examples:

           I.   **Est-ce que vous connaissez Paris?**

           2.   **Est-ce que vous parlez anglais?**

           3.   **Qu'est-ce que vous allez prendre?**

Connaissez-vous Londres?

d) The sound **r** as in **Angleterre, bizarre, noir, heure, bonjour.**

I. **A l'hôtel d'Angleterre.**

2. **C'est bizarre.**

3. **Un café noir.**

4. **Il est huit heures.**

5. **Bonjour monsieur.**

6. **Au revoir, il va pleuvoir.**

7. **Par terre, il y a un tapis vert.**

NOTE: that **r** at the end of a word is not always pronounced,

e.g. **rencontrer, neiger, la salle à manger, le petit déjeuner, une taie d'oreiller.**

Comptine:

Bonjour Madame.
Quelle heure est-il?
Il est midi!
Qui est-ce qui l'a dit?
La petite souris. — MOUSE
Où donc est-elle?
Dans la chapelle.
Que fait-elle?
De la dentelle!
Pour qui?
Pour toutes les dames de Paris!

Part Three Section Trois
Functional Dialogues Dialogues Fonctionnels

I.

| | Philip is ordering his breakfast. The waitress | **Philip commande son petit déjeuner. La serveuse = La S.** |

La S:	Good morning, sir.	**Bonjour, monsieur.**
Philip:	Good morning.	**Bonjour, mademoiselle.**
La S:	What will you have for breakfast? Coffee? Tea? Chocolate?	**Qu'est-ce que vous allez prendre pour le petit déjeuner? du café? du thé? du chocolat?**
Philip:	I'll have a coffee, please.	**Je vais prendre un café, s'il vous plaît.**
La S:	Black or white?	**Un café noir ou un café au lait?**
Philip:	Black, please.	**Un café noir, s'il vous plaît.**
La S:	Would you like some croissants?	**Voulez-vous des croissants?**
Philip:	Yes. I'd like two croissants.	**Oui. Je veux bien deux croissants.**

2.

| | The waitress is talking to Philip. | **La serveuse parle à Philip.** |

La S:	Where do you live?	**Où est-ce que vous habitez?**
Philip:	I live in England, in London. Do you know London?	**J'habite en Angleterre, à Londres. Vous connaissez Londres?**
La S:	No, unfortunately. Do you know Paris?	**Non, malheureusement. Est-ce que vous connaissez Paris?**
Philip:	No. This is my first visit.	**Non, c'est ma première visite.**

3.

| | The waitress continues the conversation with Philip. | **La serveuse poursuit la conversation avec Philip.** |

La S:	Are you English?	**Vous êtes anglais?**
Philip:	Yes. I am English.	**Oui, je suis anglais.**
La S:	You speak French very well.	**Mais vous parlez très bien français.**
Philip:	No. I understand if you speak slowly but I don't speak it very well. What about you? Do you speak English?	**Non, je comprends si vous parlez lentement mais je ne parle pas très bien. Et vous, est-ce que vous parlez anglais?**

La S:	No. I speak Spanish well and I can understand Italian quite well.	**Non monsieur. Je parle bien espagnol et je comprends assez bien l'italien.**
Philip:	Maybe you are Spanish?	**Vous êtes espagnole peut-être?**
La S:	No. I'm French but I often go to Spain and Italy.	**Non, je suis française mais je vais souvent en Espagne et en Italie.**

4.	Philip and Madame Marat are talking about the weather.	**Philip et Madame Marat parlent du temps.**

Il fait du soleil.

Philip:	What's the weather like today?	**Quel temps fait-il aujourd'hui?**
Mme M:	It isn't raining and it's sunny.	**Il ne pleut pas et il fait du soleil.**
Philip:	The weather's fine, then?	**Alors il fait beau?**
Mme M:	No, it's windy.	**Non, il y a du vent.**
Philip:	But it's going to be fine this afternoon, isn't it?	**Mais cet après-midi, il va faire beau, n'est-ce pas?**
Mme M:	No. According to the weather forecast, it's going to rain or snow.	**Non hélas, d'après la météo, il va pleuvoir ou neiger.**
Philip:	But isn't the weather always nice in Paris in the spring?	**Mais il ne fait pas toujours beau à Paris au printemps?**
Mme M:	No. Unfortunately it often rains.	**Non, il pleut souvent malheureusement.**
Philip:	Oh well. It's just like in England.	**Alors, c'est comme en Angleterre.**

5.	Philip is telling Jacqueline about the hotel.	**Philip parle de l'hôtel à Jacqueline.**

J:	Well then, is the room comfortable?	**Alors, la chambre est confortable?**
Philip:	Yes. There's a bed, a table with two white chairs and a nice, blue carpet on the floor.	**Oui. Il y a un lit, une table avec deux chaises blanches et par terre un joli tapis bleu.**
J:	Is it clean?	**Est-ce que c'est propre?**
Philip:	Yes. The pillow-case and sheets are white and clean.	**Oui. La taie d'oreiller et les draps sont blancs et propres.**
J:	Is there a bathroom?	**Est-ce qu'il y a une salle de bains?**
Philip:	Yes. There's a bath and a toilet but there isn't a shower.	**Oui. Il ya une baignoire et des toilettes mais il n'y a pas de douche.**

Part Four : Personalised Dialogues
Section Quatre : Dialogues

a) Ordering breakfast.

La serveuse:	**Bonjour.**
Vous:	(Say 'Good Morning'.)
La serveuse:	**Qu'est-ce que vous allez prendre pour le petit déjeuner?**
	Du café? du thé? du chocolat?
Vous:	(Say you'll have a coffee.)
La serveuse:	**Un café noir ou un café au lait?**
Vous:	(Say you'd like a black coffee.)
La serveuse:	**Voulez-vous des croissants?**
Vous:	(Say you'd like two croissants.)

b) You are talking to the waitress about where you come from.

La serveuse:	**Où est-ce que vous habitez?**
Vous:	(Say where you live [country and town].)
	and ask if she knows the place.)
La serveuse:	**Non, malheureusement.**
	Est-ce que vous connaissez Paris?
Vous:	(Say no and that this is your first visit.)

c) You are talking with the waitress about speaking foreign languages.

La serveuse:	**Vous êtes anglais/e?**
Vous:	(Say what your nationality is.)
La serveuse:	**Mais vous parlez très bien français.**
Vous:	(Say that you understand if she speaks slowly but that you don't speak it very well. Then ask if she speaks English.)
La serveuse:	**Non monsieur. Je parle bien espagnol et je comprends assez bien l'italien.**
Vous:	(Suggest that maybe she is Spanish.)
La serveuse:	**Non, je suis française mais je vais souvent en Espagne et en Italie.**

Du café?   *Du thé?*   *Du chocolat?*

d)   You are talking with Madame Marat about the weather.

Vous:	(Ask what the weather is like today.)
Mme Marat:	**Il ne pleut pas et il fait du soleil.**
Vous:	(Ask if the weather is fine.)
Mme Marat:	**Non, il y a du vent.**
Vous:	(Suggest that it is going to be nice weather this afternoon.)
Mme Marat:	**Non. D'après la météo, il va pleuvoir ou neiger.**
Vous:	(Ask if the weather isn't always nice in Paris in the Spring.)
Mme Marat:	**Non, il pleut souvent malheureusement.**
Vous:	(Say that it's just like in England.)

e)   You are telling Jacqueline about the hotel.

Jacqueline:	**Alors, la chambre est confortable?**
Vous:	(Say yes and that there is a bed, a table and [with] two white chairs and a nice blue carpet on the floor.)
Jacqueline:	**Est-ce que c'est propre?**
Vous:	(Say that the pillow-case and sheets are white and clean.)
Jacqueline:	**Est-ce qu'il y a une salle de bains?**
Vous:	(Say that there's a bath and a toilet but that there is no shower.)

THE EIFFEL TOWER

Part Five   : Grammar
Section Cinq : Grammaire

1.   PLURALS

REMEMBER: To make nouns plural, can't you guess?
Say **DES** or **LES** and add an **S.**

                                           ┌? some

e.g.   **un croissant**   —   **des croissants**
                      le croissant   —   **les croissants**

                      une serviette   —   **des serviettes**
                      la serviette   —   **les serviettes**

The plural of nouns often sounds the same as the singular, so you will have to listen very carefully to find out for example if it's **LE** or **LES**.

To use an adjective to describe a plural noun, just add an **s** as well:

e.g.   **Les draps sont bleus.**
                    Les serviettes sont grandes.

As with any rule, there are exceptions:

                    les yeux   —   (singular — **un oeil**)
                    les cheveux *– Hair* —   (singular — **un cheveu**)
                    les rideaux *– curtains* —   (singular — **un rideau**)

2.   ADJECTIVES

REMEMBER: When you speak or write words down,
In general, adjective follows noun.

e.g.   **les cheveux blonds**
                    les yeux verts   *pretty*

But some common adjectives, **beau, grand, petit, joli** come in front of the noun:

e.g.   **Un joli corsage blanc.**

NOTE: Certain adjectives have an irregular feminine form:

e.g.   **bon**   —   **bonne**
                    beau   —   **belle**
                    blanc   —   **blanche**

3. **SON/SA** — His or Her

REMEMBER: **SON** can mean 'his' or 'her' and so can **SA**
It's not the owner's sex that counts
But whether what he owns is **LE** or **LA**

e.g. **Le dentifrice** — **la brosse à dents**

So you must say:

**Philip sort son dentifrice
et sa brosse à dents.
Jacqueline sort son dentifrice
et sa brosse à dents.**

la jupe — **le corsage**

**La serveuse porte sa jupe noire
et son corsage blanc.**

4. **DU / DE LA** — Some

You have seen that gender is a very important concept in French:

<u>THE</u>	<u>A</u>
LE / LA	**UN / UNE**
(m) (f)	(m) (f)

When you want to talk about an indefinite quantity of certain 'uncountable' things such as bread or jam, for example, you must say:

<u>SOME</u>

DU pain (m) — bread
DE LA confiture (f) — jam

For words that begin with a vowel such as **eau**, you must say **DE L'**, de l'eau (f).

5. **NE . . . PAS** — Negative

REMEMBER: In a negative sentence, you will find
NE just before the verb and **PAS** behind.

e.g. **Il ne pleut pas.
Je ne parle pas très bien.
Il ne fait pas toujours beau à Paris.**

6. **ALLER** — To go

Here are some examples of the present tense of this important verb:

Je vais	—	I go/am going *
il/elle va	—	he/she goes/is going
vous allez	—	you go/are going

You use this verb in the same way as the English verb 'to go':

(a)   When talking about going somewhere:

e.g.   **Il va à la salle de bains.**
       Je vais en Espagne.

(b)   When saying that someone is going to do something or that something is going to happen:

e.g.   **Je vais prendre un café.**
       Il va neiger.

7. **AVOIR FAIM/AVOIR SOIF/AVOIR CHAUD/AVOIR FROID**

NOTE: You must use the verb **AVOIR** when you talk about being hungry, thirsty, hot/warm or cold:

e.g.   **Il a faim et il a soif.**
       He is hungry and thirsty.

       Il a chaud sous les couvertures.
       He is warm under the covers.

To say that you are cold, use the expression **avoir froid:**

       J'ai froid.
       I am cold.

You will have to use **AVOIR** when talking about being lucky or unlucky:

e.g.   **Vous avez de la chance.**
       You are lucky.

       Vous n'avez pas de chance.
       You are unlucky.

Also use **AVOIR** when saying your age:

       J'ai vingt-trois ans.
       I am 23 years old.

*   See Grammar Tables at the back of the book.

Vous avez de la chance.

8.   **SE/S'**

You will have noticed the little word **SE**, or its abbreviation **S'** in front of certain verbs:

e.g.   **Philip se réveille.**
                      Il se lave.
                      Il s'habille.

So, as you might have guessed, **SE** or **S'** means himself or herself, as is clear in the sentence **il se lave.**

NOTE: In French it is used with certain verbs even when 'himself' or 'herself' is missing in English.

e.g.   **Il s'asseoit.**
                      He sits down.

                      La serveuse s'approche.
                      The waitress comes up to Philip.

Il mange trois tartines.

Part Six : Key Phrases
Section Six : Expressions Utiles

1. **Il Y A . . .**

This phrase is used in the same way as English 'There is . . .' or 'There are . . .'

e.g.
Il y a une table.
There is a table.

Il y a deux chaises.
There are two chairs.

You make it negative this way:

Il n'y a pas de table.
There isn't a table.

Il n'y a pas deux chaises.
There aren't two chairs.

Il n'y a pas de douche.
There isn't a shower.

Il n'y a plus de croissants.
There are no more croissants.

2. **. . . N'EST-CE PAS?**

In English we can add various question tags to the end of our sentences:

e.g.
The weather's fine, isn't it?
You're Spanish, aren't you?

Good news: in French, you only need one question tag for any situation:

N'est-ce pas?

Il fait beau, n'est-ce pas?
Vous êtes espagnol, n'est-ce pas?

3. IL FAIT ...

When talking about the weather, you can use **Il fait ...** where in English you would say 'It's ...'

e.g.

Il fait du soleil.
It's sunny.

Il fait beau.
It's fine.

Other examples are:

Il fait chaud.
It's hot.

Il fait froid.
It's cold.

NOTE: Certain expressions, you can use either **Il fait ...** or **Il y a ...**

e.g.

Il fait du vent.
Il y a du vent.
It's windy.

NOTE ALSO the difference between:

Il fait chaud.
It's hot (weather).

Il a chaud.
He's hot (person).

Il fait du vent.

4. EN ...

If you want to say that you are going TO or have been IN a country, you use **EN** with the names of most countries:

e.g.
en France, en Angleterre, en Italie, en Espagne

BUT NOTE that we say:

au Canada, au Portugal

5. VOULEZ-VOUS ...

Whenever you are enquiring if somebody would like something, start your sentence with **voulez-vous ...?**

e.g.
Voulez-vous des croissants?
Voulez-vous encore du café?

Part Seven : Games
Section Sept : Jeux

1.   **Le jeu des 7 erreurs:**

   **Regardez les deux dessins. Le dessinateur a fait sept erreurs dans
   le dessin numéro deux.**
   Can you spot the seven mistakes and say what they are in French?

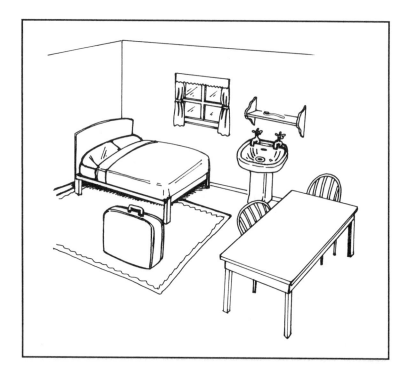

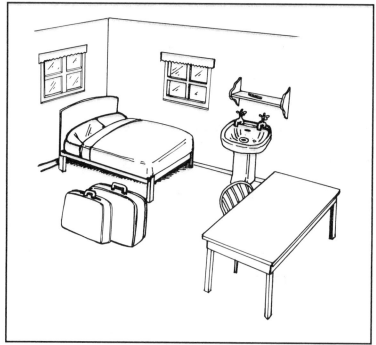

Let's do the first one together:
There is no carpet in the second picture, is there? So what should you say?
Il n'y a pas de tapis.
Now go on and do the rest then check your answers at the back of the book.

2. **Quel temps fait-il ce matin? Quel temps va-t-il faire ce soir?**

What's the weather like this morning and what is it going to be like this evening?

Look at the weather map 1 and say what the weather is like in each of these French towns this morning and then do the same for map 2, saying what the weather is going to be like in the evening.

Here is an example for you:

A Paris, il fait beau ce matin mais il va pleuvoir ce soir.

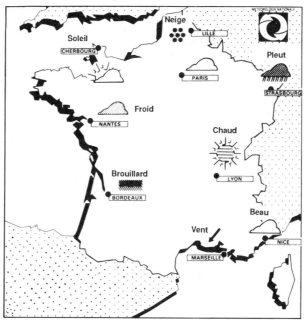

Quel temps fait-il ce matin?

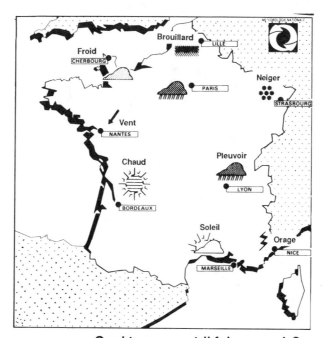

Quel temps va-t-il faire ce soir?

Check your answers at the back of the book.

3. **Le petit déjeuner:**

At the Hotel d'Angleterre, the night porter has got his breakfast orders completely mixed up. Help him to sort things out by following the lines and telling him who wants what.

For example: **Pour Monsieur West, c'est du café et des croissants.**

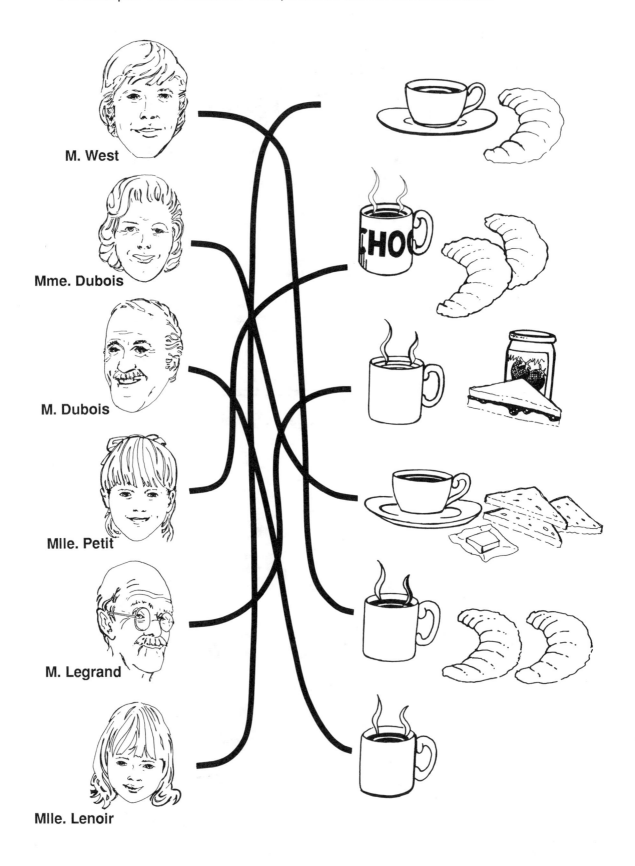

Check your answers at the back of the book.

4. **Voyage autour du monde:**

You are going to travel around the world. Find out first where you are:

e.g. **en France, au Maroc, aux Etats-Unis,** etc... Then imagine you can speak the language of the country.

Here are a few countries and languages you have not yet met but will need for the following activities:-

L'Allemagne	—	**allemand**
Le Japon	—	**japonais**
L'Egypte	—	**égyptien**
La Grèce	—	**grec**
La Russie	—	**russe**
La Chine	—	**chinois**
Le Mexique	—	**mexicain**

En France, je parle français.

1.

2.

3.

4.

5.

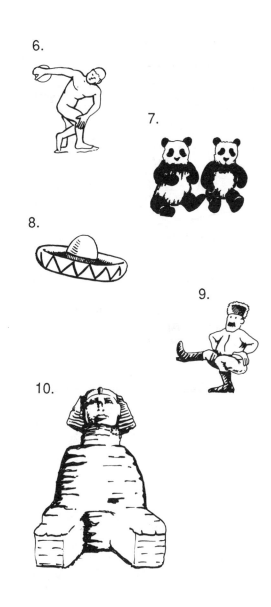

6.

7.

8.

9.

10.

BONUS

1. Can you solve this riddle? It is what Philip might say to himself in France.

J' ♡ le ☕ au 🛏 avec des 🥐🥐

mais je ✗♡ le ☕ au [LAIT UHT]

2. **Voici un proverbe;**

Après la pluie, le beau temps.

3. It helps to speak more than one language!

Un Américain, un Français, un Allemand, un Italien et un Mexicain s'asseoient à une table. L'Américain parle seulement anglais; le Français parle français et espagnol; l'Allemand parle allemand et français; l'Italien parle italien et anglais; le Mexicain parle espagnol et italien.

Que fait l'Américain pour parler à l'Allemand?

The answers are at the back of the book.

ACT 3 ACTE 3
Scene I Scène 1

Philip and Jacqueline go shopping (Tuesday morning).	**Philip et Jacqueline font les courses (Mardi matin).**
Philip goes down the rue Bonaparte.	**Philip descend la rue Bonaparte.**
'I'm going to buy some flowers for Jacqueline,' he says to himself.	**'Tiens, je vais acheter des fleurs pour Jacqueline,' se dit-il,**
He goes into a florist's shop.	**Il entre chez une fleuriste.**

Florist:	Good morning, sir. Can I help you?	**Bonjour, monsieur. Que désirez-vous?**
Philip:	Good morning. I'd like a bunch of flowers for a young lady, please.	**Bonjour, madame. Je voudrais un bouquet de fleurs pour une jeune femme, s'il vous plaît.**
Florist:	Would you like some roses or some tulips?	**Voulez-vous des roses ou des tulipes?**
Philip:	I prefer the roses.	**Je préfère les roses.**
Florist:	The red ones or the white ones?	**Les rouges ou les blanches?**
Philip:	Give me three red roses and two white ones, please. How much is that?	**Donnez-moi trois roses rouges et deux roses blanches, s'il vous plaît. Ça fait combien?**
Florist:	Sixty francs, (60F) sir.	**Soixante francs (60F), monsieur.**
Philip:	There you are. Good-bye.	**Voilà madame. Au revoir madame.**
Florist:	Thank you very much. Good-bye.	**Merci beaucoup monsieur. Au revoir monsieur.**

Philip leaves the shop. He looks at his watch.	**Philip sort de la boutique. Il regarde sa montre.**
'Gosh! It's ten past ten. I'm going to be late.'	**'Zut! il est dix heures dix. Je vais être en retard.'**
He begins to run towards the rue Madame.	**Il commence à courir vers la rue Madame.**

Scene 2   **Scène 2**

Five minutes later,   **Cinq minutes plus tard,**
he rings the bell at Jacqueline's house.   **il sonne chez Jacqueline.**
Jacqueline opens the door.   **Jacqueline ouvre la porte.**

Jacqueline:	Hello, Philip.	**Bonjour, Philip.**
	How are you	**Comment allez-vous**
	this morning?	**ce matin?**
Philip:	Fine thanks.	**Très bien, merci.**
	And yourself?	**Et vous?**
Jacqueline:	I'm fine, thanks.	**Ça va bien, merci.**
Philip:	I'm not late,	**Je ne suis pas en retard**
	I hope?	**j'espère?**
Jacqueline:	No. You're early.	**Mais non, vous êtes en avance.**
Philip:	What time is it?	**Quelle heure est-il?**
Jacqueline:	It's five to ten.	**Il est dix heures moins cinq.**
Philip:	Really?	**Ah! bon?**
	My watch is fast then.	**Ma montre avance alors.**

(note in illustration: Comment allez-vous ce matin?)

Philip gives the bunch of   **Philip offre le bouquet de**
roses to Jacqueline.   **roses à Jacqueline.**

Philip:	This is for you.	**Tenez, c'est pour vous.**
Jacqueline:	They're lovely!	**Elles sont superbes.**
	It's very kind of you.	**Vous êtes trop gentil.**
	Thank you very much.	**Merci beaucoup**
	Come in, please.	**Entrez s'il vous plaît.**

Philip and Jacqueline go   **Philip et Jacqueline entrent**
into the living-room.   **dans le salon.**
Jacqueline puts the flowers   **Jacqueline met les fleurs**
in a vase,   **dans un vase,**
then she turns round   **puis elle se retourne**
to Philip.   **vers Philip.**

Jacqueline:	I'm sorry.	**Je suis désolée.**
	My uncle isn't here yet.	**Mon oncle n'est pas encore là.**
	Will you stay	**Voulez-vous rester**
	another day or two?	**un ou deux jours de plus?**
Philip:	Yes, of course,	**Mais bien sûr,**
	I'd be delighted to.	**avec plaisir.**

Jacqueline:	Well you're going to	**Eh! bien vous allez**
	stay for lunch.	**rester déjeuner.**
	But first of all,	**Mais d'abord,**
	I am going to do	**je vais faire**
	the shopping.	**des courses.**
	Would you like to come	**Voulez-vous venir**
	with me?	**avec moi?**
Philip:	Certainly.	**Je veux bien.**

Scene 3 / **Scène 3**

Jacqueline and Philip leave the house.
They go down the rue Madame.

Jacqueline et Philip quittent la maison.
Ils descendent la rue Madame.

Jacqueline: I always do my shopping locally. I don't like supermarkets. I prefer the local shops and the market in the rue de Buci.

Jacqueline: **Je fais toujours mes courses dans le quartier. Je n'aime pas les supermarchés. Je préfère les petits commerçants du quartier et le marché de la rue de Buci.**

They walk to the traffic lights to go across the Boulevard St Germain.

Ils se dirigent vers les feux rouges pour traverser le Boulevard Saint Germain.

Jacqueline: What do you want for lunch - fish or meat?
Philip: I don't mind.

Jacqueline: **Qu'est-ce que vous voulez manger à midi? Du poisson ou de la viande?**
Philip: **Ça m'est égal.**

They stop outside the fish shop.

Ils s'arrêtent devant la poissonnerie.

Philip: It doesn't smell very nice, does it?
Jacqueline: That's true. Let's go to the butcher's.

Philip: **Ça ne sent pas très bon, n'est-ce-pas?**
Jacqueline: **C'est vrai. Allons chez le boucher.**

Il est grand et fort.

Mr Tranchesec, the butcher, knows Jacqueline very well.

Monsieur Tranchesec, le boucher, connaît bien Jacqueline.

He's a big, burly man. His face and hands are red and he has a loud voice.

Il est grand et fort. Il a le visage et les mains rouges et une grosse voix.

Mr Tranchesec: What would you like today, Mlle Dubois?
Jacqueline: I'd like two nice steaks, please.

Mr Tranchesec: **Qu'est-ce que vous désirez, aujourd'hui, Mademoiselle Dubois?**
Jacqueline: **Je voudrais deux biftecks bien tendres, s'il vous plaît.**

Mr Tranchesec:	Will there be anything else?	**Et avec ça?**
Jacqueline:	That's all.	**C'est tout.**
	How much is that?	**Ça fait combien?**
Mr Tranchesec:	Eighteen francs fifty (18.50F).	**Ça fait dix-huit francs cinquante (18.50F).**
Jacqueline:	There's a twenty franc note (20F).	**Tenez, voilà un billet de vingt francs (20F).**
Mr Tranchesec:	Thank you, and there's your change.	**Merci mademoiselle et voilà la monnaie.**

	In the street, next to the butcher's, there is a fruit and vegetable seller.	**Dans la rue, à côté de la boucherie, il y a un marchand de fruits et légumes.**

Jacqueline:	How much are the tomatoes?	**C'est combien les tomates?**
Seller:	Seventeen (17F) francs a kilo.	**Dix-sept francs (17F) le kilo.**
	They're expensive but they're nice.	**Elles sont chères, mais elles sont belles.**
Jacqueline:	Well, give me a pound of tomatoes, please.	**Eh bien, mettez-moi une livre de tomates, s'il vous plaît.**
Seller:	Anything else?	**Et avec ceci?**
Jacqueline:	I'd like a kilo of French beans, a lettuce and a pound of onions.	**Je voudrais un kilo de haricots verts, une laitue et une livre d'oignons.**
Seller:	There you are, Miss.	**Voilà, Mademoiselle.**
	Is that all?	**C'est tout?**
	That's thirty-two francs (32F) then.	**Alors, ça fait trente deux francs (32F).**
	You pay at the cash-desk, please.	**Vous payez à la caisse, s'il vous plaît.**

	Jacqueline goes and pays at the cash-desk, then she turns to Philip.	**Jacqueline va payer à la caisse, puis elle se tourne vers Philip.**

Jacqueline:	The fruit isn't very good just now.	**En ce moment, les fruits ne sont pas bons.**
	We'll buy a cake at the cake-shop.	**Nous allons acheter un gâteau à la pâtisserie.**
	But before that, we're going to stop off at the dairy.	**Mais avant, on va s'arrêter à la crémerie.**
Shopkeeper:	Good morning. Can I help you?	**Bonjour, Messieurs-Dames. Vous désirez?**

Jacqueline:	I'd like a litre of milk, half a pound of butter, two strawberry yoghurts and a dozen eggs.	**Je voudrais un litre de lait, une demi-livre de beurre, deux yaourts à la fraise et une douzaine d'oeufs.**
Shopkeeper:	There you are. Is there anything else?	**Voilà. Et avec ça?**
Jacqueline:	I'll have some cheese. Philip, what sort of cheese do you like?	**Je vais prendre du fromage. Philip, qu'est-ce que vous aimez comme fromage?**
Philip:	I like brie and camembert.	**J'aime bien le brie et le camembert.**
Jacqueline:	Do you like roquefort?	**Vous aimez le roquefort?**
Philip:	No, I don't like strong cheeses at all.	**Ah! non, je n'aime pas du tout les fromages forts.**
Jacqueline:	Do you like gruyère then?	**Alors vous aimez le gruyère?**
Philip:	Oh yes, I love that.	**Oh! oui, j'adore ça.**
Jacqueline:	All right. I'll buy a camembert and a bit of gruyère.	**Bon, eh bien je vais acheter un camembert et un morceau de gruyère.**

Jacqueline buys the cheese and they leave the shop.   **Jacqueline achète le fromage et ils sortent de la boutique.**

Philip:	What about the bread?	**Et le pain?**
Jacqueline:	We'll buy a stick at the baker's in the rue Madame.	**On va acheter une baguette à la boulangerie de la rue Madame.**

Scene 4   **Scène 4**

At a quarter to twelve, they get back to the house.   **A midi moins le quart, ils sont de retour à la maison.**

Jacqueline:	Go and sit in the living-room and listen to some records if you want. I'm going to get the meal ready.	**Asseyez-vous dans le salon et écoutez des disques si vous voulez. Moi, je vais préparer le repas.**
Philip:	Can I help you?	**Je peux vous aider?**

Une douzaine d'oeufs.

55

Jacqueline:	No. It's all right.	**Non, non, ça va.**
	There isn't much to be done.	**Il n'y a pas beaucoup de choses à préparer.**
	Would you like something to drink?	**Voulez-vous boire quelque chose?**
Philip:	Yes please.	**Volontiers.**
Jacqueline:	What will you have?	**Qu'est-ce que vous voulez prendre?**
Philip:	I'd love a cup of tea.	**Je voudrais bien une tasse de thé,**
	I'm very thirsty.	**j'ai très soif.**
Jacqueline:	Tea!	**Du thé!**
	You're in France.	**Mais vous êtes en France.**
	Have an aperitif,	**Prenez donc un apéritif,**
	a Pastis 51,	**un Pastis 51,**
	for example.	**par exemple.**
Philip:	What's that?	**Qu'est-ce que c'est?**
Jacqueline:	It's an aniseed drink.	**C'est une boisson alcoolisée à l'anis.**
	It's alcoholic.	
Philip:	All right,	**Eh bien,**
	I'll try that.	**je vais essayer ça.**
	What are you going to have?	**Et vous, qu'allez-vous prendre?**
Jacqueline:	I'm going to have a Dubonnet.	**Moi, je vais prendre un Dubonnet.**

	Jacqueline goes to the kitchen.	**Jacqueline va à la cuisine.**
	Three minutes later,	**Trois minutes plus tard,**
	she comes back	**elle revient**
	with the aperitifs	**avec les apéritifs**
	and she gives a glass of Pastis to Philip.	**et donne le verre de Pastis à Philip.**

Jacqueline:	Cheers.	**A votre santé.**
Philip:	Cheers.	**A la vôtre.**

A votre santé.

MORE TIPS FOR RAPID LEARNING

1. An excellent way to acquire vocabulary is to write words you especially want to remember on post cards with the translations on the back. You can use otherwise wasted time to 'revise' these words.

   Just 10 words a day learned gives you over 3,000 words in a year - the basis of an entire language.

2. Make sure you act out the dialogues as expressively as possible - the more you physically act out the language the better you'll learn it.

3. Make up post-it notes of objects you see around the house in French. Every time you see the object it's a reminder of the word, e.g. door, kitchen, bathroom. Use your dictionary or the glossary.

4. Look back over the Radio Play and pick out 10 words to represent visually. The quality of the drawing doesn't matter - it's the action of pictorialising the word that creates memory for the vocabulary.

5. Go back over the Radio Play and select the 10 French words you think will be the most useful - then rank them in order of importance.

6. Underline or highlight the particular words and phrases you want to fix in your memory. And remember that <u>writing</u> down words and sentences while you say them aloud combines visual, auditory and physical memory. Such words are well remembered.

7. When you've finished each Act, close your eyes and visualise the scenes - then describe <u>out loud</u> in your new language what happened. Use your own words, don't try to repeat phrases 'parrot fashion'. It's vital you take every opportunity to talk <u>out loud</u> in your new language.

IMPORTANT ☞ **You should do these seven additional exercises for each and every Act.**

ACTE 3 (i)

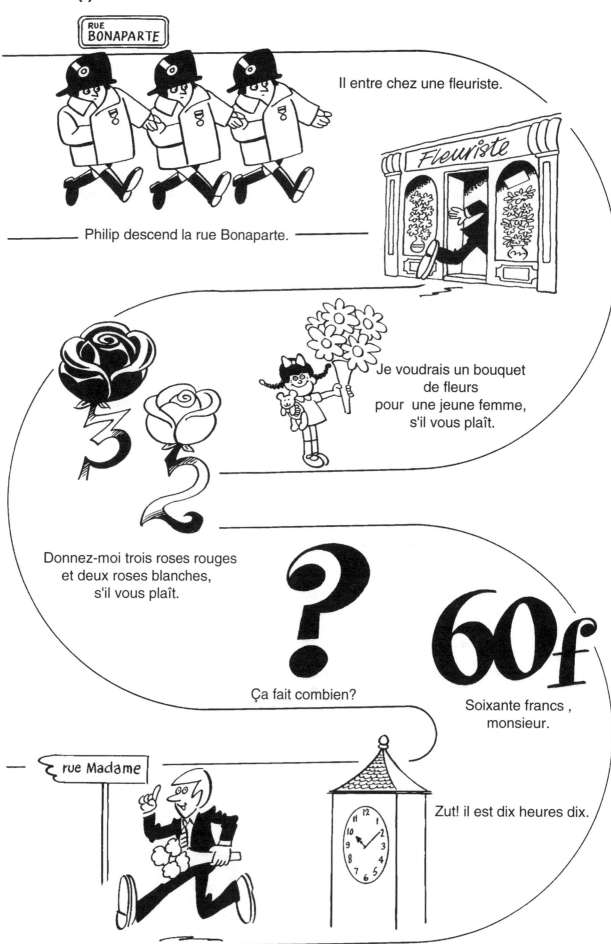

RUE BONAPARTE

Il entre chez une fleuriste.

Fleuriste

Philip descend la rue Bonaparte.

Je voudrais un bouquet de fleurs pour une jeune femme, s'il vous plaît.

Donnez-moi trois roses rouges et deux roses blanches, s'il vous plaît.

Ça fait combien?

60f

Soixante francs, monsieur.

rue Madame

Zut! il est dix heures dix.

Il commence à courir vers la rue Madame.

ACTE 3 (ii)

il sonne chez Jacqueline.

Cinq minutes plus tard.

Jacqueline ouvre la porte.

Bonjour, Philip, comment allez-vous ce matin?

Très bien, merci. Et vous?

Ma montre avance alors.

Tenez, c'est pour vous.

Jacqueline

Elle met les fleurs dans un vase.

ACTE 3 (iii)

Je vais faire des courses.

Voulez-vous rester un ou deux jours de plus?

Voulez-vous venir avec moi?

Je fais toujours mes courses dans le quartier.

Je préfère le marché de la rue de Buci.

60

BOUCHERIE

Allons chez le boucher.

Il est grand et fort.

Il y a un marchand de fruits et légumes.

Nous allons acheter un gâteau à la pâtisserie.

Philip, qu'est-ce que vous aimez comme fromage?

A votre santé.

A la vôtre.

Asseyez-vous dans le salon et écoutez des disques.

Part Two : Pronunciation and Intonation
Section Deux : Prononciation et Intonation

Many sounds in French, especially vowel sounds, are very different from English.

Listen to the difference between these English and French words which are very similar:

café / **café**   Dubonnet / **Dubonnet**   tulip / **tulipe**

a)   The sound **i** as in **il, midi, bifteck, ceci, kilo.**

        I.   **Quelle heure est-il?**
                  Il est dix heures dix.

        2.   **Non, il est midi.**

        3.   **Deux biftecks, s'il vous plaît.**

        4.   **Et avec ceci?**
                  Un kilo de haricots verts.

b)   The sound **u** as in **jupe, laitue, Dubonnet.**

        I.   **Elle a une jupe.**

        2.   **Mettez-moi une laitue.**

        3.   **Zut! c'est un Dubonnet.**

c)   Contrast between the **i** and **u** sounds in the same sentence:

        I.   **Il n'y a plus de confiture.**

        2.   **Philip achète des tulipes.**

        3.   **Dix minutes plus tard, il allume la lumière.**

        4.   **Les légumes du marché de Buci sont superbes.**

d)   **Comptines**

I.   **Mirlababi surlababo**
        Mirliton ribon ribette;
        Surlababi mirlababo
        Mirliton ribon ribo.

                        Victor Hugo

2.   **A Paris**
        Sur un cheval gris;
        A Saumur
        A vive allure;
        A Sully
        Au ralenti.
        Ah! qu'il est beau! qu'il est gentil!

e)   **Liaisons**

Remember to make the liaison with:

— Words ending with **s, x** or **z**.

I.   **Elle revient avec les‿apéritifs.**

2.   **Vous‿êtes trop gentil.**

3.   **Vous‿aimez le roquefort?**

4.   **Il est dix‿heures dix.**

5.   **Il entre chez‿une fleuriste.**

— Words ending with **t**.

I.   **Quel temps fait‿il?**

2.   **Cet‿après-midi.**

3.   **Ça m'est‿égal.**

4.   **C'est‿une boisson alcoolisée.**

But remember never to pronounce the **t** in **et**.
e.g.   **une laitue et/une livre d'oignons.**

— Words ending with **n**

1.   **Prenez donc un‿apéritif.**

2.   **J'habite en‿Angleterre.**

3.   **Mon‿oncle n'est pas là.**

Il est dix heures dix.

63

Part Three   Section Trois
Functional Dialogues   Dialogues Fonctionnels

1.	Philip arrives at Jacqueline's house.	**Philip arrive chez Jacqueline.**

J:	Good morning, Philip. How are you this morning?	**Bonjour Philip. Comment allez-vous ce matin?**
Philip:	Fine thanks. And yourself?	**Très bien, merci. Et vous?**
J:	I'm fine thanks.	**Ça va bien, merci.**
Philip:	I hope I'm not late?	**Je ne suis pas en retard, j'espère?**
J:	No, you're early.	**Mais non, vous êtes en avance.**
Philip:	What time is it?	**Quelle heure est-il?**
J:	It's five to ten.	**Il est dix heures moins cinq.**
Philip:	Really? My watch is fast then.	**Ah! bon? Ma montre avance alors.**

2.	Jacqueline offers Philip an apéritif.	**Jacqueline offre l'apéritif à Philip.**

J:	Would you like something to drink?	**Voulez-vous boire quelque chose?**
Philip:	Yes, please.	**Volontiers.**
J:	What will you have?	**Qu'est-ce que vous voulez prendre?**
Philip:	I'd love a Pastis 51. What are you going to have?	**Je voudrais bien un Pastis 51. Et vous, qu'allez-vous prendre?**
J:	I'm going to have a Dubonnet. Cheers.	**Moi, je vais prendre un Dubonnet. A votre santé.**
Philip:	Cheers.	**A la vôtre.**

3.	Jacqueline goes into the butcher's shop.	**Jacqueline entre chez le boucher.** **Le Boucher = Le B.**

Le B:	What will you have today, Miss Dubois?	**Qu'est-ce que vous désirez aujourd'hui Mlle Dubois?**
J:	I'd like two nice steaks, please.	**Je voudrais deux biftecks bien tendres, s'il vous plaît.**
Le B:	Will there be anything else?	**Et avec ça?**
J:	That's all. How much is that?	**C'est tout. Ça fait combien?**
Le B:	Eighteen francs fifty.	**Ça fait dix-huit francs cinquante.**
J:	There's a twenty franc note.	**Tenez, voilà un billet de vingt francs.**
Le B:	Thank you and there's your change.	**Merci mademoiselle et voilà la monnaie.**

4.

| | Jacqueline buys some vegetables. (The Seller) | **Jacqueline achète des légumes.** **Le Marchand = Le M.** |

J: How much are the tomatoes? **C'est combien les tomates?**

Le M: Seventeen francs a kilo. **Dix-sept francs le kilo.**

J: Well, give me a pound of tomatoes, please. **Eh bien, mettez-moi une livre de tomates, s'il vous plaît.**

Le M: Anything else? **Et avec ceci?**

J: I'd like a kilo of French beans, a lettuce and a pound of onions. **Je voudrais un kilo de haricots verts, une laitue et une livre d'oignons.**

Le M: There you are, Miss. Is that all? **Voilà mademoiselle. C'est tout?**

J: Yes, that's all. How much is that? **Oui c'est tout. Ça fait combien?**

Le M: Thirty two francs. You pay at the cash-desk, please. **Ça fait trente deux francs. Vous payez à la caisse, s'il vous plaît.**

5.

| | Jacqueline goes to the dairy with Philip. | **Jacqueline va à la crémerie avec Philip.** |

J: What sort of cheese do you like? **Qu'est-ce que vous aimez comme fromage?**

Philip: I like brie and camembert. **J'aime bien le brie et le camembert.**

J: Do you like roquefort? **Vous aimez le roquefort?**

Philip: No, I don't like strong cheeses at all. **Ah! non, je n'aime pas du tout les fromages forts.**

J: Do you like gruyère then? **Alors vous aimez le gruyère?**

Philip: Yes, I love that. **Oh! oui, j'adore ça.**

J: All right. I'll buy a camembert and a bit of gruyère. **Bien, alors je vais acheter un camembert et un morceau de gruyère.**

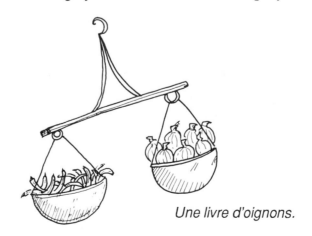

Une livre d'oignons.

Un kilo de haricots verts.

Part Four : Personalised Dialogues
Section Quatre : Dialogues

a) You arrive at Jacqueline's house and greet her.

Jacqueline:	**Bonjour. Comment allez-vous ce matin?**
Vous:	(Say you're fine thanks and ask how she is.)
Jacqueline:	**Ça va bien, merci.**
Vous:	(Say that you hope you are not late.)
Jacqueline:	**Mais non, vous êtes en avance.**
Vous:	(Ask what time it is.)
Jacqueline:	**Il est dix heures moins cinq.**
Vous:	(Say your watch is fast.)

b) Jacqueline offers you an aperitif.

Jacqueline:	**Voulez-vous boire quelque chose?**
Vous:	(Say yes please.)
Jacqueline:	**Qu'est-ce que vous voulez prendre?**
Vous:	(Say what you would like to drink, then ask Jacqueline what she is having.)
Jacqueline:	**Moi, je vais prendre un Dubonnet. A votre santé.**
Vous:	(Say cheers.)

c) You go to the butcher's.

Le boucher:	**Qu'est-ce que vous désirez?**
Vous:	(Say you would like two nice steaks.)
Le boucher:	**Et avec ça?**
Vous:	(Say that's all and ask how much it is.)
Le boucher:	**Ça fait dix-huit francs cinquante.**
Vous:	(Give the butcher a twenty franc note and say so.)
Le boucher:	**Merci et voilà la monnaie.**

d) You are buying some vegetables.

Vous:	(Ask how much the tomatoes are.)
Le marchand:	**Dix-sept francs le kilo.**
Vous:	(Tell him to give you a pound of tomatoes.)
Le marchand:	**Et avec ceci?**
Vous:	(Say you would like a kilo of French beans, a lettuce and a pound of onions.)
Le marchand:	**Voilà. C'est tout?**
Vous:	(Say that's all and ask how much it is.)
Le marchand:	**Ça fait trente-deux francs. Vous payez à la caisse, s'il vous plaît.**

e)   You go into the dairy with Jacqueline.

Jacqueline:	**Qu'est-ce que vous aimez comme fromage?**
Vous:	(Say you like brie and camembert.)
Jacqueline:	**Vous aimez le roquefort?**
Vous:	(Say that you do not like strong cheeses at all.)
Jacqueline:	**Alors vous aimez le gruyère?**
Vous:	(Say you love that.)
Jacqueline:	**Bien, alors je vais acheter un camembert et un morceau de gruyère.**

Part Five : Grammar
Section Cinq : Grammaire

1. **ILS/ELLES ... —ENT** — They are ... —ing.

When you are talking about at least two people doing something, the verb often sounds the same as when only one person is involved:

> e.g. **Philip quitte la maison.**
> **Jacqueline et Philip quittent la maison.**

You will notice, however, that the spelling is different. When more than one person is involved, the verb ends in **-ENT**.

> NOTE: With certain verbs you can always hear the difference:

> e.g. **Il sort / Ils sortent**
> **Elle descend / Elles descendent.**

This is particularly true of common irregular verbs:

> **Il est / Ils sont (être)**
> **Il a / Ils ont (avoir)**
> **Il va / Ils vont (aller)**
> **Il fait/ Ils font (faire)**

Similarly, if you wish to say 'they' it does not matter if the people you are referring to are all male or a mixture of male and female, you must use **ILS** which will sound just like **IL** (he), unless the next word begins with a vowel.

e.g.	**Il quitte**	—	**Ils quittent**
but	**Il entre**	—	**Ils entrent**

The same applies to **ELLE/ELLES** — she/they

e.g.	**Elle entre**	—	**Elles entrent**

> REMEMBER: When you add **-S** to **IL** or **ELLE**
> The verb takes on **-ENT** as well.
> But in verbs of a certain sort
> you can hear the difference:
> **Il sort — Ils sortent.**

2.   **NOUS/ON** — We

There are two ways of expressing the word 'we' in French:

(a)   use **NOUS,** and add **-ONS** to the verb:

Nous allons acheter un gâteau.

(b)   use **ON,** but now the verb has the same ending as for **IL** or **ELLE.**

On va acheter un gâteau.

REMEMBER: 'We' can be either **NOUS** or **ON**

So **on va** is the same as **nous allons.**

3.   **—ONS** — Let's

REMEMBER: When suggesting what to do
                   Just forget about the **NOUS.**

e.g.   **Allons chez le boucher.**
                   Let's go to the butcher's.

4.   **—EZ** — Giving instructions

REMEMBER: When telling someone what to do,
                   You do not need to start with **VOUS.**

e.g.   **Entrez, je vous prie.**
                   Mettez-moi une livre de tomates.
                   Asseyez-vous dans le salon.

This applies when you are talking to someone you do not know very well or to a group of people.

In the last example, **Asseyez-vous**, there is a **vous** but it comes after the verb. This is because it is a 'reflexive verb'; it is as though you were saying 'Sit yourself down'.

Mettez-moi une livre de tomates.

5.   **DE/D'** after expressions of quantity

To talk about unspecified quantities or numbers of things (or people), you already know to use **DU/DE, LA/DE, L'/DES** in front of the noun:

e.g.

DU lait	—	(some) milk
DE LA viande	—	(some) meat
DE L'eau	—	(some) water
DES fleurs	—	(some) flowers

But when you mention any given quantity, such as 'a bouquet', 'a litre', 'a dozen' or 'a lot' or even 'a bit', all you need to use after these expressions is **DE** or **D'**:

e.g.

Un litre <u>de</u> lait
Une douzaine <u>d'</u>oeufs
Un morceau <u>de</u> gruyère
Un bouquet <u>de</u> fleurs
Un kilo <u>de</u> viande
Beaucoup <u>de</u> choses.

6.   Using **VOULOIR** with another verb

You can also use the verb **VOULOIR** together with another verb:

(a)   when you are asking if someone wants to do something:

e.g.

Voulez-vous boire quelque chose?
Voulez-vous venir avec moi?

(b)   when you are asking someone what he or she wants to do or eat, etc:

e.g.

Qu'est-ce que vous voulez manger?

Un bouquet de fleurs

Part Six   :   **Key Phrases**
Section Six   :   **Expressions Utiles**

1.   **JE VOUDRAIS** . . . — I would like . . .

To ask politely for something, as well as saying **s'il vous plaît** you can begin by saying
'**Je voudrais . . .**'

> e.g.   **Je voudrais un bouquet de fleurs.**
>   **Je voudrais deux biftecks bien tendres.**

And to emphasise your request, you might add '**bien**':

> e.g.   **Je voudrais bien une tasse de thé.**

2.   **CHEZ** . . .

To say that you are AT or are going TO someone's place, all you need to use is **CHEZ** together
with their name:

> e.g.   **Philip sonne chez Jacqueline.**
>   Philip rings the doorbell at Jacqueline's house.
>
>   **Allons chez le boucher.**
>   Let's go to the butcher's.

3.   **C'EST/ÇA FAIT COMBIEN . . .?** — How much . . .?

When you want to ask the price of something, you can start by saying either of these phrases then
adding what you want to know the price of:

> e.g.   **C'est combien les tomates?**
>   **Ça fait combien les biftecks?**

4.   **QU'EST-CE QUE . . .COMME . . .?** — What sort of . . .?

This is a phrase you can use when you want to find out what someone likes or prefers:

> e.g.   **Qu'est-ce que vous aimez comme fromages?**
>   **Qu'est-ce que vous voulez comme fruits?**
>   **Qu'est-ce que vous préférez comme fleurs?**

Je voudrais deux biftecks bien tendres.

Part Seven : Games
Section Sept : Jeux

1. Hidden word among the fruit and vegetables:

    Write the name of the fruit or vegetable underneath each picture and you will discover what
    Jacqueline wants in the frame. Where is she going to buy it?

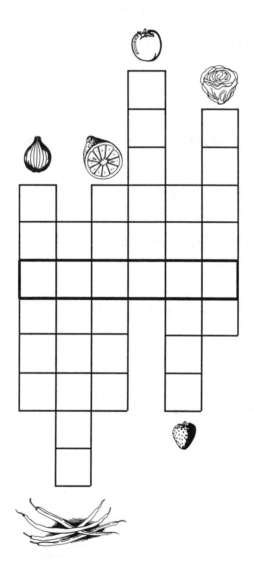

The answers are at the back of the book.

2. The sign-writer was not very good at spelling and got these shop signs wrong. Can you correct them?

1. RISTUFELE
2. ENPRISONIESO
3. CHEROBUIE
4. CHREMA
5. PHARMUCRESE
6. STRIPEASIE
7. MERCERIE
8. BLUERAINOGE

3. In each of the following groups of four words, one word is the 'odd man out'. Can you say which one it is in each case?

1.	pain	croissants	fraises	baguette
2.	bifteck	sucre	café	chocolat
3.	camembert	roquefort	beurre	brie
4.	roses	tulipes	oeillets	tomates
5.	oeufs	haricots	fromage	yaourt

4. Which words in the left-hand column match up with the ones in the right-hand column?

1. un verre		1. Pastis
2. un kilo		2. oeufs
3. une douzaine		3. fleurs
4. un bouquet	de	4. lait
5. un morceau		5. sucre
6. un paquet		6. tomates
7. un litre		7. fromage

5. Jacqueline scribbled down the following shopping list. Can you say which shops she is going to and which items she is going to buy in each shop? Remember! She doesn't like supermarkets!

Tarte aux pommes	*saucisses*	*bifteck*	*tomates*
rosbif	*crème fraîche*	*côtes d'agneau*	*ail*
lait	*bananes*	*salade*	*gruyère*
baguette	*oeufs*	*beurre*	*pommes*
	yaourts	*carottes*	

For example: **Elle va acheter une tarte aux pommes à la pâtisserie.**

Remember to use one of these words in front of each item:
un/une/du/de la/de l'/des and one of these in front of the name of the shop or shop-owner: **au/à la/chez.**

6.   Here are the main features of telling the time in French and not included in Act 3.

Huit heures et quart.   **Huit heures et demie.**   **Neuf heures moins le quart.**
Huit heures quinze.   **Huit heures trente.**   **Huit heures quarante-cinq.**

Now test your skill in the following account of Philip's morning. From each picture can you say what Philip is doing at the particular time?

1.   **A huit heures il se lève.**

2.

3.

4.

5.

6.

Philip gets organised
(Tuesday afternoon).

**Philip s'organise
(Mardi après-midi).**

Philip and Jacqueline are finishing their
meal.

**Philip et Jacqueline finissent
le repas.**

Philip:

What a lovely meal!
I'm beginning to
appreciate France.
By the way, I must phone
my parents.
They think I'm coming
back to London
this evening.
Have you got a 'phone?

**Quel bon repas!
Je commence à
apprécier la France.
Au fait, je dois téléphoner
à mes parents.
Ils pensent que je rentre à
Londres
ce soir.
Vous avez le téléphone?**

Jacqueline:

Yes. It's over there
by the door.

**Oui, il est là-bas
près de la porte.**

Philip:

Can I use
your telephone, please?

**Est-ce que je peux utiliser
votre téléphone, s'il vous plaît?**

Jacqueline:

Yes, of course.
Do you know how to phone
England?

**Oui, bien sûr.
Savez-vous téléphoner
en Angleterre?**

Philip:

No, what do I have
to do?

**Non, qu'est-ce que je dois
faire?**

Jacqueline:

You have to dial
nineteen (19) then
forty four (44)
for England.

**Vous devez composer
le dix-neuf (19) puis
le quarante-quatre (44)
pour l'Angleterre.**

Philip:

And for London?

Et pour Londres?

Jacqueline:

You dial one (1),
I think.

**Vous faites le un (1),
je crois.**

*Savez-vous téléphoner
en Angleterre?*

Philip picks up the phone
and dials the number.
His mother answers the phone
and he explains that he has to stay
a little longer in Paris.
He puts the phone down
and turns to Jacqueline.

**Philip décroche le téléphone
et compose le numéro.
Sa mère répond au téléphone
et il explique qu'il doit rester
un peu plus longtemps à Paris.
Il raccroche le téléphone
et se retourne vers Jacqueline.**

Philip:

Well, that's that.
But now there's
another problem.
As I have to stay
longer, I need to buy
some more clothes
so I must go and get
some money from
the bank.

**Bon, voilà, c'est fait,
mais maintenant, il y a encore
un problème.
Comme je dois rester plus
longtemps, j'ai besoin d'acheter
d'autres vêtements
donc je dois aller chercher de
l'argent à
la banque.**

Jacqueline:	Don't worry. There are lots of banks and shops in this district. We can go there now if you want.	**Ne vous en faites pas. Il y a beaucoup de banques et de magasins dans le quartier. On peut partir maintenant si vous voulez.**
Philip:	All right. Let's go.	**D'accord. Allons-y.**

	Scene 2	**Scène 2**
	Philip and Jacqueline are outside the bank.	**Philip et Jacqueline sont devant la banque.**

Jacqueline:	What money have you got?	**Qu'est-ce que vous avez comme argent?**
Philip:	I have seventy five (75) pound in traveller's cheques. Do you think that's enough for two days?	**J'ai soixante-quinze (75) livres en chèques de voyage. Vous croyez que c'est assez pour deux jours?**
Jacqueline:	I don't think so.	**Je crois que non.**
Philip:	Well, I can always write out a Eurocheque.	**Alors, je peux toujours faire un Eurochèque.**

	They go into the bank. Philip goes up to a desk.	**Ils entrent dans la banque. Philip se dirige vers un guichet.**

Philip:	I'd like to change these traveller's cheques, please. What is the exchange rate for the pound today?	**Je voudrais changer ces chèques de voyage, s'il vous plaît. Quel est le cours de la livre aujourd'hui?**
Clerk:	Eleven francs ten, sir.	**Il est à onze francs dix monsieur.**
Philip:	Ah, thank you. Do you accept Eurocheques?	**Bien merci. Est-ce que vous acceptez les Eurochèques?**
Clerk:	Yes, sir.	**Oui, monsieur.**

Philip:	Right then, here are the traveller's cheques and a Eurocheque for one thousand francs.	**Bon. Eh bien, voilà les chèques de voyage et un Eurochèque pour mille francs.**
Clerk:	Have you got your Eurocheque card and your passport?	**Vous avez votre carte eurochèque et votre passeport?**
Philip:	Yes. Here they are.	**Oui. Voilà madame.**
Clerk:	Thank you, sir. You can go to the cash-desk.	**Merci monsieur. Vous pouvez passer à la caisse.**

Vous avez votre carte eurochèque?

	Two minutes later, the cashier gives Philip one thousand eight hundred and thirty two francs fifty cents (1832F50). Philip puts his money in his wallet and says to Jacqueline with a grin:	Deux minutes plus tard, le caissier donne mille huit cent trente-deux francs cinquante (1.832F50) à Philip. Philip met son argent dans son porte-feuille et dit à Jacqueline avec un grand sourire,
	Now I can have a change of shirt!	Maintenant, je vais pouvoir changer de chemise!

Scene 3 — Scène 3

	Philip and Jacqueline are walking along the rue Saint Sulpice. There are lots of clothes shops. They look in the shop-windows.	Philip et Jacqueline se promènent dans la rue Saint Sulpice. Il y a beaucoup de magasins de vêtements. Ils regardent les vitrines.
Jacqueline:	What do you want to buy Philip?	Que voulez-vous acheter Philip?
Philip:	I need a shirt, some underwear and socks.	J'ai besoin d'une chemise, de sous-vêtements et de chaussettes.
	They stop in front of a shop-window where there are lots of nice clothes.	Ils s'arrêtent devant une vitrine où il y a beaucoup de jolis vêtements.
Jacqueline:	Look at that striped shirt. It's very nice, isn't it?	Regardez cette chemise rayée, elle est très belle, n'est-ce pas?
Philip:	Yes and it's not too expensive. Shall we go in?	Oui et elle n'est pas trop chère. On entre?
	They go into the shop. An assistant comes up.	Ils entrent dans le magasin. Une vendeuse s'approche.
Assistant:	Good afternoon. Can I help you?	Bonjour, Messieurs Dames. Est-ce que je peux vous aider?
Philip:	Can I try on the striped shirt which is in the shop-window?	Est-ce que je peux essayer la chemise rayée qui est en vitrine?

Assistant:	Yes, of course.	Oui, bien sûr.
	The shirt at eighty francs (80F)?	La chemise à quatre-vingts francs (80F)?
Philip:	Yes, that's it.	Oui, c'est ça.
Assistant:	What size do you take?	Vous faites du combien?
Philip:	Thirty-nine (39), I think.	Du trente-neuf (39), je crois.
Assistant:	It's your size.	Alors, c'est votre taille.
	Wait a moment please.	Attendez un instant, s'il vous plaît.
	There you are, sir.	Voilà Monsieur.
	You can go to the changing-room.	Vous pouvez passer au salon d'essayage.

	Philip goes and tries on the shirt.	Philip va essayer la chemise.
	He comes back two minutes later and asks Jacqueline her opinion.	Il revient deux minutes plus tard et demande l'avis de Jacqueline.

Philip:	What do you think of it?	Qu'est-ce que vous en pensez?
Jacqueline:	It suits you.	Ça vous va bien.
	You look very elegant.	Vous êtes très élégant.
	Now you need a plain tie to go with that shirt.	Maintenant, vous avez besoin d'une cravate unie pour aller avec cette chemise.
Philip:	Do you think so?	Vous croyez?
Jacqueline:	Yes. Look. There's a nice, grey tie.	Oui. Tenez, voilà une belle cravate grise.
	It's very smart.	Elle est très chic.
Philip:	It's a bit light, don't you think?	Elle est un peu claire, vous ne trouvez pas?
Jacqueline:	No. I think it's just the right colour.	Ah! non, moi, je trouve que c'est la bonne couleur.
	It goes very well with the shirt.	Elle va très bien avec la chemise.
Philip:	How much is it?	Elle coûte combien?

Assistant:	You are lucky, sir, it's a reduced price, twenty francs(20). It's a bargain.	Vous avez de la chance, Monsieur, elle est en solde, à vingt francs (20F), c'est une affaire.
Philip:	All right then, I'll have the tie as well.	Bon, eh bien, je vais prendre la cravate aussi.
Assistant:	Do you need anything else?	Vous avez besoin d'autre chose?
Philip:	Yes, I need a pair of white underpants and a white T-shirt and two pairs of socks.	Oui, j'ai besoin d'un slip et d'un maillot de corps blancs et de deux paires de chaussettes.
Assistant:	What size shoes do you take?	Vous chaussez du combien?
Philip:	Forty one (4l).	Du quarante et un (41).
Assistant:	And what colour do you want?	Et quelle couleur voulez-vous?

Philip:	Dark grey, please.	**Gris foncé, s'il vous plaît.**
Assistant:	Right, there are your socks,	**Bon, alors voilà vos chaussettes,**
	your underwear,	**vos sous-vêtements,**
	your shirt	**votre chemise**
	and your tie.	**et votre cravate.**
	That's the lot, isn't it?	**C'est tout, n'est-ce pas?**
Philip:	Yes, that's everything.	**Oui, c'est tout.**
Assistant:	Very good, sir.	**Très bien, Monsieur,**
	That'll be two hundred and one (201F) francs.	**alors ça fait deux cent un francs (20lF).**
	Will you pay by cheque or cash?	**Vous réglez par chèque ou en espèces?**
Philip:	Cash.	**En espèces.**

Philip pays, picks up his parcels and goes out with Jacqueline.	**Philip paie, ramasse ses paquets et sort avec Jacqueline.**

J'ai soixante-quinze livres en chèques de voyage.

ACTE 4 (i)

Philip et Jacqueline finissent le repas.

Au fait, je dois téléphoner à mes parents.

Philip décroche le téléphone et compose le numéro.

Est-ce que je peux utiliser votre téléphone, s'il vous plait?

Il explique qu'il doit rester un peu plus longtemps à Paris.

J'ai besoin d'acheter d'autres vêtements

donc je dois aller chercher de l'argent à la banque.

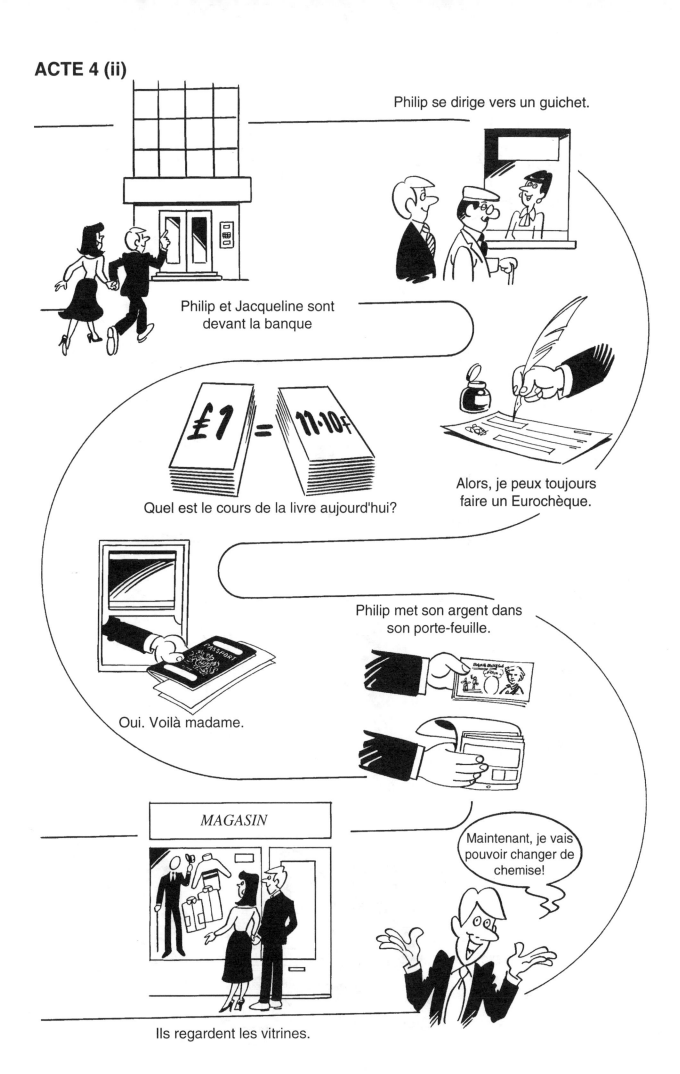

Philip se dirige vers un guichet.

Philip et Jacqueline sont devant la banque

Quel est le cours de la livre aujourd'hui?

£1 = 11·10f

Alors, je peux toujours faire un Eurochèque.

Philip met son argent dans son porte-feuille.

Oui. Voilà madame.

MAGASIN

Maintenant, je vais pouvoir changer de chemise!

Ils regardent les vitrines.

ACTE 4 (iii)

J'ai besoin d'une chemise,
de sous-vêtements et de chaussettes.

Une vendeuse
s'approche.

Vous faites du combien?

Il va essayer
la chemise

Vous êtes
très élégant.

Tenez, voilà
une belle cravate grise.

C'est tout,
n'est pas?

Philip paie, ramasse ses
paquets et sort avec
Jacqueline.

MAGASIN

82

Part Two : Pronunciation and Intonation
Section Deux : Prononciation et Intonation

Consonants: **p / t / k**

a) The sound **p** as in Paris:

Note the difference between these English and French words which are very similar:

pair / **paire**   Paris / **Paris**   passport / **passeport**

Some examples:

I. **C'est possible?**

2. **Passez-moi votre passeport.**

3. **Je peux payer en espèces?**

4. **On peut partir un peu plus tard?**

A tongue-twister:

La pipe du papa du pape pue.

b) The sound **t** as in **tard** or **thé**:

Note the differences between these English and French words which sound similar:

tar / **tard**   Tay / **taie**   telephone / **téléphone**

Some examples:

I. **Est-ce tard?**

2. **Est-ce tout?**

3. **Quelle heure est-il?**
   Il est huit heures.

4. **Une tasse de thé?**
   Non, un Pastis 5l.

A tongue-twister:

Ton thé t'a-t-il ôté ta toux?
Mon thé ne m'a rien ôté du tout.

c) The sound **k** as in **carte**, **que** or **kilo**:

Note the differences between these English and French words which sound similar:

cart / **carte**   come / **comme**   key / **qui**

Some examples:

I.   **Est-ce confortable?**

2.   **Ça coûte combien?**

3.   **Qu'est-ce que vous avez comme argent?**

4.   **Passez à la caisse avec votre carte eurochèque.**

Comptines:

I.   **Une poule sur un mur**
        Qui picote du pain dur,
        Picoti, Picota,
        Lève la queue et puis s'en va!

2.   **Voulez-vous des pommes d'api,**
        D'api, d'api rouges?
        Voulez-vous des beaux tapis,
        Tapis, tapis gris?
        Tapis, tapis rouges!
        Tapis, tapis gris!

Part Three Section Trois
Functional Dialogues Dialogues Fonctionnels

I.	Philip is phoning to England.	**Philip téléphone en Angleterre.**

Philip:	I must phone my parents. Have you got a phone?	**Je dois téléphoner à mes parents. Vous avez le téléphone?**
J:	Yes, it's over there by the door. Do you know how to phone to England?	**Oui, il est là-bas près de la porte. Savez-vous téléphoner en Angleterre?**
Philip:	No, what do I have to do?	**Non, qu'est-ce que je dois faire?**
J:	You have to dial nineteen then forty four for England.	**Vous devez composer le dix-neuf puis le quarante quatre pour l'Angleterre.**
Philip:	And for London?	**Et pour Londres?**
J:	You dial one, I think.	**Vous faites le un , je crois.**

2.	At the bank: Philip and the bank clerk.	**A la banque: Philip et l'employée de banque. L'employée deBanque = L'E B.**

Philip:	I'd like to change these traveller's cheques, please. What is the exchange rate for the pound today?	**Je voudrais changer ces chèques de voyage, s'il vous plaît. Quel est le cours de la livre aujourd'hui?**
L'E B:	Eleven francs ten, sir.	**Il est à onze francs dix, monsieur.**
Philip:	Ah, thank you. Do you accept Eurocheques?	**Bien, merci. Est-ce que vous acceptez les Eurochèques?**
L'E B:	Yes, sir.	**Oui, monsieur.**
Philip:	Right then, here are the traveller's cheques and a Eurocheque for one thousand francs.	**Bon. Eh bien, voilà les chèques de voyage et un Eurochèque pour mille francs.**
L'E B:	Have you got your Eurocheque card and your passport?	**Vous avez votre carte eurochèque et votre passeport?**
Philip:	Yes, here they are.	**Oui. Voilà madame.**
L'E B:	Thank you, sir.	**Merci monsieur.**

Quel est le cours de la livre aujourd'hui?

85

3.

Philip goes into a clothes shop.
Philip entre dans un magasin de vêtements.

The Saleswoman
La Vendeuse = La V.

La V:	Can I help you?	**Est-ce que je peux vous aider?**
Philip:	Can I try on that striped shirt which is in the shop-window?	**Est-ce que je peux essayer la chemise rayée qui est en vitrine?**
La V:	Yes, of course. The shirt at eighty francs?	**Oui, bien sûr. La chemise à quatre-vingts francs?**
Philip:	Yes, that's it.	**Oui, c'est ça.**
La V:	What size do you take?	**Vous faites du combien?**
Philip:	Thirty nine. I think.	**Du trente neuf , je crois.**
La V:	It's your size. There you are, sir. You can go to the changing-room.	**Alors, c'est votre taille. Voilà, monsieur. Vous pouvez passer au salon d'essayage.**

4.

Philip tries on a shirt and tie.
Philip essaie une chemise et une cravate.

Philip:	What do you think of it?	**Qu'est-ce que vous en pensez?**
J:	It suits you. You look very elegant.	**Ça vous va bien. Vous êtes très élégant.**
Philip:	Do you think so?	**Vous croyez?**
J:	Yes. The grey tie goes well with that shirt.	**Oui. La cravate grise va bien avec cette chemise.**
Philip:	It's a bit light, don't you think?	**Elle est un peu claire, vous ne trouvez pas?**
J:	No. I think it's just the right colour. It's very smart.	**Ah! non, moi, je trouve que c'est la bonne couleur. Elle est très chic.**

Vous devez composer le dix-neuf puis le quarante-quatre.

5.

	Philip buys some other clothes.	**Philip achète d'autres vêtements.**
La V:	Do you need anything else?	**Vous avez besoin d'autre chose?**
Philip:	Yes, I need a pair of white underpants and a white T-shirt and two pairs of socks.	**Oui, j'ai besoin d'un slip et d'un maillot de corps blancs et de deux paires de chaussettes.**
La V:	What size shoes do you take?	**Vous chaussez du combien?**
Philip:	Forty one.	**Du quarante et un.**
La V:	And what colour do you want?	**Et quelle couleur voulez-vous?**
Philip:	Dark grey, please.	**Gris foncé, s'il vous plaît.**

Philip achète d'autres vêtements.

FONTAINEBLEAU

Part Four : Personalised Dialogues
Section Quatre : Dialogues

a)   You are asking Jacqueline how to phone to England.

Vous:	(Say you must phone your uncle and ask if there is a phone.)
Jacqueline:	**Oui, il est là-bas près de la porte.**
	Savez-vous téléphoner en Angleterre?
Vous:	(Say no and ask what you must do.)
Jacqueline:	**Vous devez composer le dix-neuf (I9)**
	puis le quarante-quatre (44) pour l'Angleterre.
Vous:	(Ask what you have to do to get your home town.)
Jacqueline:	**Vous faites le un, je crois.**

b)   At the bank.

Vous:	(Say you'd like to change some traveller's cheques
	and ask what the exchange rate for the pound is today.)
L'employée:	**Il est à onze francs dix.**
Vous:	(Say thank you and ask if they accept Eurocheques.)
L'employée:	**Oui, bien sûr.**
Vous:	(Explain that you are giving the traveller's cheques
	and a Eurocheque for one thousand francs.)
L'employée:	**Vous avez votre carte eurochèque et votre**
	passeport?
Vous:	(Say yes and hand them over.)
L'employée:	**Merci.**

c)   You are in a clothes-shop.

La vendeuse:	**Est-ce que je peux vous aider?**
Vous:	(Ask if you can try on the pair of grey trousers
	which are in the shop-window.)
La vendeuse:	**Le pantalon à deux cent cinquante (250) francs?**
Vous:	(Say yes that's right.)
La vendeuse:	**Vous faites du combien?**
Vous:	(Say what size you take.)
La vendeuse:	**Alors, c'est votre taille. Voilà.**

d)   You are trying on a shirt and tie and discussing them with Jacqueline.

Vous:	(Ask Jacqueline what she thinks of them.)
Jacqueline:	**Ça vous va bien.**
	Vous êtes très élégant.
Vous:	(Ask if she really thinks so.)
Jacqueline:	**Oui. La cravate grise va bien avec cette chemise.**
Vous:	(Ask if she doesn't think the tie is a bit light.)
Jacqueline:	**Ah! non, moi, je trouve que c'est la bonne couleur.**
	Elle est très chic.

e)   You are buying some other clothes.

La vendeuse:	**Vous avez besoin d'autre chose?**
Vous:	(Say yes and ask for a white T-shirt and a pair of socks.)
La vendeuse:	**Vous chaussez du combien?**
Vous:	(Say what size shoes you take.)
La vendeuse:	**Et quelle couleur voulez-vous?**
Vous:	(Say what colour you want.)

Part Five   : Grammar
Section Cinq : Grammaire

1.   The Present tense of **-ER, -IR** and **-RE** verbs.

As we pointed out in Act 1, there are three main groups of verbs in French which are defined by the infinitive endings: **-ER, -IR, -RE.** The **-ER** group accounts for the majority of French verbs.

Below are complete examples of the Present Tense in each group:

DONNER — to give

je donne	nous donnons
tu donnes	vous donnez
il/elle/on donne	ils/elles donnent

FINIR — to finish

je finis	nous finissons
tu finis	vous finissez
il/elle/on finit	ils/elles finissent

REPONDRE — to answer

je réponds	nous répondons
tu réponds	vous répondez
il/elle/on répond	ils/elles répondent

NOTE: The **TU** form is a familiar you form to be used with close friends and relations. We shall see more of this in Act 9 when Philip has got to know Jacqueline a bit better!

THE NAME GAME

You would now benefit a lot from reading through the Name Game again.

Are you remembering to make up a mnemonic dictionary for those words where there are no linguistic associations?

2. **CE/CETTE** or **CES** — This or That/These or Those

To single out certain nouns, referring to them, for example, as 'this person' or 'that time' and 'these people' or 'those things', you use **CE/CETTE** or **CES**. Which word you use will depend upon the gender (masculine or feminine) and whether the people or things concerned are singular or plural:

e.g.
Je rentre à Londres CE soir.
(Masculine singular)
I return to London tonight.

. . . pour aller avec CETTE chemise.
(Feminine singular)
. . . to go with this shirt.

Je voudrais changer CES chèques de voyage.
(Plural)
I would like to change these traveller's cheques.

NOTE: There is another form — **CET** — which is used before masculine singular nouns that begin with a vowel sound:

e.g.
CET homme (this or that man)

3. **SON/SA** or **SES** — His/Her

You have seen that **SON** and **SA** can mean either 'his' or 'her', depending upon the gender of the singular noun to which they refer. If the noun is plural, you must use **SES**.

e.g.
Philip sort SON dentifrice et SA brosse à dents.
Il ramasse SES paquets.

4. **MON/MA or MES** — My

To translate English 'my', you also have three possible versions:

MON with **LE** nouns (masculine singular)
MA with **LA** nouns (feminine singular)
MES with **LES** nouns (plural nouns)

e.g.
Voilà MON passeport.
C'est MA première visite.
Je dois téléphoner à MES parents.

Note that **MON** and **SON** are used before all singular nouns that begin with a vowel sound, with a change in pronunciation:

e.g.
Mon oncle   **Son argent**

5. **VOTRE/VOS** — Your

To translate English 'your', you can use either **VOTRE** or **VOS** depending upon whether what you are referring to is singular or plural, no matter what the gender:

e.g. **Voilà VOS chaussettes, VOS sous-vêtements,
VOTRE chemise et VOTRE cravate.**

REMEMBER: For 'this' or 'that'   *
Say **CE** and **CETTE**
For 'these' or 'those'
Say **CES**
For 'his' or 'her'
Say **SON** — **SA** — **SES**
For 'my'
Say **MON** — **MA** — **MES**
'Your' is slightly simpler, though:
Just say either **VOTRE** or **VOS**.   *

6. **...QUE** — That

QUE is often used as a connecting word, like the English 'that' in the following sentences:

Ils pensent QUE je rentre à Londres ce soir.
They think (that) I'm coming back to London this evening.

Il explique QU'il doit rester un peu plus longtemps.
He explains (that) he has to stay a bit longer.

Je trouve QUE c'est la bonne couleur.
I think (that) it's just the right colour.

Vous croyez QUE c'est assez?
Do you think (that) it's enough?

NOTE: Whilst in English you may omit 'that' in these examples, in French always use **QUE** to link the two parts of the sentence.

J'ai besoin d'acheter d'autres vêtements.

Part Six   : Key Phrases
Section Six   : Expressions Utiles

1.   **JE PEUX . . ./VOUS POUVEZ . . .(Pouvoir)**

When you are seeking or giving permission to do something, you can use these phrases followed by the infinitive of a verb:

    e.g.   **Est-ce que je peux utiliser votre téléphone, s'il vous plaît?**   *
         Can I (May I) use your phone, please?

         Vous pouvez passer au salon d'essayage.
         You can (You may) go to the changing room.

2.   **JE DOIS . . ./VOUS DEVEZ . . .(Devoir)**

When you want to say that something must be done, you can use these phrases followed by the infinitive of a verb:

    e.g.   **Je dois téléphoner à mes parents.**   *
         I must phone my parents.

         Vous devez composer le 19.
         You have to dial 19.

3.   **SAVEZ-VOUS . . .? (Savoir)**

When you want to find out if someone knows how to do something, you can use this phrase followed by an infinitive:

    e.g.   **Savez-vous téléphoner en Angleterre?**
         Do you know how to phone England?

    NOTE: The following example:

         Savez-vous parler français?
         Can you (i.e. Do you know how to) speak French?   *

4.   **AVOIR BESOIN DE . . .**
To say that you need something or that you need to do something, you can use this expression followed by either a noun or by the infinitive of a verb:

    e.g.   **J'ai besoin d'une chemise.**
         I need a shirt.

         Vous avez besoin d'autre chose?
         Do you need anything else?

         J'ai besoin d'acheter d'autres vêtements.
         I need to buy some more clothes.

    NOTE: **J'ai besoin de** is literally 'I have need of'.

Part Seven : Games
Section Sept : Jeux

1. Pyramid

   Can you fill in the pyramid from the clues by adding one letter each time? We have helped you with the first one.

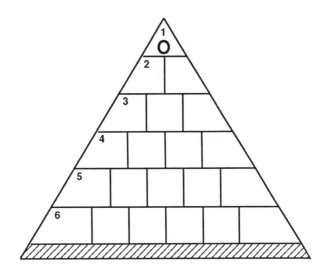

   1. Letter.
   2. Can replace 'nous'.
   3. Equals 'mine'.
   4. A mountain: e.g. - - - - **Blanc.**
   5. Philip goes upstairs.
   6. You can tell the time by it.

2. Number Game

   Complete the sequence as near to 100 as you can.

   a. **trois, six, douze ...**
   b. **deux, deux, quatre — trois, trois, neuf — ...**
   c. **deux, trois, cinq, neuf...**

3.   Can you read the numbers on the bank notes?

4. **Mon / Ma / Mes et Son / Sa / Ses**

Whose clothes are they?

A man's and a woman's clothes have been mixed up. According to your sex, say which is yours and which is the other person's.

e.g.

If you are a woman: **C'est mon collant mais c'est ses chaussettes.**
If you are a man: **C'est son collant mais c'est mes chaussettes.**

1.

2.

3.

4.

5. You have bought some of the clothes that you saw in the shop and are showing them to Jacqueline. Ask her what she thinks of them.

Example:

Mon chapeau, il est chic, vous ne trouvez pas?

Now carry on, using the words in brackets and making them 'agree' with the things that they are describing. Remember also to use the correct version of **Mon/Ma/Mes.**

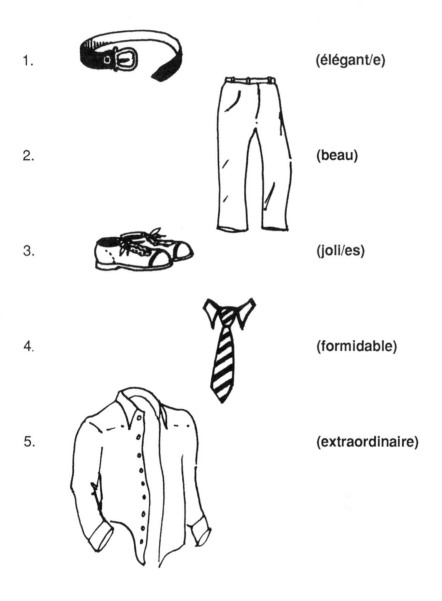

1. (élégant/e)

2. (beau)

3. (joli/es)

4. (formidable)

5. (extraordinaire)

The answers are at the back of the book.

6. Find the price:

You are looking in a shop window where the clothes have no price tags. You go into the shop and ask for the price of certain items.

Example:

Ce chapeau, il coûte combien?

Remember, when you are pointing to the various items to use the correct version of **CE/CET/CETTE/CES** and **IL/S/ELLE/S.**

1.

2.

3.

4.

5.

6.

7.

8.

7. **L'immeuble:**

Saturday morning in an apartment block in Paris.

What are they doing? In answering you will practise the present tense of some of the main verb groups and if you are stuck, look up the tables.

e.g. **Monsieur Dupont regarde l'immeuble.**

Here are the verbs you will need:

répondre, se laver, ouvrir, dormir, passer l'aspirateur, mettre, prendre, finir, se raser, prendre.

Au rez-de-chaussée:	**Madame Dupont...**
	Monsieur Lachaise...
Au premier étage:	**Monsieur Blanc...**
	Madame Blanc...
	Madame Sauge...
Au deuxième étage:	**Mademoiselle Lenoir...**
	Nicolas Lenoir...
	Monsieur Lenoir...
Au troisième étage:	**Monsieur et Madame Roux...**
	Madame Lebrun...

ACT 5 ACTE 5
Scene I Scène I

An evening with Jacqueline (Tuesday evening).	**Une soirée avec Jacqueline (Mardi soir).**

It is five o'clock in the evening. Jacqueline and Philip are tired. They are thirsty and they decide to stop at the Café des Sports.

Il est cinq heures du soir. Jacqueline et Philip sont fatigués. Ils ont soif et ils décident de s'arrêter au Café des Sports.

Jacqueline: There's an empty table on the terrace. Let's go there.

Il y a une table libre à la terrasse. Allons-y.

Ils sont fatigués.

They sit down and Jacqueline calls the waiter.

Ils s'assoient et Jacqueline appelle le garçon.

Jacqueline: Waiter, please, an orange juice and a beer.

Garçon, s'il vous plaît, un jus d'orange et une bière.

Philip: What do you like doing in your spare time?

Qu'est-ce que vous aimez faire de votre temps libre?

Jacqueline: I like the theatre and I love baroque music. What about you?

J'aime bien le théâtre et j'adore la musique baroque. Et vous?

Philip: I prefer jazz and modern painting. Do you like the cinema?

Moi, je préfère la musique de jazz et la peinture moderne. Aimez-vous le cinéma?

Jacqueline: Yes. I love American films.

Oui. J'aime beaucoup les films américains.

Philip: So do I. Do you like Hitchcock's films?

Moi aussi. Vous aimez les films de Hitchcock?

Jacqueline: Oh no. I hate thrillers. I prefer comedies.

Oh! non, je déteste les films à suspense. Je préfère les films comiques.

Philip: Are you free this evening? Do you want to go to the theatre or to a concert?

Etes-vous libre ce soir? Voulez-vous aller au théâtre ou au concert?

Jacqueline: Yes, but for that you have to book in advance. and it's too late for this evening.

Oui, mais pour cela, il faut louer les places à l'avance et c'est trop tard pour ce soir.

Philip:	Let's go to the cinema then.	Alors, allons au cinéma.
	What's on	Qu'est-ce qu'on joue
	in the local cinemas?	dans le quartier?
Jacquleine:	They're showing Woody	On joue le dernier film de Woody
	Allen's latest film.	Allen.
	Do you want to see it?	Voulez-vous le voir?
Philip:	All right and afterwards	D'accord et après je vous invite
	I'll stand you dinner at	à dîner
	a restaurant.	au restaurant.
Jacqueline:	What a good idea!	Quelle bonne idée!
	I know a nice little	Je connais un petit
	restaurant	restaurant
	in the rue des Canettes.	dans la rue des Canettes.
	It's good and	C'est bon et ce n'est
	not expensive.	pas cher.
Philip:	What time is the next	A quelle heure est la prochaine
	programme?	séance de cinéma?
Jacqueline:	At six fifteen (6.l5)	A dix-huit heures quinze. (18h 15).
	Let's go straight away.	Allons-y tout de suite.
	Waiter! The bill,	Garçon! l'addition,
	please!	s'il vous plaît.

Scene 2   Scène 2

	Jacqueline and Philip arrive at	Jacqueline et Philip arrivent à
	six o'clock (6)	dix-huit heures (18h)
	at the Danton cinema.	devant le cinéma Danton.
	There is a crowd	Il y a beaucoup de monde
	and they have to queue.	et il faut faire la queue.

	When they reach the box-office	Quand ils arrivent à la caisse
	Philip buys two tickets	Philip prend deux places
	and they go	et ils entrent
	into the cinema.	dans la salle de cinéma.
	An usherette takes them	Une ouvreuse les amène
	to their seats.	à leur place.

Usherette:	This way.	Par ici, Messieurs Dames.
	Your tickets, please.	Vos billets, s'il vous plaît.
Philip:	What does she want?	Qu'est-ce qu'elle veut?
Jacqueline:	You've got to show	Il faut montrer
	the tickets.	les billets.
Philip:	Oh! right.	Ah! bon, eh bien,
	Here they are.	les voilà.
	What is she waiting for	Mais qu'est-ce qu'elle attend
	now?	maintenant?
Jacqueline:	You've got to give her	Il faut lui donner
	a tip.	un pourboire.

Philip:	A tip for the usherette?	**Un pourboire à l'ouvreuse?**
Jacqueline:	Yes, it's the done thing.	**Oui, c'est normal.**
Philip:	O.K.	**Bon.**
	How much must I give?	**Et combien faut-il donner?**
Jacqueline:	Two francs.	**Deux francs.**

The usherette takes the money
and goes away.
After a few adverts
the film begins.

**L'ouvreuse prend l'argent
et s'en va.
Après quelques publicités
le film commence.**

Scene 3   **Scène 3**

Two hours later
Jacqueline and Philip
are in the rue des Canettes
outside Chez Tante Marie.
It is a small,
friendly restaurant.
The tablecloths and napkins
are red and white checked
and there is a candle and
some flowers on each table.
They go in.

**Deux heures plus tard,
Jacqueline et Philip
sont dans la rue des Canettes,
devant Chez Tante Marie.
C'est un petit
restaurant sympathique.
Les nappes et les serviettes
sont à carreaux rouges et blancs
et il y a une bougie et
des fleurs sur chaque table.
Ils entrent.**

Waiter:	A table for two?	**Une table pour deux?**
Jacqueline:	Yes, please.	**Oui, s'il vous plaît.**
Waiter:	There you are. Sit here.	**Tenez! Mettez-vous ici.**

Philip and Jacqueline sit down
and the waiter gives them the menu.
Five minutes later, he comes back.

**Philip et Jacqueline s'installent
et le serveur leur donne le menu.
Cinq minutes plus tard, il revient.**

Waiter:	Can I take your order?	**Je peux prendre votre commande?**
Philip:	Yes. We'll have the sixty (60) franc menu.	**Oui. Nous allons prendre le menu à soixante francs (60F).**
Waiter:	What will you have to start?	**Qu'est-ce que vous prenez comme entrée?**
Jacqueline:	I'm going to have a mushroom soufflé	**Je vais prendre un soufflé aux champignons.**
Philip:	And I'm going to have duck pâté	**Moi, je vais prendre du pâté de canard.**
Waiter:	And for the main course?	**Et comme plat principal?**
Jacqueline:	Roast veal for me.	**Pour moi, du rôti de veau.**
Waiter:	And Sir?	**Et pour monsieur?**

Philip:	An entrecôte steak for me.	**Pour moi, une entrecôte.**
Waiter:	How would you like your entrecôte?	**Vous la voulez comment votre entrecôte?**
	Medium, well done or rare?	**A point, bien cuite ou saignante?**
Philip:	Well done, please.	**Bien cuite, s'il vous plaît.**
Waiter:	What sort of vegetables do you want?	**Qu'est-ce que vous voulez comme légumes?**
Philip:	I'll have chips.	**Je vais prendre des frites.**
	What about you Jacqueline?	**Et vous, Jacqueline?**
Jacqueline:	I'll have peas.	**Moi, je vais prendre des petits pois.**
Waiter:	What would you like to drink with it?	**Et avec ça, qu'est-ce que vous buvez?**
	Wine? Beer? Mineral water?	**Du vin, de la bière, de l'eau minérale?**
Jacqueline:	Wine.	**Du vin.**
Waiter:	Red, rosé or white?	**Du rouge, du rosé ou du blanc?**
Jacqueline:	Have you any Beaujolais?	**Vous avez du Beaujolais?**
Waiter:	No, I haven't any Beaujolais	**Non, je n'ai pas de Beaujolais**
	but I've got a nice Côtes du Rhône.	**mais j'ai un bon Côtes du Rhône.**
Jacqueline:	Well, bring us a bottle of Côtes du Rhône and a jug of water.	**Eh bien, apportez nous une bouteille de Côtes du Rhône et une carafe d'eau.**
Waiter:	Right, Miss.	**Bien mademoiselle.**
	Don't you want an aperitif?	**Vous ne voulez pas d'apéritif?**
Jacqueline:	Yes.	**Si,**
	Give us two Martinis.	**donnez-nous deux Martinis.**

Scene 4 **Scène 4**

Three-quarters of an hour later. **Trois quarts d'heure plus tard.**

Philip:	This meat is very tasty.	**Cette viande a vraiment bon goût.**

He puts down his knife and fork and picks up the menu. **Il pose son couteau et sa fourchette et prend le menu.**

Philip:	Now then, what is there for dessert?	**Voyons... Qu'est-ce qu'il y a comme dessert?**
	Crème caramel, chocolate mousse, apple tart or ice cream.	**Crème caramel, mousse au chocolat, tarte aux pommes ou glaces.**

Jacqueline:	We must have cheese first.	**Il faut prendre le fromage avant.**
	You are in France!	**Vous êtes en France.**
Philip:	Ah yes, of course.	**Ah! oui, bien sûr.**

Philip and Jacqueline take a bit of brie and a bit of goat's cheese. Then Jacqueline orders crème caramel and Philip a vanilla ice-cream. When the waiter comes back with their dessert Philip asks for the bill.	**Philip et Jacqueline prennent un morceau de brie et un morceau de chèvre. Puis Jacqueline commande une crème caramel et Philip une glace à la vanille. Quand le garçon revient avec leurs desserts, Philip lui demande l'addition.**

Philip:	Jacqueline, is the service included?	**Jacqueline, est-ce que le service est compris?**
Jacqueline:	No, not in this restaurant. You usually have to leave a fifteen percent (15%) tip.	**Non, pas dans ce restaurant. En principe, il faut laisser quinze pour cent (15%) de pourboire.**

Philip pays and they leave the restaurant. Outside it's mild. The moon is shining. Philip and Jacqueline walk slowly back to the rue Madame.	**Philip paie et ils sortent du restaurant. Dehors, il fait doux. La lune brille. Philip et Jacqueline rentrent lentement Rue Madame.**

Il est cinq heures du soir.

Jacqueline et Philip
sont fatigués.

Ils s'assoient et Jacqueline
appelle le garçon.

Garçon, s'il vous plaît,
un jus d'orange
et une bière.

J'adore la musique
baroque. Et vous?

Moi, je préfère la musique
de jazz et la peinture moderne.

ACTE 5 (iii)

Après quelques publicités le film commence.

Les nappes et les serviettes sont à carreaux rouges et blancs,

et il y a une bougie et des fleurs sur chaque table.

Une table pour deux?

Chez Tante Marie

60f

Menu

Oui. Nous allons prendre le menu à soixante francs.

Je vais prendre un soufflé aux champignons.

Pour moi, du rôti de veau.

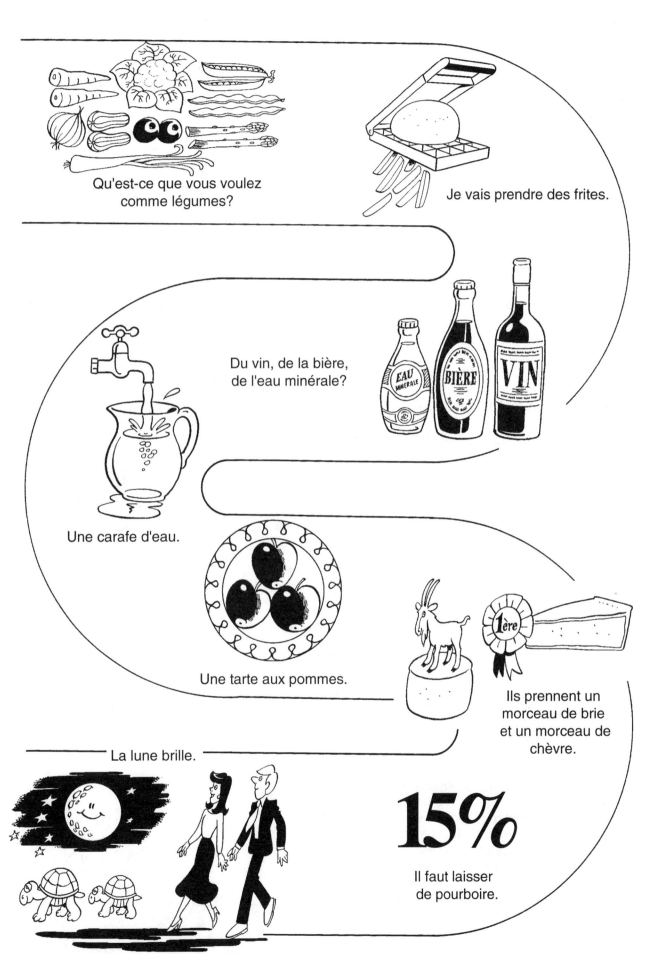

Qu'est-ce que vous voulez comme légumes?

Je vais prendre des frites.

Du vin, de la bière, de l'eau minérale?

EAU MINÉRALE

BIÈRE

VIN

Une carafe d'eau.

Une tarte aux pommes.

1ère

Ils prennent un morceau de brie et un morceau de chèvre.

La lune brille.

15%

Il faut laisser de pourboire.

Ils rentrent lentement rue Madame.

Part Two : Pronunciation and Intonation
Section Deux : Prononciation et Intonation

a) The sound **é** as in **café, aller, tenez, et** or **les**:

    I.   **Voulez-vous aller dîner?**

    2.   **Quelle bonne idée!**

    3.   **Vous aimez le café?**

    4.   **Vous détestez les soufflés?**

    5.   **Tenez, prenez du pâté.**

b) The sound **o** as in **hôtel, chaud, beau** or **trop**:

Listen to the differences between these English and French words:

bow / **beau**   pose / **pose**   show / **chaud**

Some sentences:

    I.   **Il fait chaud.**   3.   **Il pose le couteau.**

    2.   **Il faut de l'eau.**   4.   **Il y a un beau rôti de veau.**

c) Further practice of the sound **r**:

Some examples:

gare / **garçon**   art / **argent**   tard / **tarte**
sert / **serveur**   pour / **pourboire**

Some sentences:

    I.   **Garçon, un jus d'orange.**

    2.   **Un pourboire pour le serveur?**

    3.   **Apportez-nous une carafe d'eau.**

    4.   **J'adore la musique baroque
         et la peinture moderne.**

Un jus d'orange.

d) **Comptine:**

Est-ce que le temps est beau?
Se demande l'escargot
Car, pour moi, s'il fait beau
C'est qu'il pleut à seaux.
J'aime qu'il tombe de l'eau.
Moi, je préfère l'été
Pour traîner dans les prés
Ou le long des allées
Où les laitues sont plantées.

Part Three
Functional Dialogues

Section Trois
Dialogues Fonctionnels

I.

Philip and Jacqueline are discussing their likes and dislikes.

Philip et Jacqueline parlent de leurs préférences.

Philip: What do you like doing in your spare time?

Philip: **Qu'est-ce que vous aimez faire de votre temps libre?**

J: I like the theatre and I love baroque music. What about you?

J: **J'aime bien le théâtre et j'adore la musique baroque. Et vous?**

Philip: I prefer jazz and modern painting. Do you like the cinema?

Philip: **Moi, je préfère la musique de jazz et la peinture moderne. Aimez-vous le cinéma?**

J: Yes. I love American films.

J: **Oui. J'aime beaucoup les films américains.**

Philip: So do I. Do you like Hitchcock's films?

Philip: **Moi aussi. Vous aimez les films de Hitchcock?**

J: Oh no! I hate thrillers. I prefer comedies.

J: **Oh! non, je déteste les films à suspense. Je préfère les films comiques.**

2.

Philip invites Jacqueline to the cinema then to the restaurant.

Philip invite Jacqueline au cinéma puis au restaurant.

Philip: Are you free this evening? Do you want to go to the theatre or to a concert?

Philip: **Etes-vous libre ce soir? Voulez-vous aller au théâtre ou au concert?**

J: You have to book in advance for that and it's too late for this evening.

J: **Pour cela, il faut louer les places à l'avance et c'est trop tard pour ce soir.**

Philip: Let's go to the cinema then. What's on in the local cinemas?

Philip: **Alors, allons au cinéma. Qu'est-ce qu'on joue dans le quartier?**

J: They're showing Woody Allen's latest film. Do you want to see it?

J: **On joue le dernier film de Woody Allen. Voulez-vous le voir?**

| Philip: | All right and afterwards I'll stand you dinner at a restaurant. | D'accord et après je vous invite à dîner au restaurant. |
| J: | What a good idea! | Quelle bonne idée! |

| 3. | At the cinema with the usherette. | Au cinéma avec l'ouvreuse. |

Philip:	What does she want?	Qu'est-ce qu'elle veut?
J:	You've got to show the tickets.	Il faut montrer les billets.
Philip:	Oh! right. Here they are. What is she waiting for now?	Ah! bon, eh bien, les voilà. Mais qu'est-ce qu'elle attend maintenant?
J:	You've got to give her a tip.	Il faut lui donner un pourboire.
Philip:	A tip for the usherette?	Un pourboire à l'ouvreuse?
J:	Yes, it's the done thing.	Oui, c'est normal.
Philip:	O.K. How much must I give?	Bon. Et combien faut-il donner?
J:	Two francs.	Deux francs.

| 4. | At the restaurant Chez Tante Marie. The Waiter | Au restaurant Chez Tante Marie. Le Serveur = Le S. |

Le S:	What will you have to start?	Qu'est-ce que vous allez prendre comme entrée?
Philip:	I'm going to have duck pâté.	Je vais prendre du pâté de canard.
Le S:	And for the main course?	Et comme plat principal?
Philip:	An entrecôte steak.	Une entrecôte.
Le S:	How do you want your entrecôte? Medium, well done or rare?	Vous la voulez comment votre entrecôte? A point, bien cuite ou saignante?
Philip:	Well done, please.	Bien cuite, s'il vous plaît.
Le S:	What sort of vegetables do you want?	Qu'est-ce que vous voulez comme légumes?
Philip:	I'll have chips.	Je vais prendre des frites.

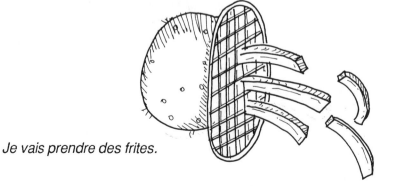

Je vais prendre des frites.

5.   Jacqueline orders something   **Jacqueline commande quelque chose**
                                  to drink.   **à boire.**

Le S:	What will you have to drink? Wine? Beer? Mineral water?	**Qu'est-ce que vous buvez? Du vin, de la bière, de l'eau minérale?**
J:	Wine.	**Du vin.**
Le S:	Red, rosé or white?	**Du rouge, du rosé ou du blanc?**
J:	Have you any Beaujolais?	**Vous avez du Beaujolais?**
Le S:	No, I haven't any Beaujolais but I've got a nice Côtes du Rhône.	**Non, je n'ai pas de Beaujolais mais j'ai un bon Côtes du Rhône.**
J:	Well, bring us a bottle of Côtes du Rhône and a jug of water.	**Eh bien, apportez-nous une bouteille de Côtes du Rhône et une carafe d'eau.**
Le S:	Right, Miss. Don't you want an aperitif?	**Bien mademoiselle. Vous ne voulez pas d'apéritif?**
J:	Yes. Give us two Martinis.	**Si, donnez-nous deux Martinis.**

Une carafe d'eau.

Part Four : Personalised Dialogues
Section Quatre : Dialogues

a) You are discussing your likes and dislikes with Jacqueline.

Vous:	(Ask Jacqueline what she likes doing in her spare time.)
Jacqueline:	**J'aime bien le théâtre**
	et j'adore la musique baroque.
	Et vous?
Vous:	(Say what you prefer e.g. jazz, modern painting, etc.)
	then ask Jacqueline if she likes the cinema.)
Jacqueline:	**Oui. J'aime beaucoup les films américains.**
Vous:	(Say you do too, then ask if she likes Hitchcock's films.)
Jacqueline:	**Oh! non, je déteste les films à suspense.**
	Je préfère les films comiques.

b) You invite Jacqueline to the cinema then to the restaurant.

Vous:	(Ask Jacqueline if she is free this evening.
	Then ask if she wants to go to the theatre
	or to a concert.)
Jacqueline:	**Pour cela, il faut louer les places à l'avance**
	et c'est trop tard pour ce soir.
Vous:	(Suggest that you go to the cinema
	and ask what is on in the local cinemas.)
Jacqueline:	**On joue le dernier film de Woody Allen.**
	Voulez-vous le voir?
Vous:	(Say all right then invite Jacqueline
	to a restaurant afterwards.)
Jacqueline:	**Quelle bonne idée!**

c) You are at the cinema and you are explaining about
the usherette to Philip.

Philip:	**Qu'est-ce qu'elle veut?**
Vous:	(Say you must show the tickets.)
Philip:	**Ah! bon, eh bien, les voilà.**
	Mais qu'est-ce qu'elle attend maintenant?
Vous:	(Say you must give a tip.)
Philip:	**Un pourboire à l'ouvreuse?**
Vous:	(Say it's the done thing.)
Philip:	**Bon. Et combien faut-il donner?**
Vous:	(Say you must give two francs.)

d) You are ordering a meal at the restaurant.

Le serveur:	**Qu'est-ce que vous allez prendre comme entrée?**
Vous:	(Say you're going to have duck pâté.)
Le serveur:	**Et comme plat principal?**
Vous:	(Say an entrecôte steak.)
Le serveur:	**Vous la voulez comment votre entrecôte?**
	A point, bien cuite ou saignante?
Vous:	(Say how you would like it.)
Le serveur:	**Qu'est-ce que vous voulez comme légumes?**
Vous:	(Say you're going to have chips.)

e) You are ordering something to drink for yourself and Jacqueline.

Le serveur:	**Qu'est-ce que vous buvez?**
	Du vin, de la bière, de l'eau minérale?
Vous:	(Say you would like wine.)
Le serveur:	**Du rouge, du rosé ou du blanc?**
Vous:	(Ask if he has any Beaujolais.)
Le serveur:	**Non, je n'ai pas de Beaujolais**
	mais j'ai un bon Côtes du Rhône.
Vous:	(Tell him to bring you a bottle of Côtes du Rhône and a jug of water.)
Le serveur:	**Bien. Vous ne voulez pas d'apéritif?**
Vous:	(Say yes and order two Martinis.)

Qu'est-ce que vous buvez?

Du vin, de la bière, de l'eau minérale?

Part Five : Grammar
Section Cinq : Grammaire

1. **LE/LA** or **LES** — Him, Her, It, Them

You know that **LE, LA** and **LES** can mean 'the' in front of a noun:

    e.g.   **LE restaurant — LA rue — LES billets.**

When you find these words in front of verbs, they mean 'him' or 'it', 'her' or 'it' and ' 'them':

    e.g.   **Voulez-vous LE voir?** (i.e. le dernier film de Woody Allen)
                                    Vous LA voulez comment, votre entrecôte?
                                      L'ouvreuse LES amène à leur place. (i.e. **Jacqueline et Philip**).

    NOTE: **LE** and **LA** become **L'** before a verb beginning with a vowel sound.

    e.g.   **Elle l'amène à sa place.**
                                    (i.e. Jacqueline OR Philip)

    REMEMBER: For 'him', 'her', 'it' and 'them', what do you say?
                                    The same as for 'the', that is, **LE — LA — LES.**

2. **LUI/LEUR** — To/for him, her, them

    REMEMBER: When saying 'to him' or 'to her',
                                    LUI is the word that should occur
                                    And if you want to say 'to them',
                                    LEUR is the word to solve the problem.

    e.g.   **Il faut lui donner un pourboire?**
                                    (i.e. to her — the usherette)

                                  Le serveur leur donne le menu.
                                    (i.e. to them — Jacqueline and Philip)

3. **VOUS — NOUS** — Saying 'To you' or ' To us'

    REMEMBER: In any situation **VOUS**
                                    Is the only word you need to translate 'you'.
                                    As for 'we' or 'us', simply say **NOUS.**

    e.g.   **Vous aimez les films de Hitchcock?**
                                  Je vous invite à diner au restaurant.
                                    . . .s'il vous plaît.

                                Nous allons prendre le menu à 60 F.
                                Apportez-nous une bouteille de Côtes du Rhône.

    NOTE: When you are giving an order, as in the last example, the **NOUS** or **VOUS** comes after the verb, just like in English.

4.   **MOI** — Saying Me

MOI means 'me', for example after prepositions like **pour**

      e.g.   **Pour MOI, du rôti de veau.**

or in phrases like   **MOI aussi** — 'me too' (or 'so do I').

MOI is also used to add emphasis alongside **je**:

      e.g.   **Moi, je préfère la musique de jazz.**
                                          Moi, je vais prendre des petits pois.

      REMEMBER: If the word **je** you wish to stress,
                                Try adding **MOI**, that should impress.

5.   **LEUR(S)**

You have just seen that **LEUR** can mean 'to/for them'. **LEUR** can also mean 'their' when it comes just before a noun:

      e.g.   **L'ouvreuse les amène à LEUR place.**

In this situation, because it is an adjective, you will add an **s** when referring to plural nouns:

      e.g.   **Le garçon revient avec leurs desserts.**

      NOTE: Unlike most adjectives, there is no special form to go with feminine nouns.

Je préfère la musique de jazz.

Part Six : Key Phrases
Section Six : Expressions Utiles

1.   **IL FAUT** + infinitive

Another way of saying that something MUST be done is to use IL FAUT plus an infinitive:

e.g.   **IL FAUT louer les places à l'avance.**
IL FAUT lui donner un pourboire.
IL FAUT prendre le fromage avant.

NOTE: It may help to think **il faut** — 'it's necessary to . . .'
You always start with **il**, but never with **je, nous, vous.**

2.   **. . .PAS DE . . ./ . . .PLUS DE . . .**

When you want to refer to unspecified quantities or numbers of things or people after negative expressions, **DU, DE LA, DE L', DES** are all reduced to **DE or D':**

e.g.   **Vous avez du Beaujolais?**
Non, je n'ai pas de Beaujolais.

Avez-vous des croissants?
Non, je n'ai plus de croissants.

3.   **QUEL/QUELLE . . .!** — What (a) . . .!

You have seen this word used just in front of nouns in questions:

e.g.   **QUELLE heure est-il?**
What time is it?

QUEL temps fait-il?
What's the weather like?

You can also use this word when you want to express pleasure or surprise as in these examples:

QUELLE bonne idée!
What a good idea!

QUEL bon repas!
What a good meal!

NOTE: If you refer to plurals, you must add an **s: QUELS/QUELLES . . .!**

e.g.   **QUELLES belles fleurs!**
What lovely flowers!

4.   AU . . ./A LA . . .

When you want to describe food items by their fillings or flavour you use
au, à la . . . or aux . . .:

e.g.
une mousse AU chocolat
une glace A LA vanille

un soufflé AUX champignons
une tarte AUX pommes

Il y a une bougie et des fleurs sur chaque table.

Part Seven : Games
Section Sept : Jeux

1. **Il faut savoir mettre la table:**

   Try to find out what you have to put on the table before starting your meal. Some of the letters are already there to help you.

   Note: Don't forget there is a glossary!

   Do you know the gender of these words?

2. Hidden phrase among cheese and wine:

   Look at the two maps opposite and fill in the appropriate names of the wine and cheeses and you will discover what Jacqueline and Philip said to each other before starting the meal.

   a.

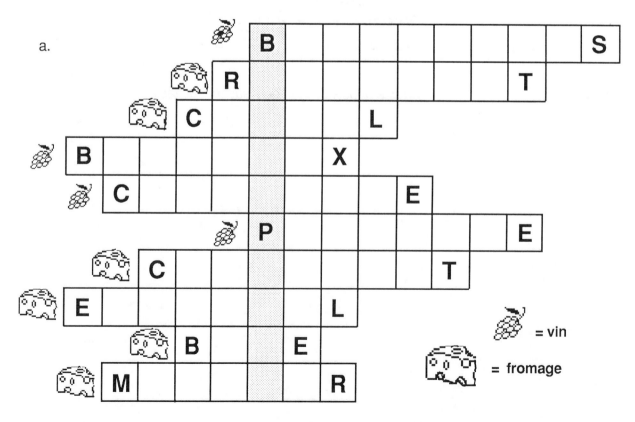

   = vin

   = fromage

120

and don't forget this recommendation:

b. **Jamais de** 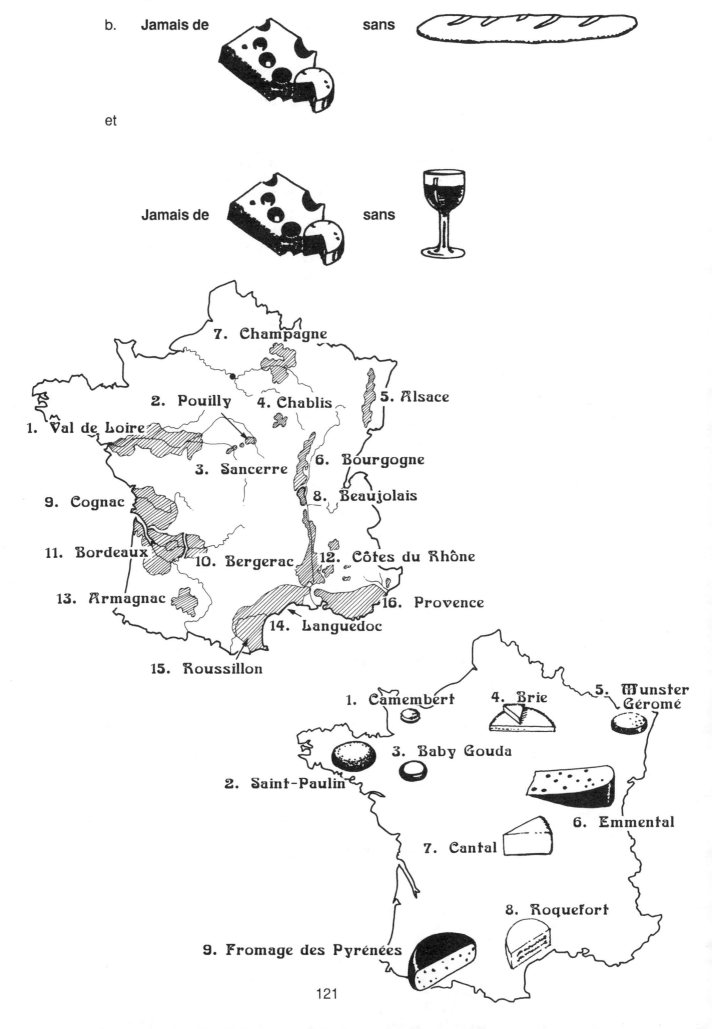 **sans**

et

Jamais de sans

7. Champagne

2. Pouilly 4. Chablis 5. Alsace

1. Val de Loire

6. Bourgogne

3. Sancerre

8. Beaujolais

9. Cognac

11. Bordeaux

10. Bergerac 12. Côtes du Rhône

13. Armagnac

16. Provence

14. Languedoc

15. Roussillon

1. Camembert 4. Brie 5. Munster Géromé

3. Baby Gouda

2. Saint-Paulin

6. Emmental

7. Cantal

8. Roquefort

9. Fromage des Pyrénées

3. **Le soufflé au fromage:**

a) Here is a recipe for a cheese soufflé for four persons. Read it carefully and put in one column the different ingredients and in the other the utensils you will need.

Faites une béchamel épaisse dans une casserole avec une bonne cuillerée à soupe d'huile, un 1/4 de litre de lait et 2 grosses cuillérées à soupe de farine. Salez et poivrez légèrement et ajoutez 75 g de gruyère râpé, une pincée de muscade et les 3 jaunes d'oeufs.

Dans un bol, battez les blancs en neige puis incorporez-les délicatement à l'aide d'une fourchette. Versez le tout dans un moule à soufflé bien beurré et mettez à four moyen pendant une bonne demi-heure. N'ouvrez jamais la porte du four pendant les vingt premières minutes de cuisson.

Les différents ingrédients	Les différents ustensiles de cuisine
1. _____	1. _____
2. _____	2. _____
3. _____	3. _____
4. _____	4. _____
5. _____	5. _____
6. _____	
7. _____	
8. _____	

b. Now replace all the imperatives by **il faut** + the infinitive:

—— ————— ————— une béchamel épaisse.

—— ————— ————— et ——————— légèrement et

——————— 75g de gruyère râpé, une pincée de muscade et les 3 jaunes

d'oeufs.

—— ———— battre les blancs en neige puis ———

—————————— délicatement.

—— ————— —————— le tout dans un moule à soufflé bien beurré

et —— ———— —— ——————— à four moyen pendant une bonne

demi-heure.

—— —— ————— —————— —————— la porte du four

pendant les vingt premières minutes de cuisson.

4.   **A l'Hôtel du Pont:**

You are having lunch at the Hôtel du Pont. Look at the menu, then tell the waitress what you would like to eat. If you are not sure what these dishes are, look at the glossary at the back of the book, then choose.

You should begin your answers with   **Je vais prendre....**   or
                                        Je voudrais...   or
                                        Donnez-moi...

La serveuse:	**Qu'est-ce que vous prenez comme hors d'oeuvre?**
Vous:	
La serveuse:	**Et comme entrée?**
Vous:	
La serveuse:	**Comme plat principal, qu'est-ce que vous voulez?**
Vous:	

As you can see, there are no details given under **Légumes**, **Fromages** and **Dessert**.

What would you ask the waitress if you wanted to know what choice there was?

And what might the waitress reply?

See if you can make up a short list under each of these headings (a glance back at Act 3 might help):

Légumes

– – – – – – – – –

– – – – – – – – –

– – – – – – – – –

– – – – – – – – –

Fromages

– – – – – – – – –

– – – – – – – – –

– – – – – – – – –

– – – – – – – – –

Dessert

– – – – – – – – –

– – – – – – – – –

– – – – – – – – –

– – – – – – – – –

HOTEL DU PONT
Logis De France

Albert Carrier
ST. PROJET DE CASSANIOUZE
15340 Calvinet

MENU à 69F50

Melon au vin de noix
ou   Jambon d'Auvergne
ou   Terrine de Campagne

Truite Meunière
ou   Six escargots
ou   Bouchée à la Reine
ou   Ecrevisses à l'américaine (supl 22F)

Pintade rôtie
ou   Gigot d'Agneau
ou   Ris de Veau sauce madère

Légumes

Plateau de fromages
et Dessert.

5.   **Qu'est-ce qu'on fait ce soir?**

You are looking through 'Pariscope', a weekly programme of shows that are on in the city, and you are discussing with Jacqueline which film to go and see. As you can see, for each film you are given the title followed by a summary and, in thick print at the end, the cinema(s) where it is showing. You can also see whether it is in a language other than French (**v.o. = version originale**).

If Jacqueline said: **J'aime les films d'aventure.**
you might say: **Allons voir 'Les sept samourais' au Rialto bananas.**

What would you say if Jacqueline said the following:

1.   **J'aime les films de Woody Allen.**
2.   **J'aime les films de François Truffaut.**
3.   **J'aime les dessins animés** (cartoons).
4.   **J'aime les films allemands en version originale.**
5.   **J'aime les films avec Bette Davis.**
6.   **J'aime les vieux films américains en noir et blanc.**

PRENDS L'OSEILLE ET TIRE-TOI. *Take the Money and Run.* 1970. 1h. 25. Comédie américaine en couleurs de Woody Allen avec Woody Allen, Janet Margolin, Marcel Hillaire, Jacquelyn Hyde, Lonny Chapman. Gangster paumé et naf, Virgil fuit la police et toutes les contingences d'un monde et d'une société hostiles. Le premier film de W.A., un ton burlesque et une verve comique très personnelle que l'on retrouve dans tous ses autres longs métrages.
Les Forums Cinémas Orient Express 3 v.o. Reflet Logos

QU'EST-IL ARRIVE A BABY JANE? *Whatever Happened to Baby Jane?* 1962. 2h. 15. Drame psychologique américain en noir et blanc de Robert Aldrich avec Bette Davies, Joan Crawford, Victor Buono. Ancienne enfant prodige obsédée par sa gloire passée, une vieille actrice sombre dans la démence, séquestrant sa soeur dont elle jalouse la célébrité.
L'affrontement de deux monstres sacrés du cinéma américain.
Saint Ambroise v.o.

LES QUATRE CENTS COUPS. 1959. 1h. 40. Drame psychologique français en noir et blanc de François Truffaut avec Jean-Pierre Léaud, Patrick Auffay, Laire Maurier, Albert Rémy, Guy Decomble.
La jeunesse d'Antoine Doinel, le premier volet de l'oeuvre du cinéaste de 'Vivement Dimanche' et du 'Dernier Métro.' Un regard bouleversant sur l'enfance. Une oeuvre importante de l'histoire du cinéma français.
Republique Cinémas.

QUERELLE. 1982. 2h. Drame psychologique allemand en couleurs de Rainer W. Fassbinder avec Brad Davis, Franco Nero, Jeanne Moreau, Laurent Malet, Hanno Poschl.
Adapté du roman de Jean Genet 'La Querelle de Brest', le portrait d'un marin homosexuel. Choquante et puissante l'oeuvre posthume d'un des grand cinéastes du cinéma allemand que déjà à Venise déclencha le scandale.
Interdit — 13 ans.
Ciné Beaubourg Les Halles, Le Grand Pavois v.o.

LE ROI ET L'OISEAU. 1979. 1h. 25. Dessin animé français en couleurs de Paul Grimault avec Les voix de Jean Martin, Pascal Mazzotti, Rauymond Bussières,Agnès Viala, Renaud Marx, Hubert Deschamps.
Le retour des personnages de 'La Bergère et le Ramoneur' pour ce grand dessin animé. En complément de programme : Petit Pierre, 8mn 30 . Court métrage de Emmanuel Clot, César 80 du meilleur court métrage documentaire.
La Boite à Films.

LES SEPT SAMOURAIS. 1954. 3h. 20. Film d'aventures japonais en noir et blanc d'Akira Kurosawa avec Toshiro Mifune, Takashi Shimura.
Dans les troubles du Moyen-Age Nippon, sept guerriers s'offrent à protéger un paisible village. Du movement, de l'action, de la vitesse, des cris, du sang. Une spectaculaire virtuosité de jongleur.
Rialto Bananas v.o.

SERENADE A TROIS. *Design for Living.* 1933. 1h. 35. Comédie américaine en noir et blanc d'Ernst Lubitsch avec Fredric March, Gary Cooper, Miriam Hopkins.
Une jeune femme s'émancipe sous l'influence d'un peintre et d'un auteur dramatique. Etourdissante comédie d'un maître du genre.
Action Christine.

6. THE CARD GAME.

Study the Grammar Notes for Act 5, 1 and 2 again.

Now try this game. You need a pack of playing cards. Take out eight and nine, Ace and King from each suit. Now divide the pack into one pile with all the cards 2-7, and one with the cards 10, Jack, Queen.

Turn over one card from each pile to determine the square across (10-Queen) and the square down (2-7). When the square is determined make sentences in French using the words indicated:

e.g. square 7/10 **Philip donne le paquet à Jacqueline.**

Now use 'it' (or 'them') instead of **le paquet**: **Philip le donne à Jacqueline.**

Now use 'to her/him' instead of **à Jacqueline/Philip**: **Philip lui donne le paquet.**

Now use both, 'it' and 'to her" **Philip le lui donne.**

or: **Jacqueline le lui donne.**

		Ten	Jack	Queen	
Un ami	2				le film
le serveur	3				l'entrecôte
	4				le vin
Philip	5				les fleurs
La serveuse	6				le pâté de canard
Philip/ Jacqueline	7				le paquet
		donner (+ à)	offrir (+ à)	recommander (+ à)	

Game devised by Lisa Schlotmann and Colin Rose

THE NAME GAME

You would now benefit a lot from reading through the Name Game again.

Are you remembering to make up a mnemonic dictionary for those words where there are no linguistic associations?

BONUS

1.   Can you solve this riddle?

It's what Philip said when he arrived at the restaurant.

2.   **Histoire drôle:**

Un petit garçon entre dans une épicerie.
— Je voudrais une bouteille de vin.
— Du blanc ou du rouge?
— Ça n'a pas d'importance, c'est pour mon grand-père et il ne voit pas bien.

3.   **Une autre histoire drôle:**

Dans un restaurant, un monsieur parle à son voisin:

'Moi, je viens ici parce que ma femme ne veut pas faire la cuisine.— Eh bien moi, c'est le contraire, c'est parce que ma femme veut toujours la faire.'

The answers are at the back of the book.

ACT 6
Scene I

ACT 6
Scène I

Another Delay (Tuesday night).

Un nouveau délai (Mardi soir).

Philip and Jacqueline
reach rue Madame.
It is ten o'clock
but Jacqueline wants to carry on their
conversation and she takes
Philip into the living-room.

Philip et Jacqueline
arrivent rue Madame.
Il est dix heures du soir
mais Jacqueline veut continuer à
parler et elle fait entrer
Philip dans le salon.

Jacqueline: | Would you like to have a drink before going back to the hotel?
Philip: | I'd love to.
Jacqueline: | Would you like a coffee?
Philip: | No. I'm sorry, I don't drink coffee in the evening.
Jacqueline: | A liqueur then? Wouldn't you like a brandy?
Philip: | Yes, I'd love one.

Avez-vous envie de prendre
quelque chose avant de
rentrer à l'hôtel?
Oui, avec plaisir.
Voulez-vous un café?
Non, je suis désolé,
je ne bois pas de café
le soir.
Un petit digestif alors?
Vous n'avez pas envie
d'un cognac?
Si, volontiers.

Ils arrivent rue Madame.

While Jacqueline is getting out
the bottle of brandy,
Philip looks around
then they both sit down
on the sofa.

Pendant que Jacqueline sort
la bouteille de cognac,
Philip regarde autour de lui,
puis ils s'installent tous les deux
sur le divan.

Philip: | You have a lovely house.
Jacqueline: | It isn't mine it belongs to my uncle. I work with him in the family business.
Philip: | Oh? What do you do?
Jacqueline: | I'm in the Import-Export business. I'm in charge of personnel. My father and my uncle founded the firm thirty years ago.
Philip: | So you work with your father as well?

Vous avez une très jolie maison.
Elle n'est pas à moi,
elle est à mon oncle.
Je travaille avec lui
dans l'entreprise familiale.
Ah! bon. Qu'est-ce que vous faites
dans la vie?
Je travaille dans
l'import-export.
Je suis chef du
personnel.
Mon père et mon oncle ont
fondé la Maison il y a
trente ans.
Alors, vous travaillez aussi
avec votre père?

127

Jacqueline:	Not any more.	**Non, plus maintenant.**
	He retired a year ago.	**Il a pris sa retraite il y a un an.**
	He bought a house	**Il a acheté une maison**
	near Cannes and lives	**près de Cannes et il vit là bas**
	there with my mother.	**avec ma mère.**
Philip:	And what exactly does	**Et votre oncle, que fait-il**
	your uncle do?	**exactement?**
Jacqueline:	He's the MD, or	**Lui il est PDG ou**
	if you prefer,	**si vous préférez**
	Managing Director.	**Président Directeur Général.**
Philip:	Do you employ a lot	**Avez-vous beaucoup**
	of people?	**d'employés?**
Jacqueline:	No, about twenty.	**Non, une vingtaine.**
	Our Sales Manager	**Nous avions un chef des ventes,**
	was an Englishman,	**un Anglais,**
	a friend of the family	**ami de la famille,**
	who died in	**qui est mort dans**
	a car-crash	**un accident de voiture**
	a month ago.	**il y a un mois.**
Philip:	How awful!	**C'est affreux.**
Jacqueline:	Yes. It's strange	**Oui et c'est curieux**
	you look a bit like him.	**vous lui ressemblez un peu.**
	Let's not speak	**Ne parlons pas**
	about that.	**de cela.**
Philip:	Well, let's talk	**Eh bien, parlons**
	about something else.	**d'autres choses.**

Il a acheté une maison
près de Cannes

	Have you always lived	**Vous avez toujours vécu à**
	in Paris?	**Paris?**
	Were you born in Paris?	**Vous êtes née à Paris?**
Jacqueline:	No. I was born	**Non, je suis née**
	in Vietnam.	**au Vietnam.**
Philip:	So when did you	**Alors, quand est-ce que vous**
	come to Paris?	**êtes venue à Paris?**
Jacqueline:	In nineteen sixty five	**En mille neuf cent soixante-cinq**
	(1965), with my parents.	**(1965) avec mes parents.**
Philip:	How old were you?	**Quel âge aviez-vous?**
Jacqueline:	I was five.	**J'avais cinq ans.**
Philip:	Are you an only child?	**Vous êtes fille unique?**
Jacqueline:	Yes.	**Oui.**
	I had an elder brother	**J'avais un frère aîné**
	but he died in nineteen	**mais il est mort en mille neuf cent**
	seventy (1970).	**soixante-dix (1970).**
	What about you?	**Et vous,**
	Have you	**avez-vous**
	any brothers or sisters?	**des frères et soeurs?**
Philip:	Yes, I have an elder	**Oui. J'ai un frère aîné**
	brother who is a doctor.	**qui est docteur.**
	He's married and has two	**Il est marié et a deux**
	children - a girl and	**enfants - une fille et**
	a boy.	**un garçon.**
	I also have a younger	**J'ai aussi une soeur cadette**
	sister who is a nurse.	**qui est infirmière.**
	She is single.	**Elle est célibataire.**

	Philip looks at his watch.	**Philip regarde sa montre.**
	It's late and he's tired.	**Il est déjà tard et il est fatigué.**
	His head is beginning to spin.	**Il a la tête qui tourne un peu.**
Philip:	I'm going to go back to the hotel now. At what time does your uncle want to see me tomorrow?	**Je vais rentrer à l'hôtel maintenant. A quelle heure est-ce que votre oncle veut me voir demain?**
Jacqueline:	At two.	**A quatorze heures.**
Philip:	All right. I'll see you tomorrow afternoon. Goodnight, Jacqueline, and thank you for the lovely evening.	**D'accord, à demain après midi. Bonne nuit Jacqueline et merci pour cette excellente soirée.**
Jacqueline:	Goodnight, Philip. See you tomorrow.	**Bonne nuit, Philip et à demain.**

Scene 2	**Scène 2**
(Wednesday)	**(Mercredi)**

The next morning Philip wakes up at a quarter to ten. He does not feel well, he has a headache and he has a pain in his stomach.

Le lendemain matin Philip se réveille à dix heures moins le quart. Il ne se sent pas bien, il a mal à la tête et il a mal au ventre.

It's too late to have breakfast and in any case he doesn't feel like eating. He gets dressed and goes downstairs. At the reception desk he sees Mme Marat.

Il est trop tard pour prendre le petit déjeuner et de toute façon, il n'a pas envie de manger. Il s'habille et il descend. A la réception, il voit Madame Marat.

Philip:	Good morning. Is there a chemist near here?	**Bonjour, madame. Est-ce qu'il y a une pharmacie près d'ici?**
Mme Marat:	Yes, there's one at the end of rue Bonaparte. Are you ill?	**Oui, au bout de la rue Bonaparte. Vous êtes malade?**
Philip:	I don't feel well but it's not serious. I have a slight headache, that's all.	**Je ne me sens pas bien mais ce n'est pas grave. J'ai un peu mal à la tête, c'est tout.**

	Philip leaves the hotel, and goes to the chemist's.	**Philip sort de l'hôtel et va à la pharmacie.**
Chemist:	Good morning.	**Bonjour, monsieur.**
Philip:	Good morning. Have you got something for a headache?	**Bonjour, madame, vous avez quelque chose contre le mal de tête?**
Chemist:	Would you like some aspirin?	**Voulez-vous de l'aspirine?**
Philip:	Yes that's fine. Give me some aspirin but I've also got a stomach-ache.	**Oui, je veux bien. Donnez-moi de l'aspirine. Mais j'ai aussi mal au ventre.**
Chemist:	Have you seen a doctor?	**Vous avez vu un médecin?**
Philip:	No.	**Non.**
Chemist:	Have you got a temperature?	**Vous avez de la fièvre?**
Philip:	No, I don't think so. I ate at a restaurant yesterday evening and I drank a little too much brandy, I think.	**Non, je ne crois pas. J'ai mangé au restaurant hier soir et j'ai bu un peu trop de cognac, je pense.**
Chemist:	I see. Feeling a bit liverish, eh? Here, take two Ventrospirine tablets now then two before meals for the next three days.	**Ah! je vois. Vous avez une crise de foie. Tenez, prenez deux comprimés de Ventrospirine tout de suite et puis deux avant chaque repas pendant trois jours.**
Philip:	Good. Thank you very much. How much is that?	**Bien, merci beaucoup. Je vous dois combien?**
Chemist:	That'll be sixteen francs seventy five cents (I6 f.75).	**Ça fait seize francs soixante-quinze (I6F 75).**

Philip pays and goes back to the hotel. He goes up to his room. He takes the medicine and as he is feeling sleepy he decides to lie down until half past one.	**Philip paie et retourne à l'hôtel. Il monte dans sa chambre. Il prend les médicaments et comme il a sommeil, il décide de s'allonger jusqu'à une heure et demie.**

Donnez-moi de l'aspirine.

130

Scene 3 **Scène 3**

It's two p.m. | Il est deux heures de l'après midi.
Philip has eaten a ham sandwich | **Philip a mangé un sandwich au jambon**
in a café and he feels | **dans un café et il se sent**
much better now. | **beaucoup mieux.**
He rings the bell at Jacqueline's house. | **Il sonne chez Jacqueline.**

Philip: | Hello, Jacqueline. | **Bonjour Jacqueline.**
 | How are you? | **Comment allez-vous?**
 | Is your uncle here? | **Votre oncle est là?**
Jacqueline: | I'm terribly sorry. | **Non, je suis vraiment désolée.**
 | He sent me a telegram | **Il m'a envoyé un télégramme**
 | this morning. | **ce matin.**
 | He's in Portugal. | **Il est au Portugal.**
 | Unfortunately, there's a | **Malheureusement, il y a une**
 | strike at Lisbon airport | **grève à l'aéroport de Lisbonne**
 | and he can't get back to | **et il ne peut pas être à**
 | Paris before | **Paris avant**
 | tomorrow evening. | **demain soir.**

Quel dommage.

Philip: | What a pity! | **Quel dommage.**
 | He really is unlucky. | **Il n'a vraiment pas de chance.**
Jacqueline: | Can you stay until | **Pouvez-vous rester jusqu'à**
 | tomorrow evening? | **demain soir?**
 | My uncle absolutely | **Mon oncle veut absolument**
 | insists on seeing you | **vous voir**
 | about the parcel. | **au sujet du paquet.**
Philip: | What is | **Mais qu'est-ce qu'il y a**
 | in that parcel? | **dans ce paquet?**
Jacqueline: | Nothing... that's to say | **Rien... c'est à dire,**
 | nothing but papers. | **rien que des papiers.**
 | Well then, you will | **Alors, vous restez,**
 | stay, won't you? | **n'est-ce pas?**

Philip thinks for a moment, | **Philip réfléchit un instant,**
the situation is getting more and more | **la situation devient de plus en plus**
mysterious but after all it's not | **mystérieuse mais ce n'est pas**
unpleasant. | **désagréable après tout.**
He looks into Jacqueline's eyes | **Il regarde Jacqueline dans les yeux**
then he smiles. | **puis il sourit.**

Philip: | Since you insist, | **Puisque vous insistez,**
 | I can't refuse. | **je ne peux pas refuser.**

ACTE 6 (i)

Ils arrrivent rue Madame.

Avez-vous envie de prendre quelque chose avant de rentrer à l'hôtel?

Qu'est-ce que vous faites dans la vie?

Vous n'avez pas envie d'un cognac?

Ils s'installent tous les deux sur le divan.

Alors, vous travaillez aussi avec votre père?

Il a pris sa retraite il y a un an.

Il a acheté une maison près de Cannes.

ACTE 6 (ii)

Lui il est PDG ou si vous préférez
Président Directeur Général.

Un ami de la famille
qui est mort dans
un accident de voiture
il y a un mois.

Vous êtes née
à Paris?

Non, je suis née au Vietnam.

Alors, quand est-ce que vous êtes
venue à Paris?

En mille neuf cent soixante-cinq
avec mes parents.

J'avais cinq ans.

J'ai un frère aîné qui est docteur.

Il est marié et a deux enfants – une fille et un garçon.

J'ai aussi une soeur cadette qui est infirmière.

Il a la tête qui tourne un peu.

Philip regarde sa montre.

A quelle heure est-ce que votre oncle veut me voir demain?

Est-ce qu'il y a une pharmacie près d'ici?

Vous êtes malade?

RÉCEPTION

Voulez-vous de l'aspirine?

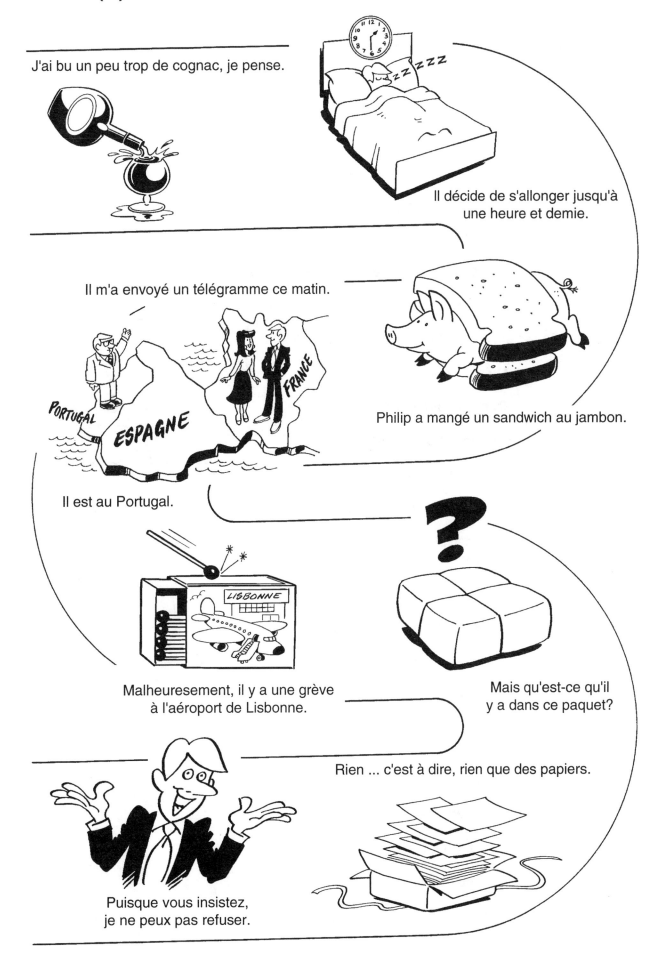

J'ai bu un peu trop de cognac, je pense.

Il décide de s'allonger jusqu'à une heure et demie.

Il m'a envoyé un télégramme ce matin.

Philip a mangé un sandwich au jambon.

PORTUGAL ESPAGNE FRANCE

Il est au Portugal.

LISBONNE

Malheuresement, il y a une grève à l'aéroport de Lisbonne.

Mais qu'est-ce qu'il y a dans ce paquet?

Rien ... c'est à dire, rien que des papiers.

Puisque vous insistez, je ne peux pas refuser.

Part Two : Pronunciation and Intonation
Section Deux : Prononciation et Intonation

a) The sound **r** as in **grave**:

1. **C'est grave?**
    Je ne crois pas.

2. **Prenez deux comprimés.**

3. **Il a pris sa retraite près de Strasbourg.**

4. **Je voudrais travailler dans votre entreprise.**

5. **Une crise de foie, c'est vraiment très désagréable.**

6. **Trois francs trente pour de la Ventrospirine, c'est trop.**

b) The sound **è** as in **père, tête, est, fait** or **paquet**:

1. **Qu'est-ce que c'est?**

2. **Que fait votre père?**

3. **Mon frère est anglais.**

4. **J'ai très mal à la tête.**

5. **C'est au sujet du paquet.**

c) Contrast between the **é** and the **è** sounds when they occur in the same sentence:

1. **Vous travaillez avec votre père?**

2. **Vous ressemblez à votre frère aîné.**

3. **Vraiment? J'en suis désolé.**

4. **Elle est mariée ou célibataire?**

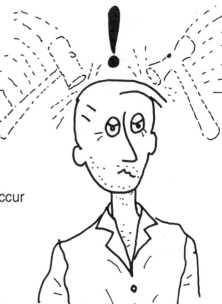

J'ai très mal à la tête.

d) The sound **o** as in **votre, bonne, comme, export** or **alors**:

1. **Alors, un cognac?**

2. **Je travaille dans l'import-export.**

3. **Il est mort à Lisbonne?**

4. **Quel dommage!**

e) Contrast between the two **o** sounds when they occur in the same sentence:

    I.   **Elle sonne à l'hôtel.**

    2.   **J'ai bu trop de cognac.**

    3.   **Lisbonne est au Portugal.**

    4.   **D'accord, parlons d'autres choses.**

f)   **Comptine:**

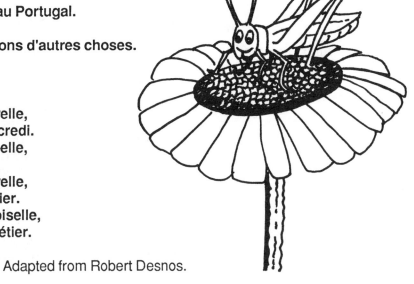

Sautez, sautez, sauterelle,
Aujourd'hui c'est mercredi.
Moi je saute, nous dit-elle,
Du lundi au samedi.
Sautez, sautez, sauterelle,
A travers tout le quartier.
Sautez donc, Mademoiselle,
Puisque c'est votre métier.

Adapted from Robert Desnos.

J'ai bu trop de cognac.

137

Part Three
Functional Dialogues

Section Trois
Dialogues Fonctionnels

I. Jacqueline is offering Philip something to drink.

Jacqueline offre à boire à Philip.

J:	Would you like something to drink?	**Avez-vous envie de prendre quelque chose?**
Philip:	I'd love to.	**Oui, avec plaisir.**
J:	Would you like a coffee?	**Voulez-vous un café?**
Philip:	No. I'm sorry, I don't drink coffee in the evening.	**Non, je suis désolé, je ne bois pas de café le soir.**
J:	A liqueur then? Wouldn't you like a brandy?	**Un petit digestif alors? Vous n'avez pas envie d'un cognac?**
Philip:	Yes, please.	**Si, volontiers.**

2. Philip is asking Jacqueline about the family business.

Philip interroge Jacqueline sur l'entreprise familiale.

Philip:	What do you do for a living?	**Qu'est-ce que vous faites dans la vie?**
J:	I'm in the Import-Export business. I'm in charge of personnel.	**Je travaille dans l'import-export. Je suis chef du personnel.**
Philip:	Do you work with your father?	**Vous travaillez avec votre père?**
J:	Not any more. He retired a year ago.	**Non, plus maintenant. Il a pris sa retraite il y a un an.**
Philip:	And what exactly does your uncle do?	**Et votre oncle, que fait-il exactement?**
J:	He's the MD, or if you prefer, Managing Director.	**Lui, il est PDG ou si vous préférez Président Directeur Général.**

Vous travaillez avec votre père?

3.

	Philip is asking Jacqueline about herself.	**Philip interroge Jacqueline sur ses origines.**

Philip:	Have you always lived in Paris?	**Vous avez toujours vécu à Paris?**
J:	No. I was born in Vietnam.	**Non, je suis née au Vietnam.**
Philip:	So when did you come to Paris?	**Alors, quand est-ce que vous êtes venue à Paris?**
J:	In nineteen hundred and sixty five (1965) with my parents.	**En mille neuf cent soixante-cinq (1965) avec mes parents.**
Philip:	How old were you?	**Quel âge aviez-vous?**
J:	I was five.	**J'avais cinq ans.**
Philip:	Are you an only child?	**Vous êtes fille unique?**
J:	I had an elder brother but he died in nineteen hundred and seventy (1970).	**J'avais un frère aîné mais il est mort en mille neuf cent soixante-dix (1970).**

4.

	Jacqueline is asking Philip about his family.	**Jacqueline interroge Philip sur sa famille.**

J:	Have you any brothers or sisters?	**Avez-vous des frères et soeurs?**
Philip:	Yes, I have an elder brother and a younger sister.	**Oui. J'ai un frère aîné et une soeur cadette.**
J:	Are they married?	**Ils sont mariés?**
Philip:	My brother is married but my sister is single.	**Mon frère est marié mais ma soeur est célibataire.**
J:	Does your brother have any children?	**Est-ce que votre frère a des enfants?**
Philip:	Yes, he has two children, a girl and a boy.	**Oui, il a deux enfants, une fille et un garçon.**

Quand est-ce que vous êtes venue à Paris?

5.

| | At the chemist's. | **A la pharmacie.** |
| | | **La Pharmacienne = La Ph.** |

La Ph: Good morning. **Bonjour monsieur.**

Philip: Good morning. **Bonjour madame.**
Have you got something **Vous avez quelque chose**
for a headache? **contre le mal de tête?**

La Ph: Would you like **Voulez-vous**
some aspirin? **de l'aspirine?**

Philip: Yes that's fine. **Oui, je veux bien.**
Give me some aspirin **Donnez-moi de l'aspirine**
but I've also got **mais j'ai aussi**
a stomach-ache. **mal au ventre.**

La Ph: Have you seen a doctor? **Vous avez vu un médecin?**

Philip: No. **Non.**

La Ph: Have you got **Vous avez de**
a temperature? **la fièvre?**

Philip: No, I don't think so. **Non, je ne crois pas.**
I ate at a restaurant **J'ai mangé au restaurant**
yesterday evening **hier soir**
and I drank a little **et j'ai bu un peu**
too much brandy. **trop de cognac.**

La Ph: I see. Feeling a bit **Ah! je vois.**
liverish, eh? **C'est une crise de foie.**
Here, take some **Tenez, prenez de la**
Ventrospirine. **Ventrospirine.**

Voulez-vous de l'aspirine?

Part Four : Personalised Dialogues
Section Quatre : Dialogues

a)   Jacqueline is offering you something to drink.

Jacqueline:	**Avez-vous envie de prendre quelque chose?**
Vous:	(Say you'd love to.)
Jacqueline:	**Voulez-vous un café?**
Vous:	(Say you're sorry but you don't drink coffee in the evening.)
Jacqueline:	**Un petit digestif alors?**
	Vous n'avez pas envie d'un cognac?
Vous:	(Say yes please.)

b)   You are asking Jacqueline about the family business.

Vous:	(Ask Jacqueline what she does for a living.)
Jacqueline:	**Je travaille dans l'import-export.**
	Je suis chef du personnel.
Vous:	(Ask if she works with her father.)
Jacqueline:	**Non, plus maintenant.**
	Il a pris sa retraite il y a un an.
Vous:	(Ask exactly what her uncle does.)
Jacqueline:	**Il est PDG.**

c)   You are asking Jacqueline about herself.

Vous:	(Ask Jacqueline if she has always lived in Paris.)
Jacqueline:	**Non, je suis née au Vietnam.**
Vous:	(Ask when she came to Paris.)
Jacqueline:	**En 1965, avec mes parents.**
Vous:	(Ask how old she was.)
Jacqueline:	**J'avais cinq ans.**
Vous:	(Ask if she is an only child.)
Jacqueline:	**J'avais un frère aîné**
	mais il est mort en 1970.

d)   Jacqueline is asking you about your family.

Jacqueline:	**Avez-vous des frères et soeurs?**
Vous:	(Say you have an elder sister and a younger brother.)
Jacqueline:	**Ils sont mariés?**
Vous:	(Say your sister is married but your brother is single.)
Jacqueline:	**Ils ont des enfants?**
Vous:	(Say your sister has six children: four girls and two boys.)

e)   You are at the chemist's.

La pharmacienne: **Bonjour.**
Vous: (Say good morning and ask if she has anything
                      for a headache.)
La pharmacienne: **Voulez-vous de l'aspirine?**
Vous: (Say yes but you also have a stomach-ache.)
La pharmacienne: **Vous avez vu un médecin?**
Vous: (Say no.)
La pharmacienne: **Vous avez de la fièvre?**
Vous: (Say you don't think so,
                      then explain that you ate at a restaurant
                      yesterday evening and that you drank a little
                      too much brandy.)
La pharmacienne: **Ah! je vois.**
                      C'est une crise de foie.
                      Tenez, prenez de la Ventrospirine.

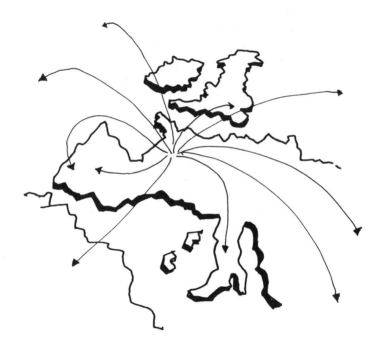

Je travaille dans l'import-export.

Part Five : Grammar
Section Cinq : Grammaire

1. THE **PASSE COMPOSE**

This is the tense the French use most of the time when speaking about the past. In fact we actually say something is **passé** meaning it is no longer current.

So **passé** means past. And there is a useful clue in the word. The **é** on the end of the verb signifies the equivalent in English of 'ed'. Similarly **composé** means 'composed'. And just as in English you can use 'to have' to express something in the past by saying 'I <u>have</u> succeeded' or 'he <u>has</u> succeeded', so in French you can also use **avoir** (to have) to compose this past tense.

Did you notice this in the story in Act 6?

Il a mangé	He <u>has</u> eaten
un sandwich au jambon.	a ham sandwich.

You use the **passé composé** to express whether someone <u>did</u> something or <u>has done</u> something. Thus 'he ate' or 'he has eaten' are both **il a mangé.**

J'ai mangé	I ate
au restaurant hier soir	at a restaurant yesterday evening.
J'ai mangé	I have eaten
au restaurant	at a restaurant.

In this sense French is easier than English.

However, you will remember that there are <u>three</u> types of verbs, those which end in **er,** in **ir** or in **re.**

Here is the rule for making the **passé composé.**

Verbs ending in	**er (donner)**	replace the ending with **é.**
Verbs ending in	**ir (finir)**	replace the ending with **i.**
Verbs ending in	**re (répondre)**	replace the ending with **u.**

So it is:
**il a donné
vous avez fini
j'ai répondu**

There are just two more points to remember when you want to make the **passé composé**.

a.   You use **avoir** to make the **passé composé** out of MOST but not <u>all</u> verbs.

Some verbs, largely those signifying movement, go with **être,** to be. So it is **il est arrivé,** he has arrived (or he arrived) and **je suis allé,** I have gone (or I went). You also use **être** for verbs like **se laver,** or **se raser**.

b.   When you make a **passé composé** with **être** you will also notice that the ending of the verb changes to agree with both the number and gender of the subject.

So it is:	**il est arrivé à Paris**
but	**elle est arrivée à Paris**
and	**je suis allé au marché**
but	**nous sommes allés au marché**

What would you say if several ladies went to the market?

Elles sont allées au marché.

Here is a little jingle to help you remember:

When you use the verb 'to be'
Subject and past participle must agree.

Anything more?

Yes. In exactly the same way as there are irregular verbs in English — so there are verbs in French which are 'irregular' when put into the past.

In English it is not 'I have gived' it is 'I have given' and it is 'I have seen' etc. French have their quota of irregular verbs too.

You possibly noticed:-

Il a pris sa retraite il y a un an.
He retired a year ago.

Vous avez toujours vécu à Paris?
Have you always lived in Paris?

Avez-vous vu un médecin?
Have you seen a doctor?

Quand est-ce que vous-êtes venue à Paris?
When did you come to Paris?

Thus, the **passé composé** of:

prendre	is	**avoir pris**
vivre	is	**avoir vécu**
voir	is	**avoir vu**
venir	is	**être venu**

You will absorb them easily enough and there is a full list in the Appendix.

2.   THE IMPERFECT TENSE

Another tense which can be used to refer to the past is the Imperfect Tense. We shall be looking at this tense in more detail in Act 7. In the meantime, note the use of the Imperfect Tense of the verb **AVOIR** in these sentences:

Nous avions un chef des ventes.
We had a Sales Manager.   *

Quel âge aviez-vous?
How old were you?

J'avais un frère aîné.
I had an elder brother.

3.   **QUI** — Who

You have seen in Act 1 that you can use **QUI** to ask a question:

e.g.   **C'est de la part de QUI?**
              QUI est-ce?

QUI is also used like the English word 'who' to link two parts of a sentence together:

e.g.   **Nous avions un chef des ventes QUI est mort**
              dans un accident de voiture.

              J'ai un frère aîné QUI est docteur.

NOTE: In this situation **QUI** can refer to things as well as people, like English 'which' or 'that':

e.g.   **Il a la tête qui tourne.**

REMEMBER: 'Who' or 'which' or 'that' can be
                  expressed by one French word, that's **QUI**.

4.   **LUI** — To/For him or her

In Act 5 you learnt that **LUI** can mean 'to or for him or her'. **LUI** can also be used, like **MOI**, after certain prepositions (**de, avec**) or to emphasise **IL**.

e.g.   **Philip regarde autour de LUI.**
              Je travaille avec LUI.
              LUI, il est PDG.

REMEMBER: In English, you can stress the pronoun 'he'
                  In French, as well as **IL**, you should say **LUI**

5. **ME (M')** — Me, to me, for me

ME or **M'** means 'to or for me' when it comes in front of a verb i.e. when it is a direct or indirect object in a sentence:

e.g. **A quelle heure est-ce que votre oncle veut me voir?**
Il m'a envoyé un télégramme ce matin.

NOTE I: **ME** is also the reflexive pronoun that goes with **JE**:

e.g. **Je ne me sens pas bien.**
I don't feel (myself) well.   *

REMEMBER: What often goes along with **JE**?
— the reflexive pronoun **ME**.

NOTE 2: When you are giving instructions, you will use **MOI** instead of **ME** and **MOI** will come <u>after</u> the verb:

e.g. **Donnez-MOI trois roses rouges.**
Donnez-MOI de l'aspirine.

6. **SI**

REMEMBER: For 'yes', in French you usually say **OUI**
But to contradict a negative, you say **SI**

e.g. **Vous n'avez pas envie d'un cognac?**
Si, volontiers.

NOTE: **SI** can also mean 'if':

e.g. **Si vous préférez.**
If you prefer.

Nous avions un chef des ventes qui est mort dans un accident de voiture.

Part Six : Key Phrases
Section Six : Expressions Utiles

1.   **AVANT (DE) . . .** — Before

Avant can be followed:

    (a)   by a noun
    (b)   by **DE** + infinitive

    e.g.   **avant chaque repas**
                                before each meal

                                avant demain soir
                                before tomorrow evening

                                avant de rentrer à l'hôtel
                                before going back to the hotel

2.   **AVOIR ENVIE DE . . .** — To feel like/want

This expression can be followed by a noun or an infinitive:

    e.g.   **Vous n'avez pas envie d'un cognac?**
                                Avez-vous envie de prendre quelque chose?
                                Il n'a pas envie de manger.

3.   **ETRE A QUELQU'UN** — To belong to someone

To indicate that something belongs to someone, all you need to use is the verb **ETRE** followed by **A** plus a noun or pronoun:

    e.g.   **Elle n'est pas à moi.**
                                  It isn't mine.

                                Elle est à mon oncle.
                                It's my uncle's.

4.   **IL Y A** — Ago

You know already that **IL Y A** can mean 'there is' or 'there are'. Used along with an expression of time, it can also mean 'ago':

    e.g.   **Mon père et mon oncle ont fondé la maison** <u>il y a</u> **trente ans.**
                                Il a pris sa retraite <u>il y a</u> **un an.**
                                Il est mort <u>il y a</u> **un mois.**

5.   **AVOIR MAL A . . .**

When you want to say that you have a pain somewhere or that some part of you is hurting, you can use **avoir mal à** — followed by the name of the offending organ!

    e.g.   **J'ai mal à la tête.**
                                  J'ai mal au ventre.
                                  J'ai mal aux dents.

Part Seven : Games
Section Sept : Jeux

1. **On déménage** (Moving house):

You are helping a friend to move house and he is telling you where to put the furniture.

Cut out the furniture on the word cards and arrange them on the empty room plans according to your friend's instructions.

Here are the instructions:—

La cuisine:

Mettez
- la table au milieu de la pièce
- les quatre chaises autour de la table
- le réfrigérateur dans le coin à droite de la fenêtre
- la cuisinière à gauche de la fenêtre
- la machine à laver dans le coin en face du frigo.

Le salon:

Mettez
- le canapé contre le mur où il y a la fenêtre
- un fauteuil à gauche et l'autre à droite du canapé
- la table basse devant le mur à droite de la porte
- la télé sur la table basse
- la bibliothéque contre le mur à droite de la fenêtre
- la chaîne hi-fi sur la bibliothèque.

La chambre:

Mettez
- la tête du lit contre le mur qui est à gauche de la fenêtre
- la table de nuit près de la tête du lit, côté fenêtre
- la lampe sur la table de nuit
- l'armoire contre le mur au pied du lit.

2. You have been walking round Paris and have met these poor people who have been suffering a lot recently. What did they say to you?

For example, Béatrice said ☐1☐ **J'ai mal au cou**.

And remember to use the right words after **'J'ai mal...'**
(i.e. **au/à la/à l'/aux**)

Béatrice

1. ....

2. ....

3. ....

Luc

4. ....

5. ....

6. ....

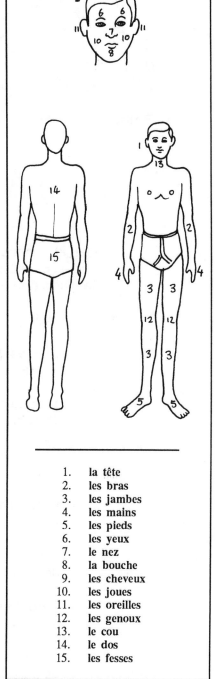

1.	la tête
2.	les bras
3.	les jambes
4.	les mains
5.	les pieds
6.	les yeux
7.	le nez
8.	la bouche
9.	les cheveux
10.	les joues
11.	les oreilles
12.	les genoux
13.	le cou
14.	le dos
15.	les fesses

3. **La famille:**

Look at this splendid family portrait! If you read the information carefully, you will be able to work out who is who in a French family.

| Bruno | Fabrice | Marie | Paul | Jean | Yvonne | Danièle | Richard | Véronique |

— Jean et Yvonne ont eu deux enfants: Danièle et Paul.
— Paul a épousé Marie; ils ont eu deux enfants: Fabrice et Bruno.
— Danièle a épousé Richard; ils ont eu une fille: Véronique.

a.   **Qui suis-je?**

    1. **Jean est mon père, Marie est ma femme, j'ai deux fils.**
       Je suis ...

    2. **Yvonne est ma mère, Richard est mon mari, j'ai une fille.**
       Je suis ...

    3. **Fabrice est mon cousin.**
       Je suis ...

    4. **Fabrice et Bruno sont mes neveux.**
       Je suis ... ou ...

    5. **Jean est mon grand-père.**
       Je suis ... ou ... ou ...

    6. **Véronique est ma petite-fille.**
       Je suis ... ou ...

    7. **Véronique est ma nièce.**
       Je suis ... ou ...

8. **Bruno est mon petit-fils.**
   Je suis ... ou ...

b. **Qui sont-ils?**

   1. **Fabrice est __ _____ de Bruno.**

   2. **Jean est __ _____ ____ de Fabrice et Bruno et de Véronique.**

   3. **Danièle est __ _____ de Paul.**

   4. **Véronique est __ _____ de Paul et Marie.**

   5. **Fabrice et Bruno sont ___ _____ ____ de Jean et Yvonne.**

   6. **Véronique est __ _____ de Fabrice et Bruno.**

   7. **Yvonne est __ _____ ____ de Véronique et de Fabrice et Bruno.**

   8. **Marie est __ _____ de Véronique.**

c. **La 'belle famille'**   (The in-laws)

Le beau —— père
         —— **frère**
         —— **fils**   = **gendre**

La belle —— **mère**
          —— **soeur**
          —— **fille**   = **bru**

Le beau-père + la belle-mère   = **les beaux-parents.**

Vrai ou Faux (True or False)

	Vrai	Faux
1.		
2.		
3.		
4.		
5.		
6.		

   1. **Jean est le beau-père de Marie**
   2. **Yvonne est la belle-mère de Paul.**
   3. **Marie est la belle-soeur de Richard.**
   4. **Danièle est la bru de Jean.**
   5. **Richard est le beau-frère de Paul.**
   6. **Richard est le gendre d'Yvonne.**

The answers are at the back of the book.

4. **Le passé composé** (Philip's diary):

Philip has been keeping a diary of his French trip. Here is the account of the second day. Try to translate it.

Tuesday 22nd April	**Mardi 22 Avril**
In the morning I had my breakfast	....
at the hotel and I spoke to the	....
waitress and to the hotel owner.	....
I gave Jacqueline a bunch of flowers	....
then we went shopping.	....
In the afternoon I phoned my parents,	....
changed some money and bought some	....
clothes.	....
In the evening Jacqueline and I went	....
to the pictures then we ate at	....
'Chez Tante Marie'.	....
After the meal we walked back to the	....
rue Madame.	....
At Jacqueline's I drank a little too	....
much brandy and we talked a lot.	....

5. **Oui ou Si: il faut savoir choisir.**

Can you match the questions and answers?

1. **Vous n'avez pas beaucoup de famille?**
2. **Vous êtes employé à l'Hôtel de France?**
3. **Vous n'avez pas de sandwich au fromage?**
4. **Vous n'avez pas un frère pharmacien?**
5. **Vous êtes né en Espagne?**
6. **Vous avez envie d'un cognac?**

a) **Si, au gruyère.**
b) **Si, à Lyon.**
c) **Oui, je suis serveur.**
d) **Oui, à Madrid.**
e) **Si, j'ai 5 frères et 4 soeurs.**
f) **Oui, volontiers.**

BONUS

1. Riddle

    **Fabrice dit que la soeur de son oncle n'est pas sa tante.
    Qui est-elle?**

2. Another Riddle

    **Je n'ai ni frère ni soeur mais le père de Jacques est le fils de mon père.
    Qui est Jacques?**

3. Can you work it out?

    **Suzanne a 40 ans. Elle est veuve depuis 8 ans. Les jumelles ont 10 ans. Elles sont
    nées 5 ans après le mariage de leurs parents.
    — A quel âge Suzanne s'est-elle mariée?
    — Quel âge avait Suzanne à la naissance des jumelles?
    — Quel âge avaient les jumelles à la mort de leur père?**

4. **Voici un petit problème.**

    **Deux mères et deux filles ont mangé trois poires sans les partager.
    Comment cela se fait-il?**

5. **Quel nom de baptème!**

    **Monsieur et Madame
    NASTIC ont la joie de
    vous annoncer la naissance
    de leur fils JIM**

    Write down his full name.

6. **Connaissez-vous votre chiffre porte-bonheur?**

    **Prenez votre date de naissance (par exemple le 24.6.69) et additionnez tous les
    chiffres (2 + 4 + 6 + 6 + 9 = 27). Puis additionnez 2 + 7 = 9. Votre chiffre porte-bonheur
    est 9. A vous maintenant de découvrir le vôtre.**

ACT 7   ACTE 7
Scene 1   Scène I

A day in Paris (Wednesday).   **Une journée à Paris (Mercredi).**

Jacqueline has persuaded Philip to stay another two days in Paris because her Uncle Anatole has not come back yet.

Jacqueline a persuadé Philip de rester encore deux jours à Paris parce que son oncle Anatole n'est pas encore rentré.

In her uncle's absence Jacqueline can look after Philip but first of all she has to write two or three letters.

En l'absence de son oncle, Jacqueline peut s'occuper de Philip mais d'abord elle doit écrire deux ou trois lettres.

Philip decides to go and visit the Louvre Museum and they arrange to meet outside the Pont Neuf metro station at five-thirty p.m.

Philip décide d'aller visiter le Musée du Louvre et ils se donnent rendez-vous à la sortie de la station Pont Neuf à dix-sept heures trente.

Jacqueline: Do you want to go to the Louvre Museum by bus or by metro?

Voulez-vous aller au Musée du Louvre en bus ou en métro?

Philip: Is there a metro station near here?

Est-ce qu'il y a une station de métro près d'ici?

Jacqueline: Yes, of course, there's Saint Sulpice station. It's five minutes' walk from here.

Oui, bien sûr, il y a la station Saint Sulpice. C'est à cinq minutes à pied.

Philip: Fine. I'll take the metro then. Which way is it?

Bon, eh bien je vais prendre le métro. C'est de quel côté?

Oui, bien sûr, il y a la station Saint Sulpice.

Jacqueline: You take the first street on the left, you go straight on and you reach the rue de Rennes.

Vous prenez la première rue à gauche, vous allez tout droit et vous arrivez à la rue de Rennes.

Philip: What then?

Et après?

Jacqueline: You're there. The metro is on the left-hand pavement.

Vous y êtes. Le métro se trouve sur le trottoir de gauche.

Philip: I've never taken the metro. What do you have to do?

Je n'ai jamais pris le métro. Qu'est-ce qu'il faut faire?

Jacqueline: First of all, you have to buy a ticket. If you ask for a book of ten tickets it's cheaper.

Il faut d'abord acheter un ticket. Si vous demandez un carnet de dix tickets, c'est moins cher.

Philip: Do I buy it at the metro station?

Je l'achète à la station de métro?

155

Jacqueline:	Yes, or at a tobacconist's, and you ask for a book of second-class tickets.	Oui, ou bien dans un bureau de tabac et vous demandez 'un carnet de seconde'.
Philip:	And to get to the Louvre what do I have to do?	Et pour aller au Louvre, qu'est-ce que je dois faire?
Jacqueline:	Here's a map of the metro. Look. We're here, at Saint Sulpice. You take the direction 'Porte de Clignancourt'.	Voilà un plan du métro. Regardez. Nous sommes ici, à Saint Sulpice. Vous prenez la direction Porte de Clignancourt.
Philip:	Do I have to change?	Est-ce que je dois changer?
Jacqueline:	Yes, you change at Châtelet station and take the direction 'Pont de Neuilly'. There's no need to change after that.	Oui, vous changez à Châtelet et vous prenez la direction Pont de Neuilly. Après, c'est direct.
Philip:	Where do I get off?	Où est-ce que je descends?
Jacqueline:	You get off at Louvre station. It's the first station after Châtelet.	Vous descendez à la station Louvre, c'est la première station après Châtelet.
Philip:	Good. I think I've understood.	Bon, je crois que j'ai compris.
Jacqueline:	And watch you don't get into a first-class compartment and don't throw away your ticket, there are sometimes inspectors.	Et attention, ne montez pas dans la voiture de première classe et ne jetez pas votre billet, il y a parfois des contrôleurs.
Philip:	All right then. Half-past five outside Pont Neuf station?	D'accord. Alors à cinq heures et demie à la station Pont Neuf?
Jacqueline:	Yes, that's right. Have a nice afternoon and good luck in the metro.	Oui, c'est entendu. Passez un bon après-midi et bonne chance avec le métro.

Scene 2   Scène 2

It is five p.m. and the Louvre Museum has just closed. Philip has just come out of the museum and is admiring the Tuileries Gardens. He's not very sure where the Pont Neuf is and decides to ask a passer-by.	Il est cinq heures de l'après-midi et le Musée du Louvre vient de fermer. Philip vient de sortir du musée et il admire le jardin des Tuileries. Il ne sait pas très bien où est le Pont Neuf et décide de demander à une passante.

Philip:	Excuse me. Can you tell me how to get to the Pont Neuf, please?	**Pardon madame, pour aller au Pont Neuf, s'il vous plaît?**
Lady:	You go straight ahead and under the clock.	**Vous allez tout droit et vous passez sous l'horloge.**
Philip:	Right. I go straight ahead and under the clock. And then?	**Alors, je vais tout droit et je passe sous l'horloge et puis?**
Lady:	Then you go across the famous Cour Carrée and turn right towards the embankment.	**Puis vous traversez la célèbre Cour Carrée et vous tournez à droite en direction des quais.**
Philip:	And when I reach the embankment, do I turn left or right?	**Et quand j'arrive aux quais, je tourne à gauche ou à droite?**
Lady:	Left.	**A gauche.**
Philip:	Is the Pont Neuf far?	**Et le Pont Neuf, c'est loin?**
Lady:	No. It's five hundred (500) metres away. Go along the Seine as far as the second set of traffic lights, then cross the street and the Pont Neuf is right in front of you.	**Non, c'est à cinq cent (500) mètres. Suivez la Seine jusqu'au deuxième feu rouge, puis traversez la rue et le Pont Neuf est juste devant vous.**
Philip:	Thank you very much.	**Merci bien.**
Lady:	Don't mention it.	**Je vous en prie.**

When he reaches the embankment, Philip stops for a few minutes outside the pet shop: there are cats, dogs, birds, mice and even snakes. On the other side of the street he notices the book-sellers.	**En arrivant sur les quais, Philip s'arrête quelques minutes devant les magasins qui vendent des animaux, des chats, des chiens, des oiseaux, des souris et même des serpents. De l'autre côté de la rue, il aperçoit les bouquinistes.**

'There are some nice engravings over there. I'm going to buy one for my parents.' Philip says to himself.	**'Tiens, il y a de jolies gravures. Je vais en acheter une pour mes parents.' se dit Philip.**

Il y a parfois des contrôleurs.

Scene 3 Scène 3

At twenty-five past five,
Philip arrives at the meeting-place.
Jacqueline is looking at
the pleasure cruisers on the Seine.

**A cinq heures vingt-cinq
Philip arrive au rendez-vous.
Jacqueline est en train de regarder
les bateaux-mouches sur la Seine.**

Philip: Have you been waiting long?
Vous attendez depuis longtemps?

Jacqueline: No, I have just arrived. What did you think of the museum?
Non, non. Je viens d'arriver. Alors, qu'avez-vous pensé du musée?

Philip: It's really big!
Qu'est-ce qu'il est grand!

Jacqueline: Did you see the Venus de Milo?
Avez-vous vu la Vénus de Milo?

Philip: Yes. It's marvellous!
Oui. Quelle merveille!

Jacqueline: Did you like the Mona Lisa?
Avez-vous aimé la Joconde?

Philip: Yes, she's really beautiful.
Oui, comme elle est belle!

Jacqueline: She has a lovely smile, hasn't she?
Elle a un beau sourire, n'est-ce pas?

Philip: Yes, wonderful and mysterious and you look a bit like her.
Oui, superbe et mystérieux et vous lui ressemblez un peu.

They both burst out laughing
and then they set out across
the Pont Neuf.
In the middle of the bridge,
Philip notices a statue.

**Ils éclatent de rire tous les deux
et ils commencent à traverser
le Pont Neuf.
Au milieu du pont,
Philip remarque une statue.**

Philip: Who is the man on the horse?
Qui est cet homme à cheval?

Jacqueline: That's King Henry IV. He was assassinated in sixteen hundred and ten (1610). They called him 'Le Vert Galant'.
C'est le roi Henri IV. Il est mort assassiné en mille six cent dix (1610). On l'appelait 'Le Vert Galant'.

Philip: What does that mean?
Qu'est-ce que ça veut dire?

Jacqueline: That means that he liked the ladies!
Ça veut dire qu'il aimait bien les femmes!

Philip: It's dangerous to like the ladies!
C'est dangereux d'aimer les femmes!

Jacqueline: Oh he didn't die because of a woman.
Oh! il n'est pas mort à cause d'une femme.

Philip: What shall we do now?
Qu'est-ce qu'on fait maintenant?

Jacqueline: Shall we go for a little walk?
Si on se promenait un peu?

Philip:	All right.	**D'accord.**
	Where shall we go?	**Où est-ce qu'on va?**
Jacqueline:	We can go and sit	**On peut aller s'asseoir**
	by the Seine	**au bord de la Seine,**
	in the little garden	**dans ce petit jardin**
	just below us.	**juste en dessous.**
	It's called the	**On l'appelle le**
	Square du Vert Galant.	**Square du Vert Galant.**
Philip:	Good idea. Let's go.	**Bonne idée. Allons-y.**

	They go down the steps	**Ils descendent les marches**
	and on to the tip of the island.	**et vont à la pointe de l'île.**
	All around them,	**Tout autour,**
	the Seine is flowing silently.	**la Seine coule silencieusement.**
	The weather is mild.	**Il fait doux.**

	The sun is shining	**Le soleil brille**
	just above the water.	**juste au dessus de l'eau.**
	The noise of the cars	**Le bruit des voitures**
	on the embankment opposite them	**sur les quais en face**
	seems to come from far away.	**semble venir de très loin.**

	Philip and Jacqueline sit down	**Philip et Jacqueline s'asseyent**
	on a bench.	**sur un banc.**

Philip:	How peaceful it is!	**Comme c'est calme!**
	It's as if we were	**C'est comme si on**
	in the country.	**était à la campagne.**
Jacqueline:	And what if we went	**Eh bien, si on**
	there tomorrow?	**y allait demain?**
	What if we had a picnic?	**Si on faisait un pique-nique?**
	Uncle Anatole has left	**Oncle Anatole m'a laissé**
	me his car-keys.	**les clés de sa voiture.**
Philip:	What a good idea.	**Quelle bonne idée!**
	I'd love to.	**Moi, je veux bien.**
Jacqueline:	All right then.	**Eh bien, c'est d'accord.**
	I'll come and fetch you	**Je viens vous chercher**
	at the hotel tomorrow	**à l'hôtel demain**
	morning at nine.	**matin à neuf heures.**
	Is that OK?	**Ça vous va?**
Philip:	Great.	**Formidable.**

*Le soleil brille
juste au dessus de l'eau.*

ACTE 7 (i)

Oncle Anatole n'est pas encore rentré.

Elle doit écrire deux ou trois lettres.

Philip décide d'aller visiter le Musée du Louvre.

Voulez-vous aller en bus ou en métro?

Vous prenez la première rue à gauche, vous allez tout droit.

Si vous demandez un carnet de dix tickets, c'est moins cher.

Ou bien dans un bureau de tabac.

160

ACTE 7 (ii)

Il y a parfois des contrôleurs.

Vous changez á Châtelet.

Bonne chance avec le métro.

Louvre

FERME

Le Musée vient de fermer.

Pour allez au Pont Neuf, s'il vous plaît?

Vous allez tout droit et vous passez sous l'horloge.

COUR CARRÉE

Puis vous traversez la célèbre Cour Carrée.

Je tourne à gauche ou à droite?

á gauche   á droite

Suivez la Seine jusqu'au deuxième feu rouge.

ACTE 7 (iii)

des chats, des chiens, des oiseaux,
des souris et même des serpents.

Il s'arrête quelques minutes devant
les magasins qui vendent des animaux.

Jacqueline est en train de regarder
les bateaux-mouches sur la Seine.

Il aperçoit les bouquinistes.

Alors, qu'avez-vous pensé du musée?

Elle a un beau sourire, n'est-ce pas?

Ils ésclatent de rire tous les deux.

ACTE 7 (iv)

Qui est cet homme à cheval?

Il est mort assassiné en 1610.

On peut aller s'asseoir au bord de la Seine, dans ce petit jardin juste en dessous.

Ils descendent les marches.

Le soleil brille juste au dessus de l'eau.

Comme c'est calme!

Oncle Anatole m'a laissé les clés de sa voiture.

Je viens vous chercher à l'hôtel demain matin.

Part Two : Pronunciation and Intonation
Section Deux : Prononciation et Intonation

a)   The sound **ou** as in **tout:**

Some examples:

bout   **vous**   **doux**   **dessous**

Some sentences:

I.   **Où allez-vous?**

2.   **Rendez-vous au Louvre.**

3.   **C'est tout doux.**

4.   **Tournez au feu rouge.**

b)   Contrast between the **u** and the **ou** sounds in the same sentence:

I.   **Cette voiture est à vous?**

2.   **Où avez-vous vu ces gravures?**

3.   **C'est tout au bout de la rue.**

4.   **Avez-vous tout vu?**

c)   Can you distinguish between **u** and **ou**? Listen to the cassette very carefully and put a tick in the box corresponding to the sound you hear first.

	u	**ou**
1		
2		
3		
4		
5		
6		
7		
8		

d)   **Comptine:**

Savez-vous planter les choux?
A la mode, à la mode,
Savez-vous planter les choux,
A la mode de chez nous?
Les choux rouges comme les choux verts,
On les plante dans la terre,
On les plante à genoux
Dans un joli petit trou.

e)   The sound **ui** as in **puis:**

Some examples:

lui   nuit   suis   puis   pluie

Some sentences:

I.   **Suivez la Seine.**

2.   **Il a dix-huit ans.**

3.   **Je suis ici depuis huit jours.**

4.   **Il y a du bruit chez lui.**

f)   **Comptine:**

Sur le Pont Neuf Henri IV
Toute la nuit toujours galope;
Ça va bien quand il fait beau,
Mais quand il tombe de la pluie
Il n'a pas de parapluie,
Il est trempé jusqu'aux os.

PONT NEUF

Part Three   Section Trois
Functional Dialogues   Dialogues Fonctionnels

I.   Jacqueline tells Philip how to get to the metro station.   **Jacqueline indique à Philip comment aller à la station de métro.**

Philip: Is there a metro station near here?   **Est-ce qu'il y a une station de métro près d'ici?**

J: Yes, of course. There's Saint Sulpice station. It's five minutes walk from here.   **Oui, bien sûr, il y a la station Saint Sulpice. C'est à cinq minutes à pied.**

Philip: Which way is it?   **C'est de quel côté?**

J: You take the first street on the left, carry straight on and you reach the rue de Rennes.   **Vous prenez la première rue à gauche, vous allez tout droit et vous arrivez à la rue de Rennes.**

Philip: What then?   **Et après?**

J: You're there. The metro is on the left-hand pavement.   **Vous y êtes, le métro se trouve sur le trottoir de gauche.**

2.   Jacqueline explains to Philip how to get about in the metro.   **Jacqueline explique à Philip comment s'orienter dans le métro.**

Philip: To get to the Louvre, what do I have to do?   **Pour aller au Louvre, qu'est-ce que je dois faire?**

J: Here's a map of the metro. Look. We're here, at Saint Sulpice. You take the direction Porte de Clignancourt.   **Voilà un plan du métro. Regardez. Nous sommes ici à Saint Sulpice. Vous prenez la direction Porte de Clignancourt.**

Philip: Do I have to change?   **Est-ce que je dois changer?**

J: Yes, you change at Châtelet station and take the direction Pont de Neuilly. There's no need to change after that.   **Oui, vous changez à Châtelet et vous prenez la direction Pont de Neuilly. Après c'est direct.**

Philip: Where do I get off?   **Où est-ce que je descends?**

J: You get off at Louvre station. It's the first station after Châtelet.   **Vous descendez à la station Louvre, c'est la première station après Châtelet.**

Philip: Good. I think I've understood.   **Bon, je crois que j'ai compris.**

Est-ce que je dois change

3.

	Philip is asking a passer-by the way.	**Philip demande son chemin à une passante.**
	The Lady	**La Femme = La F.**

Philip:	Excuse me. Can you tell me how to get to the Pont Neuf, please?	**Pardon madame, pour aller au Pont Neuf, s'il vous plaît?**
La F:	You go straight ahead and under the clock.	**Vous allez tout droit et vous passez sous l'horloge.**
Philip:	Right. I go straight ahead and under the clock. And then?	**Alors, je vais tout droit et je passe sous l'horloge et puis?**
La F:	Then you go across the famous Cour Carrée and turn right towards the embankment.	**Puis vous traversez la célèbre Cour Carrée et vous tournez à droite en direction des quais.**
Philip:	And when I reach the embankment, do I turn left or right?	**Et quand j'arrive aux quais, je tourne à gauche ou à droite?**
La F:	Left.	**A gauche.**
Philip:	Is the Pont Neuf far?	**Et le Pont Neuf, c'est loin?**
La F:	No. It's 500 metres away.	**Non, c'est à 500 mètres.**
Philip:	Thank you very much.	**Merci bien.**
La F:	Don't mention it.	**Je vous en prie.**

4.

	Philip is talking about the Louvre Museum.	**Philip donne ses impressions sur le Musée du Louvre.**

J:	What did you think of the museum?	**Alors, qu'avez-vous pensé du musée?**
Philip:	It's really big!	**Qu'est-ce qu'il est grand!**
J:	Did you see the Venus de Milo?	**Avez-vous vu la Vénus de Milo?**
Philip:	Yes. It's marvellous!	**Oui. Quelle merveille!**
J:	Did you like the Mona Lisa?	**Avez-vous aimé la Joconde?**
Philip:	Yes, she's really beautiful!	**Oui, comme elle est belle!**
J:	She has a lovely smile, hasn't she?	**Elle a un beau sourire, n'est-ce pas?**
Philip:	Yes, wonderful and mysterious and you look a bit like her.	**Oui, superbe et mystérieux et vous lui ressemblez un peu.**

5. Jacqueline is suggesting some activities. **Jacqueline suggère quelque chose à Philip.**

Philip: What shall we do now? **Qu'est-ce qu'on fait maintenant?**

J: Shall we go for a little walk? **Si on se promenait un peu?**

Philip: All right. Where shall we go? **D'accord, où est-ce qu'on va?**

J: We can go and sit in the Square du Vert Galant. **On peut aller s'asseoir dans le Square du Vert Galant.**

Philip: Good idea. Let's go. It is as if we were in the country. **Bonne idée. Allons-y. C'est comme si on était à la campagne.**

J: And what if we went there tomorrow? What if we had a picnic? **Eh bien, si on y allait demain? Si on faisait un pique-nique?**

Philip: What a good idea! I'd love to. **Quelle bonne idée! Moi, je veux bien.**

HENRI IV

Part Four : Personalised Dialogues
Section Quatre : Dialogues

a)   Asking how to get to the metro station.

Vous:	(Ask if there is a metro station near here.)
Jacqueline:	**Oui, bien sûr, il y a la station Saint Sulpice. C'est à cinq minutes à pied.**
Vous:	(Ask which way it is.)
Jacqueline:	**Vous prenez la première rue à gauche, vous allez tout droit et vous arrivez à la rue de Rennes.**
Vous:	(Ask what then.)
Jacqueline:	**Vous y êtes. Le métro se trouve sur le trottoir de gauche.**

b)   Asking how to get about in the metro.

Vous:	(Ask what you have to do to get to the Louvre.)
Jacqueline:	**Vous prenez d'abord la direction Porte de Clignancourt.**
Vous:	(Ask if you have to change.)
Jacqueline:	**Oui, vous changez à Châtelet et ensuite vous prenez la direction Pont de Neuilly.**
Vous:	(Ask where you get off.)
Jacqueline:	**Vous descendez au Louvre.**
Vous:	(Say thank you and that you think you have understood.)

c)   Asking the way in the street.

Vous:	(Stop the passer-by, then ask how to get to the Pont Neuf.)
La passante:	**Vous allez tout droit et vous passez sous l'horloge.**
Vous:	(Repeat what she has said then ask what next.)
La passante:	**Puis vous traversez la Cour Carrée et vous tournez à droite en direction des quais.**
Vous:	(Ask if you turn left or right when you reach the embankment.)
La passante:	**A gauche.**
Vous:	(Ask if the Pont Neuf is far.)
La passante:	**Non, c'est à cinq cents mètres.**
Vous:	(Say thank you.)
La passante:	**Je vous en prie.**

d)   Talking about the Louvre Museum.

Jacqueline:	**Qu'avez-vous pensé du musée?**
Vous:	(Say that it's really big.)
Jacqueline:	**Avez-vous vu la Vénus de Milo?**
Vous:	(Say yes it's marvellous.)
Jacqueline:	**Avez-vous aimé la Joconde?**
Vous:	(Say yes she is really beautiful.)
Jacqueline:	**Elle a un beau sourire, n'est-ce pas?**
Vous:	(Say that it's wonderful and mysterious.)

e)   Suggesting some activities.

Philip: **Qu'est-ce qu'on fait maintenant?**
Vous: (Suggest that you go for a little walk.)
Philip: **D'accord. Où est-ce qu'on va?**
Vous: (Say that you can go and sit in the park.)
Philip: **Bonne idée. Allons-y.**
          C'est comme si on était à la campagne.
Vous: (Suggest you go there tomorrow.
          Suggest you go for a picnic.)
Philip: **Quelle bonne idée!**
          Moi, je veux bien.

LOUVRE MUSEUM

170

Part Five : Grammar
Section Cinq : Grammaire

MORE ABOUT TENSES . . .

1.   THE IMPERFECT TENSE

In the last Act, we briefly introduced this tense and showed you three examples with the verb **avoir**, remember?

NOW we want to look at this tense more closely.

a)   When and in which situations is it used, for example?

   You can use this tense, whenever you want to talk
   about general conditions in the past. It may also
   refer to habitual actions in the past, where in
   English you would say 'used to'.

e.g.   **On l'appelait 'Le Vert Galant'.**
                        Il aimait bien les femmes.

NOTE: You can also use it to refer to continuous actions in the past, where in English you
           would say 'was'/'were . . .ing'.

b)   The next thing is how to form the Imperfect Tense?

It is quite simple: all you have to do is to remove the —**ONS** ending from the **nous** part of the
present tense of the verb (e.g. **nous donnons** - **donn-**) and add instead these endings:

e.g.   **je donn**   **—AIS**   **nous donn**   **—IONS**   *
           tu donn   **—AIS**   **vous donn**   **—IEZ**
           il/elle donn   **—AIT**   **ils/elles donn —AIENT**

A notable exception is **ETRE: j'ETais, nous ETions**, etc.

   REMEMBER: From the **NOUS** part of the present tense
                         Remove the —**ONS** from all the ends
                         Then add —**AIS**, —**AIT**, —**AIENT** with
                         JE, TU, IL(S), ELLE(S).
                         With **VOUS** add —**IEZ** and **NOUS** add —**IONS**.

Avez-vous aimé la Joconde?

171

2. MORE ABOUT THE **PASSE COMPOSE**

When you want to make a negative statement using the **passé composé,**
i.e. 'have not/has or did not', you place **NE** in front of and **PAS** after the verb **AVOIR** or **ETRE.**
This rule also applies to other negative expressions like **NE . . . PLUS** 'not any more' or
NE . . . JAMAIS 'never'!

e.g. **Il N'est PAS mort à cause d'une femme.**
Je N'ai JAMAIS pris le métro.

NOTE: To ask a question of the **avez-vous** type in the **passé composé,** you simply add the past participle after **vous:**

e.g. **Qu'avez-vous PENSE du musée?**
Avez-vous VU la Vénus de Milo?
Avez-vous AIME la Joconde?

3. **DEPUIS** — For/since

In French, you must use the PRESENT tense with **DEPUIS,** which you can use to mean either 'for' or 'since'.

e.g. **Vous attendez depuis longtemps?**
Have you been waiting for a long time?

Thus, you use **DEPUIS,** plus the PRESENT tense to:-

State that someone has been doing
something for a period of time.

Ask if something has been going on
for a particular time in the past.

REMEMBER: For English speakers, it may not make sense
But with **DEPUIS** you use the PRESENT tense.

4. **VENIR (DE)** + infinitive — Has just

As you know the verb **VENIR** usually means 'to come':

e.g. **Venez à la maison demain matin.**
Come to the house tomorrow morning.

Si je venais vous chercher à l'hôtel?
Shall I come and fetch you at the hotel?

However, you can use **VENIR,** followed by **DE,** plus an infinitive to say that someone HAS JUST done something or that something HAS JUST happened:

e.g. **Je viens d'arriver.**
I've just arrived.

Le Musée du Louvre vient de fermer.
The Louvre Museum has just closed.

REMEMBER: **Je viens . . .** means 'I'm coming . . .'
That's a 'must'
But if you add a **DE** plus infinitive
It's 'I've just . . .'

5. **Y . . .**

Y can be used to replace **A** (at or to) together with the name of a place. It can often be translated by the English word 'there':

e.g.	**Vous Y êtes**	—	**Vous êtes à la rue de Rennes.**
	Allons — Y	—	**Allons au Square du Vert Galant.**

REMEMBER: Why not save your energy?
Instead of **A** plus place, say **Y**.

Le Musée du Louvre vient de fermer.

Part Six   :   Key Phrases
Section Six   :   Expressions utiles

1.   ETRE EN TRAIN DE . . .

When you want to stress the fact that something is happening at this particular moment, instead of just using the present tense, you can use **être en train de:**

> e.g.   **Jacqueline est en train de**
>   **regarder les bateaux-mouches.**
>   (i.e. she is doing this when Philip arrives)

2.   SI JE/ON/ etc . . . + Imperfect Tense — Making suggestions

A simple way of making suggestions is to start with **SI** 'if' then continue with a verb in the Imperfect Tense:

> e.g.   **Si on se promenait un peu?**
>   Shall we go for a little walk?
>
>   **Si on faisait un pique-nique?**
>   What if we had a picnic?
>
>   **Si je venais vous chercher à l'hôtel?**
>   Shall I come and fetch you at the hotel?

3.   QU'EST-CE QUE/COMME . . .!

You have seen that one way of expressing pleasure or surprise is to use the word **QUEL/QUELLE** followed by a noun or adjective plus noun:

> e.g.   **QUELLE merveille!**
>   **QUEL bon repas!**

Here are two other ways of making similar exclamations about things that have already been mentioned:

> **e.g.**   **QU'EST-CE QU'il est grand!**   (i.e. **le musée du Louvre**)
>   **COMME elle est belle!**   (i.e. **La Joconde**)

Part Seven : Games
Section Sept : Jeux

1. Can you find your way around the metro?

Here is a simplified map of the metro.

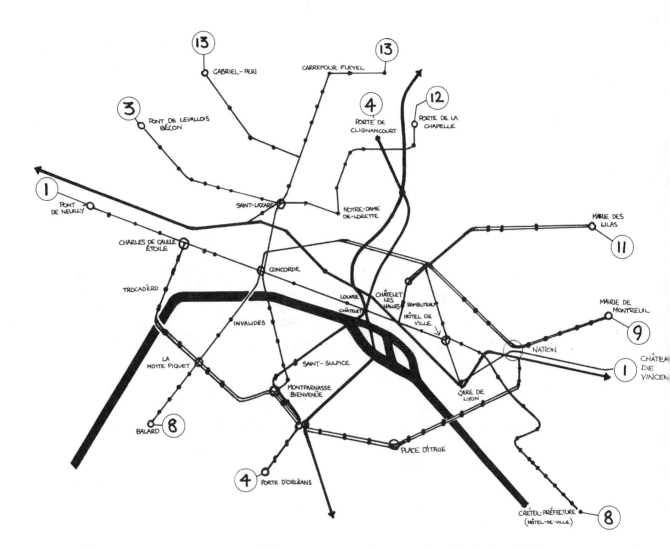

1. **Pour commencer, faites le même trajet que Philip — allez de Saint-Sulpice au Louvre.**
2. **Est-ce direct pour aller du Louvre à Charles de Gaulle-Etoile?**
   Quelle direction devez-vous prendre?
3. **Vous allez ensuite au Trocadéro pour voir la Tour Eiffel.**
   Quelle direction prenez-vous? Combien y a-t-il de stations?
4. **Vous voulez visiter le tombeau de Napoléon — vous reprenez le métro pour descendre à la station Invalides. Où devez-vous changer?**
5. **La visite est terminée. Vous décidez de rentrer à votre hôtel près de Rambuteau. Où allez-vous changer? Quelles directions allez-vous prendre?**

2. Did you manage to get there?

2. Did you manage to get there?

Voici le plan d'une petite ville de province:

You have asked the way to various places on the map below. Where did you ask to go?

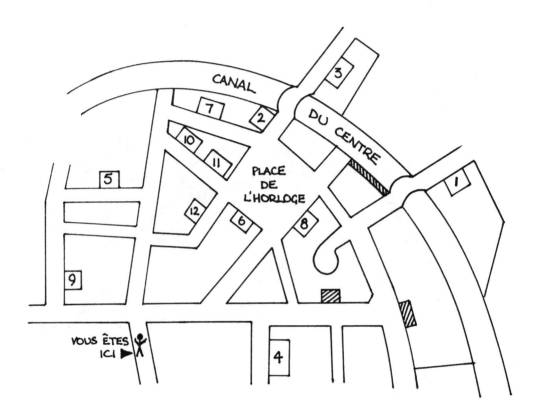

1.	**Le commissariat de police.**	7.	**La pharmacie.**
2.	**Le bureau de tabac.**	8.	**Le restaurant de l'Horloge.**
3.	**Le garage Peugeot.**	9.	**La gare.**
4.	**L'Hôtel de France.**	10.	**Le musée**
5.	**La poste.**	11.	**L'église.**
6.	**Le Syndicat d'Initiative.**	12.	**La banque.**

1. **Pour aller ...?**
   Vous prenez la troisième rue à gauche, vous continuez tout droit et c'est sur votre droite.

2. **Pour aller ...?**
   Vous tournez à droite puis vous prenez la première à droite et c'est à 200 mètres à gauche.

3. **Pour aller ...?**
   Vous prenez la première rue à droite puis la première à gauche. Vous allez tout droit jusqu'à la Place de l'Horloge et c'est juste en face sur le trottoir de droite.

4. **Pour aller ...?**
   Vous allez à droite, vous continuez jusqu'au bout puis vous tournez à gauche. Vous prenez la première à droite, vous traversez le canal et c'est à droite, juste après le pont.

5. **Pour aller ...?**
   Vous prenez la deuxième rue à droite puis la première à gauche et c'est à droite à côté du musée.

6. **Pour aller ...?**
   Vous prenez la quatrième rue à droite, vous passez devant la pharmacie et vous arrivez à la Place de l'Horloge. Vous tournez à gauche et c'est juste avant le pont sur votre gauche.

Si vous avez bien compris toutes les indications, vous avez la permission de vous y arrêter!

3. Who is sitting where?

Hier soir Jacqueline a fait un repas de famille.
Voilà la table avec les invités. Pouvez-vous retrouver le nom de chaque invité?

Oncle Antoine

1. **Arthur était en face de l'oncle Antoine.**
2. **Jacqueline était à droite d'Arthur.**
3. **Tante Marie était entre Arthur et Philip.**
4. **Nicole était à gauche de Philip.**
5. **Jean-Luc était en face de Philip.**
6. **Sophie était à côté de Jean-Luc.**

4. 10 o'clock **chez** Jacqueline.

Use the appropriate one of the following expressions to describe Jacqueline's situation at 10 a.m. each morning of the week.

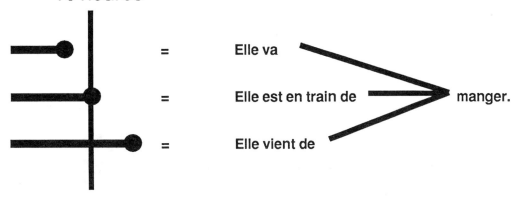

e.g. **10 heures**

= **Elle va**

= **Elle est en train de** > **manger.**

= **Elle vient de**

10 heures

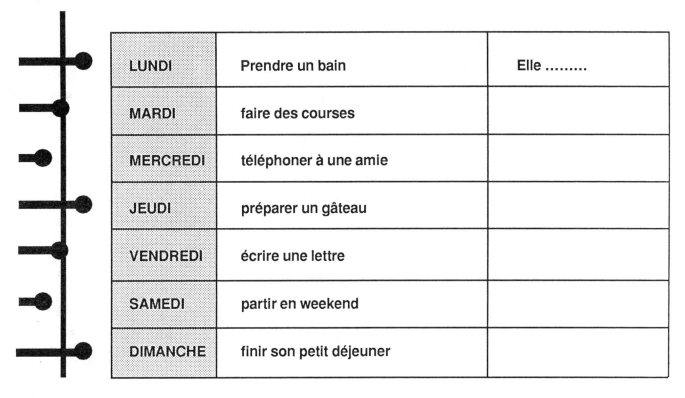

LUNDI	Prendre un bain	**Elle ………**
MARDI	faire des courses	
MERCREDI	téléphoner à une amie	
JEUDI	préparer un gâteau	
VENDREDI	écrire une lettre	
SAMEDI	partir en weekend	
DIMANCHE	finir son petit déjeuner	

Did you figure out the difference between **va, en train de** and **vient**?

5. Jacqueline is taking you for a drive around Paris to show you the sights. Express your surprise, delight, disappointment, etc., as you see each sight.

Use these words: **haut/e, beau/belle, magnifique, grand/e, moche, moderne, vieux/vieille, impressionnant/e.**

e.g. **Jacqueline:** **Voilà la Tour Eiffel.**

Vous: **Qu'est-ce qu'elle est haute!**

1. **Jacqueline:** **Ça, c'est l'Arc de Triomphe.**

Vous: ....

2. **Jacqueline:** **Nous voilà devant le Sacré Coeur.**

Vous: ....

3. **Jacqueline:** **Voici la statue d'Henri IV.**

Vous: ....

4. **Jacqueline:** **Voilà Notre Dame.**

Vous: ....

5. **Jacqueline:** **Et ça, c'est un agent de police!**

Vous: ....

6. **Trouvez l'animal.**

Each sentence tells you something about one of the animals below.
Can you match them up?

1. **C'est un animal qui habite à la maison. Il aime boire du lait et manger du poisson.**
2. **Cet animal est grand et fort. Autrefois, l'homme avait besoin de lui pour faire son travail et pour voyager.**
3. **C'est un animal qui nous donne du lait.**
4. **Cet animal peut être dangereux pour l'homme. Il est long et mince et il n'a pas de pieds.**
5. **Si vous voulez des oeufs, il faut avoir cet animal.**
6. **C'est un animal doux et timide. Il peut vivre dans la nature ou à la maison. On utilise sa peau pour faire des manteaux.**
7. **On appelle cet animal 'le meilleur ami de l'homme'.**
8. **C'est un tout petit animal qui fait souvent peur aux dames. Il aime bien le fromage.**
9. **Cet animal nous donne de la laine pour faire des pullovers.**
10. **C'est un animal avec un très long cou.**

une vache

un lapin

un chat

un chien

un cheval

un serpent

un mouton

une poule

une souris

une girafe

BONUS

1. This is how the French describe each other sometimes:

Têtu comme un âne.

Malin comme un singe.

Doux comme un agneau.

Gai comme un pinson.

Bête comme une oie.

2. Country Wisdom!

Un monsieur se promène dans la campagne. Il ne trouve plus son chemin.
Au bout d'une heure, il rencontre enfin un paysan.

— **S'il vous plaît, est-ce que je suis sur la bonne route pour aller à Marsac?**
— **Je ne sais pas.**
— **Et le prochain village est loin?**
— **Je n'en sais rien.**
— **Mais cette route, où est-ce qu'elle conduit?**
— **Aucune idée.**
— **Il y a longtemps que vous habitez ici?**
— **J'y suis né, monsieur, il y a 50 ans.**
— **Eh bien, vous n'êtes pas très intelligent, vous ne connaissez même pas les**
  routes de votre pays!
— **Peut-être, mais moi, je ne me suis jamais perdu!**

3. More about locations:

    Read this first:

dans la boîte	in the box
sur la table	on the table
sous la chaise	under the chair
derrière le mur	behind the wall
devant la porte	in front of the door.

    Now look at the picture and fill in the gap:

    1. **Le chien est — — — — — — — la table.**

    2. **Le vase est — — — la table.**

    3. **Les fleurs sont — — — — le vase.**

    4. **Le chat est — — — — la table.**

    5. **L'assiette est — — — — — — le chat.**

4. **Connaisez-vous ce proverbe?**

    —**Le chat parti, les souris dansent.**

5. Playing cards: **Voulez-vous jouer aux cartes?**

    These 4 cards will give you the names of the 4 suits and the court cards if you ever want to play cards in French.

| Roi de trèfle | Dame de pique | Valet de carreau | As de coeur |

WORD WEB

An excellent way to learn and revise vocabulary is to make up your own 'Word Webs'. There is one below. You simply take a topic, in this case shopping, and choose some sub-heads on that subject. We chose shopping for clothes, for food, at the chemist, and at the cafe, since these subjects have been covered already.

Then you just write in the words that occur to you when you think of that topic - free assocation. You'll find you soon build up logical groups of associated words which is a great way to build vocabulary.

We strongly suggest you add words to this Word Web. Better yet, go back and make up some of your own Word Webs for the previous four Acts. And continue to make up at least one Word Web per Act. It's a very memorable way to create a visual memory for your language.

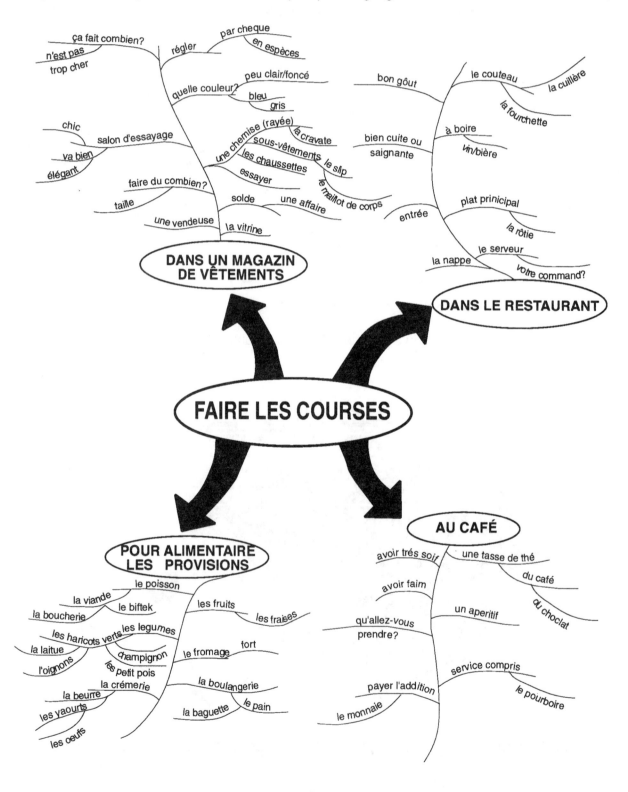

ACT 8 ACTE 8
Scene 1 Scène 1

A day in the country (Thursday).	Une journée à la campagne (Jeudi).

At nine o'clock in the morning Jacqueline arrives at the hotel. Philip is waiting for her in the foyer.	A neuf heures du matin, Jacqueline arrive à l'hôtel. Philip l'attend dans le hall.

Philip:	Good morning Jacqueline. How are you?	Bonjour Jacqueline. Comment allez-vous?
Jacqueline:	Fine thanks. And you? Are you ready?	Bien merci. Et vous? Vous êtes prêt?
Philip:	Yes. Let's go. Where have you parked the car?	Oui. Allons-y. Où avez-vous garé la voiture?
Jacqueline:	There. Just outside the door.	Là, juste devant la porte.

Philip l'attend dans le hall.

They go out of the hotel and Philip sees a beautiful, brand new Porsche. He gasps in admiration.	Ils sortent de l'hôtel et Philip voit une belle Porsche toute neuve. Il pousse un cri d'admiration.

Philip:	Well now, I say! Is that your uncle's car? Business must be doing well.	Eh bien, dites donc! C'est ça la voiture de votre oncle? Les affaires marchent bien.
Jacqueline:	Would you like to drive it?	Vous voulez la conduire?
Philip:	I'd love to but . . .	J'aimerais bien mais . . .
Jacqueline:	You can't drive?	Vous ne savez pas conduire?
Philip:	Yes, I can but I don't know the road.	Si, je sais conduire mais je ne connais pas la route.
Jacqueline:	How long have you been driving?	Vous conduisez depuis combien de temps?
Philip	I've had my driving licence for two years.	J'ai mon permis de conduire depuis deux ans.
Jacqueline:	So you're not a beginner.	Alors, vous n'êtes pas un débutant?
Philip:	No but I'd never know how to get out of Paris.	Non, mais je ne saurais pas sortir de Paris.
Jacqueline:	All right then, I'll drive. Go on, get in.	Bon. Eh bien je conduirai. Allez, montez.

	It's the rush hour.	**C'est l'heure d'affluence.**
	There are traffic jams everywhere	**Il y a des embouteillages partout**
	but Jacqueline keeps calm.	**mais Jacqueline ne s'énerve pas.**
	Slowly she heads for	**Elle se dirige lentement vers**
	the ring road.	**le boulevard périphérique.**

Philip:	This traffic is incredible.	**C'est incroyable cette circulation.**
	If I had to drive in Paris I would be scared.	**Si je devais conduire dans Paris, j'aurais peur.**
Jacqueline:	It's a question of habit.	**C'est une question d'habitude.**
Philip:	You haven't told me yet where we're going. Is it far?	**Vous ne m'avez pas encore dit où nous allons. C'est loin?**
Jacqueline:	It's a surprise.	**C'est une surprise.**
Philip:	Give me some clues.	**Donnez-moi quelques indications.**
Jacqueline:	If you watch the road signs maybe you'll guess.	**Si vous regardez les panneaux, vous devinerez peut-être.**
Philip:	If you gave me a bit of help it would be easier.	**Si vous m'aidiez un petit peu, ça serait plus facile.**
Jacqueline:	All right. I'll help you. It's about fifty kilometres from Paris and it's where Napoleon said good-bye to his troops.	**D'accord, je vais vous aider. C'est à une cinquantaine de kilomètres de Paris et c'est là où Napoléon a dit adieu à ses troupes.**
Philip:	Ah! I've got it. It's Fontainebleau.	**Ah! j'y suis. C'est Fontainebleau.**
Jacqueline:	Well done. You've guessed right. We shall be there for eleven o'clock.	**Bravo. Vous avez bien deviné. Nous y serons pour onze heures.**
Philip:	And what will we do then?	**Et après, que ferons-nous?**
Jacqueline:	We'll visit the house then we'll have a picnic and after that...	**Nous visiterons le château puis nous pique-niquerons et ensuite . . .**
Philip:	And after that? Another surprise?	**Et ensuite quoi? Une autre surprise?**
Jacqueline:	You'll see.	**Vous verrez bien.**

'Jacqueline is still as mysterious as ever,' thinks Philip, 'but she is so charming.'	**'Décidément, Jacqueline est toujours aussi mystérieuse,' pense Philip, 'mais elle est tellement charmante.'**

Fifty minutes later they arrive outside the château. They manage to park easily as it is the middle of the week and the car park is almost empty. Jacqueline buys the tickets to visit the château.	Au bout de cinquante minutes, ils arrivent devant le château. Ils trouvent facilement à se garer car c'est le milieu de la semaine et le parking est presque vide. Jacqueline achète les tickets pour la visite du château.

Scene 2 **Scène 2**

Two hours later. Philip and Jacqueline have finished the visit. As it is time to eat they get back into the car to look for a nice little spot for a picnic in the forest of Fontainebleau. It is warm for a spring day. The sky is blue and there is not a single cloud.	**Deux heures plus tard, Philip et Jacqueline ont fini la visite. Comme il est l'heure de manger, ils reprennent la voiture et cherchent un joli petit coin pour pique-niquer dans la forêt de Fontainebleau. Il fait chaud pour un jour de printemps. Le ciel est bleu et il n'y a pas un seul nuage.**

Philip: It's odd, all these big rocks in this forest. **C'est curieux tous ces gros rochers dans cette forêt.**

Jacqueline: Yes, indeed. Lots of Parisians come out here in the autumn and spring to do some rock climbing. Do you go in for that? **Oui, effectivement. Beaucoup de Parisiens viennent ici en automne et au printemps pour faire de l'escalade. Vous en faites, vous?**

Philip: Me? Rock-climbing? Never in your life! I don't want to get killed! **Moi? de l'escalade? Jamais de la vie. Je n'ai pas envie de me tuer!**

Jacqueline: What sports do you go in for? **Qu'est-ce que vous faites comme sport?**

Philip: I always play tennis in the summer and in winter I often go jogging. That's more than enough for me. What about you? Are you the sporting type? **Je joue toujours au tennis en été et en hiver je fais souvent du jogging. Ça me suffit largement. Et vous? vous êtes sportive?**

Je joue toujours au tennis en été.

Jacqueline:	Sporting? That's putting it a bit strong. I like playing tennis and now and again I go swimming.
	Sportive, c'est beaucoup dire. J'aime bien jouer au tennis et je fais de la natation de temps en temps.
Philip:	And what about jogging?
	Et du jogging, vous en faites?
Jacqueline:	No. I never go jogging.
	Ah! non. Je ne fais jamais de jogging.
Philip:?	Well, if your uncle goes on playing hide and seek and if I have to stay another fortnight in Paris, we could have a game of tennis one afternoon. What do you think of that?
	Eh bien, si votre oncle continue à jouer à cache-cache et si je dois rester encore *quinze jours à Paris, on pourra faire une partie de tennis un après midi. Qu'en pensez-vous?
Jacqueline:	Why not?
	Pourquoi pas?
	Ah!
	Tiens!
	Here's the ideal spot.
	Voilà le coin idéal.
	Let's stop here.
	Arrêtons-nous ici.

* quinze jours
= 15 days
= 14 nights

Jacqueline takes out the basket. They set up everything for their picnic and start eating.

Jacqueline sort le panier. Ils installent leur pique-nique et commencent à manger.

Scene 3   **Scène 3**

An hour later they have finished eating and they get back into the car.

Une heure plus tard, ils ont fini de manger et ils remontent dans la voiture.

Jacqueline: And now I'm going to take you to a pretty little village where someone is expecting us for coffee.

Et maintenant, je vais vous emmener dans un joli petit village où quelqu'un nous attend pour prendre le café.

Ten minutes later they reach Barbizon. At a crossroads Jacqueline turns right and stops outside an old house.

Dix minutes plus tard, ils arrivent à Barbizon. A un carrefour, Jacqueline tourne à droite et s'arrête devant une vieille maison.

Ils installent leur pique-nique.

| | On the garden gate there is a sign saying 'Beware of the dog'. She rings the bell without hesitating. A man in his early thirties comes to open the gate. He is accompanied by a big, black dog. | Sur la porte du jardin on peut lire 'Chien méchant'. Elle sonne sans hésiter. Un homme d'une trentaine d'années vient ouvrir la porte. Il est accompagné d'un gros chien noir. |

Henri:	Hello Jacqueline. How are you? I'm pleased to see you.	Bonjour Jacqueline. Comment vas-tu? Je suis content de te voir.
Jacqueline:	Hello, Henri. Let me introduce Philip West, an English friend. Philip, this is Henri Dubois, my cousin.	Bonjour Henri. Je te présente Philip West, un ami anglais. Philip, je vous présente Henri Dubois, mon cousin.
Henri:	Pleased to meet you.	Enchanté de faire votre connaissance.
Philip:	Pleased to meet you.	Enchanté Monsieur.
Henri:	Come in, please, and don't be afraid of the dog.	Entrez, je vous prie et n'ayez pas peur du chien.

| | As the weather is fine, they sit out on the patio. While Philip is admiring the blossoming trees Henri studies him closely. | Puisqu'il fait beau, ils s'installent sur la terrasse. Pendant que Philip admire les arbres en fleurs, Henri le regarde avec intérêt. |

Henri:	Well now. Tell me a bit about yourself. Where are you from?	Eh bien, parlez-moi un peu de vous. Vous êtes d'où?
Philip:	I'm from London.	Je suis de Londres.
Henri:	And what do you do for a living?	Que faites-vous dans la vie?
Philip:	I'm completing my studies at London University.	Je termine mes études à l'université de Londres.
Henri:	And what would you like to do later on?	Que voudriez-vous faire plus tard?
Philip:	If possible, I'd like to work in the import-export business.	Si c'était possible, j'aimerais bien travailler dans l'import-export.
Henri:	Well, that's funny. I work for an import-export firm.	Tiens, c'est drôle. Moi, je travaille dans une Maison d'import-export.
Philip:	Really? What a coincidence! So does Jacqueline.	Ah oui? Quelle coïncidence! Jacqueline aussi.

Jacqueline:	No, it isn't a coincidence. Henri works with me.	**Non, ce n'est pas une coïncidence. Henri travaille avec moi.**
Philip:	Is that so? Why didn't you mention it before?	**Ah bon? Pourquoi est-ce que vous ne m'en avez pas parlé avant?**
Jacqueline:	Don't worry. I'll explain it all to you later.	**Ne vous en faites pas. Je vous expliquerai tout plus tard.**

All three of them have coffee and Henri goes on asking Philip lots of questions. 'Why does he want to know so much? What do they want of me?' wonders Philip, who is more and more mystified.	**Ils prennent le café tous les trois et Henri continue à poser beaucoup de questions à Philip. 'Pourquoi veut-il savoir tant de choses? Qu'est-ce qu'ils attendent de moi?' se demande Philip, de plus en plus intrigué.**

Ils s'installent sur la terrasse.

ACTE 8 (i)

Jacqueline arrive à l'hôtel.

Philip l'attend dans le hall.

Où avez-vous garé la voiture?

Là, juste devant la porte.

Vous voulez la conduire?

Mais je ne connais pas la route.

C'est l'heure d'affluence. Il y a des embouteillages partout.

C'est là où Napoléon a dit adieu à ses troupes.

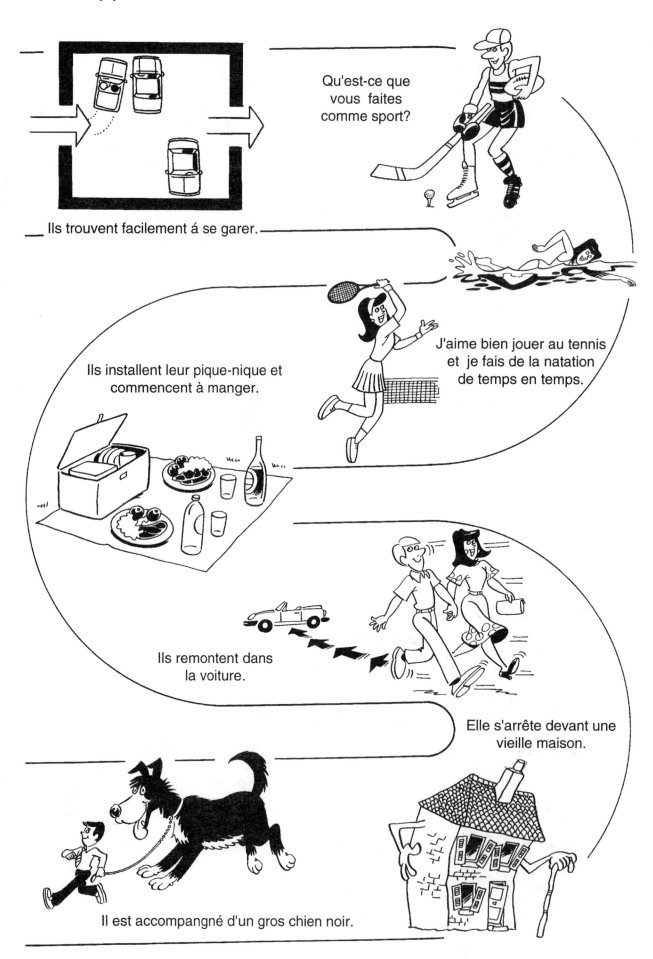

Ils trouvent facilement á se garer.

Qu'est-ce que vous faites comme sport?

J'aime bien jouer au tennis et je fais de la natation de temps en temps.

Ils installent leur pique-nique et commencent à manger.

Ils remontent dans la voiture.

Elle s'arrête devant une vieille maison.

Il est accompangné d'un gros chien noir.

ACTE 8 (iii)

Je vous présente mon cousin.

Puisqu'il fait beau
ils s'installent sur la terrasse.

Je termine mes études
à l'université de Londres.

J'aimerais bien travailler
dans l'import-export

Henri travaille avec moi.

Qu'est-ce qu'ils
attendent de moi?

Se demande, Philip
de plus en plus intrigué.

Henri continue à poser
beaucoup de questions à Philip.

Part Two : Pronunciation and Intonation
Section Deux : Prononciation et Intonation

Nasals

a)   The sound **an** as in **dans, campagne, souvent** or **temps:**

Some sentences:

      I.   **Qu'en pensez-vous?**

      2.   **Vous en faites souvent?**

      3.   **Enchanté de faire votre connaissance.**

b)   The sound **on** as in **bon, combien** or **question:**

Some sentences:

      I.   **Allons-y.**

      2.   **Montez donc.**

      3.   **Nous y serons pour onze heures.**

      4.   **Il a une maison à Barbizon.**

c)   The sound **in** as in **matin, import, un, main, bien** or **coin:**

Some sentences:

      I.   **Un jeudi matin.**

      2.   **C'est loin ce coin?**

      3.   **Quelqu'un vient avec un chien.**

d)   Listen to the cassette very carefully to spot the difference between **an** and **on**:

	an	**on**
1		
2		
3		
4		
5		
6		

How many did you get right?

e)   Spot the difference between an and in:

	an	**in**
1		
2		
3		
4		
5		
6		

Did you manage a higher score on this game?

f)   **Comptine:**

Près de la maison,
Cinq petits lapins
Mangeaient des oignons,
Comme cinq petits coquins,
La pipe à la bouche
Le verre à la main,
En disant gaiement:
Ah! le bon vin blanc,
Buvons en tout plein.

Part Three Section Trois
Functional Dialogues Dialogues Fonctionnels

I.

Jacqueline is asking Philip if he can drive.

Jacqueline demande à Philip s'il sait conduire.

J:	Do you want to drive the car?	**Vous voulez conduire la voiture?**
Philip:	I'd love to but ...	**J'aimerais bien, mais . . .**
J:	You can't drive?	**Vous ne savez pas conduire?**
Philip:	Yes, I can but I don't know the road.	**Si, je sais conduire mais je ne connais pas la route.**
J:	How long have you been driving?	**Vous conduisez depuis combien de temps?**
Philip:	I've had my driving licence for two years.	**J'ai mon permis de conduire depuis deux ans.**
J:	So you're not a beginner?	**Alors, vous n'êtes pas un débutant?**
Philip:	No, but I'd never know how to get out of Paris.	**Non mais je ne saurai pas sortir de Paris.**
J:	All right then, I'll drive. Go on, get in.	**Bon. Eh bien je conduirai. Allez, montez.**

2.

Philip is trying to guess where Jacqueline is taking him.

Philip essaie de deviner où Jacqueline l'emmène.

Je ne connais pas la route.

Philip:	You haven't told me yet where we're going. Is it far?	**Vous ne m'avez pas encore dit où nous allons. C'est loin?**
J:	It's a surprise.	**C'est une surprise.**
Philip:	Give me some clues.	**Donnez-moi quelques indications.**
J:	If you watch the road signs maybe you'll guess.	**Si vous regardez les panneaux, vous devinerez peut-être.**
Philip:	If you gave me a bit of help it would be easier.	**Si vous m'aidiez un petit peu, ça serait plus facile.**
J:	All right, I'll help you. It's about fifty kilometres from Paris and it's where Napoleon said good-bye to his troops.	**D'accord, je vais vous aider. C'est à une cinquantaine de kilomètres de Paris et c'est là où Napoléon a dit adieu à ses troupes.**
Philip:	Ah! I've got it. It's Fontainebleau.	**Ah! j'y suis. C'est Fontainebleau.**
J:	Well done. You've guessed right.	**Bravo. Vous avez bien deviné.**

3. Jacqueline and Philip are discussing sport. **Jacqueline et Philip parlent du sport.**

J: What sports do you go in for? **Qu'est-ce que vous faites comme sport?**

Philip: I always play tennis in the summer and in winter I often go jogging. What about you? Are you the sporting type? **Je joue toujours au tennis en été et en hiver je fais souvent du jogging. Et vous? Vous êtes sportive?**

J: I like playing tennis and now and again I go swimming. **J'aime bien jouer au tennis et je fais de la natation de temps en temps.**

Philip: And what about jogging? **Et du jogging, vous en faites?**

J: No. I never go jogging. **Ah, non. Je ne fais jamais de jogging.**

Philip: Well, what would you say to a game of tennis this afternoon? **Eh bien, si on faisait une partie de tennis cet après midi. Qu'en pensez-vous?**

J: Why not? **Pourquoi pas?**

4. Introducing people. **Les présentations.**

J: Hello, Henri. Let me introduce Philip West, an English friend. Philip, this is Henri Dubois, my cousin. **Bonjour Henri. Je te présente Philip West, un ami anglais. Philip, je vous présente Henri Dubois, mon cousin.**

Henri: Pleased to meet you. **Enchanté de faire votre connaissance.**

Philip: Pleased to meet you. **Enchanté Monsieur.**

Je fais de la natation de temps en temps.

5.

	Henri is trying to get to know Philip.	**Henri cherche à connaître Philip.**
Henri:	Well now, tell me a bit about yourself. Where are you from?	**Eh bien, parlez-moi un peu de vous. Vous êtes d'où?**
Philip:	I'm from London.	**Je suis de Londres.**
Henri:	And what do you do for a living?	**Que faites-vous dans la vie?**
Philip:	I'm completing my studies at London University.	**Je termine mes études à l'université de Londres.**
Henri:	What would you like to do later on?	**Que voudriez-vous faire plus tard?**
Philip:	If possible, I'd like to work in the import-export business.	**Si c'était possible, j'aimerais bien travailler dans l'import-export.**

*Je termine mes études
à l'université de Londres.*

Part Four : Personalised Dialogues
Section Quatre : Dialogues

a) Talking about being able to drive.

Jacqueline:	**Voulez-vous conduire la voiture?**
Vous:	(Say you'd love to but...)
Jacqueline:	**Vous ne savez pas conduire?**
Vous:	(Say yes but you don't know the road.)
Jacqueline:	**Vous conduisez depuis combien de temps?**
Vous:	(Say how long you've had your driving licence.)
Jacqueline:	**Alors, vous n'êtes pas un débutant?**
Vous:	(Say no but that you would not know how to get out of Paris.)
Jacqueline:	**Bon. Eh bien, je conduirai.** **Allez, montez.**

b) Trying to guess where Jacqueline is taking you.

Vous:	(Say that Jacqueline has not told you where you're going and ask if it is far.)
Jacqueline:	**C'est une surprise.**
Vous:	(Ask her to give you some clues.)
Jacqueline:	**Si vous regardez les panneaux, vous devinerez peut-être.**
Vous:	(Say that if she helped you a bit, it would be easier.)
Jacqueline:	**D'accord, je vais vous aider.** **C'est à une cinquantaine de kilomètres de Paris et c'est là où Napoléon a dit adieu à ses troupes.**
Vous:	(Say you've got it and that it's Fontainebleau.)
Jacqueline:	**Bravo. Vous avez bien deviné.**

c) Talking about sport.

Jacqueline:	**Qu'est-ce que vous faites comme sport?**
Vous:	(Say what sports you do [tennis, jogging] then ask Jacqueline if she does any sports.)
Jacqueline:	**J'aime bien jouer au tennis et je fais de la natation de temps en temps.**
Vous:	(Ask if she goes jogging.)
Jacqueline:	**Ah non! Je ne fais jamais de jogging.**
Vous:	(Suggest that you have a game of tennis this afternoon.)
Jacqueline:	**Pourquoi pas?**

d) Introducing people (Henri to Philip West).

Vous:	(Say hello to Henri, then introduce Philip West, an English friend.)
Henri:	**Enchanté de faire votre connaissance.**
Vous:	(Introduce Henri, your cousin, to Philip.)
Philip:	**Enchanté, monsieur.**

e) Trying to get to know somebody.

Vous:	(Ask Philip to tell you a bit about himself. Ask him where he's from.)
Philip:	**Je suis de Londres.**
Vous:	(Ask him what he does for a living.)
Philip:	**Je termine mes études à l'Université de Londres.**
Vous:	(Ask him what he would like to do later on.)
Philip:	**Si c'était possible, j'aimerais bien travailler dans l'import-export.**

Part Five : Grammar
Section Cinq : Grammaire

1.   THE FUTURE TENSE — Will

In French, to talk about things that WILL happen, you only have to use another set of endings with the verb.

There is no separate word like 'will' or 'shall' as in English. The endings which are added to the infinitive of most verbs are as follows:

je donner	—AI	nous donner	—ONS
tu donner	—AS	vous donner	—EZ
il/elle donner	—A	ils/elles donner	—ONT

e.g.   **nous visiterons**
              we will visit   (**visiter** — to visit)   *

              vous devinerez
              you will guess   (**deviner** — to guess)

NOTE: With —**RE** verbs, you simply drop the **E:**

e.g.   **je conduirai**
              I will drive   (**conduire** — to drive)

NOTE: There are a few common verbs whose Future Tense is not formed by adding these endings to the Infinitive:

e.g. instead of: **AVOIR**   you change to   **AUR— ai, as, a, ons, ez, ont**
                  ETRE   **SER-**
                  SAVOIR   **SAUR-**
                  FAIRE   **FER-**
                  VOIR   **VERR-**
                  POUVOIR   **POURR-**
                  VOULOIR   **VOUDR-**   *

REMEMBER: You've got to know the endings
            To make the Future Tense:
            When added to the Infinitive
            Together they make sense.

Je conduirai

2. THE CONDITIONAL TENSE — Would

The Conditional Tense (where in English you use 'would') is formed by adding the endings to the Infinitive as below:

je donner	—AIS	nous donner	—IONS
tu donner	—AIS	vous donner	—IEZ
il/elle donner	—AIT	ils/elles donner	—AIENT

e.g. **j'aimerais bien travailler**
I would like to work

You have noticed that these are the same endings as the ones used for the Imperfect Tense but note that they are added to the Infinitive.

NOTE: For those few common verbs we have just seen, you replace the future endings with the conditional ones:

e.g. **J'aurais peur**   *
I would be scared

Ça serait plus facile
It would be easier

Que voudriez-vous faire?
What would you like to do?

3. **SI . . . — If . . .**

When you are stating conditions, using **SI . . .**, the tenses of the verbs are just as in English.

The Future Tense must be used along with **SI** plus the Present Tense:

e.g. **SI vous regardez les panneaux, vous devinerez peut-être.**
If you watch the road signs maybe you'll guess.

The Conditional Tense must be used along with **SI** plus the Imperfect Tense:

e.g. **SI vous m'aidiez un petit peu, ça serait plus facile.**
If you gave me a bit of help, it would be easier.

4. **TU/TE**

As you have seen in Act 4, in French there are two forms for the English word 'you':

VOUS — when you are talking to a person who you do not know very well OR to more than one person. **TU/TE** — when you are talking to a close friend, a relative or a child.

You have seen that **VOUS** covers all situations. **TU** is only used as the subject form and another form, **TE**, is used as direct or indirect object.

> e.g.   Henri says to Jacqueline, his cousin:

> **Comment vas-tu? Je suis content de <u>te</u> voir.**

> and Jacqueline says to Henri:

> **Je <u>te</u> présente Philip West.**

> but to Philip she says:

> **Je <u>vous</u> présente Henri Dubois.**

As you will see, things will change in the next Act as they get to know one another better.

> REMEMBER: Use **TU** or **TE** for 'you' in conversation
> With children, friends or a relation.

5. **EN**

You have seen this word used together with the names of countries:

> **en Angleterre, en France.**

The word **EN** can be used to replace **DE** plus noun as in:

Qu'en pensez-vous?

> **Vous en faites, vous?**
> **(Vous faites de l'escalade?)**
> Do you go in for that?
> (Do you do rock climbing?)

> **Qu'en pensez-vous?**
> **(Que pensez-vous d'une partie de tennis?)**
> What do you think of that?
> (What do you think about a game of tennis?)

> **Vous ne m'en avez pas parlé.**
> **(Vous ne m'avez pas parlé d'Henri et de son travail.)**
> You didn't mention it.
> (You didn't mention Henri and his job.)

> REMEMBER: Repeating **DE** + noun? No need.
> Use **EN** instead, to gain some speed.

203

Part Six : Key Phrases
Section Six : Expressions Utiles

1. ADVERBS

There are many common adverbs which have a special form which must be learned individually:

    e.g.   **bien** (well), **souvent** (often), **toujours** (always)

Apart from these, there is a simple way of forming adverbs; you simply add the ending —**MENT** to the feminine form of the adjective (just as in English you add —**LY** to the adjective — quick, quickly).

facile	—**MENT**	—	easily
lente	—**MENT**	—	slowly

In ACT 8, you have several examples (which incidentally are not all translated by an English adverb ending in —LY):

telle	—**MENT**	—	so
effective	—**MENT**	—	indeed
large	—**MENT**	—	more than enough

2. **JOUER A . . ./FAIRE DE . . .**

When talking about taking part in a sporting activity, you can usually use one of these expressions along with the name of the sport concerned:

e.g.	**faire de l'escalade**	(to climb)
	jouer au tennis	(to play tennis)
	faire du jogging	(to jog)
	faire de la natation	(to swim)

3. **POUR** + Infinitive — 'In order to'

You have seen many examples of **POUR**, meaning 'for' as in **POUR mon oncle, POUR moi,** etc., **POUR** can also be followed by an infinitive, in which case it means 'in order to':

    e.g.   **POUR chercher un joli petit coin**
                POUR faire un pique-nique
                POUR faire de l'escalade.

    NOTE: After verbs of movement, like **aller** or **venir**, you do not need to use **POUR** to express the idea of purpose:

    e.g.   **Un homme vient ouvrir la porte.**
             A man comes to open the gate.

Part Seven : Games
Section Sept : Jeux

1. **Bon voyage:**

   Here is a map of France with some of the main cities.
   Where are they in relation to Paris?

   e.g. **Fontainebleau est au sud de Paris.**

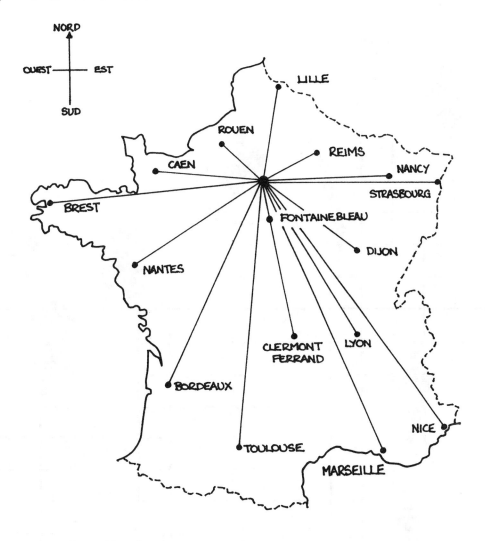

   1. **Brest est __ __ __ __ __ __ __.**

   2. **Toulouse est __ __ __ __ __.**

   3. **Lille est __ __ __ __ __ __.**

   4. **Strasbourg est __ __ __ __ __.**

   5. **Lyon est __ __ __ __ __ __ __ __ __.**

   6. **Rouen est __ __ __ __ __ __ __ __ __ __ __ __.**

   7. **Reims est __ __ __ __ __ __ __ __ __ __.**

   8. **Bordeaux est __ __ __ __ __ __ __ __ __ __ __.**

2. **Quel sport font-ils?**

Here is a list of sports for you to place in the grid. To help you there is a picture to indicate the right place. The numbered letters will give you an expression used by spectators. It can be applied to you if you get this right.

tennis, rugby, natation, voile, gymnastique, escalade, vélo, jogging, cheval, basket, course, judo, ski.

3. **Les mois et les saisons:**

This calendar lists the Saint's Days and special days. Were you born on a Saint's Day?

With the help of the calendar, re-arrange the letters of each group to make the name of a month or a season. Note the days

1. **AMI**
2. **TEE**
3. **RAMS**
4. **LUIJELT**
5. **TOMNEAU**
6. **PEMTRESBE**
7. **VERIFER**
8. **STRIPPEMN**
9. **VRAIL**
10. **TOUA**
11. **VIRNAJE**
12. **VRIHE**

Quand commence le printemps? l'été? l'automne? l'hiver?
Quelle est la date de la Fête Nationale?
A quoi correspond Easter **et** Whitsun**?**

JANVIER		FEVRIER		MARS	
1	JOUR DE L'AN	1	Ella	1	Aubin
2	Basile	2	Présentation	2	Charles le Bon
3	Geneviève	3	Blaise	3	Guénolé
4	Odilon	4	Véronique	4	Casimir
5	Edouard	5	Agathe	5	Olive
6	Epiphanie	6	Gaston	6	Colette
7	Raymond	7	Eugénie	7	Félicité
8	Lucien	8	Jacqueline	8	Jean de Dieu
9	Alix	9	Apolline	9	Françoise
10	Guillaume	10	Arnaud	10	Vivien
11	Paulin	11	Lourdes	11	Rosine
12	Tatiana	12	Félix	12	Justine
13	Bapt. du S.	13	Béatrice	13	Rodrigue
14	Nina	14	Valentin	14	Mi-Carême
15	Remi	15	Claude	15	Louise
16	Marcel	16	Julienne	16	Bénédicte
17	Roseline	17	Alexis	17	Patrice
18	Prisca	18	Bernadette	18	Cyrille
19	Marius	19	Mardi gras	19	Joseph
20	Sébastien	20	Cendres	20	Herbert
21	Agnès	21	Pierre Damien	21	Clémence
22	Vincent	22	Isabelle	22	Léa
23	Barnard	23	Lazare	23	Victorien
24	François Sales	24	Carême	24	Catherine Su.
25	Conv.S. Paul	25	Roméo	25	Annonciat.
26	Paule	26	Nestor	26	Larissa
27	Angèle	27	Honorine	27	Habib
28	Thomas d'Aq.	28	Romain	28	Gontran
29	Gildas			29	Gwladys
30	Martine			30	Amédée
31	Marcelle			31	Rameaux

Printemps: 20 mars à 16h 14mn

AVRIL		MAI		JUIN	
1	Hugues	1	F.TRAVAIL	1	Justin
2	Sandrine	2	Boris	2	F. des Mères
3	Richard	3	Jacques/Phil.	3	Kévin
4	Isidore	4	Sylvain	4	Clotilde
5	Vend St.	5	Judith	5	Igor
6	Marcellin 7	6	Prudence	6	Norbert
7	PAQUES	7	Gisèle	7	Gilbert
8	Julie	8	VICTOIRE 1945	8	Médard
9	Gautier	9	Pacôme	9	FETE DIEU
10	Fulbert	10	Solange	10	Landry
11	Stanislas	11	Estelle	11	Barnabé
12	Jules	12	Fête J. d'Arc	12	Guy
13	Ida	13	Rolande	13	Antoine de P.
14	Maxime	14	Matthias	14	Sacré-Coeur
15	Paterne	15	Denise	15	Germaine
16	Benoit-J.L.	16	ASCENSION	16	Fête des Pères
17	Anicet	17	Pascal	17	Hervé
18	Parfait	18	Eric	18	Léonce
19	Emma	19	Yves	19	Romuald
20	Odette	20	Bernardin	20	Silvère
21	Anselme	21	Constantin	21	Rodolphe
22	Alexandre	22	Emile	22	Alban
23	Georges	23	Didier	23	Audrey
24	Fidèle	24	Donatien	24	Jean-Bapt.
25	Marc	25	Sophie	25	Prosper
26	Alida	26	PENTECOTE	26	Anthelme
27	Zita	27	Augustin	27	Fernand
28	Souv.Dép.	28	Germain	28	Irénée
29	Cath.Sien	29	Aymar	29	Pierre et Paul
30	Robert	30	Ferdinand	30	Martial
		31	Visitation		

Eté: 21 juin à 10h 45mn

JUILLET		AOUT		SEPTEMBRE	
1	Thierry	1	Alphonse	1	Gilles
2	Martinien	2	Julien	2	Ingrid
3	Thomas	3	Lydie	3	Grégoire
4	Florent	4	J. —M. Vianney	4	Rosalie
5	Antoine—M.	5	Abel	5	Rassa
6	Mariette	6	Transfigur	6	Bertrand
7	Raoul	7	Gaétan	7	Reine
8	Thibaut	8	Dominique	8	Nativité N. —D.
9	Amandine	9	Amour	9	Alain
10	Ulrich	10	Laurent	10	Inès
11	Benoit	11	Claire	11	Adelphe
12	Olivier	12	Clarisse	12	Apollinaire
13	Henri/Jol	13	Hippolyte	13	Aimé
14	FETE NATION.	14	Evrard	14	Sainte Croix
15	Donald	15	ASSOMPTION	15	Roland
16	ND Mt Carmel	16	Armel	16	Edith
17	Charlotte	17	Hyacinthe	17	Renaud
18	Frédéric	18	Hélène	18	Nadège
19	Arsène	19	Jean Eudes	19	Emilie
20	Marina	20	Bernard	20	Davy
21	Victor	21	Christophe	21	Matthieu
22	Marie-Mad.	22	Fabrice	22	Maurice
23	Brigitte	23	Rose	23	Constant
24	Christine	24	Barthélemy	24	Thècle
25	Jacques Maj.	25	Louis	25	Hermann
26	Anne	26	Natacha	26	Côme/Damien
27	Nathalie	27	Monique	27	Vincent de P.
28	Samson	28	Augustin	28	Venceslas
29	Marthe	29	Sabine	29	Michel
30	Juliette	30	Fiacre	30	Jérôme
31	Ignace de L.	31	Aristide		

Automne: 23 sept. à 2h 07mn

OCTOBRE		NOVEMBRE		DECEMBRE	
1	Thérèse E-J	1	TOUSSAINT	1	Advent
2	Léger	2	Défunts	2	Viviane
3	Gérard	3	Hubert	3	Franç. Xav.
4	François Ass.	4	Charles Bor.	4	Barbara
5	Fleur	5	Sylvie	5	Gérald
6	Bruno	6	Bertille	6	Nicolas
7	Serge	7	Carine	7	Ambroise
8	Pélagie	8	Geoffroy	8	Imm. Concept.
9	Denis	9	Théodore	9	Pierre F.
10	Ghislain	10	Léon	10	Romary
11	Firmin	11	VICT. 1918	11	Daniel
12	Wilfried	12	Christian	12	Chantal
13	Géraud	13	Brice	13	Lucie
14	Juste	14	Sidoine	14	Odile
15	Thérèse d'Av.	15	Albert	15	Ninon
16	Edwige	16	Marguerite	16	Alice
17	Baudouin	17	Elisabeth	17	Judical
18	Luc	18	Aude	18	Gatien
19	René	19	Tanguy	19	Urbain
20	Adeline	20	Edmond	20	Théophile
21	Céline	21	Présent. N. —D.	21	Pierre Canis.
22	Salomé	22	Cécile	22	Françoise-X.
23	Jean de Cap.	23	Clément	23	Hartmann
24	Florentin	24	Christ-Roi	24	Adèle
25	Crépin	25	Cath. Lab.	25	NOEL
26	Dimitri	26	Delphine	26	Etienne
27	Emeline	27	Séverin	27	Jean Apôtre
28	Simon	28	Jacq. de la M.	28	Innocents
29	Narcisse	29	Saturnin	29	Ste Famille
30	Bienvenue	30	André	30	Roger
31	Quentin			31	Sylvestre

Hiver: 21 décembre à 22h 08mn

4. Adverbs:

Fill in the spaces with adverbs in French corresponding to the clues.
If you get the answers the letter in the outlined column will give another adverb
to be found in the text.

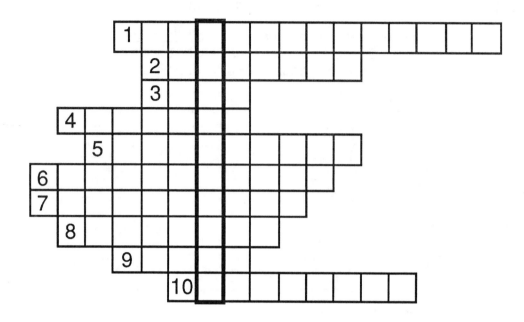

1. **Oui, _ _ _ _ _ _ _ _ _ _ _ _ _.**

2. **Il y a des embouteillages _ _ _ _ _ _ _.**

3. **Beaucoup de Parisiens viennent _ _ _ en automne.**

4. **Moi? de l'escalade? _ _ _ _ _ _ de la vie.**

5. **Mais elle est _ _ _ _ _ _ _ _ _ charmante.**

6. **Et _ _ _ _ _ _ _ _ _ _ _ _, je vais vous emmener dans un joli petit village.**

7. **Elle se dirige _ _ _ _ _ _ _ _ _ _ vers le boulevard périphérique.**

8. **En hiver je fais _ _ _ _ _ _ _ du jogging.**

9. **Pourquoi veut-il savoir _ _ _ _ de choses?**

10. **Je joue _ _ _ _ _ _ _ _ au tennis en été.**

What is the opposite of **lentement**?

208

5. **Le jeu des 'si':**

Match up phrases in each column to make sentences.

1. **S'il fait beau demain,**
2. **Si j'étais riche,**

3. **Si vous aimez jouer au tennis,**
4. **S'il y avait un chien méchant,**
5. **Si vous regardez les panneaux,**
6. **Si tu avais de la farine,**

7. **Si j'ai mal aux dents,**
8. **S'il y avait un bon film,**

A. **j'irai chez le dentiste.**
B. **nous ferons une partie un après-midi.**
C. **je ferais un gâteau.**
D. **on irait au cinéma.**
E. **vous trouverez votre route.**
F. **vous auriez peur de rentrer dans la maison.**
G. **j'achèterais un château.**
H. **on ira pique-niquer à la campagne.**

6. **Le Code de la Route:**

Do you know your Highway Code? Can you match these sentences with the road-signs?

1. **Il faut tourner à droite.**
2. **Vous ne devez pas stationner.**
3. **Il faut céder le passage.**
4. **Vous ne pouvez pas entrer dans cette rue.**
5. **Vous ne devez pas dépasser les autres voitures.**
6. **Vous devez faire attention aux animaux sauvages.**
7. **Il faut vous arrêter.**
8. **Vous pouvez téléphoner ici.**
9. **Les autobus ne peuvent pas passer par là.**
10. **Il ne faut pas klaxonner.**

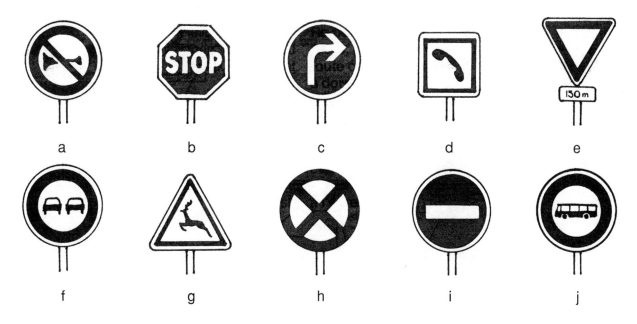

a b c d e

f g h i j

BONUS

1. **Les jours de la semaine:**

   Bonjour lundi.
   Comment va mardi?
   — Très bien, mercredi,
   Dites à jeudi.
   De la part de vendredi.
   De venir samedi.
   Pour danser dimanche.

2. Dog story (not shaggy)

   Un monsieur arrive chez un ami. Sur la porte du jardin il lit:
   'Attention au chien'.   Il entre et demande à son ami:
   Pourquoi as-tu mis cette pancarte? Ton chien est tellement petit, on le voit à peine...
   Justement, j'ai peur qu'on marche dessus.

3. A seasonal joke

   En hiver, on dit souvent: 'Fermez la porte, il fait froid dehors!'
   Mais quand la porte est fermée, il fait toujours aussi froid dehors.

4. **Proverbes**

   Une hirondelle ne fait pas le printemps.
   En mai, fais ce qu'il te plaît.

ACT 9   ACTE 9
Scene I   Scène I

Back to Paris (Thursday evening).   **Retour à Paris (Jeudi soir).**

After coffee,
as the weather was so fine,
Henri suggested
a walk round Barbizon.
Jacqueline and Philip agreed
and the three of them went off,
with Youki, the dog, of course.
When they came back from their walk
Henri asked them to stay for
dinner.
To please Jacqueline
he prepared a Vietnamese dish.

**Après le café,
comme il faisait toujours beau,
Henri a proposé de faire
le tour de Barbizon.
Jacqueline et Philip ont accepté
et ils sont partis tous les trois
avec Youki le chien bien sûr.
En rentrant de leur promenade,
Henri leur a demandé de rester
dîner.
Pour faire plaisir à Jacqueline,
il a préparé un plat vietnamien.**

During the meal Henri and Jacqueline
spoke about their childhood in
Vietnam.
Henri was very amusing
and Philip now found
him much nicer
After a while
Henri said to Philip:

**Pendant le repas, Henri et Jacqueline
ont parlé de leur enfance au
Vietnam.
Henri était très amusant
et Philip le trouvait maintenant
beaucoup plus sympathique.
Au bout d'un moment,
Henri a dit à Philip:**

Henri: Why are we using **vous** to one another? We could use **tu**, couldn't we?

Pourquoi est-ce qu'on se vouvoie? On pourrait se tutoyer, n'est-ce pas?

Philip: Yes, if you wish Mr Dubois. Sorry, I mean Henri.

Oui, si vous voulez. Oh! pardon, si tu veux.

Jacqueline: And what if we did the same, Philip?

Et si on se disait 'tu' nous aussi Philip?

Philip: All right, let's use **tu**. Oh! Have you seen the time?

Moi, je veux bien. Alors, on se tutoie. Oh! tu as vu l'heure?

Ils sont partis tous les trois.

Jacqueline: Heavens! It's quarter past nine. We must get back to Paris. My uncle will be waiting for us.

Mon dieu! il est neuf heures et quart. Il faut rentrer à Paris, mon oncle va nous attendre.

Philip: Ah yes, the phantom of the rue Madame. At last I'm going to meet him.

Ah! oui, le fantôme de la rue Madame! Je vais enfin le rencontrer!

211

Henri:	Don't worry.	**Ne t'inquiète pas.**
	My father will be there.	**Mon père sera là.**
	He told me so this	**Il me l'a dit**
	morning over the phone.	**ce matin au téléphone.**
Jacqueline:	Let's hurry, then.	**Dépêchons-nous alors.**

	Henri goes with Jacqueline and	**Henri accompagne Jacqueline et**
	Philip to the car.	**Philip jusqu'à la voiture.**
	It is cool and misty.	**Il fait frais et il y a de la brume.**

Henri:	Be careful on the	**Sois prudente sur**
	motorway.	**l'autoroute.**
Jacqueline:	Don't worry.	**Ne t'en fais pas.**
Philip:	Good-bye Henri	**Allez, au revoir Henri**
	and thanks.	**et merci.**
Henri:	Bye. I'll be seeing you.	**Salut et à un de ces jours.**
Jacqueline:	I'll give you a ring.	**Je te téléphonerai.**
Henri:	Right.	**Entendu.**

Scene 2   **Scène 2**

	Before reaching the motorway	**Avant d'arriver sur l'autoroute,**
	Jacqueline stops at a	**Jacqueline s'arrête à une**
	petrol station	**station-service**
	to buy some petrol.	**pour prendre de l'essence.**

Attendant:	How much would you like?	**Combien je vous en mets?**
Jacqueline:	Fill her up,	**Faites le plein,**
	please.	**s'il vous plaît.**
Attendant:	Shall I check the oil	**Je vérifie l'huile**
	and water	**et l'eau**
	and the tyre pressures?	**et la pression des pneus?**
Jacqueline:	No thanks.	**Non, merci.**
	It's all right.	**Ça va.**
	How much is that?	**Je vous dois combien?**
Attendant:	Fifty litres . . .	**cinquante litres . . .**
	that'll be three hundred	**Ça fait trois cents**
	francs, please.	**francs, s'il vous plaît.**
Jacqueline:	There you are.	**Voilà.**
Attendant:	Thank you,	**Merci**
	safe journey.	**et bonne route.**

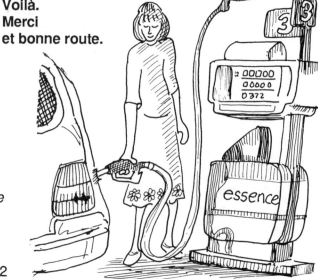

Jacqueline s'arrête à une station-service.

| | Jacqueline gets back into the car. As they drive off, she notices that Philip is not wearing his safety-belt. | Jacqueline remonte dans la voiture. En démarrant, elle remarque que Philip n'a pas mis sa ceinture de sécurité. |

Jacqueline: Fasten your safety-belt, Philip.
Philip, mets ta ceinture,

It's compulsory.
c'est obligatoire.

Philip: Oh yes. I forgot.
Ah! oui, j'ai oublié.

Jacqueline is in a hurry to get to Paris.
Jacqueline est pressée d'arriver à Paris.

Soon they are on the motorway.
Bientôt ils sont sur l'autoroute.

She moves into the fast lane and drives along at top speed.
Elle se met dans la file de gauche et roule à toute vitesse.

Philip: Be careful, it's foggy.
Fais attention, il y a du brouillard.

Don't drive so fast.
Ne roule pas si vite.

Jacqueline: It's all right.
Ça va.

Don't be frightened.
N'aie pas peur.

Philip: Isn't there a speed limit on the motorway?
Il n'y a pas de limite de vitesse sur l'autoroute?

Jacqueline: Yes, the speed limit is one hundred and thirty (130) km/h.
Si, la vitesse est limitée à cent trente (130) km/heure.

Philip: Do you know you're doing one hundred and eighty (180)?
Tu sais que tu fais du cent quatre-vingt (180)?

Jacqueline: Gosh! You're right.
Mince! c'est vrai.

I didn't realise.
Je ne m'en rendais pas compte.

Philip: You'd better slow down or you'll be fined.
Tu ferais bien de ralentir sinon tu vas avoir une amende.

She puts on the brakes and moves over into the middle lane. A few minutes later a police car overtakes them. Jacqueline looks at Philip and smiles.
Jacqueline freine un peu et se met dans la file du milieu. Quelques minutes plus tard, une voiture de police les double. Jacqueline regarde Philip en souriant.

Jacqueline: Thanks to you we won't have a fine.
Grâce à toi, on n'aura pas d'amende.

A little further on everyone has to slow down as the road is blocked.
Un peu plus loin, tout le monde doit ralentir parce qu'il y a un bouchon.

Philip: What's up?
Qu'est-ce qu'il y a?

Jacqueline: I don't know.
Je ne sais pas.

Probably an accident.
Probablement un accident.

They move forward very slowly
and after twenty minutes,
they see a sign
marked 'diversion'.
A policeman is standing
beside it.

Ils avancent très lentement
et après vingt minutes,
ils voient un panneau
marqué 'déviation'.
Un agent de police se trouve
à côté.

Philip:	What has happened?	Qu'est-ce qui s'est passé?
Policeman:	There's been an accident involving a lorry and a motor-bike. The lorry has overturned and it is holding up the traffic.	Il y a eu un accident entre un camion et une moto. Le poids lourd s'est renversé et il bloque la circulation.
Philip:	Is it serious?	C'est grave?
Policeman:	Yes, unfortunately.	Oui, malheureusement.
Philip	Has anyone been injured?	Est-ce qu'il y a des blessés?
Policeman:	Yes two people. The ambulance has just taken them to the hospital.	Oui, il y en a deux. L'ambulance vient de les emmener à l'hôpital.

Il y a eu un accident entre un camion et une moto.

Scene 3　Scène 3

Because of the diversion
Jacqueline and Philip
lose time.

A cause de la déviation,
Jacqueline et Philip
prennent du retard.

Jacqueline:	Dash it! We're going to be very late. What is Uncle Anatole going to think?	Zut! nous allons être très en retard. Que va penser l'oncle Anatole?
Philip:	He'll probably be tired and will have gone to bed. Do you want to bet?	Il sera probablement fatigué et il se sera couché. Tu paries?

The lights of the capital
are shining in the distance.
Philip recognises several monuments –
The Eiffel Tower, the Sacré Coeur and
Notre Dame.

Les lumières de la capitale
brillent dans le lointain.
Philip reconnaît quelques monuments
– la Tour Eiffel, le Sacré Coeur et
Notre Dame.

Eleven o'clock is striking
at the church of St Germain des Prés
when they reach rue Madame.
There is a light on in the hall
and they hurry in.

Onze heures sonnent à l'église
de Saint Germain des Prés
quand ils arrivent rue Madame.
Le vestibule est éclairé
et ils se dépêchent d'entrer.

Jacqueline:	Uncle Anatole, it's us.	**Oncle Anatole, c'est nous.**
Philip:	Keep quiet.	**Tais-toi.**
	You'll wake him up.	**Tu vas le réveiller.**

	There is no reply.	**Personne ne répond.**
	She goes quickly into the sitting room	**Elle se précipite dans le salon.**
	On the coffee table,	**Sur la table basse,**
	she finds a note.	**elle trouve un mot.**

	'I am dead tired	**'Je suis mort de fatigue,**
	so I'm going to bed.	**je vais me coucher.**
	See you tomorrow morning at	**Rendez-vous demain matin à**
	ten thirty.'	**dix heures trente.'**
	Uncle Anatole.	**Oncle Anatole.**

Philip:	You see?	**Tu vois?**
	I told you so.	**Je te l'avais bien dit.**
Jacqueline:	You were right, Philip.	**Tu avais raison Philip.**
	You won't meet my	**Ce n'est pas encore aujourd'hui**
	uncle today but tomorrow	**que tu rencontreras mon oncle,**
	morning without fail	**mais demain matin sans faute,**
	he'll be here.	**il sera là.**
Philip:	I'll believe it	**J'y croirai**
	when I see him.	**quand je le verrai!**

Je suis mort de fatigue.

ACTE 9 (i)

Ils sont partis tous les trois avec
Youki le chien bien sûr.

Il a prépare un plat
Vietnamien.

On pourait se tutoyer, n'est-ce pas?

Le fantôme de la rue
Madame!

Mon père sera là.
Il me l'a dit ce matin
au téléphone.

Sois prudente sur l'autoroute.

Jacqueline s'arrête à une station-service
pour prendre de l'essence.

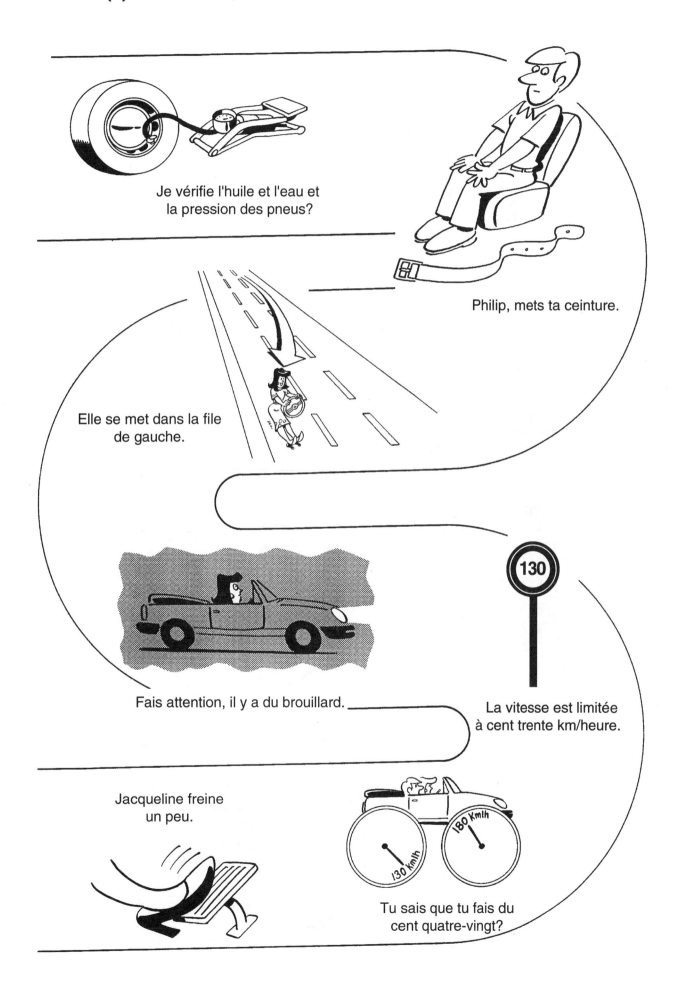

ACTE 9 (iii)

Quelques minutes plus tard, une voiture de police les double.

Je ne sais pas.

Qu'est-ce qu'il y a?

Tout le monde doit ralentir parce qu'il y a un bouchon.

Déviation

Il y a eu un accident entre un camion et une moto.

Un agent de police se trouve à côté.

Le poids lourd s'est renversé et il bloque la circulation.

Oui, il y en a deux.

HÔPITAL +

Les lumières de la capitale
brillent dans le lointain.

L'ambulance vient de les
emmener à l'hôpital.

Philip reconnaît quelques
monuments.

Le vestibule est éclairé

Je suis mort de
fatigue, je vais
coucher. Rendez-
vous demain
matin à 10.30

et ils se dépêchent d'entrer.

Part Two : Pronunciation and Intonation
Section Deux : Prononciation et Intonation

The sound **e** as in **le** or **je**.

a)   When to swallow it:

1.   **Moi, j(e) veux bien.**

2.   **Alors, on s(e) tutoie?**

3.   **A un d(e) ces jours.**

4.   **J(e) vous dois combien?**

5.   **Qu'est-c(e) q'il y a?**

6.   **Tu sais qu(e) tu fais du I80?**

7.   **Tu vas l(e) réveiller.**

8.   **Tu f(e)rais bien d(e) ralentir.**

9.   **J(e) vais enfin l(e) rencontrer d(e)main.**

Some more examples:

1.   **Il frein(e) un peu.**

2.   **Il s'arrêt(e) à une station-service.**

3.   **Grâc(e) à toi, on n'aura pas d'amende.**

4.   **Que va penser l'oncl(e) Anatole?**

b)   When not to swallow it:

— in words like:

   probabl<u>e</u>ment — rencontr<u>e</u>ras — cent quatr<u>e</u>-vingts.

— in expressions like:

   J(e) t<u>e</u> l'avais bien dit.

   J<u>e</u> n(e) sais pas.

220

c) When you don't hear it, cross it off!

Je te donne pour ta fête
Un grand chapeau de paille
Pour te mettre sur la tête,
Un petit éventail
Pour le tenir à la main;
Une robe en mousseline
Toute ornée de satin,
Une écharpe en hermine
Et des chaussures blanches;
Ne les mets que le dimanche.

ST. GERMAIN DES PRES

221

Part Three   Section Trois
Functional Dialogues   Dialogues Fonctionnels

1.   Using **vous** and **tu**. L'emploi de 'vous' et 'tu'.

Henri:	Why are we saying **vous** to one another?	Pourquoi est-ce qu'on se vouvoie?
	We could use **tu**, couldn't we?	On pourrait se tutoyer, n'est-ce pas?
Philip:	Yes, if you wish.	Oui, si vous voulez.
	Sorry I mean Henri.	Oh! pardon, si tu veux.
J:	And what if we did the same, Philip?	Et si on se disait 'tu' nous aussi Philip?
Philip:	All right, let's use **tu**.	Moi, je veux bien. Alors, on se tutoie.

2.   Jacqueline is taking leave of Henri. Jacqueline prend congé d'Henri.

J:	Bye then and thanks.	**Allez, au revoir et merci.**
Henri:	Bye. I'll be seeing you.	**Salut et à un de ces jours.**
J:	I'll give you a ring.	**Je te téléphonerai.**
Henri:	Right.	**Entendu.**

3.   At the petrol-station. **A la station-service.**
                  Pump Attendant **Le Pompiste = Le P.**

Le P:	How much would you like?	**Combien je vous en mets?**
J:	Fill her up, please.	**Faites le plein, s'il vous plaît.**
Le P:	Shall I check the oil and water and the tyre pressures?	**Je vérifie l'huile et l'eau et la pression des pneus?**
J:	No, it's all right. How much is that?	**Non, merci. Ça va. Je vous dois combien?**
Le P:	50 litres ... that'll be 300 francs please.	**50 litres ... Ça fait 300 francs, s'il vous plaît.**
J:	There you are.	**Voilà.**
Le P:	Thanks and safe journey.	**Merci et bonne route.**

4.   Philip is telling Jacqueline **Philip dit à Jacqueline**
     to drive carefully. **d'être prudente.**

Philip: Be careful. It's foggy. **Fais attention, il y a du brouillard.**
              Don't drive so fast. **Ne roule pas si vite.**
J: It's all right. **Ça va.**
              Don't be frightened. **N'aie pas peur.**
Philip: Isn't there a speed limit **Il n'y a pas de limite de vitesse**
              on the motorway? **sur l'autoroute?**
J: Yes, the speed limit is **Si, la vitesse est limitée à**
              130 km/h. **130 km/heure.**
Philip: Do you know you're doing 180? **Tu sais que tu fais du 180?**
J: Gosh! You're right. **Mince! c'est vrai.**
              I didn't realise. **Je ne m'en rendais pas compte.**
Philip: You'd better slow down **Tu ferais bien de ralentir**
              or you'll be fined. **sinon tu vas avoir une amende.**

5.   Philip is asking about **Un accident — Philip demande**
     an accident. **ce qui s'est passé.**
     Policeman **L'agent.**

Philip: What has happened? **Qu'est-ce qui s'est passé?**
L'agent: There's been an accident **Il y a eu un accident**
              involving a lorry **entre un camion**
              and a motor-bike. **et une moto.**
Philip: Is it serious? **C'est grave?**
L'agent: Yes, unfortunately. **Oui, malheureusement.**
Philip: Has anyone been injured? **Est-ce qu'il y a des blessés?**
L'agent: Yes, two people. **Oui, il y en a deux.**
              The ambulance has just **L'ambulance vient**
              taken them to **de les emmener**
              the hospital. **à l'hôpital.**

L'ambulance vient de les emmener à l'hôpital.

Part Four : Personalised Dialogues
Section Quatre : Dialogues

a)   Using **vous** and **tu.**

Vous:	(Suggest to Henri that you use **tu** with one another.)
Henri:	**Oui, si vous voulez.**
	Oh pardon, si tu veux.
Vous:	(Suggest to Jacqueline that she and you might also use **tu.**)
Jacqueline:	**Alors, on se tutoie.**

b)   Taking leave of a friend.

Vous:	(Say goodbye and thank you.)
Henri:	**Salut et à un de ces jours.**
Vous:	(Say that you will phone.)
Henri:	**Entendu.**

c)   At the petrol-station.

Le pompiste:	**Combien je vous en mets?**
Vous:	(Tell him to fill her up.)
Le pompiste:	**Je vérifie l'huile et l'eau**
	et la pression des pneus?
Vous:	(Say no thank you, it's all right.
	Then ask how much you owe him.)
Le pompiste:	**50 litres . . . ça fait 300 francs, s'il vous plaît.**
Vous:	(Hand over the money.)
Le pompiste:	**Merci et bonne route.**

d)   Warning someone to drive carefully.

Vous:	(Tell Jacqueline to be careful because it's foggy
	and tell her not to drive so fast.)
Jacqueline:	**Ça va. N'aie pas peur.**
Vous:	(Ask if there isn't a speed limit on the motorway.)
Jaqueline:	**Si, la vitesse est limitée à l30 km/heure.**
Vous:	(Point out that she's doing l80.)
Jacqueline:	**Mince! c'est vrai.**
	Je ne m'en rendais pas compte.
Vous:	(Tell her she'd better slow down or she'll be fined.)

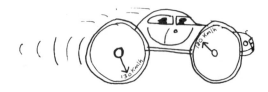

e)   Asking about an accident.

Vous: (Ask what has happened.)
L'agent: **Il y a eu un accident
                                   entre un camion et une moto.**
Vous: (Ask if it is serious.)
L'agent: **Oui, malheureusement.**
Vous: (Ask if anyone has been injured.)
L'agent: **Oui, il y en a deux.
                                   L'ambulance vient de les emmener
                                   à l'hôpital.**

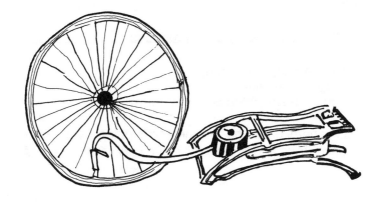

Je vérifie la pression des pneus?

Part Five : Grammar
Section Cinq : Grammaire

1. TO GIVE INSTRUCTIONS USING **TU**

In Act 8, you learnt the personal use of **TU**. The French have a special verb for this:

tutoyer	—	to use **tu**.
vouvoyer	—	to use **vous**.

When you are giving instructions to a child, a friend or relative, you simply use the **tu** form of the verb without the **tu**.

e.g. **Mets ta ceinture.**
Fais attention.
Ne roule pas si vite.

REMEMBER: To tell a close friend what to do
Use the verb without the **TU**.

NOTE: There are special forms for **ETRE** and **AVOIR**:

e.g. **SOIS prudente sur l'autoroute.**
N'AIE pas peur.

2. MORE ABOUT REFLEXIVES

You are already familiar with the following reflexive pronouns:

ME/M'	**Je ne ME sens pas bien.**
SE/S'	**Philip SE réveille.**
SE/S'	**Jacqueline et Philip SE dépêchent .**

Pronouns come in front of the verb, but when a command is being given they come after the verb. You will remember when Jacqueline told Philip to sit down in Act 3 she said: '**Asseyez-vous.**'

Philip se réveille.

226

In this Act you have met:

NE T'inquiète pas.
Tais-TOI.
Dépêchons-NOUS.

NOTE 1:   When the command is negative, the pronoun goes in front of the verb as in **Ne T'inquiète pas.**

NOTE 2:   When the command is positive the **TE/T'** becomes **TOI** as in **TAIS-TOI.**

REMEMBER: Reflexive **NOUS** goes along with **NOUS**
VOUS is the same, it goes with **VOUS**
So **JE** goes with **ME**
and **TU** goes with **TE**
but **IL(S)** and **ELLE(S)**
both go with **SE**

3.   ORDER OF PRONOUNS

REMEMBER: The pronouns **NOUS, VOUS, ME, TE, SE**   *
Come in front of **LES, LA, LE**
These in turn precede **LEUR** or **LUI**
Which always come in front of **Y**
And **EN** comes last inevitably.

e.g.   **Il ME L'a dit ce matin au téléphone.**
Je ne M'EN rendais pas compte.
Combien je VOUS EN mets?
Je TE L'avais bien dit.

L'ouvreuse les amène à leur place.

227

4.   **EN . . . —ANT** — The —ing form

In French, the ending **—ANT** is the equivalent of the English form —ing. So take the **NOUS** form of the Present Tense, remove **—ONS** and put **—ANT** instead.

e.g.	**nous donnons**	—	**donnANT**
	nous finissons	—	**finissANT**
	nous prenons	—	**prenANT**

NOTE: As usual there are exceptions:

e.g.	**(être)**	—	**étant**
	(avoir)	—	**ayant**
	(savoir)	—	**sachant**

Very often, another **EN** comes in front as in these examples from Act 9:

EN rentrANT de leur promenade.
When they come back from their walk.
On returning from . . .

Jacqueline regarde Philip EN souriANT.
Jacqueline looks at Philip and smiles.
While at the same time smiling.

EN démarrANT, elle remarque . . .
As they drive off, she notices . . .
On/While driving off . . .

REMEMBER: In French, the —ing form is **—ANT**
Often with **EN** as company
The English 'while' to represent
For two happenings or events
More or less at the same moment.

5.   **QUAND** + The Future Tense — When

In English, we use the Present Tense with WHEN:

e.g.   I'll believe it when I see him.

The French, however, use the Future Tense with **Quand**:

e.g.   **J'y croirai quand je le VERRAI.**

REMEMBER: With WHEN in English
Use the Present Tense
But French with **QUAND**
Use Future Tense.

Part Six : Key Phrases
Section Six : Expressions Utiles

1. GRACE A . . .

This expression is used in exactly the same way as the English 'Thanks to . . .'

     e.g.   **Grâce à toi**   —   Thanks to you

You can also use it with names:

     e.g.   **Grâce à Philip**   —   Thanks to Philip

With feminine nouns, the pattern is similar:

     e.g.   **Grâce à la ceinture de sécurité.**

     NOTE: If you use it followed by a masculine singular or all plural nouns, you must say **Grâce AU . . .** or **Grâce AUX . . .**

     e.g.   **Grâce au panneau**
                        Grâce aux agents de police

But remember to say:

                        Grâce à l'agent de police.

2. IL Y EN A — (+ number)

In English, when you are talking about a certain number of people or things that have already been mentioned, you would just say:

                        'There's one' or 'There are two', etc . . .

In French, you must always include the pronoun **EN**:

     e.g.   **Il y a des blessés?**   **Oui, il y EN a deux.**
                        (There are two — understand 'of them')

                        Il y a des voitures?   **Oui, il y EN a quatre.**

3. TU FERAIS BIEN DE . . .

When you want to persuade someone to do something, you can use this expression followed by an infinitive:

     e.g.   **TU FERAIS BIEN DE ralentir.**
                        You'd better slow down.

You can also say **Tu ferais mieux de . . .** and you can use the expression with different subjects:

                        Je ferais bien de . . .
                        Vous feriez bien de . . .

Part Seven : Games
Section Sept : Jeux

1. Jacqueline is a remarkably busy young lady. She always seems to be doing two things at once. Look at the pictures and say what she is doing.

Elle mange en regardant la télévision.

1. ....

2. ....

3. ....

4. ....

5. ....

2. If Philip had known what was going to happen to him before he left on his trip, what might he have said about the scenes below?

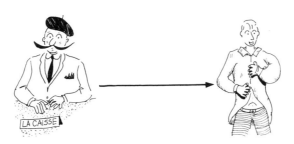

Quand j'aurai de l'argent, j'achèterai une chemise.

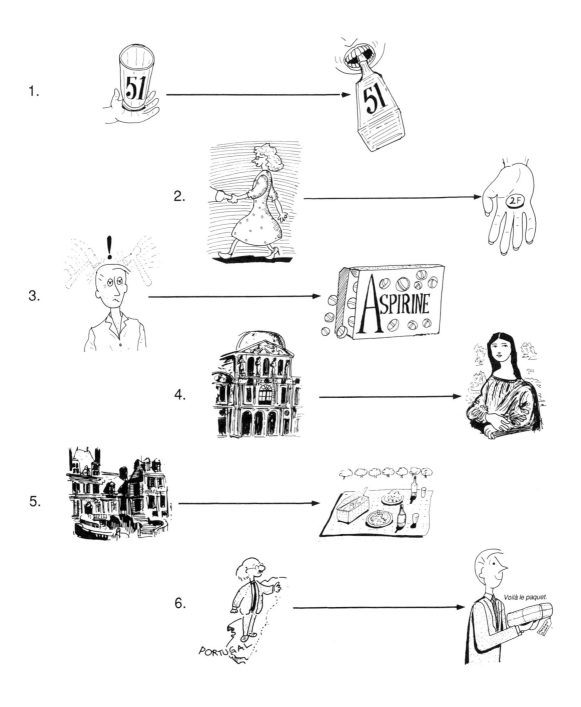

1.

2.

3.

4.

5.

6.

231

3.   Can you remember what Philip does first thing every morning?

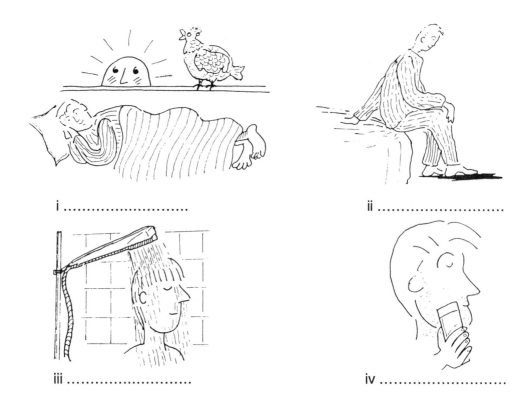

i ....   ii ....

iii ....   iv ....

a.   Now ask him at what time he wakes up (you don't know him very well, so use '**vous**').
b.   What would Philip's answer be if he wakes up at 7.30?
c.   What would you say if you wanted to tell Philip to get up?
d.   How would you say the same thing if you knew him well?
e.   And finally, if you wanted to see what he looked like with a beard, how would you tell him not to shave? (You would obviously know him very well if you said such a thing!)

4.   **Tu** or **Vous?**

Use the appropriate one in the following sentences.

1.   Ask a child his name.
2.   Tell your boss you will phone him this evening.
3.   Ask a good friend how he is.
4.   Ask your cousin if she wants to play tennis tomorrow.
5.   In a restaurant ask the waiter if he can bring you the bill.
6.   Tell your wife/husband to hurry.
7.   Ask a tourist you've just met if he likes Paris.
8.   An old woman is carrying a heavy suitcase, you offer to help.
9.   A policeman asks you if you know you were doing 180 km/h.
10.   Tell your son not to worry.

The answers are at the back of the book.

BONUS

1. **Un train Paris-Marseille qui est parti à 21.05 roule à une vitesse de 120 km/heure. Un autre train Marseille-Paris est parti 30 minutes plus tard et fait du 130 km/heure. Quand ils se rencontreront, quel train sera plus près de Paris?**

2. **Histoire belge.**

    Un agent de police arrête un automobiliste belge:
    Vous rouliez à plus de 160 km/heure!
    Qu'est-ce que vous pouvez en savoir? Ça ne fait même pas une demi-heure que je suis parti de chez moi!

3. Your Car

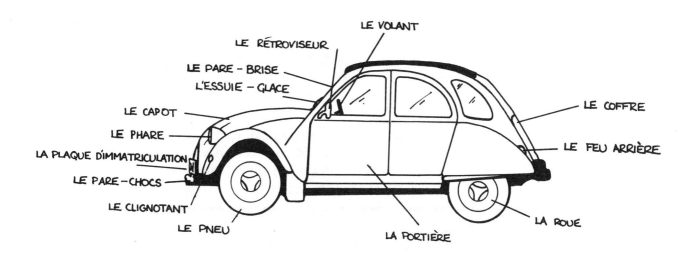

and its insides:

le réservoir d'essence	petrol tank
la courroie	fan belt
la boîte de vitesse	gearbox
la batterie	battery
la bougie	plug
les amortisseurs	shock absorbers
le carburateur	carburettor

REMINDER

* Are you following the Step by Step instruction sheet?

* Don't forget the visualisation exercise — the exercise where you close your eyes and describe what is happening during the Act — <u>using your own words in French</u>.

* Also don't forget to treat your tape recorder as your partner — using the pause button to answer before the presenter does.

* And don't forget to 'act out' the scenes.

If you do all this, you will ensure visual, sound and physical associations are formed with your French.

ACT 10 ACTE 10
Scene I Scène 1

	Uncle Anatole (Friday).	Oncle Anatole (Vendredi).

It was a big day for Philip.
At last he was going to meet
Jacqueline's uncle
and maybe find out what was
in the package.
At about ten thirty
he rang the bell at rue Madame.
The cleaning lady
opened the door

C'était un grand jour pour Philip.
Il allait enfin rencontrer
l'oncle de Jacqueline
et peut-être savoir ce qu'il y
avait dans le paquet.
Vers dix heures trente,
il a sonné rue Madame.
La femme de ménage a
ouvert la porte.

Mme Brossetout:

Good morning, Mr West.
Please come in.
Mr Dubois is waiting for
you in his study.

Bonjour Monsieur West.
Entrez, s'il vous plaît.
Monsieur Dubois vous attend
dans son bureau.

Through the half-open door
he could see Uncle Anatole.
He was an absolute giant of a man!
He was at least
six foot tall
and weighed at least one hundred and ten
(II0) kilos!
Philip immediately noticed
his eyes sparkling behind
his glasses,
his big, black moustache
and his jolly, reassuring appearance.

Par la porte entrouverte,
Philip apercevait l'oncle Anatole.
C'était un véritable colosse!
Il mesurait au moins un mètre quatre-
vingt-dix
et pesait bien cent dix
(110) kilos!
Philip a tout de suite remarqué
ses yeux pétillants derrière
ses lunettes,
sa grosse moustache noire
et son air jovial et rassurant.

Uncle Anatole:

Hello Philip.
I'm sorry to have kept
you waiting
for several days.

Bonjour Philip.
Je regrette de vous avoir
fait attendre
pendant plusieurs jours.

Philip: That's quite all right.

Ce n'est pas grave.

Uncle Anatole: I was delayed in
Portugal,
as you know.

J'ai été retardé au
Portugal,
comme vous le savez.

Philip: Yes, I know it isn't
your fault.

Oui, je sais bien que ce n'est pas de
votre faute.

Uncle Anatole: So you're not too angry
with me?

Alors, vous ne m'en voulez pas trop?

Philip:	Of course not.	**Bien sûr que non.**
	I'm not at all angry with you.	**Je ne vous en veux pas du tout.**
Uncle Anatole:	At least you've had time to visit Paris.	**Au moins, vous avez eu le temps de visiter Paris?**
Philip:	Yes, that's right.	**Oui, c'est exact.**
	It was very nice being a tourist and especially with Jacqueline as a guide.	**C'était très agréable de faire le touriste, surtout avec Jacqueline comme guide.**
Uncle Anatole:	All good things come to an end!	**Toutes les bonnes choses ont une fin!**
	Tomorrow you must leave for Geneva.	**Demain, vous devez partir pour Genève.**
Philip:	For Geneva? To do what?	**Pour Genève? Et pour quoi faire?**
Uncle Anatole:	I'll explain.	**Je vais vous expliquer.**

Uncle Anatole went over to his desk and took two packages out of a drawer.
The first was the one that Philip had brought to Paris.
The second was smaller and was tied up with red string.
Philip had never seen it before.

**L'oncle Anatole s'est approché de son bureau et il a sorti deux paquets d'un tiroir.
Le premier était celui que Philip avait apporté à Paris.
Le deuxième était plus petit et entouré d'une ficelle rouge.
Philip ne l'avait jamais vu.**

Uncle Anatole:	These two packages must be at the lawyer Henri Simenon's office by one o'clock tomorrow afternoon.	**Ces deux paquets doivent être chez Maître Henri Simenon demain avant treize heures.**
Philip:	Sorry? Where? I didn't understand.	**Pardon? Chez qui? Je n'ai pas compris.**
Uncle Anatole:	Have you got a paper and pencil?	**Vous avez un papier et un crayon?**
Philip:	Yes, here we are.	**Oui, voilà.**
Uncle Anatole:	Well, then. It's at Mr Henri Simenon's office.	**Alors, c'est chez Maître Henri Simenon.**
Philip:	Simenon? Can you spell that, please?	**Simenon? Vous pouvez épeler, s'il vous plaît?**
Uncle Anatole:	S I M E N O N. Simenon. He lives at twelve rue Jean-Jacques Rousseau.	**S I M E N O N. Simenon. Il habite au douze rue Jean-Jacques Rousseau.**

Philip:	Can you speak more slowly, please?	Pouvez-vous parler moins vite, s'il vous plaît?
Uncle Anatole:	Yes, of course. 12 rue...Jean... Jacques...Rousseau.	Mais oui, bien sûr. 12 rue... Jean... Jacques... Rousseau...

Philip:	Rousseau. That's spelt R O U S S E A U, isn't it?	Rousseau, ça s'écrit R O U S S E A U, n'est-ce pas?
Uncle Anatole:	Yes, that's right. I'll put them in this briefcase, it'll be less cumbersome. And here's some money to cover your travel expenses.	Oui, c'est ça. Je vais les mettre dans ce porte-documents, ce sera moins encombrant. Voilà aussi de l'argent pour couvrir vos frais de voyage.

Philip thanked Uncle Anatole and they carried on talking a bit more. But he was asking himself all sorts of questions: Why go to Geneva? Why not post these packages? What on earth was in them? Suddenly Uncle Anatole looked at his watch.	Philip a remercié l'oncle Anatole et ils ont continué à discuter. Mais il se posait toutes sortes de questions, Pourquoi aller à Genève? Pourquoi ne pas poster ces paquets? Que contenaient-ils donc? Soudain, l'oncle Anatole a regardé sa montre.

Uncle Anatole:	It's time for lunch. I'm going to take you to a nice little restaurant which is quite near here. I think Jacqueline will be coming with us.	Il est l'heure de déjeuner. Je vais vous emmener dans un petit bistro très sympathique qui se trouve tout près d'ici. Je pense que Jacqueline nous accompagnera.

Scene 2	Scène 2

After lunch, Philip decided to see to his plane ticket. That very morning, Uncle Anatole had phoned Air France at the Porte Maillot to book a seat. Philip took the bus to the terminal building and arrived at Porte Maillot twenty minutes later. He went up to a hostess who was behind the desk.	Après le déjeuner, Philip a décidé de s'occuper de son billet d'avion. L'oncle Anatole avait téléphoné le matin même à l'agence d'Air France à la Porte Maillot pour réserver une place. Il a pris l'autobus jusqu'au terminus et est arrivé à la Porte Maillot vingt minutes plus tard. Il s'est dirigé vers une hôtesse qui était derrière le comptoir.

Hostess:	Can I help you?	**Est-ce que je peux vous aider?**
Philip:	I've come to fetch my plane ticket.	**Je viens chercher mon billet d'avion.**
	It's a return ticket, Paris to Geneva.	**C'est un aller-retour Paris-Genève.**
Hostess:	What's your name?	**C'est à quel nom?**
Philip:	West.	**West.**
Hostess:	Just wait a minute, please.	**Attendez une minute, s'il vous plaît.**
	Ah, here it is.	**Ah! le voici.**
	Air France flight 125, (one hundred and twenty five) leaving Charles de Gaulle airport at eleven o'clock. tomorrow morning.	**C'est le vol Air France 125 (cent vingt-cinq) qui part de l'aéroport Charles de Gaulle à onze heures demain matin.**
Philip:	What time does it arrive in Geneva.	**A quelle heure est-ce qu'on arrive à Genève?**
Hostess:	At five past twelve.	**A midi cinq.**
Philip:	And what about the return flight?	**Et mon vol de retour,**
	What time is it?	**A quelle heure est-il?**
Hostess:	Quarter past five.	**A dix-sept heures quinze.**
	You'll be in Paris for six-twenty	**Vous serez à Paris pour dix-huit heures vingt.**
Philip:	How do you get to the airport?	**Comment est-ce qu'on se rend à l'aéroport?**
Hostess:	There are coaches that go direct from here to Charles de Gaulle.	**Il y a des cars qui vont directement d'ici à Charles de Gaulle.**
Philip:	When do they leave?	**Quand est-ce qu'il y en a?**
Hostess:	There's one every quarter of an hour.	**Il y en a un tous les quarts d'heure.**
Philip:	And how long does it take to get from here to the airport?	**Et combien de temps faut-il pour aller d'ici à l'aéroport?**

Voilà aussi de l'argent pour couvrir vos frais de voyage.

Hostess:	Thirty to forty five minutes.	**Entre trente et quarante cinq minutes.**
Philip:	Which one should I take, do you think?	**Lequel est-ce que je devrais prendre à votre avis?**
Hostess:	I advise you to take the nine o'clock one.	**Je vous conseille de prendre celui de neuf heures.**
Philip:	Isn't that too early?	**Ce n'est pas trop tôt?**
Hostess:	If you don't want to miss your plane, you have to be at the airport an hour before take-off.	**Si vous ne voulez pas manquer votre avion, il faut être à l'aéroport une heure avant le départ.**
Philip:	Good. Thanks very much.	**Bien, merci beaucoup.**

Scene 3   **Scène 3**

When Philip left the terminal building, it was only four-thirty. As he was not in a hurry, he walked back up the Avenue de la Grande Armée towards the Arc de Triomphe.

Quand Philip est sorti de l'aérogare, il n'était que seize heures trente. Comme il n'était pas pressé, il a remonté l'Avenue de la Grande Armée en direction de l'Arc de Triomphe.

In a tobacconist's he bought some postcards of Paris to send to his parents and friends and he asked for some stamps.

Dans un bar tabac il a acheté quelques cartes postales de Paris pour envoyer à ses parents et à ses amis et il a demandé des timbres.

Philip:	How much is it to send a post-card to England?	**C'est combien pour envoyer une carte postale en Angleterre?**
Tobacconist:	Two francs fifty.	**C'est deux francs cinquante.**
Philip:	Can I have four stamps at two francs fifty please?	**Vous pouvez me donner quatre timbres à deux francs cinquante, s'il vous plaît?**
Tobacconist:	Yes. Oh! I'm sorry, I haven't any left.	**Oui... Ah! je regrette, je n'en ai plus.**
Philip:	Is there a post office in the district?	**Est-ce qu'il y a une poste dans le quartier?**
Tobacconist:	There's one in the first street on the right.	**Oui, il y en a une dans la première rue à droite.**
Philip:	Thank you.	**Merci beaucoup.**

After posting his cards	**Après avoir posté ses cartes,**
Philip walked back to the hotel	**Philip est rentré à l'hôtel à pied.**
down the Avenue des Champs	**Il a descendu l'Avenue des Champs**
Elysées and through the	**Elysées et il a traversé**
Tuileries Gardens.	**le Jardin des Tuileries.**
As he walked past the	**En passant devant**
Square du Vert Galant	**le Square du Vert Galant,**
he began to daydream....	**il s'est mis à rêver....**
about whom....?	**De qui....?**
about Jacqueline, of course.	**mais de Jacqueline bien sûr.**

LES QUAIS

A REMINDER

Are you still doing the 'extra exercises' we described on page 69, i.e.

1. Making up post cards to revise with.

2. Acting out the Dialogues expressively.

3. Putting up post-it notes around the house or office or even in the car!

4. Representing at least 10 words visually.

5. Selecting the 10 most useful words per Act. (That gets you reviewing them all!)

6. Underlining, highlighting and <u>writing down</u> key words and sentences.

7. Describing the scenes out loud in your new language.

8. Making a Word Web for each Act.

ACTE 10 (i)

La femme de ménage a ouvert la porte.

ENTREZ

Philip a tout suite remarqué son air jovial et rassurant

Monsiuer Dubois vous attend dan son bureau.

C'était un véritable colosse!

Alors, vous ne m'en voulez pas trop?

Demain, vous devez partir pour Genève.

C'était très agréable de faire le touriste.

GENÈVE

Il a sorti deux paquets d'un tiroir.

13:00

ME HENRI SIMEONE NOTAIRE

Ces deux paquets doivent être chez Maître Henri Simenon demain avaint treize heures.

Je vais les mettre dans ce porte-documents.

ACTE 10 (ii)

Pourquoi ne pas poster ces paquets?

Je vais vous emmener dans un petit bistro très sympathique.

Philip a décidé de s'occuper de son billet d'avion.

PARIS A GENEVA
AIR FRANCE

L'oncle Anatole avait téléphoné le matin même à l'agence d'Air France à la Porte Maillot

PHILIP

pour réserver une place.

Il a pris l'autobus jusqu'au terminus.

Ah! le voici. C'est le vol Air France 125.

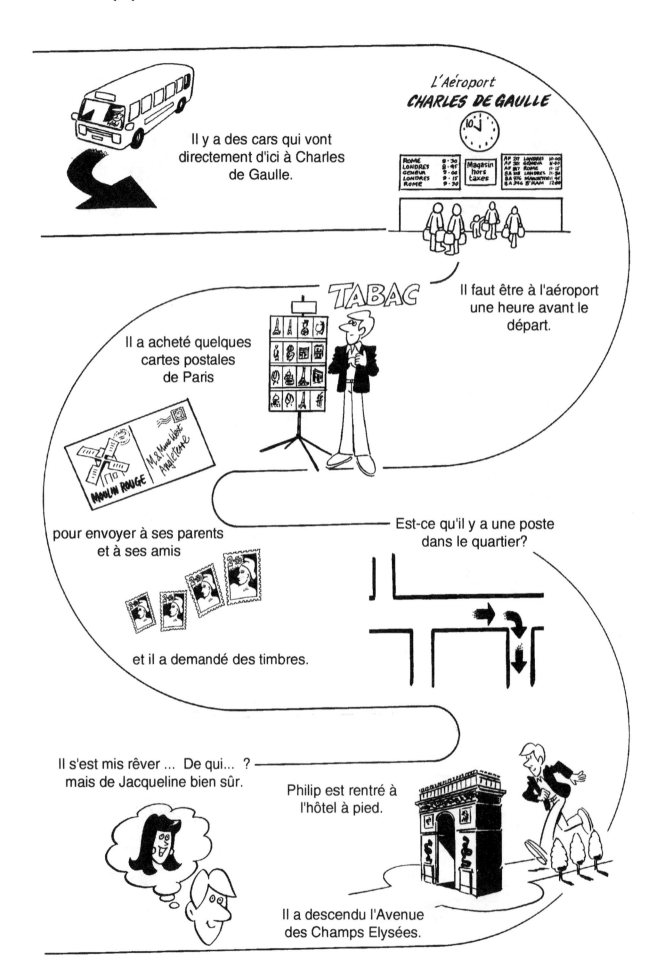

Il y a des cars qui vont directement d'ici à Charles de Gaulle.

L'Aéroport **CHARLES DE GAULLE**

Il faut être à l'aéroport une heure avant le départ.

Il a acheté quelques cartes postales de Paris

pour envoyer à ses parents et à ses amis

et il a demandé des timbres.

Est-ce qu'il y a une poste dans le quartier?

Il s'est mis rêver ... De qui... ? mais de Jacqueline bien sûr.

Philip est rentré à l'hôtel à pied.

Il a descendu l'Avenue des Champs Elysées.

Part Two : Pronunciation and Intonation
Section Deux : Prononciation et Intonation

a)   The French alphabet:

A B C / D E F / G H I / J K L / M N O / P Q R /

S T U / V W X / Y Z.

b)   The French alphabet the P. et T. ⊤ way:

A comme Anatole	I comme Irma	R comme Raoul
B comme Berthe	J comme Joseph	S comme Suzanne
C comme Célestin	K comme Kléber	T comme Thérèse
D comme Désiré	L comme Louis	U comme Ursule
E comme Eugène	M comme Marcel	V comme Victor
é comme émile	N comme Nicolas	W comme William
F comme François	O comme Oscar	X comme Xavier
G comme Gaston	P comme Pierre	Y comme Yvonne
H comme Henri	Q comme Quintal	Z comme Zoé

c)   Spelling the P.T.T. ☎ way:

Dubois   **West**   **Brossetout**

Note that for double letters as in Brossetout,
we say '**Suzanne deux fois**'.

⊤   Postes et Télécommunications

☎   Postes, Télégraphe, Téléphone

245

d)   **Comptine:**

A B C D

Elle n'a pas voulu céder,

E F G H

Elle a pris une hache,

I J K L

Pour lui couper les ailes

M N O P

Pour lui couper les pieds,

Q R S T

Rien ne lui est resté,

U V W X

Sauf une idée fixe.

Et...Y Z!

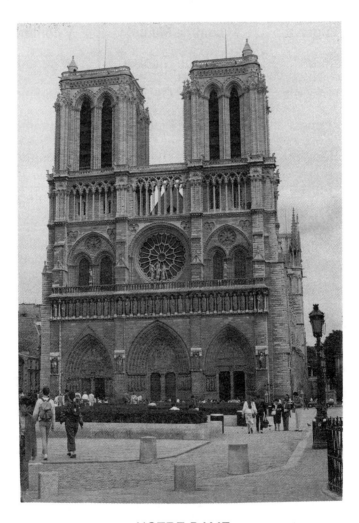

NOTRE DAME

Part Three   Section Trois
Functional Dialogues   Dialogues Fonctionnels

1.

Uncle Anatole is apologising for having kept Philip waiting.

Oncle Anatole s'excuse d'avoir fait attendre Philip.

Oncle A:	Hello Philip.	**Bonjour Philip.**
	I'm sorry to have kept you waiting for several days.	**Je regrette de vous avoir fait attendre pendant plusieurs jours.**
Philip:	That's quite all right.	**Ce n'est pas grave.**
Oncle A:	I was delayed in Portugal, as you know.	**J'ai été retardé au Portugal, comme vous le savez.**
Philip:	Yes, I know it isn't your fault.	**Oui, je sais bien que ce n'est pas de votre faute.**
Oncle A:	So you're not too angry with me?	**Alors, vous ne m'en voulez pas trop?**
Philip:	Of course not. I'm not at all angry with you.	**Bien sûr que non. Je ne vous en veux pas du tout.**

2.

Philip asks Uncle Anatole how to spell a name and address.

Philip demande à l'oncle Anatole d'épeler nom et adresse.

Oncle A:	These two packages must be at Mr Henri Simenon's office by one p.m. tomorrow.	**Ces deux paquets doivent être chez Maître Henri Simenon demain avant 13 heures.**
Philip:	Sorry? Where? I didn't understand.	**Pardon? Chez qui? Je n'ai pas compris.**
Oncle A:	Have you got a paper and pencil?	**Vous avez un papier et un crayon?**
Philip:	Yes, here we are.	**Oui, voilà.**
Oncle A:	Well then, it's at Mr. Henri Simenon's office.	**Alors, c'est chez Maître Henri Simenon.**
Philip:	Simenon? Can you spell that, please?	**Simenon? Vous pouvez épeler, s'il vous plaît?**

Je n'ai pas compris.

247

Oncle A:	S I M E N O N. Simenon. He lives at 12 rue Jean-Jacques Rousseau.	**S I M E N O N. Simenon. Il habite au 12 rue Jean-Jacques Rousseau.**
Philip:	Can you speak more slowly, please?	**Pouvez-vous parler moins vite, s'il vous plaît?**
Oncle A:	Yes, of course. 12... rue... Jean... Jacques... Rousseau.	**Mais oui, bien sûr. 12... rue... Jean... Jacques... Rousseau.**
Philip:	Rousseau, that's spelt R O U S S E A U, isn't it?	**Rousseau. Ça s'écrit R O U S S E A U, n'est-ce pas?**
Oncle A:	Yes, that's right.	**Oui, c'est ça.**

3.	Philip is collecting his plane ticket. The Air Hostess	**Philip vient chercher son billet d'avion. L'hôtesse = L'h.**

L'h:	Can I help you?	**Est-ce que je peux vous aider?**
Philip:	I've come to fetch my plane ticket. It's a return ticket, Paris to Geneva.	**Je viens chercher mon billet d'avion. C'est un aller retour Paris-Genève.**
L'h:	What's your name?	**C'est à quel nom?**
Philip:	West.	**West.**
L'h:	Just wait a minute, please. Ah! here it is. Air France flight 125, leaving Charles de Gaulle airport at eleven o'clock tomorrow morning.	**Attendez une minute, s'il vous plaît. Ah! le voici. C'est le vol Air France 125 qui part de l'aéroport Charles de Gaulle à 11 heures demain matin.**
Philip:	What time does it arrive in Geneva?	**A quelle heure est-ce qu'on arrive à Genève?**
L'h:	At five past twelve.	**A midi cinq.**
Philip:	And what about the return flight? What time is it?	**Et mon vol de retour, à quelle heure est-il?**
L'h:	Quarter past five. You'll be in Paris for six-twenty.	**A 17 heures 15. Vous serez à Paris pour 18 heures 20.**

Je viens chercher mon billet d'avion.

4.   Philip is inquiring about   **Philip veut savoir comment se**
                                getting to the airport.   **rendre à l'aéroport.**

Philip:	How do you get to the airport?	**Comment est-ce qu'on se rend à l'aéroport?**
L'h:	There are coaches that go direct from here to Charles de Gaulle.	**Il y a des cars qui vont directement d'ici à Charles de Gaulle.**
Philip:	When do they leave?	**Quand est-ce qu'il y en a?**
L'h	There's one every quarter of an hour.	**Il y en a un tous les quarts d'heure.**
Philip:	And how long does it take to get from here to the airport?	**Et combien de temps faut-il pour aller d'ici à l'aéroport?**
L'h:	30 to 45 minutes.	**Entre 30 et 45 minutes.**
Philip:	Which one should I take, do you think?	**Lequel est-ce que je devrais prendre à votre avis?**
Hostes:	I advise you to take the 9 o'clock one.	**Je vous conseille de prendre celui de 9 heures.**
Philip:	Isn't that too early?	**Ce n'est pas trop tôt?**
L'h:	If you don't want to miss your plane, you have to be at the airport an hour before take-off.	**Si vous ne voulez pas manquer votre avion, il faut être à l'aéroport une heure avant le départ.**
Philip:	Good. Thanks very much.	**Bien, merci beaucoup.**

5.   Philip is buying stamps.   **Philip achète des timbres.**

Philip:	How much is it to send a post-card to England?	**C'est combien pour envoyer une carte postale en Angleterre?**
La V:	2 francs 50.	**C'est 2 francs 50.**
Philip:	Can I have four stamps at 2F50, please?	**Vous pouvez me donner quatre timbres à 2 francs 50, s'il vous plaît?**
La V:	Yes. Oh! I'm sorry, I haven't any left.	**Oui. Ah! je regrette, je n'en ai plus.**
Philip:	Is there a post-office in the district?	**Est-ce qu'il y a une poste dans le quartier?**
La V:	There's one in the first street on the right.	**Oui, il y en a une dans la première rue à droite.**
Philip:	Thanks a lot.	**Merci beaucoup.**

*C'est combien pour envoyer
une carte postale en Angleterre?*

Part Four : Personalised Dialogues
Section Quatre : Dialogues

a)   Apologising for having kept someone waiting.

Vous:	(Tell Jacqueline you're sorry you've kept her waiting.)
Jacqueline:	**Ce n'est pas grave.**
Vous:	(Explain that you were delayed [in London].)
Jacqueline:	**Oui, je sais bien que ce n'est pas votre faute.**
Vous:	(Ask if she's not too angry with you.)
Jacqueline:	**Bien sûr que non.**
	Je ne vous en veux pas du tout.

b)   Spelling out a name and address.

Oncle Anatole:	**Ces deux paquets doivent être chez Maître Simenon demain avant 13 heures.**
Vous:	(Apologise and ask where, explaining that you did not understand.)
Oncle Anatole:	**Vous avez un papier et un crayon?**
Vous:	(Say yes, here they are.)
Oncle Anatole:	**Alors c'est chez Maître Henri Simenon.**
Vous:	(Ask Uncle Anatole to spell the name 'Simenon'.)
Oncle Anatole:	**S I M E N O N. Simenon.** **Il habite au 12 rue Jean-Jacques Rousseau.**
Vous:	(Ask him to speak more slowly.)
Oncle Anatole:	**Mais oui, bien sûr.** **12... rue... Jean... Jacques... Rousseau...**
Vous:	(Check the spelling of the name 'Rousseau'.)
Oncle Anatole:	**Oui, c'est ça.**

c)   Collecting a plane ticket.

Hôtesse:	**Est-ce que je peux vous aider?**
Vous:	(Say you've come to fetch your plane ticket and that it's a return ticket, Paris to Geneva.)
Hôtesse:	**C'est à quel nom?**
Vous:	(Give your name.)
Hôtesse:	**Attendez une minute, s'il vous plaît.** **Ah! Le voici. C'est le vol Air France 125 qui part de l'aéroport Charles de Gaulle à 11 heures demain matin.**
Vous:	(Ask what time it reaches Geneva.)
Hôtesse:	**A midi cinq.**
Vous:	(Ask her what time your return flight is.)
Hôtesse:	**A 17 heures 15. Vous serez à Paris pour 18 heures 20.**

d) Enquiring about getting to the airport.

Vous: (Ask how you get to the airport.)
Hôtesse: **Il y a des cars qui vont directement d'ici à Charles de Gaulle.**

Vous: (Ask when they leave.)
Hôtesse: **Il y en a un tous les quarts d'heure.**
Vous: (Ask how long it takes to get from here to the airport.)
Hôtesse: **Entre 30 et 45 minutes.**
Vous: (Ask which one you should take.)
Hôtesse: **Je vous conseille de prendre celui de 9 heures.**
Vous: (Ask if that's not too early.)
Hôtesse: **Si vous ne voulez pas manquer votre avion, il faut être à l'aéroport une heure avant le départ.**

Vous: (Say thank you.)

e) Buying stamps.

Vous: (Ask how much it is to send a post-card to England.)
La vendeuse: **C'est 2 francs 50.**
Vous: (Ask if you can have four stamps at 2 francs 50.)
La vendeuse: **Oui. Ah! je regrette, je n'en ai plus.**
Vous: (Ask if there is a post office in the district.)
La vendeuse: **Il y en a une dans la première rue à droite.**
Vous: (Say thank you.)

*C'est le vol Air France 125 qui part de l'aéroport
Charles de Gaulle à 11 heures demain matin.*

Part Five : Grammar
Section Cinq : Grammaire

1. THE PLUPERFECT TENSE — Had done

This tense is used in the same way as its English equivalent i.e. when you use 'had' in front of the verb.

> e.g. **L'Oncle Anatole avait téléphoné le matin même.**
> That very morning Uncle Anatole had phoned.

It is made up of the Imperfect Tense of **AVOIR** or **ETRE** together with the Past Participle.

> REMEMBER: Take **AVOIR** or **ETRE** in the Imperfect
> Then add a Past Participle to make the Pluperfect.

2. THE PERFECT INFINITIVE — After doing something

When you want to say 'After doing something . . .', you start with **Après** and go on with the Perfect Infinitive i.e. **avoir/être** + past participle:

> e.g. **Après avoir posté ses cartes . . .**

You can also use this construction when you want to say that you are sorry for having done something:

> e.g. **Je regrette de vous avoir fait attendre.**
> I'm sorry to have kept you waiting.

3. AVOIR OR ETRE?

In ACT 6, you saw that you had to use **être** to make up the **passé composé** of a small number of verbs such as **aller, venir,** etc . . .

Note, however, that some of these verbs can also be found with **avoir** in the **passé composé** when they have a direct object:

> **Il est sorti.**
> He went out.
>
> **Il a sorti deux paquets.**
> He took out two packages.

Il a sorti deux paque

252

4. **CELUI QUE/CELUI DE** — The one that/the one of

This word is usually followed by **que** or **de** and means 'the one that' or 'the one of'. **CELUI** is the masculine singular form. In Act 12 you will learn the feminine form.

REMEMBER:	The masculine 'one' for all to see Is clearly marked by **CELUI**.
e.g.	**Le premier était celui que Philip avait apporté à Paris.** (referring to the package)
	Je vous conseille de prendre celui de neuf heures. (referring to the Air France coach)

5. **LEQUEL?**

This is the masculine singular form of the question word you should use when you want to ask 'Which one?', referring to either people or things:

e.g.	**A votre avis, lequel est-ce que je devrais prendre?** (asking about the Air France coach)
REMEMBER:	When 'which one' you cannot tell You need only ask **LEQUEL**?
NOTE:	**LAQUELLE** is the feminine singular form. The plurals are **LESQUELS** and **LESQUELLES**.

6. **PLUS/MOINS** — More/Less

This is the equivalent of English 'more', 'less' or '-er'.

REMEMBER:	**PLUS** or **MOINS** with adjective Will make it a comparative.
e.g.	**Le deuxième était plus petit.** **Ce sera moins encombrant.**

plus beau	—	more beautiful
moins encombrant	—	less cumbersome
plus petit	—	smaller

NOTE 1: 'more and more' is **DE PLUS EN PLUS**
'less and less' is **DE MOINS EN MOINS**

as in Act 8: **. . .se demande Philip de plus en plus intrigué.**

NOTE 2: **PLUS** and **MOINS** can also be used with adverbs:

e.g. **Pouvez-vous parler moins vite, s'il vous plaît?**
Il est arrivé à la Porte Maillot 20 minutes plus tard.

Part Six : **Key Phrases**
Section Six : **Expressions Utiles**

1. **JE DEVRAIS . . .** — I should or I ought to . . .

Note the use of the Conditional Tense of **DEVOIR** to convey the idea that one should or ought to do something:

> e.g. **Lequel est-ce que je devrais prendre?**
> Which one should I (ought I to) take?

2. **NE . . .QUE** — Only

You have seen that **NE** is used with **PAS** to make a negative statement.

Instead of **PAS** you can put **QUE** and this will serve to express the English idea of 'only':

> e.g. **Il n'était que 16 heures 30.**
> It was only 4.30 p.m.

3. HEIGHT AND WEIGHT

When you want to say how tall a person is or what his/her weight is, you can use the verbs **mesurer** and **peser** respectively together with the appropriate figures:

> e.g. **Il mesure 1m 90.**
> **Il pèse 110 kilos.**

For height or weight, you can also use **faire**. As you already know, **faire** is really the **passe-partout** verb in French, like 'to get' in English.

> So you can say:
>
> **Il fait 1m 90.**
> **Il fait 110 kilos.**

4. **TOUS LES . . ./TOUTES LES . . .** — Every . . .

To tell or ask people how often things occur, you can use **TOUS** or **TOUTES**:

> e.g. **Il y en a un tous les quarts d'heure.**
> There's one every quarter of an hour.

> or **Il y en a un toutes les cinq minutes.**
> There's one every five minutes.

Il mesure 1m 90.

Part Seven : Games
Section Sept : Jeux

1. Describing people

Here are some more terms:

Il a le visage

rond   **ovale**   **allongé**   **carré**   **triangulaire**

Hair: always plural in French

Il a les cheveux   **courts et frisés**

Elle a les cheveux   **longs et bouclés**

Il a les cheveux   **mi-longs et raides**

Il n'a plus de cheveux   **il est chauve**

Colour:

Il a
Elle a
les cheveux
blonds
bruns
noirs
roux
poivre et sel
gris
blancs

Eyes:

Ces yeux sont

  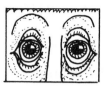

grands   **petits**   **ronds**

Colour:

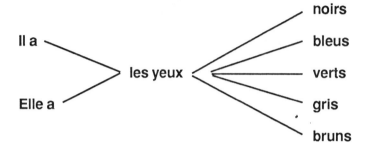

Il a

Elle a

les yeux

noirs

bleus

verts

gris

bruns

Height and weight: in general terms you can say

Ils sont

grands et minces   **de taille moyenne**   **petits et forts**

2.   **Le portrait de Léonie:**

Read the following description carefully.

Léonie est <u>âgée,</u> <u>elle</u> a <u>plus de 70 ans</u>.
<u>Elle</u> est <u>petite</u> et <u>mince</u>.
<u>Elle</u> est <u>veuve</u> et porte des vêtements <u>foncés</u>.
<u>Elle</u> est <u>triste</u> et <u>pleure</u> souvent.
<u>Elle</u> habite <u>à la campagne</u> et mène une vie très <u>calme</u>.
<u>Elle</u> <u>déteste</u> lire mais regarde <u>beaucoup</u> la télévision.

Now change all the words that are underlined because her grandson, Richard, is her opposite. After writing out his description, you might like to draw your own picture of him.

Richard est ....

....

....

Le portrait de Richard

257

3. **Les moyens de transport:**

Here are some pictures to help you fill in the grid.
A few of the words you know already and others are like their English counterparts.

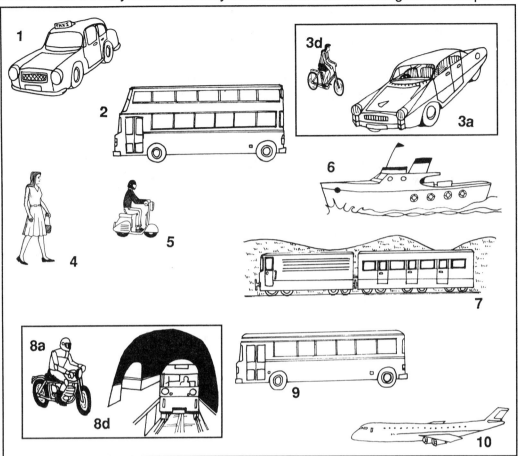

In France this is how we travel:

On voyage:

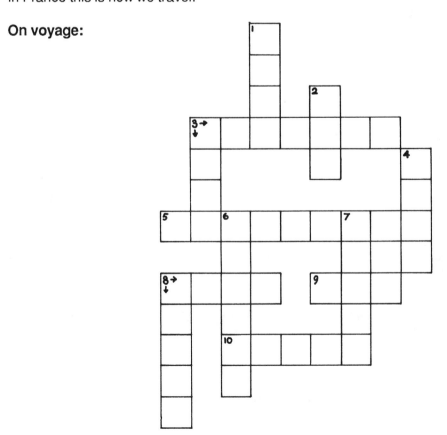

4. The time:

In France the various transport systems normally use the twenty-four hour clock. The strange clock on the right will help you.

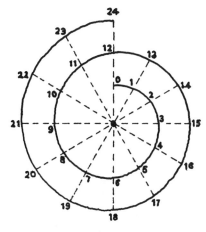

1. Philip is at the station enquiring about trains to Dijon in the morning:

e.g. 8 a.m. **'Est-ce qu'il y a un train qui arrive vers huit heures?'**

How would he ask about the following times?

a. 8.30 a.m.
b. 9.15 a.m.
c. 10.45 a.m.
d. 12 noon

2. Now he is enquiring about his return journey in the evening:

e.g. 6 p.m. **'Est-ce qu'il y a un train qui part vers dix-huit heures?'**

How would he check on the following times?
(Remember to use the 24 hour clock)
a. 7.30 p.m.
b. 8.15 p.m.
c. 9.45 p.m.
d. midnight

The answers are at the back of the book.

5. **Au guichet de la gare de Reims:**

Here is a conversation between a passenger (**un voyageur**) and a railway man (**un employé de la S.N.C.F.**).*

Unfortunately the questions and answers have got mixed up. Can you sort them out?

1.	Le voyageur:	Je voudrais un billet pour Châlons-sur-Marne.
2.	Le voyageur:	Merci bien, monsieur.
3.	L'employé:	A 12h.50.
4.	L'employé:	Un aller simple?
5.	Le voyageur:	A quelle heure est le prochain train?
6.	Le voyageur:	En seconde. Ça fait combien?
7.	Le voyageur:	Et le suivant?
8.	L'employé:	37 F.
9.	L'employé:	Vous en avez un qui part à 16h.42.
10.	L'employé:	En quelle classe?
11.	Le voyageur:	Non, un aller-retour.
12.	Le voyageur:	A quelle heure est-ce qu'il arrive à Châlons?
13.	L'employé:	A 17h.24.

* S.N.C.F. = Société nationale des Chemins de fer français.

1 ....

2 ....

3 ....

4 ....

5 ....

6 ....

7 ....

8 ....

9 ....

10 ....

11 ....

12 ....

13 ....

6. Philip wants to buy some stamps but the **tabac** has not got the values that he wants. He will have to buy several stamps at a lower value to make up what he needs.

First of all here is what he wants:

4 x    6 x

a. How would he ask for these?

The **tabac** only has these stamps available:

b. How many of each of these should Philip ask for?

BONUS

1. **Proverbe**

    Can you find an English proverb that is the equivalent of:

    Oeil pour oeil, dent pour dent.

2. **Qui est qui?**

    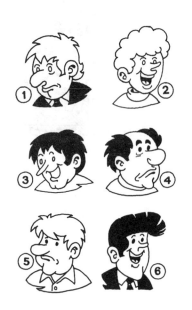

    Paul, Jean et Léon sont blonds.

    Pierre, Paul et Marc rient.

    Lucien, Marc et Léon ont les yeux noirs.

    Jean, Lucien et Léon ont un gros nez.

    Pouvez-vous retrouver le prénom de chaque

    personnage?

3. **Histoire belge**

    Deux amis se retrouvent en vacances et se racontent les événements de l'année.
    Quand je pense, dit l'un, qu'à un numéro près, je gagnais 300 millions au loto!
    Pas possible, répond l'autre, à un seul numéro près?
    Oui. Le gagnant habite au 26, boulevard du Roi, et moi j'habite au 27.

4. **Connaissez-vous ce personnage célèbre?**

5. **Le cyclope n'en avait qu'un! Oui ... mais un quoi?**
    Prenez votre calculatrice et faites l'opération suivante:
    Multipliez quatre cents par vingt.
    Enlevez neuf cents.
    Ajoutez trente.
    Faites le total.
    Retournez votre calculatrice.
    Que voyez-vous?

ACT 11   ACTE 11
Scene I   Scène I

The Departure for Geneva (Saturday).	**Départ pour Genève (Samedi).**

The Air France coach is speeding along the Northern motorway towards Charles de Gaulle Airport at Roissy.	**Le car d'Air France roule à toute vitesse sur l'autoroute du Nord en direction de l'aéroport Charles de Gaulle à Roissy.**

Seated by a window Philip is watching the flat, mournful countryside go by. On his knees he is holding the precious briefcase containing the packages with which Uncle Anatole has entrusted to him.

Assis près d'une fenêtre, Philip regarde passer le paysage triste et plat. Sur ces genoux il tient le porte-documents précieux contenant les paquets que l'oncle Anatole lui a confiés.

His mouth is rather dry and his hands damp. He is not afraid of taking the plane but he would just like to know what is in the packages.

Il a la bouche un peu sèche et les mains moites. Il n'a pas peur de prendre l'avion mais il aimerait seulement savoir ce que contiennent ces paquets.

The coach arrives at the airport. Philip gets off and walks over to the Air France desk. He shows his ticket to a hostess, goes through passport control, then goes to the luggage registration desk.

Le car arrive à l'aéroport. Philip descend et se dirige vers le comptoir d'Air France. Il présente son billet à une hôtesse, passe au contrôle des passeports puis se dirige vers le comptoir d'enregistrement.

Hostess: What luggage have you got?

Qu'est-ce que vous avez comme bagages?

Philip: Just this briefcase.

Je n'ai que ce porte-documents.

Hostess: Smoker or non-smoker?

Fumeur ou non fumeur?

Philip: Non-smoker.

Non fumeur.

Hostess: Right, here's your boarding card.

Bon, voilà votre carte d'accès à bord.

Philip: Thank you. What time do we board the plane?

Merci bien. A quelle heure est-ce qu'on monte dans l'avion?

Hostess: Twenty minutes before departure.

Vingt minutes avant le départ.

	Philip goes into the departure lounge, sits down in a comfortable seat and begins to read a paper. He has scarcely sat down when somebody taps him on the shoulder. When he turns round, he sees Henri, Jacqueline's cousin.	**Philip passe dans la salle d'embarquement, s'asseid dans un fauteuil confortable et commence à lire un journal. Il est à peine installé que quelqu'un lui tape sur l'épaule. En se retournant, il voit Henri, le cousin de Jacqueline.**
Philip:	Goodness! Henri! What are you doing here?	**Ça alors! Henri! Qu'est-ce que tu fais là?**
Henri:	I'm going to Geneva and you?	**Je vais à Genève, et toi?**
Philip:	Me too. What are you going to Geneva for?	**Moi aussi. Pourquoi vas-tu à Genève?**
Henri:	Because I've got a lunch appointment with a very good customer. He's the one who buys most of our stuff from the Far East. And why are you taking this plane?	**Parce que j'ai un déjeuner d'affaires avec un très bon client. C'est lui qui achète la plupart de nos produits qui viennent d'Extrème Orient. Et toi, pourquoi prends-tu cet avion?**
Philip:	Because your father asked me to.	**Parce que ton père me l'a demandé.**
Henri:	He didn't mention it to me.	**Tiens, il ne m'en a rien dit.**

	Philip was more and more convinced that Henri knew why he was going to Geneva but he didn't give anything away.	**Philip était de plus en plus persuadé qu'Henri savait pourquoi il allait à Genève mais il n'a rien laissé paraître.**
Henri:	Do you mind if I sit here?	**Je peux m'asseoir ici, tu permets?**
Philip:	Please do.	**Je t'en prie.**
Henri:	You don't mind if I smoke, do you?	**Ça ne t'ennuie pas que je fume?**
Philip:	No, you can if you want to.	**Non, tu peux si tu veux.**
Henri:	You're not bothered by the smell of cigars?	**L'odeur du cigare ne te dérange pas?**
Philip:	No, it's all the same to me. Go ahead.	**Non, ça m'est absolument égal. Vas-y.**

	Just then, they hear a voice announcing:	A ce moment là, ils entendent une voix qui annonce:

'Would passengers for Geneva Air France Flight 125 (one hundred and twenty five) please go to gate number ten. Boarding now.'

'Les passagers à destination de Genève Vol Air France 125 (cent vingt cinq) sont priés de se présenter à la porte numéro dix pour embarquement immédiat.'

Philip and Henri make for gate number ten and board the plane.

Philip et Henri se dirigent vers la porte numéro dix et montent dans l'avion.

Scene 2   Scène 2

After take-off, Henri notices that there is an empty seat next to Philip and asks the air hostess if he can change places.

Après le décollage, Henri constate qu'il y a une place libre à côté de Philip et il demande à l'hôtesse de l'air s'il peut changer de place.

Henri:	Excuse me, Miss, can I sit over there?	Pardon mademoiselle, est-ce que je peux me mettre là?
Hostess:	Yes, sir, since there's nobody there.	Oui monsieur, puisqu'il n'y a personne.
Henri:	Am I allowed to smoke here?	Est-ce qu'il est permis de fumer ici?
Hostess:	No, sir, there's no smoking. This is the non-smokers section.	Non monsieur, c'est interdit. Ici, c'est le côté non fumeurs.
Henri:	Oh well, that's too bad, but I can have a drink, nevertheless?	Ah bon, tant pis, mais j'ai le droit de boire tout de même?
Hostess:	Yes, of course. What would you like?	Oui, bien sûr. Qu'est-ce que vous voulez?
Henri:	I'll have a coffee. What about you, Philip?	Moi, je prendrai un café. Et toi Philip?
Philip:	The same.	La même chose.
Henri:	How long must you stay in Geneva?	Tu dois rester combien de temps à Genève?
Philip:	Until this evening.	Jusqu'à ce soir.
Henri:	Are you absolutely obliged to go back this evening?	Tu es vraiment obligé de repartir ce soir?
Philip:	Yes, I've got to be in London the day after tomorrow.	Oui, il faut que je sois à Londres après demain.

J'ai le droit de boire tout de même?

Henri:	Well then, you can easily stay until tomorrow. We could have dinner together this evening and afterwards go to a night-club.	Alors, tu peux bien rester jusqu'à demain? On pourrait dîner ensemble ce soir et après aller en boîte.
Philip:	Yes, but I haven't booked a room.	Oui, mais je n'ai pas retenu de chambre.
Henri:	Don't worry. I can book you one when I get to my hotel.	Ne t'en fais pas. Je peux t'en retenir une en arrivant à mon hôtel.
Philip:	Which hotel do you go to?	A quel hôtel descends-tu?
Henri:	I always go to the Hotel des Alpes. It's a big hotel overlooking Lake Geneva.	Je descends toujours à l'Hôtel des Alpes. C'est un grand hôtel qui donne sur le Lac Léman.
Philip:	And what about changing my plane ticket?	Et pour changer mon billet d'avion?
Henri:	No problem. I'll see to that. You'll stay then?	Il n'y a aucun problème. Je m'en charge. Alors, tu restes?
Philip:	O.K.	Bon, d'accord.
Henri:	So shall we meet outside the Hotel des Alpes at six o'clock?	Alors, on se retrouve devant l'Hôtel des Alpes à dix-huit heures?
Philip:	All right.	Entendu.

	They carry on talking about one thing and the other until the journey is over. As the plane lands five minutes late, Philip gets out of the plane quickly.	Ils continuent à parler de choses et d'autres jusqu'à la fin du voyage. Comme l'avion atterrit avec cinq minutes de retard, Philip se dépêche de descendre de l'avion.

Philip:	Excuse me, Henri, I'm in a hurry. I mustn't arrive late for my appointment. See you this evening.	Excuse moi, Henri, je suis pressé. Il ne faut pas que j'arrive en retard à mon rendez-vous. A ce soir.

*C'est un grand hôtel
qui donne sur le Lac Léman.*

266

Scene 3   **Scène 3**

After showing his passport
Philip went on to the customs desk.

**Après avoir montré son passeport,
Philip est passé à la douane.**

Customs Officer:	Is that all your luggage?	**C'est tout ce que vous avez comme bagages?**
Philip:	Yes. I've only got this briefcase.	**Oui, je n'ai que ce porte-documents.**
Customs Officer:	Have you anything to declare?	**Vous avez quelque chose à déclarer?**
Philip:	No, nothing.	**Non, rien.**
Customs Officer:	What's in that?	**Et qu'est-ce qu'il y a là-dedans?**
Philip:	There are only two little packages.	**Il n'y a que deux petits paquets.**
Customs Officer:	Show me them.	**Montrez-les moi.**
Philip:	There they are.	**Les voilà.**
Customs Officer:	Will you open them, please?	**Voulez-vous les ouvrir?**
Philip:	Do I absolutely have to?	**Est-ce que c'est absolument nécessaire?**
	I'm already late.	**Je suis déjà en retard.**
Customs Officer:	Yes sir, I'm afraid so.	**Oui monsieur, je regrette.**

This was awful:
exactly what Philip was afraid of.
He undid the two packages,
his heart beating because he was sure
he was going to get into trouble.

**C'était affreux, c'était juste
ce que Philip redoutait.
Il a défait les deux paquets
le coeur serré parce qu'il était sûr
qu'il allait avoir des ennuis.**

But no . . .
Uncle Anatole had sworn
that the packages only contained
papers
and it was true -
there was nothing but papers.
What a relief!
The customs officer seemed satisfied.

**Mais non . . .
L'oncle Anatole avait juré
que les paquets ne contenaient que
des papiers
et c'était vrai -
il n'y avait rien que des papiers.
Ouf! quel soulagement.
Le douanier semblait satisfait.**

Philip quickly put all the papers
back into the briefcase
and made his way out
to get a taxi.
As he left the airport,
he looked at his watch:

**Philip a vite remis tous les papiers
dans le porte-documents
et s'est dirigé vers la sortie
pour prendre un taxi.
En sortant de l'aéroport,
il a regardé sa montre:**

'Twenty-five past twelve,
I only have
thirty-five minutes
left to reach
Mr Simenon's office.
I must get a move on,'
he said to himself.

**'Midi vingt-cinq,
il ne me reste plus que
trente cinq minutes
pour arriver au
bureau de Maître Simenon.
Il faut que je fasse vite,'
se dit-il.**

Assis près d'une fenêtre, Philip regarde passser le paysage triste et plat.

Il passe au contrôle des passeports puis se dirige vers le comptoir d'enregistrement.

Fumeur ou non fumeur?

Je n'ai que ce porte-documents.

Je vais à Genève, et toi?

En se retournant, il voit Henri, le cousin de Jaqueline.

LE FIGARO

Parce que ton père me l'a demande.

Pourquoi prends-tu cet avion?

Parce que j'ai un dejeuner d'affaires avec un tres bon client

ACTE 11 (iii)

C'est tout ce que vous avez comme baggages?

Voulez-vous les ouvrir?

Le coeur serre parce qu'il était sur qu'il allait avoir des ennuis.

Il n'ya rien que des papiers.

Philip a vite remis tous les papiers dans le porte documents

Philip s'est dirigé vers la sortie por prendre un taxi.

Il a regardé sa montre.

Part Two : Pronunciation and Intonation
Section Deux : Prononciation et Intonation

a)   Linking:

1.   **Moi aussi.**

2.   **Ça alors!**

3.   **Je prendrai un café.**

4.   **Tu es vraiment obligé de repartir ce soir?**

5.   **Il n'y a aucun problème.**

6.   **Je suis déjà en retard.**

b)   **Testez-vous** — Revision exercises.

— Asking questions:

1.   **Vous avez quelque chose à déclarer?**

2.   **Voulez-vous les ouvrir?**

3.   **Pourquoi vas-tu à Genève?**

4.   **A quel hôtel descends-tu?**

5.   **Est-ce que c'est absolument nécessaire?**

6.   **Qu'est-ce que tu fais là?**

7.   **A quelle heure est-ce qu'on monte dans l'avion?**

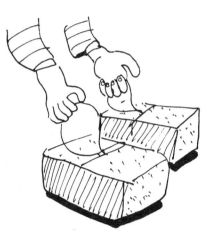

Voulez-vous les ouvrir?

— Make the liaison when necessary:

1.   **C'est interdit.**

2.   **C'est un grand hôtel.**

3.   **Alors, devant l'hôtel des Alpes à l8 heures?**

4.   **Je peux t'en retenir une en arrivant à mon hôtel.**

5.   **On pourrait dîner ensemble et après aller en boîte.**

— Drop the **e** when possible:

1. **Je peux m'asseoir ici?**

2. **Il faut que je fasse vite.**

3. **Il ne me reste plus que 35 minutes.**

4. **On se retrouve devant l'hôtel.**

5. **Ça ne t'ennuie pas que je fume?**

6. **Est-ce que je peux me mettre là?**

7. **J'ai le droit de boire tout de même?**

c)   Poem:

Le hareng saur

> Il était un grand mur blanc — nu, nu, nu,
> Contre le mur une échelle — haute, haute, haute,
> Et par terre, un hareng saur — sec, sec, sec.
>
> Il vient, tenant dans ses mains — sales, sales, sales,
> Un marteau lourd, un grand clou — pointu, pointu, pointu,
> Un peloton de ficelle — gros, gros, gros.
>
> Alors, il monte à l'échelle — haute, haute, haute,
> Et plante le clou pointu — toc, toc, toc,
> Tout en haut du grand mur blanc — nu, nu, nu.
>
> Il laisse aller le marteau — qui tombe, qui tombe, qui tombe.
> Attache au clou la ficelle — longue, longue, longue,
> Et, au bout, le hareng saur — sec, sec, sec.
>
> J'ai composé cette histoire — simple, simple, simple,
> Pour mettre en fureur les gens — graves, graves, graves,
> Et amuser les enfants — petits, petits, petits.

> Charles Cros.
> (adapted)

Part Three — Section Trois
Functional Dialogues — Dialogues Fonctionnels

1. Philip is talking to the hostess at the luggage registration desk. — **Philip parle à l'hôtesse au comptoir d'enregistrement. L'hôtesse = L'h.**

L'h:	What luggage have you got?	**Qu'est-ce que vous avez comme bagages?**
Philip:	Just this briefcase.	**Je n'ai que ce porte-documents.**
L'h	Smoker or non-smoker?	**Fumeur ou non fumeur?**
Philip:	Non-smoker.	**Non fumeur.**
L'h:	Right, here's your boarding-card.	**Bon, voilà votre carte d'accès à bord.**
Philip:	Thank you. What time do we board the plane?	**Merci bien. A quelle heure est-ce qu'on monte dans l'avion?**
L'h:	20 minutes before departure.	**20 minutes avant le départ.**

2. Philip allows Henri to join him and to smoke. — **Philip donne à Henri la permission de s'asseoir et de fumer.**

Henri:	Do you mind if I sit here?	**Je peux m'asseoir ici, tu permets?**
Philip:	Please do.	**Je t'en prie.**
Henri:	You don't mind if I smoke, do you?	**Ça ne t'ennuie pas que je fume?**
Philip:	No, you can if you want to.	**Non, tu peux si tu veux.**
Henri:	You're not bothered by the smell of cigars?	**L'odeur du cigare ne te dérange pas?**
Philip:	No, it's all the same to me. Go ahead.	**Non, ça m'est absolument égal. Vas-y.**

Philip donne à Henri la permission de s'asseoir.

3.   Henri is asking the air hostess for permission to change seats.   **Henri demande à l'hôtesse de l'air la permission de changer de place.**

Henri: Excuse me, Miss, can I sit over there?   **Pardon mademoiselle, est-ce que je peux me mettre là?**

L'h: Yes, sir, since there's nobody there.   **Oui monsieur, puisqu'il n'y a personne.**

Henri: Am I allowed to smoke here?   **Est-ce qu'il est permis de fumer ici?**

L'h: No, sir, there's no smoking. This is the non-smokers section.   **Non monsieur, c'est interdit. Ici, c'est le côté non fumeurs.**

Henri: Oh well that's too bad but I can have a drink, nevertheless?   **Bon, tant pis, mais j'ai le droit de boire tout de même?**

L'h: Yes, of course.   **Oui, bien sûr.**

4.   Henri is persuading Philip to stay a little longer in Geneva.   **Henri persuade Philip de rester un peu plus longtemps à Genève.**

Henri: How long must you stay in Geneva?   **Tu dois rester combien de temps à Genève?**

Philip: Until this evening.   **Jusqu'à ce soir.**

Henri: Are you absolutely obliged to go back this evening?   **Tu es vraiment obligé de repartir ce soir?**

Philip: Yes, I've got to be in London the day after tomorrow.   **Oui, il faut que je sois à Londres après demain.**

Henri: Well then, you can easily stay until tomorrow.   **Alors, tu peux bien rester jusqu'à demain?**

Philip: O.K.   **Bon, d'accord.**

Alors, tu peux bien rester jusqu'à demain?

5.

	At the customs.	**A la douane.**
	Philip goes to the customs desk.	**Philip passe à la douane.**
	Customs Officer	**Le Douanier = Le D.**

Le D:	Is that all your luggage?	**C'est tout ce que vous avez comme bagages?**
Philip:	Yes, I've only got this briefcase.	**Oui, je n'ai que ce porte-documents.**
Le D:	Have you anything to declare?	**Vous avez quelque chose à déclarer?**
Philip:	No, nothing.	**Non, rien.**
Le D:	What's in that?	**Et qu'est-ce qu'il y a là-dedans?**
Philip:	There are only two little packages.	**Il n'y a que deux petits paquets.**
Le D:	Show me them.	**Montrez-les moi.**
Philip:	There they are.	**Les voilà.**
Le D:	Will you open them?	**Voulez-vous les ouvrir?**
Philip:	Do I absolutely have to? I'm already late.	**Est-ce que c'est absolument nécessaire? Je suis déjà en retard.**
Le D:	Yes, sir, I'm afraid so.	**Oui monsieur, je regrette.**

Philip passe à la douane.

Part Four : Personalised Dialogues
Section Quatre : Dialogues

a) At the luggage registration desk.

L'hôtesse:	**Qu'est-ce que vous avez comme bagages?**
Vous:	(Say you've only got this briefcase.)
L'hôtesse:	**Fumeur ou non-fumeur?**
Vous:	(Say non-smoker.)
L'hôtesse:	**Bon, voilà votre carte d'accès à bord.**
Vous:	(Say thank you then ask what time you board the plane.)
L'hôtesse:	**Vingt minutes avant le départ.**

b) Giving somebody permission to smoke.

Henri:	**Je peux m'asseoir ici, vous permettez?**
Vous:	(Say please do [using **vous**].)
Henri:	**Ça ne vous ennuie pas que je fume?**
Vous:	(Tell him he can if he wants to.)
Henri:	**L'odeur du cigare ne vous dérange pas?**
Vous:	(Say that it's all the same to you and tell him to go ahead.)

c) Asking permission (to change seats, smoke).

Vous:	(Say excuse me to the hostess then ask if you can sit over there.)
L'hôtesse:	**Oui, puisqu'il n'y a personne.**
Vous:	(Ask if you are allowed to smoke here.)
L'hôtesse:	**Non, c'est interdit.** **Ici, c'est le côté non-fumeurs.**
Vous:	(Say that's too bad then ask whether you can nevertheless have a drink.)
L'hôtesse:	**Oui, bien sûr.**

d) Persuading somebody to stay a little longer (in London).

Vous:	(Ask Jacqueline how long she must stay in London using **vous**.)
Jacqueline:	**Jusqu'à ce soir.**
Vous:	(Ask if she is absolutely obliged to go back this evening.)
Jacqueline:	**Oui, il faut que je sois à Paris après demain.**
Vous:	(Say that she can easily stay until tomorrow.)
Jacqueline:	**Bon, d'accord.**

e)   At the customs.

Le douanier:	**C'est tout ce que vous avez comme bagages?**
Vous:	(Say yes, you've only got this briefcase.)
Le douanier:	**Vous avez quelque chose à déclarer?**
Vous:	(Say no, nothing.)
Le douanier:	**Et qu'est-ce qu'il y a là-dedans?**
Vous:	(Say there are only two little packages.)
Le douanier:	**Montrez-les moi.**
Vous:	(Say there they are.)
Le douanier:	**Voulez-vous les ouvrir?**
Vous:	(Ask if you absolutely have to and point out you are already late.)
Le douanier:	**Oui, je regrette.**

Ça ne vous ennuie pas que je fume?

Part Five : Grammar
Section Cinq : Grammaire

1. USE OF **LE**, **LA**, **LES** WITH PARTS OF THE BODY

When talking about parts of the body in English, we normally indicate 'ownership' by using words like 'my', 'his', 'your', etc.

In French, **LE**, **LA**, **LES** are used instead, especially when 'ownership' is obvious:

e. g. **Il a LA bouche un peu sèche et LES mains moites.**

If there is any risk of confusion, you can use **MON**, **MA**, **MES**, etc., as in Act10:

e. g. **Philip a remarqué ses yeux pétillants, sa grosse moustache.**
(i. e. Philip is not the owner of the eyes or moustache)

Another way of indicating ownership is to use **LE**, **LA**, **LES** together with **me**, **lui**, **leur**, etc.

e. g. **Quelqu'un lui tape sur l'épaule.**

REMEMBER: Referring to the body
You should use **le**, **la**, **les**
Instead of, for example,
Mon, **ma**, **mes**, or **son**, **sa**, **ses**.

2. NEGATIVE EXPRESSIONS

You always need **NE** in a negative sentence but often **PAS** can be replaced by other words meaning, for example, 'nothing', 'nobody', etc. :

e. g. **Il ne m'en a rien dit.** (nothing)
... puisqu'il n'y a personne. (nobody)
... il n'y avait rien que des papiers. (nothing but)
... Il ne me reste plus que 35 minutes. (no more than)
Il n'y a aucun problème. (no)

REMEMBER: **Plus**, **rien**, **personne** and **aucun** go with **ne**
In exactly the same way as **pas** and **que**.

3. **CE QUE**

If a question is not asked directly, but 'reported', for example, **Il a demandé . . . CE QUE** can be used instead of **Qu'est-ce que**:

e. g. **Il aimerait savoir CE QUE contiennent ces paquets.**
C'était juste CE QUE Philip redoutait.

NOTE ALSO the use of **CE QUE** after **tout** to translate 'all that'.

e. g. **C'est tout CE QUE vous avez comme bagages?**

Part Six : **Key Phrases**
Section Six : **Expressions Utiles**

1. **IL FAUT QUE . . .**

You learnt in Act 5 that **IL FAUT** together with an Infinitive says that something must be done.

IL FAUT can also be followed by **QUE** in which case a special form of the verb (the subjunctive) might be used:

e. g. **Il faut que je sois à Londres après demain.**   *
Il faut que je fasse vite.

2. **ETRE OBLIGE DE . . .**

An alternative to using **IL FAUT** to express the idea of having to do something is to use **ETRE OBLIGE DE** followed by an infinitive:

e. g. **Tu es obligé de repartir ce soir?**

3. **C'EST LUI QUI . . .**

NOTE: This way of stressing 'he' in French:

e. g. **C'est lui qui achète la plupart de nos produits.**

LUI can be replaced by **moi, toi, elle, nous, vous** or **eux** but remember to make the verb agree with the pronoun:

e. g. **C'est nous** qui achetons . . .   It's us who buy . . .
C'est vous qui achetez . . .   It's you who buy . . .
C'est eux qui achètent . . .   It's them who buy . . .

C'est tout ce que vous avez comme bagages?

279

Part Seven : Games
Section Sept : Jeux

1 Sign language:

Know your signs! What do these mean?
Answer in English.

1. _ _ _ _ _ _ _ _ _ _ _ _ _ _ _ _

PRIERE DE NE PAS STATIONNER — **SORTIE DE VOITURES**

INTERDIT AUX PIÉTONS

2. _ _ _ _ _ _ _ _ _ _ _ _ _ _ _

FIN D'INTERDICTION DE STATIONNER

3. _ _ _ _ _ _ _ _ _ _ _ _ _

Entrée réservée aux voyageurs munis de billets

4. _ _ _ _ _ _ _ _ _ _ _ _ _ _ _

5. _ _ _ _ _ _ _ _ _ _ _ _ _

N'OUBLIEZ PAS DE COMPOSTER VOTRE BILLET

SALLE D'ATTENTE

6. _ _ _ _ _ _ _ _ _ _ _ _ _ _

7. **Une place libre — une place occupée**

2. **La carte postale:**

Chère tante Marie,
Nous passons d'excellentes vacances sur la Côte d'Azur. .... il fait très beau et nous sommes sur la plage.
.... 3 jours nous avons fait une belle promenade en bateau. .... Arthur a attrapé un bon coup de soleil et il a encore le nez tout rouge ! .... nous irons visiter le musée Picasso à Antibes. La fin des vacances approche et c'est bien triste. .... nous serons de retour à Paris et nous viendrons te dire un petit bonjour. Nous t'embrassons très affectueusement.
À bientôt.
Julie + Arthur.

Madame Coquelicot

12 RUE DES CHAMPS

75008 PARIS

Can you fill in this holiday postcard with the appropriate words from the following list:

cet après-midi,

après-demain,

aujourd'hui,

la semaine prochaine,

il y a,

avant-hier.

281

3. Jacqueline is planning a dinner-party. Philip and Henri are asking who is going to do what?

What does Jacqueline reply?   (Use **C'est moi qui ... C'est toi qui ...** etc., to start each answer)

1. Philip: **C'est Madame Brossetout qui fait les courses?**
   Jacqueline: **Oui,**

2. Henri: **Qu'est-ce que j'apporte, moi?**
   Jacqueline:

3. Henri: **Et Philip?**
   Jacqueline:

4. Philip: **Qui fait la cuisine?**
    Jacqueline:

5. Henri: **Et qui fait la vaisselle?**
    Jacqueline:

BONUS

1. **Voici une devinette:**

   Avant de prendre l'avion pour un voyage d'affaires, un PDG passe très tôt à son usine. Quand il arrive, le veilleur de nuit lui dit:

   'Monsieur, ne partez pas! Mes rêves ne me trompent jamais et je viens de rêver que vous aviez été tué dans un accident d'avion.'

   Le directeur, inquiet, décide de prendre le train. Le soir même, il apprend que l'avion qu'il devait prendre s'est écrasé au sol et qu'il n'y a aucun survivant. A son retour, il remercie vivement le veilleur de nuit et le renvoie. Pourquoi?

2. **Il y a deux proverbes cachés dans cette carte. Si vous partez des mots soulignés et si vous sillonnez bien la France, vous découvrirez ces deux proverbes.**

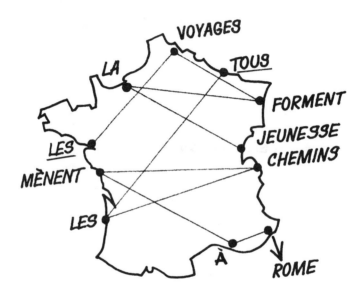

3. **Histoire drôle**

   En France, dans tous les autobus, on peut lire sur une pancarte:

   'Il est défendu de parler au chauffeur.'

   Mais à Marseille, les gens aiment beaucoup parler: ils sont très bavards. Là-bas, la pancarte dit:

   'Il est défendu de répondre au chauffeur.'

ACT 12 ACTE 12
Scene 1 Scène 1

	The key to the puzzle (Saturday).	**La clé de l'énigme (Samedi).**
	Philip has just found a taxi.	**Philip vient de trouver un taxi.**

Taxi driver,	Where are you going?	**Où allez-vous?**
Philip:	Rue Jean-Jacques Rousseau.	**Rue Jean-Jacques Rousseau.**
Taxi-driver:	What number?	**Quel numéro?**
Philip:	Twelve.	**Douze.**
Taxi-driver:	Do you know Geneva?	**Vous connaissez Genève?**
Philip:	No, not at all. I'm from London.	**Non, pas du tout. Je suis de Londres.**
Taxi-driver:	Our town is smaller than London but it's the most beautiful in the world. Are you going to stay long?	**Notre ville est plus petite que Londres mais c'est la plus belle du monde. Vous allez rester longtemps?**
Philip:	No, I go back tomorrow.	**Non, je repars demain.**
Taxi-driver:	Eight, ten, twelve. Here's the building, sir.	**Huit, dix, douze. Voilà l'immeuble, monsieur.**
Philip:	Thanks. How much is that?	**Merci, je vous dois combien?**
Taxi-driver:	Thirty eight francs, sir.	**Trente-huit francs, Monsieur.**
Philip:	Here. There's forty francs. Keep the change.	**Tenez, voilà quarante francs. Gardez la monnaie.**
Taxi-driver:	Thank you sir. Sir! Your brief-case.	**Merci, monsieur. Monsieur! Votre porte-documents.**
Philip:	Oh, thanks ...	**Oh, merci ...**
Taxi-driver:	At your service.	**A votre service.**

La clé de l'énigme

When Philip gets out of the taxi, it is ten to one. Outside the main door he spots a name plate,	**Quand Philip descend du taxi, il est une heure moins dix. Devant la porte d'entrée, il repère une plaque:**
Henri Simenon Solicitor 3rd floor.	**Etude de Me Henri Simenon Notaire 3ème étage.**

	As the lift is out of action,	**L'ascenseur étant en panne,**
	Philip has to go up the stairs.	**Philip doit prendre l'escalier.**
	When he reaches the door,	**En arrivant devant la porte,**
	he rings the doorbell and waits.	**il sonne et attend.**
	A man who is about sixty years old	**·Un monsieur d'une soixantaine**
	opens the door.	**d'années ouvre la porte.**

Philip:	Mr. Simenon, please?	**Maître Simenon, s'il vous plaît?**
Mr Simenon:	Yes, that's me.	**Oui, c'est moi.**
Philip:	Hello,	**Bonjour Maître,**
	I'm Philip West.	**Je suis Philip West.**
	Mr. Dubois sent me.	**Je viens de la part de**
		Monsieur Dubois.
Mr Simenon:	Ah! Hello.	**Ah! Bonjour monsieur.**
	Please come in.	**Entrez, s'il vous plaît.**
Philip:	Thank you.	**Merci bien.**
Mr Simenon:	Have you had a	**Vous avez fait**
	good trip?	**bon voyage?**
Philip:	Very nice, thanks.	**Très bon, merci.**
Mr Simenon:	How is Monsieur Dubois?	**Comment va Monsieur Dubois?**
Philip:	Very well.	**Très bien.**
	He sends his regards	**Il vous donne le bonjour**
	and has asked me	**et m'a chargé de**
	to give you	**vous remettre**
	these two packages.	**ces deux paquets.**

Philip opens the brief-case	**Philip ouvre le porte-documents**
and puts the packages on the desk.	**et pose les paquets sur le bureau.**

Philip:	Please excuse the way	**Je vous prie d'excuser**
	they look but the	**la présentation mais le**
	customs officer made me	**douanier m'a obligé à**
	open them.	**les ouvrir.**
Mr Simenon:	That doesn't matter.	**Ça ne fait rien.**
	Let me just	**Laissez-moi le temps de**
	examine them.	**les examiner.**

Philip is beginning to	**Philip commence à être impatient**
grow impatient and to wonder	**et à se demander où**
what all this is leading up to.	**tout cela va le mener.**

Mr Simenon:	Can I see your passport,	**Puis-je voir votre passeport,**
	please?	**s'il vous plaît?**

Philip pose les paquets sur le bureau.

Philip is at a complete loss but he hands his passport to Mr Simenon. The latter gives it a quick look then hands it back to Philip with a smile.	Philip ne comprend plus rien mais il tend son passeport à Me Simenon. Celui-ci le regarde rapidement puis le redonne à Philip en souriant.

Mr Simenon:	I'm pleased to inform you that, from this day on, you are a partner in the firm of Dubois Ltd.	J'ai l'honneur de vous annoncer qu'à partir d'aujourd'hui, vous êtes un associé de la Maison Dubois.
Philip:	What did you say? I am a partner in Dubois Ltd?	Qu'est-ce que vous dites? Moi, un associé de la Maison Dubois?
Mr Simenon:	Yes, you are indeed.	Oui, vous même.
Philip:	I can't get over it. But why? How? I just don't understand.	Je n'en reviens pas. Mais pourquoi? Comment? Je n'y comprends rien.
Mr Simenon:	Let me explain, about a month ago, a certain Mr. Watson, the sales manager and a partner in this firm, died in a car accident.	Laissez-moi vous expliquer, il y a un mois environ, un certain Monsieur Watson, chef des ventes et associé de cette compagnie, est mort dans un accident de voiture.
Philip:	Mr Watson?	Monsieur Watson?
Mr Simenon:	Yes, he was English. You didn't know him but you were related. He was a distant relation and in his will he left you his shares and a nice little house in Barbizon.	Oui, c'était un Anglais. Vous ne le connaissiez pas mais vous étiez parents. C'était un cousin éloigné et dans son testament, il vous a légué ses actions et une jolie petite maison à Barbizon.
Philip:	How about that! Am I dreaming or something?	Ça alors! Je rêve ou quoi?
Mr Simenon:	Oh no. You're not dreaming. I assure you that all this belongs to you.	Mais non, vous ne rêvez pas. Je vous assure que tout cela vous appartient.
Philip:	It's incredible!	Ce n'est pas croyable!

He fills up and signs the required papers then he takes leave of Mr Simenon.	Il remplit et signe les papiers nécessaires puis il prend congé de Me Simenon.

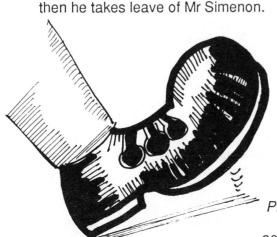

Philip commence à être impatient.

Scene 2   **Scène 2**

As he has some time to spare,	**Comme il a du temps devant lui,**
he uses it to visit Geneva	**il en profite pour visiter Genève**
and admire the banks of Lake Geneva.	**et admirer les bords du Lac Léman.**
As he goes past a post office,	**En passant devant une poste,**
he suddenly	**une idée lui vient**
has an idea.	**soudain à l'esprit.**

'I'm going to phone Jacqueline.	**'Je vais téléphoner à Jacqueline.**
She's bound to know all about this.	**Elle est sûrement dans le coup.**
She owes me an explanation.'	**Elle me doit une explication.'**
Philip says to himself.	**se dit Philip.**
He goes in and goes up to a desk.	**Il entre et s'approche d'un guichet.**

Philip:	Good afternoon.	**Bonjour, madame.**
Telephonist:	Good afternoon, sir.	**Bonjour, monsieur.**
Philip:	I'd like to make a	**Je voudrais**
	phone-call to Paris,	**téléphoner à Paris,**
	please.	**s'il vous plaît.**
Telephonist:	Yes sir.	**Oui monsieur.**
	What number,	**C'est quel numéro,**
	please?	**s'il vous plaît?**
Philip:	Forty three,	**Quarante-trois,**
	seventy seven,	**soixante-dix-sept,**
	sixty nine,	**soixante-neuf,**
	ninety nine.	**quatre-vingt-dix-neuf.**
Telephonist:	43.77.69.99.	**C'est le 43.77.69.99**
	Is that right?	**C'est bien ça?**
Philip:	Yes, that's it.	**Oui. C'est ça.**
Telephonist:	Hello? Paris?	**Allô? Paris?**
	Hold the line please.	**Ne raccrochez pas, s'il vous plaît.**
	You have a call.	**On vous parle.**
	Booth six, sir,	**Cabine six, monsieur,**
	please.	**s'il vous plaît.**
Philip:	Thank you.	**Merci bien.**
Mme Brossetout:	Hello?	**Allô? J'écoute.**
Philip:	Hello? Is that	**Allô? Je suis bien**
	Mr Dubois' place?	**chez Monsieur Dubois?**
Mme Brossetout:	Yes.	**Oui monsieur.**
Philip:	I'd like to speak to	**Je voudrais parler à**
	Jacqueline, please.	**Jacqueline, s'il vous plaît.**
Mme Brossetout:	Who's speaking?	**Qui est à l'appareil?**
Philip:	This is Philip West.	**C'est Philip West.**

*Je voudrais parler
à Jacqueline*

Mme Brossetout:	Hold on,	**Ne quittez pas,**
	I'll get her for you...	**je vous la passe ....**
	I'm sorry, she's out.	**Je suis désolée, elle est sortie.**
	Would you like to leave	**Voulez-vous laisser**
	a message?	**un message?**
Philip:	No, it doesn't matter.	**Non, ça ne fait rien,**
	I'll call back later.	**je rappellerai plus tard.**
	Good-bye	**Au revoir**
	Madame Brossetout.	**Madame Brossetout.**
Mme Brossetout:	Good-bye Mr West.	**Au revoir Monsieur West.**

Scene 3   **Scène 3**

Disappointed but keen to have
an explanation,
Philip makes his way to the hotel
so as not to be late.
From the distance, he notices Henri,
sitting on the terrace
which overlooks the lake.

**Déçu mais avide d'avoir
des explications,
Philip se dirige vers l'hôtel
pour ne pas être en retard.
De loin, il aperçoit Henri,
assis à la terrasse
qui donne sur le bord du lac.**

The setting is magnificent
and the hotel is splendid.
Henri is speaking to a
very elegant young woman
but, as she has her back towards him,
Philip cannot see her face.

**Le cadre est magnifique
et l'hôtel splendide.
Henri parle à une
jeune femme très élégante
mais comme elle est de dos,
Philip ne peut pas voir son visage.**

'What if it were Jacqueline?'
he says to himself.
Just as he comes up to
the table,
the young woman turns round.

**'Et si c'était Jacqueline?'
se dit-il.
Au moment où il s'approche de
la table,
la jeune femme se retourne.**

Philip:	Jacqueline! You here!	**Jacqueline! Toi ici.**
	I thought as much.	**Je m'en doutais.**
Jacqueline:	Philip! How nice	**Philip!**
	to see you again!	**Quel plaisir de te revoir.**
Henri:	Hello again, Philip.	**Re-bonjour Philip.**
Philip:	Well then, why did you	**Alors, pourquoi avez-vous inventé**
	make up all that	**toute cette histoire**
	crazy story?	**à dormir debout?**
Henri:	You mustn't forget	**Il ne faut pas oublier**
	that it's a family	**qu'il s'agit**
	business.	**d'une entreprise familiale.**
Jacqueline:	We wanted to get to know	**On voulait te connaître davantage**
	you better and the best	**et la meilleure façon,**
	way was to put you	**c'était de te mettre**
	to the test.	**à l'épreuve.**

Henri:	You've displayed patience and composure and we congratulate you. Now, after a week, we know that you are capable of working with us and taking poor Bobby Watson's place.	**Tu as fait preuve de patience et de sang froid et nous t'en félicitons. Maintenant, après une semaine, nous savons que tu es capable de travailler avec nous et de remplacer ce pauvre Bobby Watson.**
Philip:	All the same, what a set-up! And why have you asked me to come here?	**Quand même, quelle mise en scène! Et pourquoi m'avez-vous demandé de venir ici?**
Henri:	To open the champagne. You're not going to refuse to drink a toast with us, are you?	**Pour sabler le champagne. Tu ne vas pas refuser de trinquer avec nous?**
Philip:	Oh no! This business has made me thirsty.	**Oh! non, cette histoire m'a donné soif!**
Henri & Jacqueline:	Here's to our future collaboration!	**A notre future collaboration!**
Philip:	To Dubois Ltd.	**A la Maison Dubois!**

Philip had never been so happy in his life. Was it the effect of the champagne? He felt drunk with joy.

Philip n'avait jamais été aussi heureux de sa vie. Etait-ce l'effet du champagne? Il se sentait ivre de joie.

He laid his hand gently on Jacqueline's and they smiled at one another knowingly.

Il a posé doucement sa main sur celle de Jacqueline et ils se sont souris d'un air complice.

As they watched the waves breaking gently below the terrace, they knew that the future belonged to them.

En regardant les vagues se briser doucement au pied de la terrasse, ils savaient que l'avenir leur appartenait.

Philip n'avait jamais été aussi heureux de sa vie.

290

ACTE 12 (i)

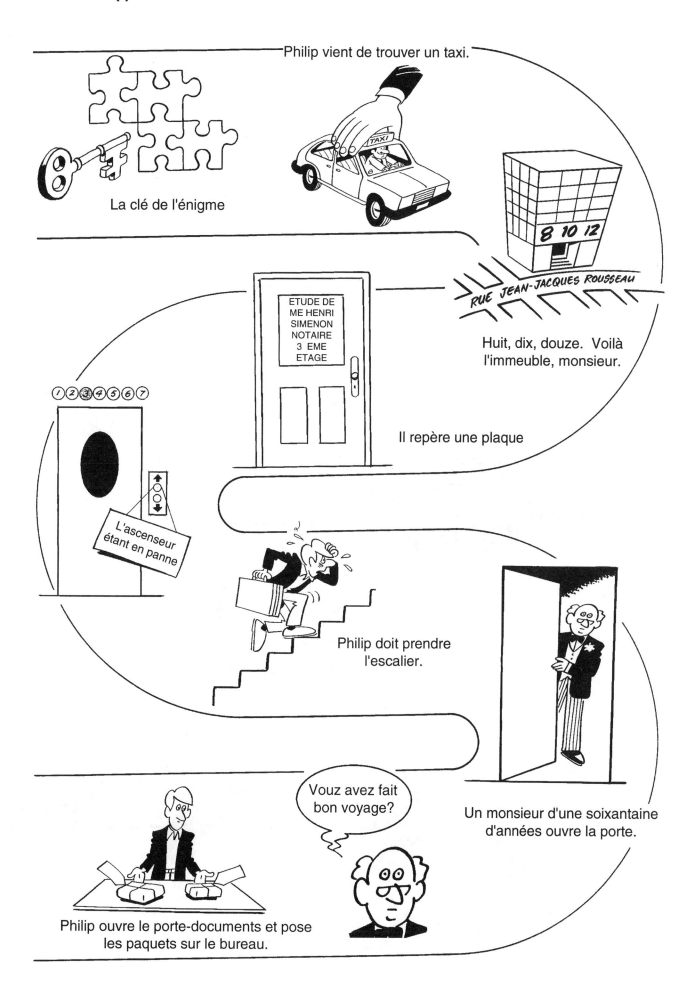

La clé de l'énigme

Philip vient de trouver un taxi.

8 10 12

RUE JEAN-JACQUES ROUSSEAU

Huit, dix, douze. Voilà l'immeuble, monsieur.

ETUDE DE ME HENRI SIMENON NOTAIRE 3 EME ETAGE

Il repère une plaque

L'ascenseur étant en panne

Philip doit prendre l'escalier.

Vouz avez fait bon voyage?

Un monsieur d'une soixantaine d'années ouvre la porte.

Philip ouvre le porte-documents et pose les paquets sur le bureau.

ACTE 12 (ii)

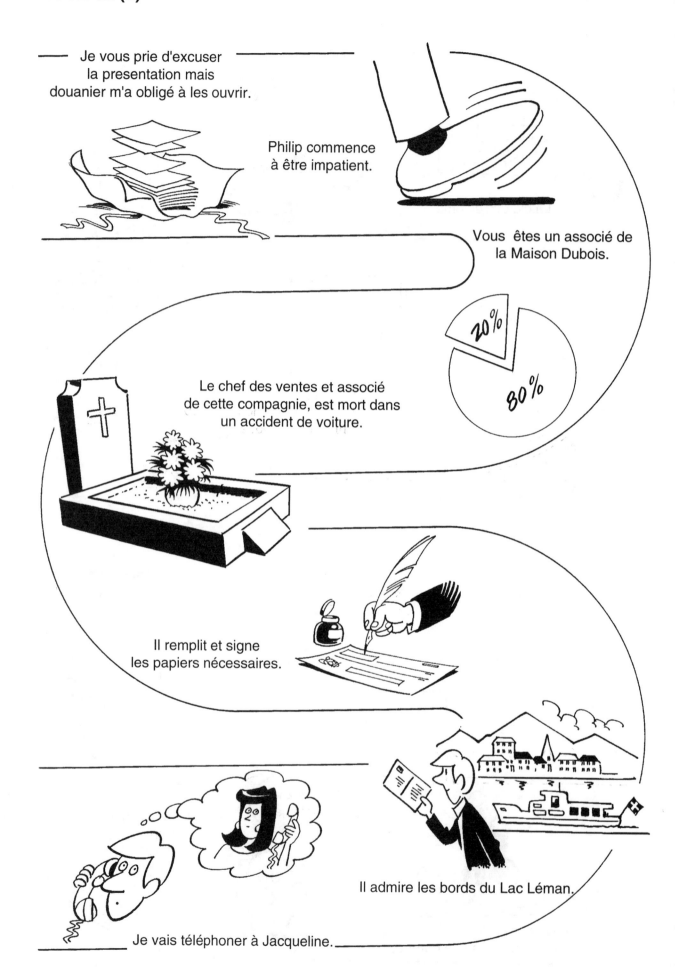

Je vous prie d'excuser la presentation mais douanier m'a obligé à les ouvrir.

Philip commence à être impatient.

Vous êtes un associé de la Maison Dubois.

20%

80%

Le chef des ventes et associé de cette compagnie, est mort dans un accident de voiture.

Il remplit et signe les papiers nécessaires.

Il admire les bords du Lac Léman.

Je vais téléphoner à Jacqueline.

De loin, il aperçoit Henri, assis à la terrasse.

Philip se dirige vers l'hotel.

Henri parle à une jeune femme très élégante mais comme elle est de dos ...

Et si c'était Jacqueline?

Il ne faut pas oublier qu'il s'agit d'une entreprise familiale.

Pour sabler le champagne.

et ils se sont souri d'un air complice.

Il a posé doucement sa main sur celle de Jacqueline

Part Two : Pronunciation and Intonation
Section Deux : Prononciation et Intonation

Numbers:

a)   Telephone numbers:

They have 8 figures grouped in twos.

e.g.	20	73	60	12	**vingt / soixante treize / soixante / douze**
1.					soixante douze / douze / trente deux / quatre vingt treize
2.					quatre vingts / treize / quarante trois / soixante quatorze
3.					soixante / quatorze / cinquante quatre / quatre vingt quinze
4.					quatre vingts / quinze / soixante cinq / soixante seize
5.					soixante / seize / soixante seize / quatre vingt dix sept
6.					quatre vingts / dix sept / quatre vingt sept /quatre vingt dix huit

b)   Can you spot the difference?

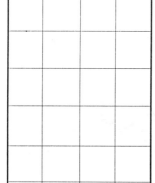

e.g.	80	16	12	74
1.				
2.				
3.				
4.				
5.				
6.				

96	12	60	14

c) **Grand Finale:**

1. Lundi ☐☐ avril ☐☐☐☐ Philip est arrivé à Paris. Il est allé au ☐☐ rue Madame puis à l'hôtel d'Angleterre au ☐☐ rue Bonaparte.

2. Mardi il a changé ☐☐ livres en chèques de voyage et un Eurochèque pour ☐☐☐☐ F. Au total, le caissier lui a donné ☐☐☐☐ F ☐☐ et il a pu s'acheter pour ☐☐☐ F. de vêtements.

3. Mardi soir à ☐☐ h ☐☐ il est allé au cinéma avec Jacqueline. Un peu plus tard, elle a parlé du Vietnam où elle est née en ☐☐☐☐ et de son arrivée à Paris en ☐☐☐☐.

4. Mercredi: Philip avait rendez-vous avec Jacqueline au Pont Neuf à ☐☐ h ☐☐ et il a remarqué la statue d'Henri IV assassiné en ☐☐☐☐.

5. Jeudi: il a visité Fontainebleau et rencontré Henri. Au retour, Jacqueline a fait du ☐☐☐ sur l'autoroute!

6. Vendredi: il a enfin rencontré l'Oncle Anatole à ☐☐ h ☐☐. Quel personnage impressionnant — ☐ m ☐☐ et ☐☐☐ kilos!

7. Samedi: il a pris le Vol Air France ☐☐☐ à ☐☐ h et est arrivé à Genève ☐☐ minutes plus tard. Il a essayé sans succès de téléphoner à Jacqueline au ☐☐—☐☐—☐☐—☐☐. A ☐☐ h ☐☐ il a sablé le champagne et est devenu un associé de la Maison Dubois fondée en ☐☐☐☐ .

QUELLE SEMAINE EXTRAORDINAIRE!

Part Three Section Trois
Functional Dialogues Dialogue Fonctionnels

I. Philip and the taxi driver. **Philip et le chauffeur de taxi.**
Le Chauffeur de Taxi = Le Ch.

Le Ch.	Where are you going?	**Où allez-vous?**
Philip:	Rue Jean Jacques Rousseau.	**Rue Jean-Jacques Rousseau.**
Le Ch.	What number?	**Quel numéro?**
Philip:	12.	**12.**
Le Ch.	Do you know Geneva?	**Vous connaissez Genève?**
Philip:	No, not at all.	**Non, pas du tout.**
	I'm from London.	**Je suis de Londres.**
Le Ch.	8, 10, 12.	**8, I0, I2.**
	Here's the building, sir.	**Voilà l'immeuble, monsieur.**
Philip:	Thanks. How much is that?	**Merci, je vous dois combien?**
Le Ch.	38 francs, sir.	**38 francs, monsieur.**
Philip:	Here. There's 40 francs.	**Tenez, voilà 40 francs.**
	Keep the change.	**Gardez la monnaie.**
Le Ch.	Thank you, sir.	**Merci monsieur.**

2. Philip is introducing himself to Mr Simenon. **Philip se présente à Me Simenon.**

Philip:	Mr Simenon, please?	**Maître Simenon s'il vous plaît?**
Me S:	Yes, that's me.	**Oui, c'est moi.**
Philip:	Hello.	**Bonjour Maître.**
	I'm Philip West.	**Je suis Philip West.**
	Mr Dubois sent me.	**Je viens de la part de Monsieur Dubois.**
Me S:	Ah! Hello.	**Ah! Bonjour monsieur.**
	Please come in.	**Entrez, s'il vous plaît.**
Philip:	Thank you.	**Merci bien.**
Me S:	Have you had a good trip?	**Vous avez fait bon voyage?**
Philip:	Very nice, thanks.	**Très bon, merci.**
Me S:	How is Mr Dubois?	**Comment va Monsieur Dubois?**
Philip:	Very well.	**Très bien.**
	He sends his regards.	**Il vous donne le bonjour.**

Voilà l'immeuble, monsieur.

3. | Philip is surprised at what has happened. | **Philip est très surpris d'apprendre ce qui lui arrive.**

Me S:	I'm pleased to inform you that, from this day on, you are a partner in the firm of Dubois Ltd.	**J'ai l'honneur de vous annoncer qu'à partir d'aujourd'hui, vous êtes un associé de la Maison Dubois.**
Philip:	What did you say? I can't get over it.	**Qu'est-ce que vous dites? Je n'en reviens pas.**
Me S:	You've been left some shares and a nice little house in Barbizon.	**On vous a légué des actions et une jolie petite maison à Barbizon.**
Philip:	How about that! Am I dreaming or something?	**Ça alors! Je rêve ou quoi?**
Me S:	Oh no. You're not dreaming. I assure you that all this belongs to you.	**Mais non, vous ne rêvez pas. Je vous assure que tout cela vous appartient.**
Philip:	It's incredible!	**Ce n'est pas croyable!**

4. | Philip is making a phone-call to Paris. The Telephonist. | **Philip demande à téléphoner à Paris. La téléphoniste = La T.**

Philip:	Good afternoon.	**Bonjour madame.**
La T:	Good afternoon, sir.	**Bonjour monsieur.**
Philip:	I'd like to make a phone-call to Paris, please.	**Je voudrais téléphoner à Paris, s'il vous plaît.**
La T:	Yes, sir. What number, please?	**Oui monsieur. C'est quel numéro, s'il vous plaît?**
Philip:	43.77.69.99.	**C'est le 43.77.69.99.**
La T:	43.77.69.99. Is that right?	**Le 43.77.69.99. C'est bien ça?**
Philip:	Yes, that's right.	**Oui, c'est ça.**
La T:	Hello? Paris? Hold the line, please. You have a call. Booth 6, sir, please.	**Allô? Paris? Ne raccrochez pas, s'il vous plaît, on vous parle. Cabine 6, monsieur, s'il vous plaît.**
Philip:	Thank you.	**Merci bien.**

On vous a légué des actions et une jolie petite maison.

5.

| | Philip asks | **Philip demande à** |
| | to speak to Jacqueline. | **parler à Jacqueline.** |

Mme B:	Hello?	**Allô? J'écoute**
Philip:	Hello?	**Allô?**
	Is that Mr Dubois' place?	**Je suis bien chez Monsieur Dubois?**
Mme B:	Yes.	**Oui monsieur.**
Philip:	I'd like to speak to	**Je voudrais parler à**
	Jacqueline, please.	**Jacqueline, s'il vous plaît.**
Mme B:	Who's speaking?	**Qui est à l'appareil?**
Philip:	This is Philip West.	**C'est Philip West.**
Mme B:	Hold on,	**Ne quittez pas,**
	I'll get her for you.	**je vous la passe.**
	...I'm sorry, she's out.	**...Je suis désolée, elle est sortie.**
	Would you like to leave	**Voulez-vous laisser**
	a message?	**un message?**
Philip:	No, it doesn't matter.	**Non, ça ne fait rien,**
	I'll call back later.	**je rappellerai plus tard.**

*Vous êtes un associé de la
Maison Dubois.*

Part Four   :   Personalised Dialogues
Section Quatre :   Dialogues

a)   Taking a taxi in Paris.

Le chauffeur de taxi:	**Où allez-vous?**
Vous:	(Say rue de Rennes.)
Le chauffeur de taxi:	**Quel numéro?**
Vous:	(Say 120.)
Le chauffeur de taxi:	**Vous connaissez Paris?**
Vous:	(Say 'not at all' and then say where you are from.)
Le chauffeur de taxi:	**Voilà l'immeuble.**
Vous:	(Say 'thank you' and ask how much you owe.)
Le chauffeur de taxi:	**Trente-huit francs.**
Vous:	(Give him 40 francs and tell him to keep the change.)
Le chauffeur de taxi:	**Merci mademoiselle.**

b)   Introducing yourself (to Me Simenon).

Vous:	(Ask if this is Me Simenon.)
Me Simenon:	**Oui c'est moi.**
Vous:	(Say 'hello' and who you are then say that Monsieur Dubois sent you.)
Me Simenon:	**Ah! Bonjour. Entrez s'il vous plaît.**
Vous:	(Say 'thank you'.)
Me Simenon:	**Vous avez fait bon voyage?**
Vous:	(Say 'very nice, thank you'.)
Me Simenon:	**Comment va Monsieur Dubois?**
Vous:	(Say 'very well' and that he sends his regards.)

c)   Expressing surprise.

Me Simenon:	**J'ai l'honneur de vous annoncer que vous êtes à partir d'aujourd'hui un associé de la Maison Dubois.**
Vous:	(Ask him what he said and say that you can't get over it.)
Me Simenon:	**On vous a légué des actions et une jolie petite maison à Barbizon.**
Vous:	(Say 'how about that!' then ask if you are dreaming or something.)
Me Simenon:	**Non, vous ne rêvez pas. Je vous assure que tout cela vous appartient.**
Vous:	(Say it's incredible.)

d)   Making a phone-call to Paris.

Vous: (Say you would like to make a phone-call to Paris.)
La téléphoniste: **Oui. C'est quel numéro, s'il vous plaît?**
Vous: (Say 4l.23.93.89)
La téléphoniste: **Le 4l.23.93.89. C'est bien ça?**
Vous: (Say that's it.)
La téléphoniste: **Allô? Paris?**
                                          Ne raccrochez pas, s'il vous plaît,
                                          on vous parle. Cabine 6.
Vous: (Say 'thank you'.)

e)   Trying to get someone on the phone.

Mme Brossetout: **Allô? J'écoute.**
Vous: (Say 'hello' and check that this is Mr. Dubois' place.)
Mme Brossetout: **Oui.**
Vous: (Say you'd like to speak to Jacqueline.)
Mme Broussetout: **Qui est à l'appareil?**
Vous: (Give your name.)
Mme Broussetout: **Ne quittez pas, je vous la passe.**
                                          ...Je suis désolée, elle est sortie.
                                          Voulez-vous laisser un message?
Vous: (Say no, it doesn't matter and that you will call back later.)

Où allez-vous?

Part Five : Grammar
Section Cinq : Grammaire

1. VERBS FOLLOWED BY **DE** OR **A** + Infinitive

In English there are many verbs which are followed by the infinitive:

> e.g.   He forced me to open the package.
> Philip is starting to get impatient.

In French these verbs are followed by **de** or **à** then the Infinitive. There is no obvious system and you will have to learn each construction as you meet it.

> **Il m'a chargé de vous remettre ces deux paquets.**
> **Je vous prie d'excuser la présentation.**
> **Le douanier m'a obligé à les ouvrir.**
> **Philip a commencé à être impatient.**
> **Pourquoi m'avez-vous demandé de travailler avec vous?**
> **Tu ne vas pas refuser de trinquer avec nous.**

2. **NE PAS** — Not to

> REMEMBER: **Ne pas** together makes a verb negative
> Only when it comes before the infinitive.

> e.g.   **Pour ne pas être en retard . . .**

3. **CELUI/CELLE**

You have already learnt in Act 10 that **CELUI** followed by **QUE** or **DE** meant 'the one that . . .' or 'the one of . . .'. The feminine form is **CELLE**:

> e.g.   **Il a posé sa main sur CELLE de Jacqueline.**

The plurals are **CEUX** and **CELLES**.

You can also add —**CI** or —**LA** to either **CELUI** or **CELLE** if you wish to distinguish between two people or things. In this situation, **CELUI-CI** or **CELLE-CI** can mean 'the former' or 'this one' and **CELUI-LA** or **CELLE-LA** can mean 'the latter' or 'that one'.

> e.g.   **CELUI-CI le regarde rapidement.**

The same goes for the plurals:

> **CELLES-CI le sentent pas très bon.**
> **CEUX-CI le regardent rapidement.**

4.   TO MAKE COMPARISONS

In Act10 you learnt how to make simple comparatives:

e.g.   **PLUS petit — MOINS encombrant.**

In this Act you have come across **PLUS petit QUE:**

e.g.   **Notre ville est <u>plus</u> petite <u>que</u> Londres.**
                    Our town is smaller than London.

The taxi driver could have said:

e.g.   **Notre ville est <u>moins</u> grande <u>que</u> Londres.**
                    Our town is not as big as London.

If you want to say 'most' or 'least', you must use **LE PLUS, LA PLUS** or
LE MOINS, LA MOINS:

e.g.   **C'est LA PLUS belle du monde.**
                    It's the most beautiful in the world.

REMEMBER: Before **PLUS** or **MOINS** put **LE, LA, LES.**
                When superlatives you want to say.

NOTE: The irregular forms of **BON** — good, are:

        MEILLEUR (QUE)   —   better (than)
        LE MEILLEUR   —   the best.

e.g.   **. . .et LA MEILLEURE façon, c'était de te mettre à l'épreuve.**

Part Six : Key Phrases
Section Six : Expressions Utiles

1. **AU MOMENT OU . . .**

This expression is used in the same way as the English 'Just as . . .':

    e.g.   **Au moment où il s'approche de la table . . .**

2. **—AINE** — Approximate numbers

If you add **—AINE** to certain numbers, you will make them approximate:

    e.g.   **Un monsieur d'une soixantAINE d'années.** (about 60)

The only numbers that can take **—AINE** are: 8, 10, 12, 15, 20, 30, 40, 50, 60 and 100.

    NOTE: Two of these, however, can be precise in special cases:

    a)   **une douzaine** for things that are sold by the dozen

    e.g.   **une douzaine d'oeufs**

    b)   **une quinzaine de jours**   —   a fortnight.

3. **—IEME** — How to say second, third . . .

If you add **—IEME** to any numbers with the exception of **UN/UNE** which becomes **PREMIER/PREMIERE**, you will get:

        deuxIEME
        dixIEME
        vingtIEME etc . . .

NOTE:	quatre	— quatrIEME
	cinq	— cinquIEME
	neuf	— neuvIEME
	onze	— onzIEME

Part Seven : Games
Section Sept : Jeux

1. **Plus ou moins?**

   Savez-vous faire des comparaisons? Par exemple:

Philip est plus jeune qu'Henri.

Philip est moins gros que l'Oncle Anatole.

Regardez les autres images et faites des comparaisons:

1. **Madame Marat** _ _ _ _ _ _ _ _ _ _ _ _ _ _ _ _ _ _ _ Jacqueline

2. **Mme Brossetout** _ _ _ _ _ _ _ _ _ _ _ _ _ _ _ _ _ _ _ Jacqueline.

3.   **Londres** _ Paris

4.   **Le métro** _ le bus

5.   **L'Arc de Triomphe** _ _ _ _ _ _ _ _ _ _ _ _ _ _ _ _ la Tour Eiffel

6.   **La cravate** _ la chemise

7.   **Woody Allen** _ _ _ _ _ _ _ _ _ _ _ _ _ _ _ _ _ _ Alfred Hitchcock

8.   **Le thé** _ le champagne.

2. **Le livre des records:**

a. **Pouvez-vous répondre aux questions suivantes?**
   Voilà les réponses — dans le désordre:

Tancarville   La Tour Eiffel

Les Beatles   Paul Getty

Boulogne   Février

La Joconde   Diego Maradonna

La Place de la Concorde   La Place Fürstenberg

   1. Quel est le plus grand port de pêche de France?
   2. Où se trouve le pont le plus long de France?
   3. Quelle est la plus petite place de Paris?
   4. Qui était l'homme le plus riche du monde?
   5. Quel est le mois le plus court de l'année?
   6. Qui est la plus belle femme du monde?
   7. Où se trouve le monument le plus ancien de Paris?
   8. Comment s'appelait le groupe 'pop' le plus célèbre du monde?
   9. Quel est le monument le plus haut de Paris?
   10. Qui était le meilleur joueur de football du monde en 1986?

b. **Et maintenant pouvez-vous compléter les phrases suivantes?**
   Exemple: L'Everest est la montagne la plus haute du monde.

   1. L'Amazone   long
   2. Le Groenland   grande
   3. La Rolls Royce   prestigieuse
   4. La Chine   peuplé
   5. Le 21 décembre   court

The answers are at the back of the book.

306

3. Philip's thoughts at the end of the week

If you take the first letter of each picture and bear in mind that one line = one word, you will discover what Philip thinks (it's a proverb).

‒ ‒ ‒ ‒   ‒ ‒ ‒   ‒ ‒ ‒ ‒   ‒ ‒ ‒   ‒ ‒ ‒ ‒ ‒   ‒ ‒ ‒ ‒

4. **Le jeu de l'oie:**

This game is an adaptation of the game of the goose which will help you to take stock of what you have learnt during the course. The throw of the dice will move your marker on an amusing journey full of adventure.

You can play on your own or with friends and the game sheet can be found in your word card folder.

a. You need one dice.
b. You need one marker for each player.
c. If you land on a goose, you double your throw and move forward.
d. But you have some obstacles to overcome. If you manage to answer — no problem. But if you don't, you will be penalised by a **gage**.
e. You must finish on 63 exactly. Keep throwing until you get the right score. But if you want to play the game strictly according to the rules, you should go back to square one (**la case 1**) if you don't reach 63 exactly.

OIE MÉTÉO

Instructions

1. **Case de départ.**
2. **Rue Madame**   Say you have an appointment with Mr. Dubois.
3. **Hotel d'Angleterre**   Ask if they have a room with shower for 2 nights.
4. Tell the waitress you want a chocolate and some bread, butter and jam.
5. **Oie météo**
6. **Le pont:**   Conjuguez le verbe 'aller' au présent.
      Gage: **vous avez oublié votre passeport à l'hôtel, retournez le chercher à la case 3.**
7. Say you don't speak Chinese.
8. **Quel temps fait-il ce matin?**
9. **Oie fleuriste**
10. Ask for a bunch of red roses.
11. Ask if you are late.
12. Say you prefer shopping at the market.
13. **Ce chiffre porte malheur — Retournez voir l'oie météo.**

OIE FLEURISTE

14. **Oie crémière**
15. Order a pound of butter and a dozen eggs.
16. **Pouvez-vous donner le nom de trois fromages français?**
17. How do you say 'Cheers' in French?
18. **Oie banquière**
19. **Le café:**   Conjuguez le verbe 'venir' au présent.
       Gage: **vous avez trop bu — Retournez voir l'oie crémière.**
20. What is the meaning of **régler en espéces**?
21. Write a cheque for 2.469F in words.
22. Tell a friend you must go to the bank this afternoon.

OIE BANQUIER

23. **Oie vendeuse.**
24. Ask if you can try on this pair of dark grey trousers.
25. Tell the shop assistant that these shoes are too expensive.
26. Ask if you can use his/her phone.
27. **Oie ouvreuse**
28. Ask what's on at the cinema.
29. Say you hate thrillers.
30 Say you love cartoons.

31. **Le puits:**   **Donnez le féminin des adjectifs: bon, gentil, frais, beau, nouveau, vieux.**

     Gage: **vous n'avez plus d'argent — Retournez voir l'oie banquière.**

32. **Oie serveuse**
33. Ask the waiter for the bill.
34. Ask if the service is included.
35. Order a bottle of Champagne.
36. **Oie infirmière**
37. Say your mother retired two years ago.
38. How do you say 'an elder sister' in French?
39. Say you don't feel very well.
40. Say that your feet are aching.

OIE INFIRMIERE

41. **Oie parisienne**
42. **Le labyrinthe:**   **Quel est le participe passé des verbes: <u>vivre</u>, <u>venir</u>, <u>voir</u>, <u>avoir</u> et <u>être</u>?**

                 Mettez ces verbes à la première personne du singulier du passé composé.

     Gage: **Vous n'avez pas trouvé votre chemin — retournez à la case 27.**

43. Ask a close friend if she/he feels like going to the Moulin Rouge.
44. How do we say 'Mona Lisa' in French?
45. **Oie sportive**
46. **A quelle époque de l'année fait-on du ski?**
47. Suggest walking along the Seine.
48. Ask Jacqueline if she has been waiting for a long time.
49. Say you have just had a game of tennis.
50. **Oie voyageuse**
51. Ask the way to the Pont Neuf.

OIE VOYAGEUSE

52. **La prison:**   **Conjuguez le verbe faire au futur et le verbe aimer au conditionnel.**

     Gage: **Vous avez insulté un gardien de prison — Retournez à la case 45.**

53. Ask for a return ticket to Geneva.
54. **Oie agent de police**
55. Ask Jacqueline if she knows how to drive.
56. Tell a very good friend not to drive too fast on the motorway.
57. **'Fin d'interdiction de stationner'** — What does it mean?
58. **La mort:**   **Conjuguez le verbe <u>se promener</u> au présent et au passé composé.**

     Gage: **Vous avez flirté avec la mort sans succès.**

                 Retournez à la case de départ.

59. **Oie suisse.**
60. What do you say when you meet someone for the first time?

61. Somebody has just told you you are a millionnaire. You are very surprised. What do you say?
62. Say you have to be at the Hôtel des Alpes at 6 p.m.
63. **Hôtel des Alpes et Champagne — Bravo et à votre santé!**

BONUS

1. **Voici un dernier proverbe:**

    On a souvent besoin d'un plus petit que soi.

2. **Devinette:**

    Du plus beau au moins beau

    Arthur est plus beau que Jacques.
    Jacques est plus beau que Pierre mais moins beau que Paul.
    Paul est plus beau que Jean mais moins beau qu'Arthur.

    1. **Quel est le plus beau?**   **C'est . . . .**
    2. **Quel est le moins beau?**   **C'est . . . .**

3. **Une dernière histoire drôle:**

    A Lyon, un taxi s'arrête devant un hôtel. Le client demande au chauffeur:

    'Je vous dois combien?'
    —'Cinquante francs vingt, monsieur.'

    Le client cherche dans ses poches puis dit au chauffeur:

    'Vous ne pouvez pas reculer d'une centaine de mètres? Je n'ai que quarante francs soixante-dix sur moi.'

The answers are at the back of the book.

4. **Drôles de cercles!**

Tout le monde s'y trompe! Et vous, êtes-vous plus fort que les autres?

**Le cercle de droite est-il plus grand que l'autre?
Oui ou non?**

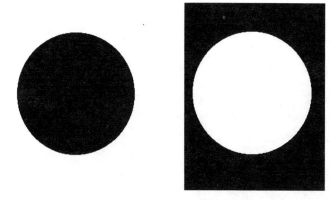

5. **A votre santé!**

Le Champagne n'est un luxe
que si la joie de vivre en est un.

SACRE COEUR

REMINDER

Are you still following all the steps?
It will fully repay you to do so.

* GRAMMAR TABLES *

i. <u>Number and Gender</u>

(a) These words need to 'agree' with the noun that follows, depending upon whether the noun is masculine/feminine and singular/plural.

	Singular				Plural
	Masculine		Feminine		
a/some	un		une		des
the	le	(l')	la	(l')	les
some/any	du	(de l')	de la	(de l')	des
to/at the	au	(à l')	à l'	(à l')	aux
this/that these/those	ce	(cet)	cette		ces
my	mon		ma	(mon)	mes
your	ton		ta	(ton)	tes
his/her/its	son		sa	(son)	ses
our	notre		notre		nos
your	votre		votre		vos
their	leur		leur		leurs

(When words begin with vowel sounds use the form in brackets e.g. **mon amie**)

(b)   Common adjectives with spelling changes.

	Singular		Plural	
	Masculine	Feminine	Masculine	Feminine
Regular endings				
good	bon	bonne	bons	bonnes
fat	gros	grosse	gros	grosses
nice	gentil	gentille	gentils	gentilles
which	quel	quelle	quels	quelles
white	blanc	blanche	blancs	blanches
soft	doux	douce	doux	douces
cool	frais	fraîche	frais	fraîches
long	long	longue	longs	longues
beautiful	beau (bel)	belle	beaux	belles
new	nouveau (nouvel)	nouvelle	nouveaux	nouvelles
old	vieux (vieil)	vieille	vieux	vieilles

(Forms in brackets are used in front of masculine singular nouns that start with vowel sounds e.g. un bel hôtel, un vieil ami.)

ii.   Pronouns

(a)

	Subject	Direct Object	Indirect Object	Reflexive	Stressed or + prepositions
I/me	je (j')	me (m')	me (m')	me (m')	moi
you	tu	te (t')	te (t')	te (t')	toi
he/him/it	il	le (l')	lui	se (s')	lui
she/her/it	elle	la (l')	lui	se (s')	elle
one/we	on	nous	nous	se (s')	nous
we/us	nous	nous	nous	nous	nous
you	vous	vous	vous	vous	vous
they/them (m)	ils	les	leur	se (s')	eux
they/them (f)	elles	les	leur	se (s')	elles

(b)   Order of Pronouns in same sentence:

1	2	3	4	5
me te nous vous se	le la les	lui leur	y	en

(c)

	Singular		Plural	
	Masculine	Feminine	Masculine	Feminine
which one (s)	lequel	laquelle	lesquels	lesquelles
the one (s)	celui	celle	ceux	celles
this one/ these ones	celui-ci	celle-ci	ceux-ci	celles-ci
that one/ those ones	celui-là	celle-là	ceux-là	celles-là

iii. <u>Verbs</u>

(a) Regular Verbs

Infinitive	**donner** — to give (typical of **er** verbs)	**répondre** — to answer (typical of **re** verbs)	**finir** — to finish (typical of **ir** verbs)
Present	je donne tu donnes il donne nous donnons vous donnez ils donnent	je réponds tu réponds il répond— nous répondons vous répondez ils répondent	je finis tu finis il finit nous finissons vous finissez ils finissent
Imperative e.g. give!	donne! donnons! donnez!	réponds! répondons! répondez!	finis! finissons! finissez!
Present Participle e.g. giving	donnant	répondant	finissant
Past Participle e.g. given	donné	répondu	fini
Passé Composé e.g. I gave I have given	j'ai donné tu as donné il a donné nous avons donné vous avez donné ils ont donné	j'ai répondu tu as répondu il a répondu nous avons répondu vous avez répondu ils ont répondu	j'ai fini tu as fini il a fini nous avons fini vous avez fini ils ont fini

Imperfect
 	
e.g. I gave
      I used to give
      I was giving
	je donnais
	tu donnais
	il donnait
	nous donnions
	vous donniez
	ils donnaient
		je répondais
		tu répondais
		il répondait
		nous répondions
		vous répondiez
		ils répondaient
			je finissais
			tu finissais
			il finissait
			nous finissions
			vous finissiez
			ils finissaient

Pluperfect e.g. I had given	j'avais donné tu avais donné il avait donné nous avions donné vous aviez donné ils avaient donné	j'avais répondu tu avais répondu il avait répondu nous avions répondu vous aviez répondu ils avaient répondu	j'avais fini tu avais fini il avait fini nous avions fini vous aviez fini ils avaient fini
Future e.g. I will give	je donnerai tu donneras il donnera nous donnerons vous donnerez ils donneront	je répondrai tu répondras il répondra nous répondrons vous répondrez ils répondront	je finirai tu finiras il finira nous finirons vous finirez ils finiront
Conditional e.g. I would give	je donnerais tu donnerais il donnerait nous donnerions vous donneriez ils donneraient	je répondrais tu répondrais il répondrait nous répondrions vous répondriez ils répondraient	je finirais tu finirais il finirait nous finirions vous finiriez ils finiraient

A   'Reflexive' verb

Infinitive	**se laver** — to wash oneself
Present	**Je me lave** **tu te laves** **il/elle se lave** **nous nous lavons** **vous vous lavez** **ils/elles se lavent**
Imperative	**lave-toi** **lavons-nous** **lavez-vous**
Present & Past Participles	**se lavant** **s'étant lavé(e)**
Passé composé	**Je me suis lavé(e)** **tu t'es lavé(e)** **il s'est lavé/elle s'est lavée** **nous nous sommes lavé(e)s** **vous vous êtes lavé(e)s** **ile se sont lavés/elles se sont lavées**
Imperfect	**Je me lavais** **tu te lavais** **il/elle se lavait** **nous nous lavions** **vous vous laviez** **ils/elles se lavaient**
Pluperfect	**Je m'étais lavé(e)** **tu t'étais lavé(e)** **il s'était lavé/elle s'était lavée** **nous nous étions lavé(e)s** **vous vous étiez lavé(e)s** **ils s'étaient lavés/elles s'étaient lavées**
Future	**je me laverai** **tu te laveras** **il/elle se lavera** **nous nous laverons** **vous vous laverez** **ils/elles se laveront**
Conditional	**je me laverais** **tu te laverais** **il/elle se laverait** **nous nous laverions** **vous vous laveriez** **ils/elles se laveraient**

(b) -er verbs with spelling changes in the stem

Infinitive	Present	Passé composé	Imperfect	Future
manger to eat	je mange tu manges il mange nous mangeons vous mangez ils mangent Like **manger** verbs ending in -**ger**	j'ai mangé tu as mangé il a mangé nous avons mangé vous avez mangé ils ont mangé	je mangeais tu mangeais il mangeait nous mangions vous mangiez ils mangeaient	je mangerai tu mangeras il mangera nous mangerons vous mangerez ils mangeront
commencer to begin	je commence tu commences il commence nous commençons vous commencez ils commencent Like **commencer** verbs ending in -**cer**	j'ai commencé tu as commencé il a commencé nous avons commencé vous avez commencé ils ont commencé	je commençais tu commençais il commençait nous commencions vous commenciez ils commençaient	je commencerai tu commenceras il commencera nous commencerons vous commencerez ils commenceront
payer to pay	je paie tu paies il paie nous payons vous payez ils paient Like **payer** verbs ending in -**yer**	j'ai payé tu as payé il a payé nous avons payé vous avez payé ils ont payé	je payais tu payais il payait nous payions vous payiez ils payaient	**je paierai** **tu paieras** **il paiera** **nous paierons** **vous paierez** **ils paieront**
acheter to buy	j'achète tu achètes il achète nous achetons vous achetez ils achètent Like **acheter**: se lever, se promener, peser	j'ai acheté tu as acheté il a acheté nous avons acheté vous avez acheté ils ont acheté	j'achetais tu achetais il achetait nous achetions vous achetiez ils achetaient	j'achèterai tu achèteras il achètera nous achèterons vous achèterez ils achèteront
espérer to hope	j'espère tu espères il espère nous espérons vous espérez ils espèrent Like **espérer**: répéter, préférer, s'inquiéter	j'ai espéré tu as espéré il a espéré nous avons espéré vous avez espéré ils ont espéré	j'espérais tu espérais il espérait nous espérions vous espériez ils espéraient	j'espérerai tu espéreras il espérera nous espérerons vous espérerez ils espéreront
appeler to call	j'appelle tu appelles il appelle nous appelons vous appelez ils appellent Like **appeler**: jeter, se rappeler	j'ai appelé tu as appelé il a appelé nous avons appelé vous avez appelé ils ont appelé	j'appelais tu appelais il appelait nous appelions vous appeliez ils appelaient	j'appellerai tu appelleras il appellera nous appellerons vous appellerez ils appelleront

Section 1. These are worth learning!

(c) Irregular verbs

Infinitive	Present	Passé composé	Imperfect	Future

aller
to go
	je vais
	tu vas
	il va
	
	nous allons
	vous allez
	ils vont
		je suis allé(e)
		tu es allé(e)
		il est allé
		elle est allée
		nous sommes
		  allé(e)s
		vous êtes
		  allé(e)(s)
		ils sont allés
		elles sont allées
			j'allais
			tu allais
			il allait
			
			nous allions
			vous alliez
			ils allaient
				j'irai
				tu iras
				il ira
				
				nous irons
				vous irez
				ils iront

avoir to have	j'ai tu as il a nous avons vous avez ils ont	j'ai eu tu as eu il a eu nous avons eu vous avez eu ils ont eu	j'avais tu avais il avait nous avions vous aviez ils avaient	j'aurai tu auras il aura nous aurons vous aurez ils auront
boire to drink	je bois tu bois il boit nous buvons vous buvez ils boivent	j'ai bu tu as bu il a bu nous avons bu vous avez bu ils ont bu	je buvais tu buvais il buvait nous buvions vous buviez ils buvaient	je boirai tu boiras il boira nous boirons vous boirez ils boiront
connaître to know	je connais tu connais il connaît nous connaissons vous connaissez ils connaissent	j'ai connu tu as connu il a connu nous avons connu vous avez connu ils ont connu	je connaissais tu connaissais il connaissait nous connaissions vous connaissiez ils connaissaient	je connaîtrai tu connaîtras il connaîtra nous connaîtrons vous connaîtrez ils connaîtront
devoir to have to	je dois tu dois il doit nous devons vous devez ils doivent	j'ai dû tu as dû il a dû nous avons dû vous avez dû ils ont dû	je devais tu devais il devait nous devions vous deviez ils devaient	je devrai tu devras il devra nous devrons vous devrez ils devront
dire to say	je dis tu dis il dit nous disons vous dites ils disent	j'ai dit tu as dit il a dit nous avons dit vous avez dit ils ont dit	je disais tu disais il disait nous disions vous disiez ils disaient	je dirai tu diras il dira nous dirons vous direz ils diront
être to be	je suis tu es il est nous sommes vous êtes ils sont	j'ai été tu as été il a été nous avons été vous avez été ils ont été	j'étais tu étais il était nous étions vous étiez ils étaient	je serai tu seras il sera nous serons vous serez ils seront

Infinitive	Present	Passé composé	Imperfect	Future
faire to do, make	**je fais** **tu fais** **il fait** **nous faisons** **vous faites** **ils font**	**j'ai fait** **tu as fait** **il a fait** **nous avons fait** **vous avez fait** **ils ont fait**	**je faisais** **tu faisais** **il faisait** **nous faisions** **vous faisiez** **ils faisaient**	**je ferai** **tu feras** **il fera** **nous ferons** **vous ferez** **ils feront**
lire to read	**je lis** **tu lis** **il lit** **nous lisons** **vous lisez** **ils lisent**	**j'ai lu** **tu as lu** **il a lu** **nous avons lu** **vous avez lu** **ils ont lu**	**je lisais** **tu lisais** **il lisait** **nous lisions** **vous lisiez** **ils lisaient**	**je lirai** **tu liras** **il lira** **nous lirons** **vous lirez** **ils liront**
savoir to know	**je sais** **tu sais** **il sait** **nous savons** **vous savez** **ils savent**	**j'ai su** **tu as su** **il a su** **nous avons su** **vous avez su** **ils ont su**	**je savais** **tu savais** **il savait** **nous savions** **vous saviez** **ils savaient**	**je saurai** **tu sauras** **il saura** **nous saurons** **vous saurez** **ils sauront**
venir to come	**je viens** **tu viens** **il vient** **nous venons** **vous venez** **ils viennent**	**je suis venu(e)** **tu es venu(e)** **il est venu** **elle est venue** **nous sommes** **venu(e)s** **vous êtes** **venu(e)(s)** **ils sont venus** **elles sont venues**	**je venais** **tu venais** **il venait** **nous venions** **vous veniez** **ils venaient**	**je viendrai** **tu viendras** **il viendra** **nous viendrons** **vous viendrez** **ils viendront**
vivre to live	**je vis** **tu vis** **il vit** **nous vivons** **vous vivez** **ils vivent**	**j'ai vécu** **tu as vécu** **il a vécu** **nous avons vécu** **vous avez vécu** **ils ont vécu**	**je vivais** **tu vivais** **il vivait** **nous vivions** **vous viviez** **ils vivaient**	**je vivrai** **tu vivras** **il vivra** **nous vivrons** **vous vivrez** **ils vivront**
voir to see	**je vois** **tu vois** **il voit** **nous voyons** **vous voyez** **ils voient**	**j'ai vu** **tu as vu** **il a vu** **nous avons vu** **vous avez vu** **ils ont vu**	**je voyais** **tu voyais** **il voyait** **nous voyions** **vous voyiez** **ils voyaient**	**je verrai** **tu verras** **il verra** **nous verrons** **vous verrez** **ils verront**

Section 2. For information

Infinitive	Present	Passé composé	Imperfect	Future
s'asseoir to sit down	je m'assieds tu t'assieds il s'assied nous nous asseyons vous vous asseyez ils s'asseyent	je me suis assis(e) tu t'es assis(e) il s'est assis elle s'est assise nous nous sommes assis(e)s vous vous êtes assis(e)(es) ils se sont assis elles se sont assises	je m'asseyais tu t'asseyais il s'asseyait nous nous asseyions vous vous asseyiez ils s'asseyaient	je m'assiérai tu t'assiéras il s'assiéra nous nous assiérons vous vous assiérez ils s'assiéront
battre to beat	je bats tu bats il bats nous battons vous battez ils battent	j'ai battu tu as battu il a battu nous avons battu vous avez battu ils ont battu	je battais tu battais il battait nous battions vous battiez ils battaient	je battrai tu battras il battra nous battrons vous battrez ils battront
conduire to drive	je conduis tu conduis il conduit nous conduisons vous conduisez ils conduisent	j'ai conduit tu as conduit il a conduit nous avons conduit vous avez conduit ils ont conduit	je conduisais tu conduisais il conduisait nous conduisions vous conduisiez ils conduisaient	je conduirai tu conduiras il conduira nous conduirons vous conduirez ils conduiront
courir to run	je cours tu cours il court nous courons vous courez ils courent	j'ai couru tu as couru il a couru nous avons couru vous avez couru ils ont couru	je courais tu courais il courait nous courions vous couriez ils couraient	je courrai tu courras il courra nous courrons vous courrez ils courront
craindre to fear	je crains tu crains il craint nous craignons vous craignez ils craignent	j'ai craint tu as craint il a craint nous avons craint vous avez craint ils ont craint	je craignais tu craignais il craignait nous craignions vous craigniez ils craignaient	je craindrai tu craindras il craindra nous craindrons vous craindrez ils craindront
croire to believe	je crois tu crois il croit nous croyons vous croyez ils croient	j'ai cru tu as cru il a cru nous avons cru vous avez cru ils ont cru	je croyais tu croyais il croyait nous croyions vous croyiez ils croyaient	je croirai tu croiras il croira nous croirons vous croirez ils croiront

Infinitive	Present	Passé composé	Imperfect	Future
dormir to sleep	**je dors** **tu dors** **il dort** **nous dormons** **vous dormez** **ils dorment**	**j'ai dormi** **tu as dormi** **il a dormi** **nous avons dormi** **vous avez dormi** **ils ont dormi**	**je dormais** **tu dormais** **il dormait** **nous dormions** **vous dormiez** **ils dormaient**	**je dormirai** **tu dormiras** **il dormira** **nous dormirons** **vous dormirez** **ils dormiront**
écrire to write	**j'écris** **tu écris** **il écrit** **nous écrivons** **vous écrivez** **ils écrivent**	**j'ai écrit** **tu as écrit** **il a écrit** **nous avons écrit** **vous avez écrit** **ils ont écrit**	**j'écrivais** **tu écrivais** **il écrivait** **nous écrivions** **vous écriviez** **ils écrivaient**	**j'écrirai** **tu écriras** **il écrira** **nous écrirons** **vous écrirez** **ils écriront**
entendre to hear	**j'entends** **tu entends** **il entend** **nous entendons** **vous entendez** **ils entendent**	**j'ai entendu** **tu as entendu** **il a entendu** **nous avons entendu** **vous avez entendu** **ils ont entendu**	**j'entendais** **tu entendais** **il entendait** **nous entendions** **vous entendiez** **ils entendaient**	**j'entendrai** **tu entendras** **il entendra** **nous entendrons** **vous entendrez** **ils entendront**
envoyer to send	**j'envoie** **tu envoies** **il envoie** **nous envoyons** **vous envoyez** **ils envoient**	**j'ai envoyé** **tu as envoyé** **il a envoyé** **nous avons envoyé** **vous avez envoyé** **ils ont envoyé**	**j'envoyais** **tu envoyais** **il envoyait** **nous envoyions** **vous envoyiez** **ils envoyaient**	**j'enverrai** **tu enverras** **il enverra** **nous enverrons** **vous enverrez** **ils enverront**
éteindre to switch off	**j'éteins** **tu éteins** **il éteint** **nous éteignons** **vous éteignez** **ils éteignent**	**j'ai éteint** **tu as éteint** **il a éteint** **nous avons éteint** **vous avez éteint** **ils ont éteint**	**j'éteignais** **tu éteignais** **il éteignait** **nous éteignions** **vous éteigniez** **ils éteignaient**	**j'éteindrai** **tu éteindras** **il éteindra** **nous éteindrons** **vous éteindrez** **ils éteindront**
falloir to be necessary	**il faut**	**il a fallu**	**il fallait**	**il faudra**

Infinitive	Present	Passé composé	Imperfect	Future
mettre to put	je mets tu mets il met nous mettons vous mettez ils mettent	j'ai mis tu as mis il a mis nous avons mis vous avez mis ils ont mis	je mettais tu mettais il mettait nous mettions vous mettiez ils mettaient	je mettrai tu mettras il mettra nous mettrons vous mettrez ils mettront
mourir to die	je meurs tu meurs il meurt nous mourons vous mourez ils meurent	je suis mort(e) tu es mort(e) il est mort elle est morte nous sommes mort(e)(s) vous êtes mort(e)(s) ils sont mort elles sont mortes	je mourais tu mourais il mourait nous mourions vous mouriez ils mouraient	je mourrai tu mourras il mourra nous mourrons vous mourrez ils mourront
naître to be born	je nais tu nais il naît nous naissons vous naissez ils naissent	je suis né(e) tu es né(e) il est né elle est née nous sommes né(e)s vous êtes né(e)(s) ils sont nés elles sont nées	je naissais tu naissais il naissait nous naissions vous naissiez ils naissaient	je naîtrai tu naîtras il naîtra nous naîtrons vous naîtrez ils naîtront
ouvrir to open	j'ouvre tu ouvres il ouvre nous ouvrons vous ouvrez ils ouvrent	j'ai ouvert tu as ouvert il a ouvert nous avons ouvert vous avez ouvert ils ont ouvert	j'ouvrais tu ouvrais il ouvrait nous ouvrions vous ouvriez ils ouvraient	j'ouvrirai tu ouvriras il ouvrira nous ouvrirons vous, ouvrirez ils ouvriront
partir to leave go away	je pars tu pars il part nous partons vous partez ils partent	je suis parti(e) tu es parti(e) il est parti elle est partie nous sommes parti(e)(s) vous êtes parti(e)(s) ils sont partis elles sont parties	je partais tu partais il partait nous partions vous partiez ils partaient	je partirai tu partiras il partira nous partirons vous partirez ils partiront

Infinitive	Present	Passé composé	Imperfect	Future
pouvoir to be able, can	**je peux** **tu peux** **il peut** **nous pouvons** **vous pouvez** **ils peuvent**	**j'ai pu** **tu as pu** **il a pu** **nous avons pu** **vous avez pu** **ils ont pu**	**je pouvais** **tu pouvais** **il pouvait** **nous pouvions** **vous pouviez** **ils pouvaient**	**je pourrai** **tu pourras** **il pourra** **nous pourrons** **vous pourrez** **ils pourront**
prendre to take	**je prends** **tu prends** **il prend** **nous prenons** **vous prenez** **ils prennent**	**j'ai pris** **tu as pris** **il a pris** **nous avons pris** **vous avez pris** **ils ont pris**	**je prenais** **tu prenais** **il prenait** **nous prenions** **vous preniez** **ils prenaient**	**je prendrai** **tu prendras** **il prendra** **nous prendrons** **vous prendrez** **ils prendront**
recevoir to receive	**je reçois** **tu reçois** **il reçoit** **nous recevons** **vous recevez** **ils reçoivent**	**j'ai reçu** **tu as reçu** **il a reçu** **nous avons reçu** **vous avez reçu** **ils ont reçu**	**je recevais** **tu recevais** **il recevait** **nous recevions** **vous receviez** **ils recevaient**	**je recevrai** **tu recevras** **il recevra** **nous recevrons** **vous recevrez** **ils recevront**
rire to laugh	**je ris** **tu ris** **il rit** **nous rions** **vous riez** **ils rient**	**j'ai ri** **tu as ri** **il a ri** **nous avons ri** **vous avez ri** **ils ont ri**	**je riais** **tu riais** **il riait** **nous riions** **vous riiez** **ils riaient**	**je rirai** **tu riras** **il rira** **nous rirons** **vous rirez** **ils riront**
suivre to follow	**je suis** **tu suis** **il suit** **nous suivons** **vous suivez** **ils suivent**	**j'ai suivi** **tu as suivi** **il a suivi** **nous avons suivi** **vous avez suivi** **ils ont suivi**	**je suivais** **tu suivais** **il suivait** **nous suivions** **vous suiviez** **ils suivaient**	**je suivrai** **tu suivras** **il suivra** **nous suivrons** **vous suivrez** **ils suivront**
vouloir to want	**je veux** **tu veux** **il veut** **nous voulons** **vous voulez** **ils veulent**	**j'ai voulu** **tu as voulu** **il a voulu** **nous avons voulu** **vous avez voulu** **ils ont voulu**	**je voulais** **tu voulais** **il voulait** **nous voulions** **vous vouliez** **ils voulaient**	**je voudrai** **tu voudras** **il voudra** **nous voudrons** **vous voudrez** **ils voudront**

(d) Verbs where the **passé composé** is formed by using the present tense of **être** along with the past participle:-

aller	**venir**
monter	**descendre**
arriver	**partir**
entrer	**sortir**
naître	**mourir**
rester	**tomber**
rentrer	**retourner**
revenir	**devenir**

+ all reflexive verbs.

e.g.

je suis descendu(e)	**je me suis levé(e)**
tu es descendu(e)	**tu t'es levé(e)**
il est descendu	**il s'est levé**
elle est descendue	**elle s'est levée**
nous sommes descendu(e)s	**nous nous sommes levé(e)s**
vous êtes descendu(e)(s)	**vous vous êtes levé(e)(s)**
ils sont descendues	**ils se sont levés**
elles sont descendues	**elles se sont levées**

Numbers:

0	**zéro**	40	**quarante**
1	**un, une**	41	**quarante et un**
2	**deux**	42	**quarante-deux**
3	**trois**	50	**cinquante**
4	**quatre**	51	**cinquante et un**
5	**cinq**	60	**soixante**
6	**six**	61	**soixante et un**
7	**sept**	70	**soixante-dix**
8	**huit**	71	**soixante et onze**
9	**neuf**	72	**soixante-douze**
10	**dix**	73	**soixante-treize**
11	**onze**	74	**soixante-quatorze**
12	**douze**	75	**soixante-quinze**
13	**treize**	76	**soixante-seize**
14	**quatorze**	77	**soixante-dix-sept**
15	**quinze**	78	**soixante-dix-huit**
16	**seize**	79	**soixante-dix-neuf**
17	**dix-sept**	80	**quatre-vingts**
18	**dix-huit**	81	**quatre-vingt-un**
19	**dix-neuf**	82	**quatre-vingt-deux**
20	**vingt**	90	**quatre-vingt-dix**
21	**vingt et un**	91	**quatre-vingt-onze**
22	**vingt-deux**	92	**quatre-vingt-douze**, etc.
23	**vingt-trois**	99	**quatre-vingt-dix-neuf**
24	**vingt-quatre**	100	**cent**
25	**vingt-cinq**	101	**cent un**
26	**vingt-six**	102	**cent deux**, etc.
27	**vingt-sept**	200	**deux cents**
28	**vingt-huit**	201	**deux cent un**, etc.
29	**vingt-neuf**	305	**trois cent cinq**
30	**trente**	1,000	**mille**
31	**trente et un**	1,001	**mille un**, etc.
32	**trente-deux**	1,100	**onze cents or mille cent***
		2,000	**deux mille**
		1,000,000	**un million**
		2,000,000	**deux millions**, etc.
		1,000,000,000	**un milliard**
		2,000,000,000	**deux milliards**, etc.

* Dates can be expressed in two ways:

1986

mille neuf cent quatre-vingt-six

or

dix-neuf cent quatre-vingt-six

Place Names

a)   For countries which are feminine, use **en**:

LA	**EN**
Belgique	Belgique
Chine	Chine
France	France
Grande-Bretagne	Grande-Bretagne
Grèce	Grèce
Hollande	Hollande
Pologne	Pologne
Russie	Russie
Suisse	Suisse

L'	**EN**
Allemagne	Allemagne
Angleterre	Angleterre
Argentine	Argentine
Australie	Australie
Ecosse	Ecosse
Espagne	Espagne
Inde	Inde
Irlande	Irlande
Italie	Italie
Union Soviétique	Union Soviétique

b)   For countries which are masculine, use **au**:

LE	**AU**
Brésil	Brésil
Canada	Canada
Danemark	Danemark
Japon	Japon
Mexique	Mexique
Pays de Galles	Pays de Galles
Portugal	Portugal

c)   For countries which are masculine and plural, use **aux**:

LES	**AUX**
Etats-Unis	Etats-Unis
Pays-Bas	Pays-Bas

Acte 1
Section Quatre: Dialogues

a)   Vous: Bonjour madame.
C'est ici la maison de Madame Dupont?
J'ai rendez-vous avec Madame Dupont.
Monsieur/Madame ......
Merci Madame.

b)   Vous: Je m'appelle ....
Non, j'arrive de (Manchester).
Oui, j'arrive de Londres.
Tenez, voilà mon passeport.
Je m'appelle ....
Je suis ....
Oui, je suis étudiant/e
et j'ai .....ans.
Merci.

c)   Vous: Non, elle est française.
Non, elle habite Paris.
Oui, elle a les yeux bleus
et les cheveux noirs.
Elle a vingt deux ans.

d)   Vous: Bonjour madame.
Vous avez une chambre pour
une nuit, s'il vous plaît?
Une chambre pour une personne
s'il vous plaît.
Monsieur/Madame ....
Bien, merci.
Au revoir madame.

e)   Vous: Bonsoir madame.
Vous avez une chambre réservée pour
Monsieur/Madame ....?
Monsieur/Madame ....
C'est à quel étage?
Merci bien.
Bonne nuit madame.

Section Sept: Jeux

1. 1. Philip regarde la maison.
    2. La maison est grande et belle.
    3. Il s'approche de la porte et sonne.
    4. Une dame âgée ouvre la porte.
    5. C'est ici la maison de Monsieur Dubois?
    6. Philip entre dans la maison.
    7. Philip donne le passeport à Jacqueline.
    8. J'habite Londres.
    9. Je m'appelle Jacqueline Dubois.
    10. Le paquet est pour Monsieur Dubois.
    11. Monsieur Dubois rentre à Paris ce soir.
    12. C'est un petit hôtel mais il est confortable.
    13. Philip arrive à l'hôtel.
    14. Vous avez une chambre réservée pour Monsieur West.
    15. Madame Marat donne la clé à Philip.
    16. Il monte l'escalier et trouve la chambre.
    17. La chambre est agréable et calme.
    18. Il est fatigué mais content.

2. Philip West, un étudiant anglais, arrive à Paris avec un paquet pour Monsieur Dubois, mais Monsieur Dubois rentre à Paris demain et Philip donne le paquet à la jeune femme, Jacqueline Dubois.

3.

1.	C	A	L	M	E					
2. E	X	T	R	A	O	R	D	I	N	A	I	R	E
3.	N	O	I	R	S					
4.	F	A	T	I	G	U	E			
5.	C	O	N	T	E	N	T	E		
6.	G	R	A	N	D	E				
7. P	E	T	I	T						
8.	A	G	E	E						
9.	B	L	E	U	S					
10. B	E	L	L	E						
11.	J	E	U	N	E					

330

4.

5.

	Vrai	Faux
1.	X	
2.		X
3.	X	
4.		X
5.		X
6.	X	
7.		X
8.		X
9.	X	
10.	X	
11.		X
12.	X	
13.		X
14.		X

Acte 2
Section Quatre: Dialogues

a)   Vous: Bonjour mademoiselle.
    Je vais prendre un café,
    s'il vous plaît.
    Un café noir, s'il vous plaît.
    Oui. Je veux bien deux croissants.

b)   Vous: J'habite en (Angleterre), à (Londres).
    Vous connaissez (Londres)?
    Non, c'est ma première visite.

c)   Vous: Oui, je suis anglais/e.
    Non, je suis italien/ne.
    Non, je comprends si vous parlez
    lentement mais je ne parle pas très bien.
    Et vous, est-ce que vous parlez anglais?
    Vous êtes espagnole peut-être?

d)   Vous: Quel temps fait-il aujourd'hui?
    Alors il fait beau?
    Mais cet après midi, il va faire beau,
    n'est-ce pas?
    Mais il ne fait pas toujours beau
    à Paris au printemps?
    Alors, c'est comme en Angleterre.

e)   Vous: Oui. Il y a un lit, une table
    avec deux chaises blanches
    et par terre un joli tapis bleu.
    Oui. La taie d'oreiller et les draps
    sont blancs et propres.
    Oui. Il y a une baignoire
    et des toilettes
    mais il n'y a pas de douche.

Section Sept: Jeux

1. Il y a une chaise.
   Il y a deux fenêtres.
   Il n'y a pas de rideaux.
   Il y a deux valises.
   Il y a un peigne.
   Il n'y a pas de brosse à dents.

2. A Bordeaux, il fait du brouillard ce matin mais il va faire chaud ce soir.
   A Marseille, if fait du vent ce matin mais il va faire du soleil ce soir.
   A Strasbourg, il pleut ce matin mais il va neiger ce soir.
   A Lille, il neige ce matin mais il va faire du brouillard ce soir.
   A Cherbourg, il fait du soleil ce matin mais il va faire froid ce soir.
   A Nantes, il fait froid ce matin mais il va faire du vent ce soir.
   A Lyon, il fait chaud ce matin mais il va pleuvoir ce soir.
   A Nice, il fait beau ce matin mais il va faire de l'orage ce soir.

3. Pour Madame Dubois, c'est du thé et du pain avec du beurre.
   Pour Monsieur Dubois, c'est du café.
   Pour Mademoiselle Petit, c'est du chocolat et des croissants.
   Pour Monsieur Legrand, c'est du café au lait et du pain avec de la confiture.
   Pour Mademoiselle Lenoir, c'est du thé et un croissant.

4. 1. En Angleterre, je parle anglais.
   2. En Italie, je parle italien.
   3. En Espagne, je parle espagnol.
   4. En Allemagne, je parle allemand.
   5. Au Japon, je parle japonais.
   6. En Grèce, je parle grec.
   7. En Chine, je parle chinois.
   8. Au Mexique, je parle mexicain.
   9. En Russie, je parle russe.
   10. En Egypte, je parle égyptien.

BONUS

1. J'aime le café au lit avec des croissants (chauds), mais je n'aime pas le café au lait.

3. L'Américain parle à l'Italien,
   l'Italien parle au Mexicain,
   le Mexicain parle au Français,
   le Français parle à l'Allemand!

Acte 3
Section Quatre: Dialogues

a)   **Vous:**   Très bien, merci. Et vous?
                           Je ne suis pas en retard j'espère?
                           Quelle heure est-il?
                           Ah! bon? Ma montre avance alors.

b)   **Vous:**   Volontiers.
                           Je voudrais bien (un Martini).
                           Et vous, qu'allez-vous prendre?
                           A la vôtre.

c)   **Vous:**   Je voudrais deux biftecks bien tendres,
                           s'il vous plaît.
                           C'est tout. Ça fait combien?
                           Tenez, voilà un billet de
                           vingt francs.

d)   **Vous:**   C'est combien les tomates?
                           Eh bien, mettez-moi une livre
                           de tomates, s'il vous plaît.
                           Je voudrais un kilo de haricots verts,
                           une laitue et une livre d'oignons.
                           Oui c'est tout. Ça fait combien?

e)   **Vous:**   J'aime bien le brie et le camembert.
                           Ah! non, je n'aime pas du tout
                           les fromages forts.
                           Oh! oui, j'adore ça.

Section Sept: Jeux

1.

Elle va acheter un gâteau
à la pâtisserie

2. 1. Fleuriste
   2. Poissonnerie
   3. Boucherie
   4. Marché
   5. Supermarché
   6. Pâtisserie
   7. Crémerie
   8. Boulangerie

3. 1. fraises
   2. bifteck
   3. beurre
   4. tomates
   5. haricots

4.   un verre de Pastis / lait.
       un kilo de sucre / tomates / fromage.
       une douzaine d'oeufs / de fleurs / tomates.
       un bouquet de fleurs.
       un morceau de sucre / beurre/ fromage.
       un paquet de sucre.
       un litre de Pastis / lait.

5.   Elle va acheter du rosbif, des saucisses, un/du bifteck et des côtes d'agneau à la boucherie (chez le boucher).
   Elle va acheter du lait, de la crème fraîche, des oeufs, des yaourts, du beurre et du gruyère à la crèmerie.
   Elle va acheter une baguette à la boulangerie.
   Elle va acheter des pommes, des bananes, une / de la salade, des carottes, des tomates et de l'ail chez le marchand de fruits et légumes.

6. 1. A huit heures il se lève.
   2. A huit heures et demie (huit heures trente) il prend son petit déjeuner.
   3. A dix heures moins vingt il entre chez une fleuriste.
   4. A dix heures moins cinq il sonne chez Jacqueline.
   5. A midi moins le quart (onze heures quarante-cinq) ils sont de retour à la maison.
   6. A midi Philip et Jacqueline prennent l'apéritif.

Acte 4
Section Quatre: Dialogues

a)　Vous:　Je dois téléphoner à mon oncle.
　　　　　Vous avez le téléphone?
　　　　　Non, qu'est-ce que je dois faire?
　　　　　Et pour (Londres)?

b)　Vous:　Je voudrais changer ces chèques de voyages,
　　　　　s'il vous plaît.
　　　　　Quel est le cours de la livre aujourd'hui?
　　　　　Bien merci.
　　　　　Est-ce que vous acceptez les Eurochèques?
　　　　　Bon. Eh bien, voilà les chèques de voyage
　　　　　et un Eurochèque pour mille francs.
　　　　　Oui. Voilà madame.

c)　Vous:　Est-ce que je peux essayer
　　　　　le pantalon gris qui est en vitrine?
　　　　　Oui, c'est ça.
　　　　　Du (quarante-deux)...

d)　Vous:　Qu'est-ce que vous en pensez?
　　　　　Vous croyez?
　　　　　La cravate est un peu claire,
　　　　　vous ne trouvez pas?

e)　Vous:　Oui, j'ai besoin d'un maillot
　　　　　de corps blanc et d'une paire
　　　　　de chaussettes.
　　　　　Du (quarante)...
　　　　　(Noir), s'il vous plaît.

Section Sept:　Jeux

1.

2. a. trois, six, douze, vingt-quatre, quarante-huit, quatre-vingt-seize.
   b. deux, deux, quatre — trois, trois, neuf — quatre, quatre, seize — cinq, cinq, vingt-cinq — six, six, trente-six — sept, sept, quarante-neuf — huit, huit, soixante-quatre — neuf, neuf, quatre-vingt-un — dix, dix, cent.
   c. deux, trois, cinq, neuf, dix-sept, trente-trois, soixante-cinq, cent vingt-neuf.

3.   a. 20 francs: quatre cent sept mille cinq cent vingt-neuf.
      b. 50 francs: six cent vingt-neuf mille trois cent dix-sept.
      c. 100 francs: cent quatre-vingt-dix mille huit cent vingt et un.

4. 1. If you are a woman: C'est ma jupe mais c'est son pantalon.
       If you are a man: C'est sa jupe mais c'est mon pantalon.

   2. If you are a woman: C'est sa chemise mais c'est mon corsage.
       If you are a man: C'est ma chemise mais c'est son corsage.

   3. If you are a woman: C'est ma robe mais c'est son écharpe.
       If you are a man: C'est sa robe mais c'est mon écharpe.

   4. If you are a woman: C'est ses chaussures mais c'est ma montre.
       If you are a man: C'est mes chaussures mais c'est sa montre.

5. 1. Ma ceinture, elle est élégante, vous ne trouvez pas?
   2. Mon pantalon, il est beau, vous ne trouvez pas?
   3. Mes chaussures, elles sont jolies, vous ne trouvez pas?
   4. Ma cravate, elle est formidable, vous ne trouvez pas?
   5. Ma chemise, elle est extraordinaire, vous ne trouvez pas?

6. 1. Cette cravate, elle coûte combien?
   2. Cette centure, elle coûte combien?
   3. Cette chemise, elle coûte combien?
   4. Cette jupe, elle coûte combien?
   5. Ce pantalon, il coûte combien?
   6. Ces chaussures, elles coûtent combien?
   7. Ce slip, il coûte combien?
   8. Ces chaussettes, elles coûtent combien?

7.   Madame Dupont passe l'aspirateur.
      Monsieur Lachaise répond au téléphone.
      Monsieur Blanc ouvre sa valise.
      Madame Blanc prend son petit déjeuner au lit.
      Madame Sauge met ses chaussures.
      Mademoiselle Lenoir prend un bain.
      Nicolas Lenoir dort.
      Monsieur Lenoir se rase.
      Monsieur et Madame Roux finissent de manger.
      Madame Lebrun se lave les cheveux.

Acte 5
Section Quatre: Dialogues

a)   Vous: Qu'est-ce que vous aimez faire
de votre temps libre?
Moi, je préfère la musique de jazz
et la peinture moderne.
Aimez-vous le cinéma?
Moi aussi.
Vous aimez les films de Hitchcock?

b)   Vous: Etes-vous libre ce soir?
Voulez-vous aller au théâtre
ou au concert?
Alors, allons au cinéma.
Qu'est-ce qu'on joue dans le quartier?
D'accord et après je vous invite
à dîner au restaurant.

c)   Vous: Il faut montrer les billets.
Il faut donner un pourboire.
Oui, c'est normal.
Il faut donner deux francs.

d)   Vous: Je vais prendre du pâté de canard.
Une entrecôte.
(Bien cuite), s'il vous plaît.
Je vais prendre des frites.

e)   Vous: Du vin.
Vous avez du Beaujolais?
Eh bien, apportez-nous une bouteille
de Côtes du Rhône et une carafe d'eau.
Si, donnez-nous deux Martinis.

Section Sept: Jeux

1.

2.a.

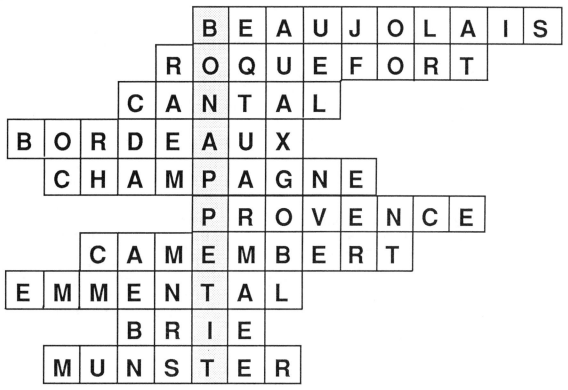

2. b. Jamais de fromage sans pain.
   et Jamais de fromage sans vin.

3. a.
   1. 1 bonne cuillerée à soupe d'huile.
   2. 1/4 de litre de lait
   3. 2 grosses cuillerées à soupe de farine
   4. sel, poivre
   5. 75g de gruyère râpé
   6. une pincée (de noix) de muscade
   7. 3 oeufs
   8. un peu de beurre.

   1. une casserole
   2. une cuillère à soupe
   3. un bol
   4. une fourchette
   5. un moule à soufflé

3. b. Il faut faire une béchamel épaisse.
   Il faut saler et poivrer légèrement et ajouter 75g de gruyère râpé, une pincée de muscade et les 3 jaunes d'oeufs.
   Il faut battre les blancs en neige puis les incorporer délicatement.
   Il faut verser le tout dans un moule à soufflé bien beurré et
   il faut le mettre à four moyen pendant une bonne demi-heure.
   Il ne faut jamais ouvrir la porte du four pendant les vingt premières minutes de cuisson.

4.   You would ask the waitress:

Qu'est-ce qu'il y a comme légumes/fromage/etc?
or Qu'est-ce que vous avez comme légumes/etc?

5. 1. **Allons voir 'Prends l'oseille et tire-toi' au Reflet Logos.**
   2. **Allons voir 'Les quatre cents coups' au République Cinémas.**
   3. **Allons voir 'Le roi et l'oiseau' à la Boîte à Films.**
   4. **Allons voir 'Querelle' au Grand Pavois**
   5. **Allons voir 'Qu'est-il arrivé à Baby Jane?' au Saint Ambroise.**
   6. **Allons voir 'Sérénade à trois' à Action Christine.**

6 | Ten | Jack

	Ten	Jack
2	**Un ami donne le film à Philip.**	**Un ami offre le film à Philip.**
3	**Le serveur donne l'entrecôte à J.**	**Le serveur offre l'entrecôte à J.**
4	**Le serveur donne le vin à J.**	**Le serveur offre le vin à J.**
5	**Philip donne les fleurs à J.**	**Philip offre les fleurs à J.**
6	**La serveuse donne le pâté de canard à J.**	**La serveuse offre le pâté de canard à J.**
7	**Philip donne le paquet à J.**	**Philip offre le paquet à J.**
7	**J. donne le paquet à Philip.**	**J. offre le paquet à Philip**

Queen

2	**Un ami recommande le film à Philip.**
3	**Le serveur recommande l'entrecôte à J.**
4	**Le serveur recommande le vin à Philip.**
5	**Philip recommande les fleurs à J.**
6	**La serveuse recommande le pâté de canard à Philip.**
7	**Philip recommande le paquet à J.**
7	**J. recommande le paquet à Philip.**

	Ten	Jack
2	**Un ami le donne à Philip.**	**Un ami offre le film à Philip.**
3	**Le serveur le donne à J.**	**Le serveur l'offre à J. (l'=le)**
4	**Le serveur le donne à J.**	**Le serveur l'offre à J.**
5	**Philip les donne à J.**	**Philip les offre à J.**
6	**La serveuse le donne à J.**	**La serveuse l'offre à J.**
7	**Philip le donne à J.**	**Philip l'offre à J.**
7	**J. le donne à Philip.**	**J. l'offre à Philip.**

Queen

2	**Un ami le recommande à Philip.**
3	**Le serveur le recommande à J.**
4	**Le serveur le recommande à Philip.**
5	**Philip les recommande à J.**
6	**La serveuse le recommande à Philip.**
7	**Philip le recommande à J.**
7	**J. le recommande à Philip.**

	Ten	Jack
2	**Un ami lui donne le film.**	**Un ami lui offre le film.**
3	**Le serveur lui donne l'entrecôte.**	**Le serveur lui offre l'entrecôte.**
4	**Le serveur lui donne le vin.**	**Le serveur lui offre le vin.**
5	**Philip lui donne les fleurs.**	**Philip lui offre les fleurs.**
6	**La serveuse lui donne le pâté de c.**	**La serveuse lui offre le pâté de c.**
7	**Philip lui donne le paquet.**	**Philip lui offre le paquet**
7.	**J. lui donne le paquet.**	**J. lui offre le paquet.**

Queen

2   Un ami lui recommande le film.
3   Le serveur lui recommande l'entrecôte.
4   Le serveur lui recommande le vin.
5   Philip lui recommande les fleurs.
6   La serveuse lui recommande le pâté de c.
7   Philip lui recommande le paquet.
7   J. lui recommande le paquet.

Ten   Jack

2   Un ami le lui donne.   Un ami le lui offre.
3   Le serveur le lui donne.   Le serveur le lui offre.
4   Le serveur le lui donne.   Le serveur le lui offre.
5   Philip les lui donne.   Philip les lui offre.
6   La serveuse le lui donne.   La serveuse le lui offre.
7   Philip le lui donne.   Philip le lui offre.
8   J. le lui donne.   J. le lui offre.

Queen

2   Un ami le lui recommande.
3   Le serveur le lui recommande.
4   Le serveur le lui recommande.
5   Philip les lui recommande.
6   La serveuse le lui recommande.
7   Philip le lui recommande.
7   J. le lui recommande.

BONUS

1.   J'ai grand appétit! (G grand, a petit)

Acte 6
Section Quatre: Dialogues

a)   **Vous:**   **Oui, avec plaisir.**
            Non, je suis désolé(e).
            je ne bois pas de café le soir.
            Si, volontiers.

b)   **Vous:**   **Qu'est-ce que vous faites dans la vie?**
            Vous travaillez avec votre père?
            Et votre oncle, que fait-il exactement?

c)   **Vous:**   **Vous avez toujours vécu à Paris?**
            Alors, quand est-ce que vous
            êtes, venue à Paris?
            Quel âge aviez-vous?
            Vous êtes fille unique?

d)   **Vous:**   **J'ai une soeur aînée**
            et un frère cadet.
            Ma soeur est mariée
            mais mon frère est célibataire.
            Ma soeur a six enfants:
            quatre filles et deux garçons.

e)   **Vous:**   **Bonjour madame,**
            vous avez quelque chose
            contre le mal de tête?
            Oui, je veux bien mais
            j'ai aussi mal au ventre.
            Non.
            Non, je ne crois pas.
            J'ai mangé au restaurant
            hier soir et j'ai bu un peu
            trop de cognac.

Section Sept: Jeux

1.   Moving House

The Kitchen

Put: The table in the middle of the room.
      The four chairs around the table.
      The 'fridge in the corner to the right of the window.
      The cooker to the left of the window.
      The washing machine in the corner opposite the 'fridge.

The Living Room

Put: The sofa against the wall by the window.
      An armchair to the left and right of the sofa.
      The coffee table by the wall to the right of the door.
      The television on the coffee table.
      The bookcase against the wall to the right of the window.
      The stereo unit on the bookcase.

The Bedroom

Put: The headboard against the wall to the left of the window.
      The bedside table at the top of the bed, on the window side.
      The light on the bedside table.
      The wardrobe against the wall at the foot of the bed.

2. 1. J'ai mal au cou.
   2. J'ai mal au genou.
   3. J'ai mal au dos.
   4. J'ai mal à l'oreille.
   5. J'ai mal au bras.
   6. J'ai mal à la main.

3. a.
   1. Paul
   2. Danièle
   3. Véronique
   4. Danièle ou Richard
   5. Bruno ou Fabrice ou Véronique
   6. Jean ou Yvonne
   7. Marie ou Paul
   8. Jean ou Yvonne

3. b.
   1. le frère
   2. le grand-père
   3. la soeur
   4. la nièce
   5. les petits-fils
   6. la cousine
   7. la grand-mère
   8. la tante

3. c.

	Vrai	Faux
1.	X	
2.		X
3.	X	
4.		X
5.	X	
6.	X	

4 Le matin, j'ai pris mon petit déjeuner
à l'hôtel et j'ai parlé à la
serveuse et à la patronne.
J'ai donné un bouquet de fleurs à Jacqueline
puis nous sommes allés faire des courses.
L'après-midi, j'ai téléphoné à mes parents,
changé de l'argent et acheté des
vêtements.
Le soir, Jacqueline et moi sommes allés
au cinéma puis nous avons mangé
'Chez Tante Marie'.
Après le repas, nous sommes rentrés
rue Madame.
Chez Jacqueline, j'ai bu un peu
trop de cognac et nous avons beaucoup parlé.

5. 1 et e)
  2 et c)
  3 et a)
  4 et b)
  5 et d)
  6 et f)

BONUS

1. Sa mère (son oncle est le frère de sa mère).

2. C'est mon fils.

3. — Suzanne s'est mariée à 25 ans.
  — Suzanne avait 30 ans à la naissance des jumelles.
  — Les jumelles avaient deux ans à la mort de leur père.

4. Il y a trois personnes: une grand-mère, sa fille et sa petite-fille.

5. Jim Nastic.

Acte 7
Section Deux : Prononciation et Intonation

c)

	u	ou
1	✔ dessus	dessous
2	rue	✔ roue
3	sais-tu?	✔ c'est tout
4	✔ but	bout
5	tu sais	✔ toussez
6	✔ vu	vous
7	✔ cure	cour
8	sûr	✔ sourd

Acte 7
Section Quatre: Dialogues

a) **Vous:** Est-ce qu'il y a une station de
métro près d'ici?
C'est de quel côté?
Et après?

b) **Vous:** Pour aller au Louvre,
qu'est-ce que je dois faire?
Est-ce que je dois changer?
Où est-ce que je descends?
Bon, merci. Je crois que j'ai compris.

c) **Vous:** Pardon madame,
pour aller au Pont Neuf, s'il vous plaît?
Alors, je vais tout droit
et je passe sous l'horloge. Et puis?
Et quand j'arrive aux quais
je tourne à gauche ou à droite?
Et le Pont Neuf, c'est loin?
Merci bien.

d) **Vous:** Qu'est-ce qu'il est grand!
Oui. Quelle merveille!
Oui, comme elle est belle!
Oui, superbe et mystérieux.

e) **Vous:** Si on se promenait un peu?
On peut aller s'asseoir
dans le parc.
Eh bien, si on y allait demain?
Si on faisait un pique-nique?

Section Sept: Jeux

1. 2. **Oui, c'est direct. Direction Pont de Neuilly.**
   3. **Direction Nation. Il y a trois stations.**
   4. **A La Motte-Piquet.**
   5. **Direction Créteil-Préfecture — changer à Concorde.**
      Direction Château de Vincennes — changer à Hôtel de Ville.
      Direction Mairie des Lilas — descendre à Rambuteau.

   illustr.

2. 1. **à la poste?**
   2. **à l'Hôtel de France?**
   3. **au restaurant de l'Horloge?**
   4. **au commissariat de police?**
   5. **à l'église?**
   6. **au bureau de tabac?**

3.

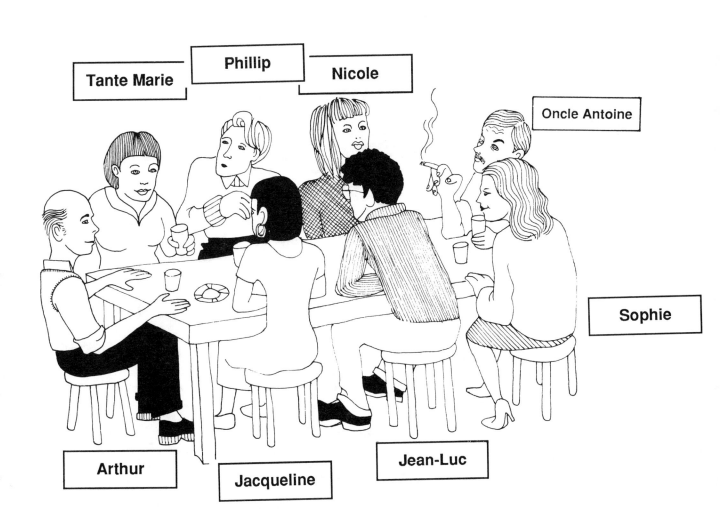

Tante Marie   Phillip   Nicole   Oncle Antoine   Sophie   Arthur   Jacqueline   Jean-Luc

347

4. **LUNDI:**   elle vient de prendre un bain.
    MARDI: elle est en train de faire des courses.
    MERCREDI: elle va téléphoner à une amie.
    JEUDI: elle vient de préparer un gâteau.
    VENDREDI: elle est en train d'écrire une lettre.
    SAMEDI: elle va partir en weekend.
    DIMANCHE: elle vient de finir son petit déjeuner.

5.   Here is what you might have said:

5. 1. **Qu'est-ce qu'il est magnifique/beau!**
   2. **Qu'est-ce qu'il est impressionnant/moche!**
   3. **Qu'est-ce qu'elle est belle/magnifique!**
   4. **Qu'est-ce qu'elle est grande/vieille!**
   5. **Qu'est-ce qu'il est beau!**

6. 1. **Un chat**
   2. **Un cheval**
   3. **Une vache**
   4. **Un serpent**
   5. **Une poule**
   6. **Un lapin**
   7. **Un chien**
   8. **Une souris**
   9. **Un mouton**
   10. **Une girafe.**

BONUS

3. 1. **derrière**
   2. **sur**
   3. **dans**
   4. **sous**
   5. **devant**

Acte 8
Section Deux : Prononciation et Intonation

d) Spot the difference between **an** and **on**

	an	on
1	Menton	✔ Montons
2	✔ content	comptons
3	✔ en été	on était
4	✔ lent	long
5	sans	✔ son
6	temps	✔ ton

e) Spot the difference between **an** and **in**

	an	in
1	cousant	✔ cousin
2	✔ m'attend	matin
3	✔ débutant	des butins
4	en été	✔ un été
5	vent	✔ vin
6	✔ l'emporter	l'importer

Acte 8
Section Quatre: Dialogues

a)   Vous: J'aimerais bien, mais...
Si, je sais conduire
mais je ne connais pas la route.
J'ai mon permis de conduire depuis deux ans.
Non, mais je ne saurai pas sortir de Paris.

b)   Vous: Vous ne m'avez pas dit où nous allons.
C'est loin?
Donnez-moi quelques indications.
Si vous m'aidiez un petit peu,
ça serait plus facile.
Ah! j'y suis — c'est Fontainebleau.

c)   Vous: Je joue au tennis/je fais du jogging.
Et vous? Vous êtes sportive?
Vous faites du jogging?
Eh bien, si on faisait une partie
de tennis cet après-midi?

d)   Vous: Bonjour Henri.
Je te présente Philip West,
un ami anglais.
Philip, je vous présente Henri,
mon cousin.

e)   Vous: Eh bien, parlez-moi un peu de vous.
Vous êtes d'où?
Que faites-vous dans la vie?
Que voudriez-vous faire plus tard?

Section Sept: Jeux

1. 1. à l'ouest.
    2. au sud.
    3. au nord.
    4. à l'est.
    5. au sud-est.
    6. au nord-ouest.
    7. au nord-est.
    8. au sud-ouest.

2.

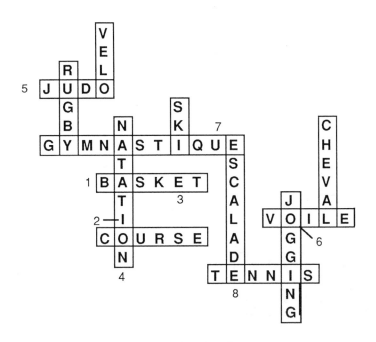

Hidden expression: **Bien joué.**

3. 1. **Mai**
   2. **Eté**
   3. **Mars**
   4. **Juillet**
   5. **Automne**
   6. **Septembre**
   7. **Février**
   8. **Printemps**
   9. **Avril**
   10. **Août**
   11. **Janvier**
   12. **Hiver.**

   Le printemps commence le 20 mars.
   L'été commence le 21 juin.
   L'automne commence le 23 septembre.
   L'hiver commence le 21 décembre.
   La Fête Nationale est le 14 juillet.
   Easter = **Pâques** et Whitsun = **Pentecôte.**

4.

```
 1 E F F E C T I V E M E N T
   2 P A R T O U T
   3   I C I
 4 J A M A I S
   5 T E L L E M E N T
 6 M A I N T E N A N T
 7 L E N T E M E N T
   8 S O U V E N T
   9 T A N T
  10 T O U J O U R S
```

The opposite of **lentement** is **rapidement**.

5.

1	2	3	4	5	6	7	8
H	G	B	F	E	C	A	D

6. 1. c)
   2. h)
   3. e)
   4. i)
   5. f)
   6. g)
   7. b)
   8. d)
   9. j)
   10. a)

Acte 9
Section Deux: Prononciation et Intonation

c)   J(e) te donn(e) pour ta fêt(e)
     Un grand chapeau d(e) paill(e)
     Pour t(e) mettr(e) sur la têt(e),
     Un p(e)tit éventail
     Pour l(e) tenir à la main;
     Un(e) rob(e) en mouss(e)line
     Tout(e) ornée d(e) satin,
     Un(e) écharp(e) en hermin(e)
     Et des chaussur(es) blanch(es);
     Ne les mets que l(e) dimanch(e).

Section Quatre: Dialogues

a)   **Vous:**   **On pourrait se tutoyer, n'est-ce pas?**
                 Si on se disait <u>tu</u> nous aussi?

b)   **Vous:**   **Allez, au revoir et merci.**
                 Je te téléphonerai.

c)   **Vous:**   **Faites le plein, s'il vous plaît.**
                 Non, merci. Ça va.
                 Je vous dois combien?
                 Voilà.

d)   **Vous:**   **Fais attention, il y a du brouillard.**
                 Ne roule pas si vite.
                 Il n'y a pas de limite de vitesse
                 sur l'autoroute?
                 Tu sais que tu fais du 180?
                 Tu ferais bien de ralentir,
                 sinon tu vas avoir une amende.

e)   **Vous:**   **Qu'est-ce qui s'est passé?**
                 C'est grave?
                 Est-ce qu'il y a des blessés?

Section Sept: Jeux

1. 1. **Elle chante en prenant sa douche.**
   or **Elle prend sa douche en chantant.**

2.   **Elle lit en faisant la cuisine.**
   or **Elle fait la cuisine en lisant.**

3.   **Elle téléphone en buvant son café.**
   or **Elle boit son café en téléphonant.**

4.   **Elle conduit en écoutant de la musique.**
   or **Elle écoute de la musique en conduisant.**

5.   **Elle apprend l'anglais en dormant.**
   or **Elle dort en apprenant l'anglais.** (which is not quite the same thing!)

2. 1. Quand Jacqueline m'offrira l'apéritif, je prendrai un Pastis.
   2. Quand j'irai au cinéma, je donnerai un pourboire à l'ouvreuse.
   3. Quand j'aurai mal à la tête, je prendrai de l'aspirine.
   4. Quand j'irai au Louvre, je regarderai la Joconde.
   5. Quand nous irons à Fontainebleau, nous ferons un pique-nique.
   6. Quand l'oncle Anatole reviendra du Portugal, je lui donnerai le paquet.

3. i   Il se réveille.
   ii Il se lève.
   iii Il se lave.
   iv Il se rase.

3. a. A quelle heure est-ce que vous vous réveillez?
   b. Je me réveille à sept heures et demie.
   c. Levez-vous.
   d. Lève-toi.
   e. Ne te rase pas.

4. 1. Quel âge as-tu?
   2. Je vous téléphonerai ce soir.
   3. Comment vas-tu?
   4. Tu veux jouer au tennis demain?
   5. Pouvez-vous m'apporter l'addition, s'il vous plaît?
   6. Dépêche-toi.
   7. Vous aimez Paris?
   8. Est-ce que je peux vous aider?
   9. Vous savez que vous faites du 180?
   10. Ne t'inquiète pas.

BONUS

1. Quand ils se recontreront, les deux trains seront forcément à la même distance de Paris!

Acte 10
Section Quatre: Dialogues

a) **Vous:** Je regrette de vous avoir fait attendre.
J'ai été retardé à Londres.
Alors, vous ne m'en voulez pas trop?

b) **Vous:** Pardon? Chez qui?
Je n'ai pas compris.
Oui, voilà.
Simenon? Vous pouvez épeler,
s'il vous plaît?
Pouvez-vous parler moins vite,
s'il vous plaît?
Rousseau. Ça s'écrit R O U S S E A U,
n'est-ce pas?

c) **Vous:** Je viens chercher mon billet d'avion.
C'est un aller retour Paris-Genève.
Monsieur/Madame ....
A quelle heure est-ce qu'on arrive à Genève?
Et mon vol de retour, à quelle heure est-il?

d) **Vous:** Comment est-ce qu'on se rend à l'aéroport?
Quand est-ce qu'il y en a?
Combien de temps faut-il pour
aller d'ici à l'aéroport?
Lequel est-ce que je devrais
prendre à votre avis?
Ce n'est pas trop tôt?
Bien, merci beaucoup.

e) **Vous:** C'est combien pour envoyer une carte postale en Angleterre?
Vous pouvez me donner quatre timbres
à 2 francs 50, s'il vous plaît?
Est-ce qu'il y a une poste dans le quartier?
Merci beaucoup.

Section Sept: Jeux

2. Richard est jeune, il a moins de 30 ans. Il est grand et fort. Il est marié et porte des vêtements clairs. Il est gai et rit souvent. Il habite en ville et mène une vie très active. Il adore lire mais regarde peu la télévision.

3.

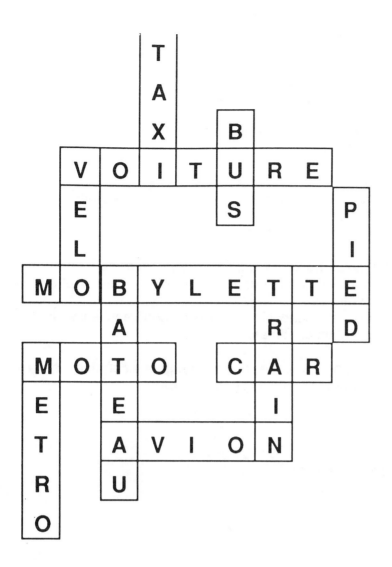

4. 1. In the morning:

   a. **vers huit heures trente or huit heures et demie.**
   b. **vers neuf heures quinze or neuf heures et quart.**
   c. **vers dix heures quarante-cinq or onze heures moins le quart.**
   d. **vers midi.**

4. 2. In the evening:

   a. **vers dix-neuf heures trente.**
   b. **vers vingt heures quinze.**
   c. **vers vingt et une heures quarante-cinq.**
   d. **minuit.**

5. 1. Le voyageur: Je voudrais un billet pour Châlons-sur-Marne.
 2. L'employé: Un aller simple?
 3. Le voyageur: Non, un aller-retour.
 4. L'employé: En quelle classe?
 5. Le voyageur: En seconde. Ça fait combien?
 6. L'employé: 37F.
 7. Le voyageur: A quelle heure est le prochain train?
 8. L'employé: A 12h.50.
 9. Le voyageur: Et le suivant?
 10. L'employé: Vous en avez un qui part à 16h.42.
 11. Le voyageur: A quelle heure est-ce qu'il arrive à Châlons?
 12. L'employé: A 17h.24.
 13. Le voyageur: Merci bien, monsieur.

6. a. Quatre timbres à deux francs soixante et six timbres à un franc quatre-vingts.

 b. 4 x 2f60 = huit à un franc, quatre à cinquante centimes et quatre à dix centimes.

  6 x 1f80 = six à un franc, six à cinquante centimes, six à vingt centimes et six à dix centimes.

  Total = quatorze à un franc, dix à cinquante centimes, six à vingt centimes et dix à dix centimes.

BONUS

1. An eye for an eye, a tooth for a tooth.

2. 1. Jean
 2. Paul
 3. Pierre
 4. Lucien
 5. Léon
 6. Marc

4. C'est le général de Gaulle.

5. Le mot oeil. Et oui, le cyclope n'avait qu'un oeil.

Acte 11
Section Quatre: Dialogues

a) **Vous:** **Je n'ai que ce porte-documents.**
Non-fumeur.
Merci bien.
A quelle heure est-ce qu'on monte
dans l'avion?

b) **Vous:** **Je vous en prie.**
Non, vous pouvez si vous voulez.
Non, ça m'est absolument égal.
Allez-y.

c) **Vous:** **Pardon mademoiselle,**
est-ce que je peux me mettre-là?
Est-ce qu'il est permis de fumer ici?
Bon, tant pis, mais j'ai le droit
de boire tout de même?

d) **Vous:** **Vous devez rester combien de temps à Londres?**
Vous êtes vraiment obligée de
repartir ce soir?
Alors, vous pouvez bien rester
jusqu'à demain?

e) **Vous:** **Oui, je n'ai que ce porte-documents.**
Non, rien.
Il n'y a que deux petits paquets.
Les voilà.
Est-ce que c'est absolument nécessaire?
Je suis déjà en retard.

Section Sept: Jeux

1. 1. No parking please — Exit used by cars.
   2. No pedestrians.
   3. End of controlled parking zone.
   4. Passengers with tickets.
   5. Don't forget to validate your ticket.
   6. Waiting room
   7. A vacant seat; an occupied seat.

2.

chère tante Marie,
  Nous passons d'excellentes vacances sur la Côte d'Azur. Aujourd 'hui il fait très beau et cet après-midi nous sommes sur la plage. Il y a 3 jours nous avons fait une belle promenade en bateau. Avant-hier Arthur a attrapé un bon coup de soleil et il a encore le nez tout rouge !
Après-demain nous irons visiter le musée Picasso à Antibes. La fin des vacances approche et c'est bien triste. La semaine prochaine nous serons de retour à Paris et nous viendrons te dire un petit bonjour. Nous t'embrassons très affectueusement. A bientôt.
       Julie + Arthur.

Madame Coquelicot

12 RUE DES CHAMPS

75008 PARIS

3. 1. **Oui, c'est elle qui fait les courses.**
  2. **C'est toi qui apportes le vin.**
  3. **C'est lui qui apporte le pain.**
  4. **C'est moi qui fais la cuisine.**
  5. **C'est vous qui faites la vaisselle.**

BONUS

1.   **Il le remercie parce qu'il lui a sauvé la vie mais il le renvoie parce qu'un veilleur de nuit ne doit pas dormir au travail.**

2. 1. **Les voyages forment la jeunesse.**
    (Travel educates the young)
  2. **Tous les chemins mènent à Rome.**
    (All roads lead to Rome)

Acte 12
Section Deux: Prononciation et Intonation

a)

I.	72	I2	32	93	soixante-douze/douze/trente-deux/quatre-vingt-treize
2.	80	I3	43	74	quatre-vingts/treize/quarante-trois/soixante-quatorze
3.	60	I4	54	95	soixante/quatorze/cinquante-quatre/quatre-vingt-quinze
4.	80	I5	65	76	quatre-vingts/quinze/soixante-cinq/soixante-seize
5.	60	I6	76	97	soixante/seize/soixante-seize/quatre-vingt-dix-sept
6.	80	I7	87	98	quatre-vingts/dix-sept/quatre-vingt-sept/quatre-vingt-dix-huit

b)

I.	77	67	80	I5	60	I7	67	95
2.	60	I8	I6	93	78	I6	80	I3
3.	6I	04	2I	30	7I	04	2I	30
4.	80	I6	I2	74	96	I2	60	I4
5.	90	II	80	I2	80	I0	II	92
6.	75	99	60	I3	60	I5	99	73

c)

1. Lundi 2 I avril I 9 8 6 Philip est arrivé à Paris. Il est allé au
   7 2 rue Madame puis à l'hôtel d'Angleterre au 9 6 rue Bonaparte.

2. Mardi il a changé 7 5 livres en chèques de voyage et un Eurochèque
   pour I 0 0 0 F. Au total, le caissier lui a donné I 8 3 2 F. 5 0 et il a
   pu s'acheter pour 2 0 I F. de vêtements.

3. Mardi soir à I 8 h I 5 il est allé au cinéma avec Jacqueline. Un
   peu plus tard, elle a parlé du Vietnam où elle est née en I 9 6 0 et
   de son arrivée à Paris en I 9 6 5.

4. Mercredi: Philip avait rendez-vous avec Jacqueline au Pont Neuf à
   I 7 h 3 0 et il a remarqué la statue d'Henri IV assassiné en I 6 I 0.

5. Jeudi: il a visité Fontainebleau et rencontré Henri. Au retour,
   Jacqueline a fait du I 8 0 sur l'autoroute!

6. Vendredi: il a enfin rencontré l'Oncle Anatole à I 0 h 3 0.
   Quel personnage impressionnant — I m 9 0 et I I 0 kilos!

7. Samedi: il a pris le Vol Air France I 2 5 à I I h et est arrivé
   à Genève 6 5 minutes plus tard. Il a essayé sans succès de téléphoner
   à Jacqueline au 4 3 — 7 7 — 6 9 — 9 9.   A I 8 h 2 0 il a sablé le
   champagne et est devenu un associé de la Maison Dubois fondée en
   I 9 5 6.
   QUELLE SEMAINE EXTRAORDINAIRE!

Section Quatre: Dialogues

a) **Vous:**   Rue de Rennes.
120.
Non, pas du tout.
Je suis de (Londres).
Merci, je vous dois combien?
Tenez, voilà 40 francs -
gardez la monnaie.

b) **Vous:**   Maître Simenon s'il vous plaît?
Bonjour Maître.
Je suis Monsieur/Madame ....
Je viens de la part de Monsieur Dubois.
Merci bien.
Très bon, merci.
Très bien. Il vous donne le bonjour.

c) **Vous:**   Qu'est-ce que vous dites?
Je n'en reviens pas.
Ça alors! Je rêve ou quoi?
Ce n'est pas croyable.

d) **Vous**   Je voudrais téléphoner à Paris,
s'il vous plaît.
C'est le 41, 23, 93, 89.
Oui, c'est ça.
Merci bien.

e) **Vous**   Allô? Je suis bien chez Monsieur Dubois?
Je voudrais parler à Jacqueline,
s'il vous plaît
Monsieur/Madame...
Non, ça ne fait rien,
je rappellerai plus tard.

Section Sept: Jeux

1. 1. est plus vieille (plus âgée) que
   2. est moins jolie (moins belle) que
   3. est moins grand que Paris. (or plus petit).
   4. est plus rapide que
   5. est moins haut que
   6. est moins chère que
   7. est plus drôle qu'
   8. est moins bon que

2. a.
1. Le plus grand port de pêche de France est Boulogne.
2. Le pont le plus long de France se trouve à Tancarville en Normandie.
3. La plus petite place de Paris est la Place Furstenberg près du Boulevard St. Germain.
4. L'homme le plus riche du monde était Paul Getty, un Américain.
5. Le mois le plus court de l'année est février avec 28 jours.
6. La plus belle femme du monde est la Joconde.
7. Le monument le plus ancien de Paris est l'Obélisque qui se trouve au milieu de la Place de la Concorde.
8. Le groupe 'pop' le plus célèbre du monde s'appelait, Les Beatles.
9. Le monument le plus haut de Paris est la Tour Eiffel qui mesure 320 mètres.
10. Le meilleur joueur de football était Diego Maradonna, l'Argentin.

2. b.
1. L'Amazone est le fleuve le plus long du monde.
2. Le Groenland est l'île la plus grande du monde.
3. La Rolls Royce est la voiture la plus prestigieuse du monde.
4. La Chine est le pays le plus peuplé du monde.
5. Le 21 décembre est le jour le plus court de l'année.

3.
TOUT	(télévision, oiseau, un, train)
EST	(escargot, souris, théière)
BIEN	(bouteille, Italie, eau, nuages)
QUI	(quinze, usine, immeuble)
FINIT	(France, igloo, Nord, île, treize)
BIEN	(bateau, idée, Espagne, nez)

4.   Le Jeu de L'Oie

4. 2. J'ai rendez-vous avec Monsieur Dubois.
3. Vous avez une chambre avec douche pour deux nuits?
4. Je voudrais un chocolat, du pain, du beurre et de la confiture.
6. <u>Le pont:</u>

je vais	nous allons
tu vas	vous allez
il va	ils vont

7. Je ne parle pas chinois.
8. Il fait du soleil.
10. Je voudrais un bouquet de roses rouges.
11. Est-ce que je suis en retard?
12. Je préfère faire mes courses au marché.
15. Donnez-moi une livre de beurre et une douzaine d'oeufs.
16. Camembert, brie, gruyère.
17. A votre santé!
19. <u>Le café:</u>

je viens	nous venons
tu viens	vous venez
il vient	ils viennent

OIE SERVEUSE

20. To pay cash.
21. Deux mille quatre cent soixante-neuf francs.
22. Je dois aller à la banque cet après-midi.
24. Est-ce que je peux essayer ce pantalon gris foncé?
25. Ces chaussures sont trop chères.
26. Est-ce que je peux utiliser votre téléphone, s'il vous plaît?
28. Qu'est-ce qu'on joue au cinéma?
29. Je déteste les films à suspense.
30. J'adore les dessins animés.

31. **Le puits:**   bon   bonne
                     gentil   gentille
                     frais   fraîche
                     beau   belle
                     nouveau   nouvelle
                     vieux   vieille
33. **L'addition, s'il vous plaît.**
34. **Le service est compris?**
35. **Apportez-moi (Donnez-moi) .une bouteille de Champagne.**
37. **Ma mère a pris sa retraite il y a deux ans.**
38. **Une soeur aînée.**
39. **Je ne me sens pas bien.**
40. **J'ai mal aux pieds.**
42. **Le labyrinthe:** vécu; venu; vu; eu; été.

                     j'ai vécu
                     je suis venu(e)
                     j'ai vu
                     j'ai eu
                     j'ai été
43. **As-tu envie d'aller au Moulin Rouge?**
44. **La Joconde.**
46. **En hiver.**
47. **Si on se promenait le long de la Seine?**
48. **Vous attendez depuis longtemps?**
49. **Je viens de faire une partie de tennis.**
51. **Pour aller au Pont Neuf, s'il vous plaît?**
52. **La prison:**   je ferai   nous ferons
                     tu feras   vous ferez
                     il fera   ils feront

                     j'aimerais   nous aimerions
                     tu aimerais   vous aimeriez
                     il aimerait   ils aimeraient

53. **Un aller-retour Genève, s'il vous plaît.**
55. **Savez-vous conduire?**
56. **Ne conduis pas trop vite sur l'autoroute.**
57. **End of controlled parking zone.**
58. **La mort:**   je me promène   nous nous promenons
                   tu te promènes   vous vous promenez
                   il se promène   ils se promènent

                   je me suis promené(e)   nous nous sommes promené(e)s
                   tu t'es promené(e)   vous vous êtes promené(e)s
                   il/elle s'est promené(e) ils/elles se sont promené(e)s.
60. **Enchanté(e) de faire votre connaissance.**
61. **Je n'en reviens pas**
  or **Ce n'est pas croyable.**
62. **Il faut que je sois à l'Hôtel des Alpes à 18 heures.**

BONUS

2. 1. **C'est Arthur.**
   2. **C'est Pierre.**

Foreword to the Glossary

In all cases throughout this glossary we have used and referred to the words and their translation within the context of this course. For additional information and/or different meanings for some of them, please refer to a dictionary.

With the adjectives we have given the feminine version abbreviated after the masculine version:

| e.g. | **jovial/e** | jolly | **joviale** | feminine adjective |
| | **merveilleux/se** | wonderful | **merveilleuse** | feminine adjective |

Abbreviations used:

(comp.)	=	comparison
(dir)	=	direction
(f)	=	feminine
(m)	=	masculine
(pl.)	=	plural
(o.s.)	=	oneself
(poss. pron)	=	possesive pronoun
(qn.) = **quelqu'un**	(s.o.)	= someone
(qch.) = **quelque chose**	(s.th)	= something

Note: Capital letters in French do not usually have an accent; so when you read the Grammar headings and explanations – **ETRE** e.g. — you should be aware that normally it is **être**.

FRENCH – ENGLISH
GLOSSARY

A

à in, at, to
à bientôt see you soon
abricot (m) apricot
absence (f) absence
absolument absolutely
accent circonflexe (m) circumflex accent
accepter to accept
accident (m) accident
accompagner to accompany
acheter to buy
à cause de because of
à côté next to, beside
actif/ve busy, active
action (f) share
adieu good-bye
addition (f) bill
additionner to add up
admiration (f) admiration
admirer to admire
adorer to love, like
aérogare (f) terminal
aéroport (m) airport
affaire (f) bargain
affaires (f) (pl) business
affectueusement fondly
affreux/se awful, dreadful
âge (m) age
âgé/e old

agence (f) agency, office
agent de police (m) policeman
s'agir (de) to concern, be the matter
agneau (m) lamb
agréable nice, pleasant
aider to help
ail (m) garlic
aile (f) wing
aimer to like, love
aîné/e elder, eldest
air (m) appearance
ajouter to add
à l'aide de with the help of
à la maison at home
à la mode de in a ... way, manner
alcoolisé/e alcoholic
allée (f) path
Allemagne (f) Germany
allemand/e German
aller to go, walk
s'en aller to go away, leave
aller bien to suit
aller (m) single ticket
aller-retour (m) return
allô hello (telephone)
s'allonger to lie down
allumer to switch on, light
allure (f) walk
alors so, then, well
ambulance (f) ambulance
aménagé/e installed

amende (f)   fine
amener   to bring, lead
américain/e   American
ami/e   friend
amusant/e   amusing
amuser   to amuse
an (m)année (f)   year
ananas (m)   pineapple
ancien/ne   old
âne (m)   ass, donkey
anglais/e   English
Angleterre (f)   England
animal (m)   animal
anis (m)   aniseed
annoncer   to announce, inform
à peine   scarcely
apercevoir   to notice, realise, perceive
apéritif (m)   aperitif
à pied   on foot, walking
appareil (m)   apparatus, appliance
appartenir à   to belong to
appeler   to call (for, in, up)
s'appeler   to be called, named
apporter   to bring
apprécier   to appreciate
s'approcher   to approach, go up to
après   afterwards, then
après-demain   day after tomorrow
après-midi (m & f)   afternoon
après tout   after all
arbre (m)   tree
arc (de cercle) (m)   curve
argent (m)   money
armoire (f)   wardrobe
s'arrêter   to stop
arriver   to arrive, come
art (m)   art
à seaux   buckets (rain)
ascenseur (m)   lift
aspirateur (m)   hoover, vacuum-cleaner
aspirine (f)   aspirin
assassiner   to assassinate, murder
s'asseoir   to sit down
assez   enough, rather, fairly
assiette (f)   plate
associé/e (m & f)   partner
assurer   to assure
attacher   to fix, attach
attention (f)   (pay) attention, care
attendre   to wait, expect
atterrir   to land
attraper   to catch
à travers   across, through
au   at, about
au bord de   by
au bout de   at the end of, after
aucun/e   anyone, any
au fait   by the way
aujourd'hui   today
au moins   at least
au ralenti   slowly, in slow motion
au revoir   good-bye
aussi   also
au sujet de qch.   about s.th., concerning
autobus (m)   bus
automne (m)   autumn
autorisé   authorised, allowed
autoroute (f)   motorway
autour de   around
autre   other

autre chose   something else
autrefois   formerly, in the past
avance (f)   advance, start
avancer   to move forward, advance
être en avance   to be fast, early
avant   before
avant-hier   day before yesterday
avec   with
avenir (m)   future
avide   keen, anxious
avion (m)   plane
avis (m)   opinion, advice
à vive allure   quickly
avoir   to have, possess
avoir besoin de   to need
avoir de l'appétit   to have an appetite
avoir de la chance   to be lucky
avoir envie de qch.   to want, have a
   fancy for s.th.
avoir faim   to be hungry
avoir mal à la tête   to have a headache
avoir mal au ventre   to have a stomach
   ache
avoir peur   to be afraid
avoir raison   to be right
avoir soif   to be thirsty
avoir sommeil   to be, feel sleepy

B

bagages (m) (pl)   luggage
baguette (f)   French stick
se baigner   to bathe
baignoire (f)   bathtub
banane (f)   banana
banc (m)   bench
banque (f)   bank
baptême (m)   christening
bar tabac (m)   tobacconist's
baroque   baroque
bas (m)   bottom
bas/se   low, deep
bateau-mouche (m)   pleasure boat
battre   to beat
bavard/e   talkative
beau, belle   beautiful, pretty, lovely
beaucoup   (very)much, a lot
beaucoup de monde   many people,
   crowd
bête (f)   animal
bête   stupid
beurre (m)   butter
beurré/e   buttered
bibliothèque (f)   bookcase
bien   well, fine
bien sûr   of course
bientôt   soon
bienvenu/e   welcome
bière (f)   beer
bifteck (m)   steak (beef)
billet (m)   (bank)note, ticket
bistro (m)   snack bar, restaurant
bizarre   funny, strange
blanc/he   white
blanc d'oeuf (m)   egg white
blessé/e   wounded, injured
bleu/e   blue
bloquer   to hold up, jam

blond/e fair
boire to drink
boisson (f) drink
boîte (f) night-club, disco
bol (m) bowl
bon/ne good, fine, right
bonjour good morning
bonsoir good evening
bord (m) side
bouche (f) mouth
bouchée à la reine (f) vol-au-vent
bouchée (f) mouthful, bite, morsel
boucher (m) butcher
boucherie (f) butcher's shop
bouchon (m) plug, stopper, cork
bouclé/e wavy
bougie (f) candle
boulangerie (f) baker's shop
boulevard (m) avenue
boulevard périphérique ring road
bouquet (m) bunch
bouquiniste (m) book-seller
bout (m) end
bouteille (f) bottle
boutique (f) shop
bras (m) arm
briller to shine
se briser to break
brosse à dents (f) toothbrush
brouillard (m) fog, mist, haze
bru (f) daughter-in-law
bruit (m) noise
brume (f) mist, haze
bureau (m) study, desk
bureau de tabac (m) tobacconist's
bus (m) bus
but (m) goal, aim
butin (m) booty, plunder

C

cabine (f) booth, phone box
cache-cache (m) hide and seek
cadeau (m) present
cadet/te younger, junior
cadre (m) setting
café (m) coffee
caisse (f) cash-desk
caissier (m) cashier
calcul (m) calculation
calculatrice (f) calculator
caleçon (m) (under-)pants, shorts
calme quiet, peaceful
ça m'est égal I don't mind
camion (m) lorry
campagne (f) country
canapé (m) sofa
canard (m) duck
capable capable, able
car (m) coach
car as, because
carafe (f) jug
carnet (m) book (of tickets)
carré/e square
carreau (m) small square
carrefour (m) crossroads
carte (f) card
carte d'accès à bord boarding card

carte postale postcard
casserole (f) saucepan
ce, cet, cette this, that, such
ceci this
céder to give way
ceinture (f) belt
ceinture de sécurité safety belt
cela, ça that
célèbre famous
célibataire single
centaine (f) about a hundred
centime (m) French currency
cercle (m) circle
c'est it is, this is
c'est à dire that is to say
certain/e certain
chaîne hi-fi (f) stereo unit
chaise (f) chair
chambre (f) bedroom, hotel room
champagne (m) champagne
champignon (m) mushroom
chance (f) chance, luck
changer to change
chanteur (m) singer
chapeau (m) hat
chapelle (f) chapel
chaque each, every
charcutier (m) pork butcher
charger to load, charge
charmant/e charming
chat (m) cat
château (m) castle, manor, palace
chaud/e warm
chauffeur (m) driver
chauffeur de taxi (m) taxi driver
chaussette (f) sock
chaussure (f) shoe
chauve bald
chef (m) head, boss
chef du personnel personnel manager
chef des ventes sales manager
chemin (m) path
chemise (f) shirt
cher, chère expensive
chercher to look (for, up), fetch, get
chèque de voyage (m) traveller cheque
cheval (m) horse
chic chic, smart
cheveux (m) (pl) hair
chèvre (f) goat
chez at, in
chien (m) dog
chiffre (m) figure, number
chocolat (m) chocolate
chose (f) thing
chou (m) cabbage
chouette great
ciel (m) sky
cigare (m) cigar
cinéma (m) cinema
cinquantaine about fifty
circulation (f) traffic
clair/e light (colour)
classe (f) class, division
clé (f) key
client (m) customer
clou (m) nail
coeur (m) heart
coiffeur (m) coiffeuse (f) hairdresser
coin (m) corner, spot

coïncidence (f) coincidence
colosse (m) giant
collaboration (f) collaboration
collant (m) tights
combien how much, many
comique funny, comic
commande (f) order
comme as, like, for
commencer to start, begin
comment how, what
commerçant/e shopkeeper, tradesman
commissariat de police (m) police-station
compagnie (f) company
compartiment (m) compartment
composer to dial
composter to stamp (ticket)
comprendre to understand
comprimé (m) tablet
compris/e included
compter to count
comptoir (m) desk
concert (m) concert
conduire to drive
confier à qn. to entrust s.o. with s.th.
confiture (f) jam
confortable comfortable
conjuguer to conjugate
connaissance (f) knowledge, acquaintance
connaître to know
conseiller to advise
constater to notice
conte (m) story, yarn, tale
contenir to contain, hold
content/e to be pleased, glad
continuer to carry on, continue
contraire opposite
contre against, for
contrôle (m) check-point, control
contrôleur (m) inspector
coquin/e sly, cheeky
corps (m) body
corsage (m) blouse
côté (m) side
cou (m) neck
se coucher to go to bed
couler to flow
couleur (f) colour
coup de soleil (m) sunburn
couper to cut
couple (m) couple
cour (f) courtyard
courir to run
cours (m) exchange rate
course (f) (sport) race
court/e short
cousin/e cousin
couteau (m) knife
coûter to cost
couverture (f) cover, blanket
couvrir to cover
cravate (f) tie
crayon (m) pencil
crème (f) cream
crémerie (f) dairy
crémière (f) dairy woman
cri (m) cry, shout
crise de foie (f) bilious attack
croire to believe, think

croissant (m) croissant
croyable credible
cuillère (f) spoon
cuillerée (f) spoonful
cuillerée à soupe soup spoonful
cuisine (f) kitchen
cuisinière (f) cooker
cuisson (f) cooking, baking
cuit/e cooked, baked
cure (f) a course of treatment
curieux/se strange
cyclope (m) cyclops

D

d'abord first (of all)
d'accord all right
dame (f) lady
dangereux/se dangerous
dans in
danser to dance
d'après according to
date de naissance (f) date of birth
davantage more
de of, from
débutant (m) beginner
décevoir to disappoint
décidément decidedly, resolutely
décider to decide
déclarer to declare
décollage (m) take-off
décrocher to pick up, unhook
dedans inside, within
défaire to undo, untie
déjà already
déjeuner (m) lunch
déjeuner d'affaires (m) business lunch
dehors outside
de la part de on behalf of
délicatement delicately, gently
délicieux/se delicious
de loin from far away
demain tomorrow
demander to ask
se demander to wonder
démarrer to start, move off
demi half
dentelle (f) lace
dentifrice (m) toothpaste
dentiste (m) dentist
départ (m) departure, take-off
dépasser to overtake
se dépêcher to hurry, hasten
de plus en plus more and more
depuis since
déranger to disturb, trouble
dernier/ière latest
derrière behind, beyond
désagréable unpleasant
descendre to go, walk down, get off
désirer to desire, want
dessert (m) dessert
en dessous below, under(neath)
au dessus above, over
de temps en temps now and then, again
détester to dislike, hate
de toute façon anyhow, in any case
devant in front of

devenir to become
déviation (f) diversion
deviner to guess
devinette (f) riddle
devoir to have to
deuxième second
dieu (m) god
différence (f) difference
digestif (m) liqueur, brandy
dimension (f) size
dîner to dine, have dinner
dire to say
direct direct
directeur (m) manager, headteacher
direction (f) direction
se diriger to make one's way, go up to, proceed
discuter to talk, discuss
disque (m) record
distance (f) distance
divan (m) sofa
diviser to divide
d'occasion secondhand
docteur (m) doctor
dommage (m) pity (what a)
donc so, therefore, well, just
donner to give
donner rendez-vous à qn. to fix, make an appointment with s.o.
dormir to sleep
dos (m) back
douane (f) customs
douanier (m) customs officer
doubler to overtake
douche (f) shower
douter to doubt
se douter de qch. to suspect
doux/ce mild, soft, sweet, gentle
douzaine (f) dozen
drap (m) sheet
droit (m) right
droite (f) right (dir.)
drôle funny
dur hard

E

eau (f) water
eau minérale mineral water
écharpe (f) scarf
échecs (m) (pl) chess
échelle (f) ladder
éclairé/e lit
éclater to burst (out), explode
école (f) school
écouter to listen (to)
s'écraser to crash
écrevisse (f) (fresh-water) crayfish
écrire to write
effectivement indeed
effet (m) effect, result
égal (all) the same, equal
église (f) church
égout (m) drain, sewer
Egypte Egypt
égyptien/ne Egyptian
élève (m & f) pupil
elle she, it

éloigné/e distant
élégant/e elegant
embarquement (m) boarding
embouteillage (m) traffic jam, bottleneck
embrasser to embrace
emmener to lead, take s.o. away, out
employé/e employee
emporter to take, carry away
en bas down (below)
enchanté/e delighted, pleased
encombrant/e cumbersome
encore still, yet, again
s'énerver to get excited
en espèces cash
en face de opposite
enfance (f) childhood
enfant (m) child
enfin at last
en haut up (above)
en hermine (f) ermine (fur)
enlever to take away, subtract
en mousseline (f) chiffon
ennui (m) worry, trouble
ennuyer to annoy, bother, worry, vex
enregistrement (m) registration
en solde 'to clear', bargain price
ensuite then, after that
entendre to hear, understand
entendu (all) right
entourer to surround, encircle
entre between
entrecôte (f) steak
entrée (f) starter, entry
entreprise (f) undertaking, firm
entrer to enter
entrouvert/e half-open, ajar
envie (f) desire, longing
en vouloir à to be angry with s.o.
envoyer to send
épais/se thick, dense
épaule (f) shoulder
épeler to spell
épicerie (f) grocer's shop
épreuve (f) test, exam
équitation (f) horse-riding
escalade (f) climbing
escalier (m) staircase, stairs
escargot (m) snail
Espagne (f) Spain
espagnol/e Spanish
espérer to hope
esprit (m) mind
essayer to try
essence (f) petrol
est is
et and
étage (m) floor, storey
été (m) summer
êtes you are
étourdissant/e staggering, astounding
être to be
être content/e to be pleased
être dans le coup to know about s.th., to be informed
être désolé/e to be sorry
être en avance to be fast, early
être en train de to be about to
être malade to be ill
être pressé/e to be in a hurry

être retardé/e   to be delayed
être en retard   to be late
étude (f)   study
étudiant/e   student
Eurochèque (m)   Eurocheque
événement (m)   event
éventail (m)   fan
éviter   to avoid
exact/e   right
exactement/e   exactly
examiner   to examine
excellent/e   excellent, lovely
s'exclamer   to exclaim
excuser   to excuse, pardon
exemple (m)   exemple
par exemple   for example
explication (f)   explanation
expliquer   to explain
exporter   to export
extraordinaire   unusual, incredible
Extrême-Orient (m)   Far East

F

facile   easy
facilement   easily
façon (f)   way, manner, mode
faim (f)   hunger
faire   to make, do, get, be
faire attention   to be careful
faire beau   to be good, nice (weather)
faire de l'escalade   to do rock climbing
faire de la natation   to go swimming
faire de la voile   sailing
faire des courses   to go shopping
faire la cour   to court
faire la cuisine   to cook
faire la queue   to queue (up)
faire la vaisselle   to wash dishes
faire un tour   to (take a) walk
familial/e   family (life, ties)
famille (f)   family
fantôme (m)   phantom
farine (f)   flour
fatigue (f)   fatigue, weariness
fatigué/e   tired, exhausted
faute (f)   mistake, fault
fauteuil (m)   chair
féliciter   to congratulate
femme (f)   woman, lady
femme de ménage (f)   cleaning lady
fenêtre (f)   window
fermé   closed
fermer   to close
fesses (f) (pl)   bottom
fête (f)   name-day, festivity
feu (m)   fire
feu rouge (m)   traffic lights (red)
feux rouges (pl)   traffic lights
fièvre (f)   temperature, fever
ficelle (f)   string
file (f)   lane
file de gauche   left-hand lane
file du milieu   middle lane
fille (f)   daughter
film (m)   film
fils (m)   son
fin (f)   end, finish
finir   to finish

fixe   fixed, permanent
fleur (f)   flower
fleuriste (m & f)   florist ('s shop)
fleuve (m)   (large) river
forcément   necessarily, inevitably
foie (m)   liver
foncé/e   dark, deep
fonder   to found
fôret (f)   forest
fort/e   strong
forcément   necessarily, inevitably
former   to shape, form
formidable   great, fantastic
four (m)   oven
fourchette (f)   fork
frais, fraîche   fresh
frais (de voyage) (m)
    (pl)   (travel)expenses
fraise (f)   strawberry
franc (m)   French currency
français/e   French
France (f)   France
freiner   to apply the brakes
frère (m)   brother
frigo (m)   fridge
frisé/e   curly
frites (f) (pl)   chips
froid/e   cold
fromage (m)   cheese
frotter   to rub
fruit (m)   fruit
fumer   to smoke
fumeur (m)   smoker
futur (m)   (life) to come

G

gage (m)   pledge, pawn
gagnant (m)   winner
gagner   to win, earn
gai/e   merry, happy
gaiement   gaily, lively
galant/e   gallant
galoper   to gallop
garage (m)   garage
garagiste (m)   garage owner
garçon (m)   waiter, boy
garder   to keep, observe
gardien de but (m)   goalkeeper
gare (f)   station (rail)
garer   to park
gâteau (m)   cake
gauche (f)   left
gendre (m)   son in law
Genève   Geneva
genou (m)   knee
genoux (pl)   knees
gens (pl)   people
gentil/le   nice, kind, friendly
gigot (m)   leg of lamb
girafe (f)   giraffe
glace (f)   ice, ice-cream
glissant/e   sliding, slippery
goût (m)   taste
grâce (f)   grace, charm, gracefulness
grâce à toi   thanks to you
grand/e   tall, big
grandeur (f)   size
grand-mère (f)   grandmother

grand-père (m) grandfather
gratuit/e free, gratis
grave serious
gravure (f) engraving
grenier (m) attic
grève (f) strike
gris/e grey
gros/se loud, rough, big, large
guichet (m) desk, (pay) desk
guide (m) guide
gymnastique (f) gymnastics

H

s'habiller to dress
habiter to live
habitude (f) habit
hache (f) axe
hall (m) hall, hotel lounge, foyer
hareng saur (m) smoked herring
haricot (m) bean
haricots verts French beans
haut (m) top
haut/e high, tall
hélas alas
Henri Henry
hésiter to hesitate
heure (f) hour, time
heure d'affluence (f) rush hour
heureux/se happy
hier yesterday
hier soir last night
hirondelle (f) swallow
histoire (f) story, history
histoire à dormir debout a tall yarn
hiver (m) winter
homme (m) man
honneur (m) honour
horloge (f) clock
hôtel (m) hotel
hôtesse (f) hostess
huile (f) oil

I

ici here
idéal/e ideal
idée (f) idea
identique identical
identité (f) identity
igloo (m) igloo
il he, it
île (f) island, isle
il faut + Inf. one has to
il y a there is, are
immédiatement immediately
immeuble (m) block of flats
impatient/e impatient
import-export (m) import-export
  (business)
importance (f) importance
important/e important
importer to import
impressionnant/e impressive
incorporer to include
incroyable incredible

indication (f) clue
infirmière (f) nurse
inquiet/ète worried, anxious
s'inquiéter to become anxious, to worry
insister to insist
s'installer to settle (down)
instant (m) moment
instituteur (m) teacher (primary school)
intelligent intelligent
interdire to forbid
interdit forbidden
intérêt (m) interest
interroger to ask
intrigué mystified
inventer to invent, make up
invité (m), invitée (f) guest
inviter to invite
Italie (f) Italy
italien/ne Italian
ivre drunk, tipsy

J

jamais never
jambe (f) leg
jambon (m) ham
Japon (m) Japan
japonais/e Japanese
jardin (m) garden
jaune yellow
jaune d'oeuf (m) egg yolk
jazz (m) jazz
je I
jeter to throw
jeune young
jeunesse (f) youth
la Joconde Mona Lisa
jogging (m) jogging
joli/e pretty, fine, nice, lovely
jouer to play
joueur (m) player
jour (m) day
journal (m) paper
journée (f) day
jovial/e jolly
jumeaux (m) (pl) twins
jumelles (f) (pl) twins
jupe (f) skirt
jurer to swear
jus d'orange (m) orange juice
juste right, just
justement exactly
jusque as far as, up to, until

K

kilo (m) kilo (2.2 lbs)
kilomètre (m) km (1000 m)
klaxonner to hoot, sound one's horn

L

là there, then, that
là-bas over, down there
lac (m) lake

Lac Léman Lake Geneva
laid ugly
laine (f) wool
laisse (f) leash
laisser to leave, to let, allow
laisser aller to let go
lait (m) milk
laitue (f) lettuce
lampe (f) lamp
lapin (m) rabbit
la plupart de most
laquelle which one
largement broadly, widely
se laver to get washed, to wash
légèrement slightly, lightly
léguer to bequeath, hand down
légume (m) vegetable
le long de along
lendemain (m) day after, next day
lent/e slow
lentement slowly
lequel which one
lettre (f) letter
se lever to get up
librairie (f) bookshop
libre free
limite (f) limit
lire to read
lit (m) bed
litre (m) litre (1.75 pts.)
livre (f) pound (Sterling)
loin far (back), distant
lointain distant
loisirs (m) (pl) leisure
Londres London
long/ue long
longtemps long, for a long time
loto (m) lotto
louer to reserve, to rent
louer à l'avance to book
lourd/e heavy
lumière (f) light
lundi (m) Monday
lune (f) moon
lunettes (f) (pl) spectacles

M

machine à laver (f) washing machine
madame (f) Mrs.
mademoiselle (f) Miss
magasin (m) shop
magnifique magnificent
maillot de corps (m) T-shirt
main (f) hand
maintenant now
mais but
maison (f) house
Maison (f) firm
mal bad
malade ill
malheureusement unfortunately
mal de tête (m) headache
malin/igne sly, cunning
manger to eat
manquer to miss
marchand (m) shopkeeper
marchand de fruits et
     légumes greengrocer

marché (m) market
marche (f) step, stair
marcher to walk, go, run, work, get along
mardi (m) Tuesday
mari (m) husband
mariage (m) marriage, wedding
marié/e married
se marier to get married
marin (m) sailor
marron brown
marteau (m) hammer
mathématiques (f) (pl) mathematics
matin (m) morning
méchant/e wicked, evil, mischievous
médicament (m) medicine
médecin (m) doctor
meilleur/e better (best)
melon (m) melon
même even, same
mener to lead
menu (m) menu, card
merci thank you
mercredi (m) Wednesday
mère (f) mother
merveille (f) marvel, wonder
merveilleux/se wonderful, fantastic
message (m) message
mesurer to measure
métal (m) metal
météo (f) weather forecast
métier (m) job, profession, trade
métro (m) underground
mettre to put, place, set
se mettre à to begin to
mettre qn. à l'épreuve (f) to put s.o. to
     the test
mettre en fureur to enrage
midi midday
mieux better, best
mince slim
mince good heavens
milieu middle
mi-long medium length
minuit midnight
minute (f) minute
mise en scène (f) set-up, staging
mobylette (f) moped
moche poor, bad, terrible
moderne modern
moi I, me
moins less, minus
moins de less than
mois (m) month
moite moist
moment (m) moment
mon, ma, mes my
monde (m) world
mon dieu good heavens
monnaie (f) change
monsieur (m) Mr.
mont (m), montagne (f) mountain
monter to go up, climb, get in
montre (f) watch
montrer to show
monument (m) monument
morceau (m) piece, bit
mort (f) death
mort/e dead
moteur (m) engine
moto (f) motor-bike

moule (m) tin, mould
mourir to die
mousse (f) mousse, cream
moustache (f) moustache
mouton (m) sheep
moyen/ne average, medium
multiplier to multiply
muni de provided, equipped with
mur (m) wall
muscade (f) nutmeg
musée (m) museum
musique (f) music
mystérieux/se mysterious

N

naissance (f) birth
naître to be born
nappe (f) tablecloth
natation (f) swimming
nature (f) nature
nécessaire necessary
neige (f) snow
neiger to snow
neuf/ve new
neveu (m) nephew
nez (m) nose
nièce (f) niece
noir/e black
noix (f) walnut
nom (m) name
non no
non fumeur non-smoker
nord (m) north
normal normal, standard
notaire (m) solicitor, lawyer
nouveau, nouvelle new, another
nouvelles (f) (pl) news
nu/e naked, bare
nuage (m) cloud
nuit (f) night
nulle part nowhere
numéro (m) number, size

O

obligatoire compulsory
obliger to oblige
occupé/e engaged, taken
s'occuper to keep o.s. busy
odeur (f) smell
oeil (m) eye
oeuf (m) egg
offrir to offer, give
oie (f) goose
oignon (m) onion
oiseau (m) bird
oncle (m) uncle
opération (f) calculation
orage (m) (thunder-) storm
oreille (f) ear
s'organiser to organise oneself, get organised
orner to adorn
ôter to remove, take off (clothes)
ou or

où where
oublier to forget
oui yes
ovale oval
ouvert/e open
ouvreuse (f) usherette
ouvrir to open

P

paille (f) straw
pain (m) bread
paire (f) pair
pancarte (f) placard, sign
panier (m) basket
panne (f) breakdown, mishap
panneau (m) sign, board
pantalon (m) trousers
papa (m) Daddy
pape (m) Pope
papier (m) paper
paquet (m) package, packet
par by, through, for, with, in, on
paraître to appear
parapluie (m) umbrella
parce que because
pardon excuse me, sorry
parent/e relative
parents (m) (pl) parents
par erreur (f) by mistake
parfois sometimes
parfum (m) perfume
parfumerie (f) perfume shop
parier to bet
parisien/ne Parisian
parking (m) car park
parler to speak, talk
part (f) part, share
partager to divide, part, share
partie (f) game
partir to leave, go (off)
à partir de from (a given time)
partout everywhere
pas (neg.) not
pas du tout not at all
passage (m) way through
passager/ère passenger
passante (f) passer-by
passeport (m) passport
passer to spend, pass (on, over, by), go
passer l'aspirateur (m) to hoover
passionnant/e exciting, thrilling
pâté (m) paté
patience (f) patience
pâtisserie (f) cake shop
pâtissier (m) pastry cook
patron/ne owner
pauvre poor
payer to pay
pays (m) country
paysage (m) countryside
paysan (m) peasant
peau (f) skin
peigne (m) comb
peinture (f) painting, picture
peloton de ficelle (m) ball of string
pendant (que) while, during
penser to think

pension (f) full board
père (m) father
permettre to permit, allow
permis (m) permit, licence
permis de conduire (m) driving licence
personnage (m) character
personne (f) person,
personne no one, nobody
persuader to persuade
peser to weigh
pétillant/e sparkling
petit/e small, little
petit déjeuner (m) breakfast
petite-fille (f) granddaughter
petit-fils (m) grandson
petits pois (m)(pl) green peas
peu little, not much
un peu a little, rather, just
peuplé/e populated
peur (f) fear, fright
peut-être perhaps
pharmacie (f) chemist's
pharmacien/ne chemist
picoter to peck (at)
pièce (f) piece, part, room
pied (m) foot
à pied on foot, walk(ing)
piéton (m) pedestrian
pincée (f) pinch
pinson (m) chaffinch
pintade (f) guinea-fowl
pipe (f) pipe
pique-nique (m) picnic
pique-niquer to have a picnic
place (f) place, seat, ticket
plafond (m) ceiling
plage (f) beach
plaire to please
plaisir (m) pleasure, delight
plan (m) street-map
planter to plant
plaque (f) (name)plate
plat (m) course, dish
plat/e flat
plateau (m) tray
plein/e full
pleurer to cry
pleuvoir to rain
pluie (f) rain
plus more
plusieurs several
plus que more than
plus tard later
poche (f) pocket
poids (m) weight
poids lourd (m) lorry
point (m) point, dot
à point medium
pointe (f) tip
pointu/e sharp, pointed
poire (f) pear
poisson (m) fish
poissonnerie (f) fishmonger, -shop
poivre (m) pepper
poivre et sel grizzly, iron-grey
poivrer to add pepper
police (f) police
pomme (f) apple
pomme d'api (f) lady-apple
pomme de terre (f) potato

pompiste (m & f) petrol pump attendant
pont (m) bridge
port de pêche (m) fishing harbour
porte (f) door
porte d'entrée front door
porte-documents (m) briefcase
porte-feuille (m) wallet
porter to carry, wear
Portugal (m) Portugal
poser to put (down), place, set, lay
possible possible
poste (f) post office
poster to post
poule (f) hen
pour for
pourboire (m) tip
pourquoi why
pousser to push, prompt, utter
pouvoir to be able, can, manage, to be allowed
pré (m) meadow
précieux/se precious, valuable
se précipiter to rush, dash, bolt
préférer to prefer
premier/ière first
prendre to take, have
prendre congé de qn. (m) to take leave of s.o.
prendre sa retraite to retire
prénom (m) Christian name
préparer to prepare
près (de) near, near(by)
présentation (f) presentation
présenter to introduce, to show
se présenter to show up
président directeur général (m) managing director
presque almost, nearly
pression (f) pressure
pression des pneus (f) tyre pressure
prestigieux/se prestigious
prêt/e ready
prêter to lend
preuve (f) proof, evidence
prier to request, ask, invite
prière de ... please
je vous en prie please do, don't mention it
principal/e main
principe (m) principle
en principe usually
printemps (m) spring
probablement probably
problème (m) problem
prochain/e next
produit (m) product
professeur (m) teacher
profiter to profit
promenade (f) walk, stroll
se promener to (go for a) walk
propre clean
propriétaire (m & f) owner
proverbe (m) proverb
prudent/e careful
publicité (f) advertisement, advertising
puer to stink
puis then, after that
puisque since

Q

quai (m) embankment
quand when
quand même all the same, nevertheless
quart (m) quarter
quartier (m) quarter, area, district
que that, which, what, than (comp.)
quel/le which, what (a)
quelque some, any
quelque chose something
quelqu'un/e someone
qu'est-ce que what
question (f) question, query
queue (f) queue
qui who, whom, which, that
quinze jours (m)(pl) fortnight
quitter to leave

R

raccrocher to hang up
raide straight, wiry
ralentir to slow down
ramasser to pick up, collect
râpé/e grated
rapide swift, fast
rapidement quickly
rappeler to ring again
se raser to shave
rasoir (m) razor
rassurant/e reassuring
rassurer to reassure
rayé/e striped
réception (f) reception
reconnaître to recognize
recouvrir to cover
reculer to move back
redonner to give, hand back
redouter to dread
réfléchir to think, reflect
réfrigérateur (m) refrigerator
refuser to refuse
regarder to look (at), watch
régler to settle, pay
regretter to regret, be sorry
rejoindre to join
remarquer to notice, realise
remercier to thank
remettre to put, bring back (again)
remonter to get back (to), walk back
remplacer to replace
remplir to fill up, in
rencontrer to meet
rendez-vous (m) meeting, appointment
se rendre to proceed
se rendre compte de qch. to realise s.th.
rentrer to return, come back
renverser to overturn
renvoyer to send back, to dismiss, sack
repartir to return
repas (m) meal
repérer to spot
répondre to answer, respond, reply
reprendre to take again
réservation (f) reservation

réservé/e reserved, booked
réserver to reserve, book
ressemblance (f) resemblance
ressembler to resemble, look alike
restaurant (m) restaurant
rester to stay (on), rest
retard (m) delay
être en retard to be late
retenir to book, reserve
retour (m) return
retourner to return, go back
se retourner to turn (round, towards, to)
retraite (f) retirement
se retrouver to meet
rêve (m) dream
se réveiller to wake up
revenir to come back, return
je n'en reviens pas I can't get over it
rêver to dream
revoir to see again
au revoir (m) good-bye
riche rich
rideau (m) curtain
rien nothing
rien du tout nothing whatsoever
rire to laugh
ris de veau (m) sweetbread
robe (f) dress
robinet (m) tap
rocher (m) rock
roi (m) king
rosbif (m) roast beef
rose (f) rose
rosé (m) rosé (wine)
rôti (m) roast (meat)
rôti/e roast
rôti de veau roast veal
roue (f) wheel
rouge red
rouler to drive, speed
route (f) way, road
roux/sse reddish-brown, red (hair)
rue (f) street, road
Russie (f) Russia
russe Russian

S

sa, son, ses her, his, its, one's
sabler le champagne to open the champagne (i.e. to celebrate)
saignant/e rare, raw (bleeding)
Saint (m) Saint
sale dirty
saler to add salt
salle (f) room, hall
salle à manger (f) dining-room
salle de bains (f) bathroom
salle d'embarquement (f) departure lounge
salon (m) living-room
salon d'essayage (m) changing room
salut (good) bye
sandwich (m) sandwich
sang froid (m) composure
sans without
sans succès without success
santé (f) health

à votre santé cheers
satin (m) satin
satisfait/e satisfied
saucisse (f) sausage
sauter to jump
sauterelle (f) grasshopper
sauvage wild
sauver to save
savoir to know, find out
savon (m) soap
séance (f) performance, session
sec, sèche dry
seconde (f) second (class)
séjour (m) living-room
sel (m) salt
semaine (f) week
sembler to seem, appear
semelle (f) sole, tread
sentir to feel, to smell
se sentir bien, mal to feel well, ill
serpent (m) snake
serrer la main to shake hands
serveur (m) waiter
serveuse (f) waitress
service (m) service
serviette (f) towel, napkin
servir to serve
seul/e single, alone
si if, yes
signer to sign
silencieusement quietly, silently
sillonner to furrow, to travel
s'il vous plaît please
simple plain, simple
singe (m) monkey
sinon otherwise,(or) else, if not
situation (f) situation
slip (m) underpants
s'occuper de to look after, be busy
soeur (f) sister
soif (f) thirst
soir (m) evening
soirée (f) evening
soixantaine (f) about sixty
sol (m) floor
soleil (m) sun
sommeil (m) drowsiness, sleepiness
sonner to ring
sorte (f) kind, sort, way
sortie (f) exit
sortir to leave, go, come out, take out
soudain suddenly
soufflé (m) soufflé
soufflé aux champignons mushroom
  soufflé
soulagement (m) relief
souligné/e underlined
sourcil (m) eyebrow
sourd/e deaf
sourire (m) smile
sourire to smile
souris (f) mouse
sous under
sous-vêtement (m) underwear
souvent often
splendide splendid
sportif/ve sporting
square (m) square, park
station (f) station (metro)
stationnement (m) parking

stationner to park
station-service (f) petrol station
statue (f) statue
sucre (m) sugar
suffire to suffice, be sufficient
suivant (m) next one
suivant/e next, following
suivre to follow
sujet (m) cause, reason, object
superbe lovely, gorgeous, great
supermarché (m) supermarket
sur on (pos.)
sûr sure, certain
surgir to loom (up), to appear
surpris/e surprised
surprise (f) surprise
surtout especially
survivant (m) survivor
suspense (m) suspense
sympathique friendly, nice, sympathetic
syndicat d'initiative (m) tourist
  information office

T

table (f) table
table basse (f) coffee table
table de nuit (f) bedside table
taie d'oreiller (f) pillow-case
taille (f) size, figure
se taire to hold one's tongue
tant so much
tante (f) aunt
tant pis what a pity, too bad
taper to tap
tapis (m) carpet
tard late
tarte (f) tart
tartine (f) slice of bread and butter
tasse (f) cup
taxi (m) taxi
télégramme (m) telegram
téléphone (m) telephone
téléphoner to telephone, ring
télévision, télé (f) television (set)
tellement so, very
témoignage (m) evidence, testimony
temps (m) time, weather
temps libre (m) spare time
tendre tender
tenir to hold, keep
tennis (m) tennis
terminer to complete
terminus (m) terminus, terminal
terrasse (f) terrace
terre (f) floor, ground
testament (m) will
tester to test
tête (f) head
têtu/e obstinate, stubborn
thé (m) tea
théâtre (m) theatre
théière (f) tea pot
ticket (m) ticket
timbre (m) stamp
timide shy
tirer to pull
tiroir (m) drawer

tomate (f) tomato
tomber to fall
tomber de l'eau to rain
ton (m) tone
tôt early
toujours always
touriste (m & f) tourist
tourner to turn, spin
tousser to cough
tout/e all, everything
tout de même nevertheless
tout de suite at once, immediately
tout droit straight on
tout le monde everyone, everybody
toute neuve (f), tout neuf (m) brand new
à toute vitesse at top speed
toux (f) cough
train (m) train
traîner to drag
trajet (m) route
travail (m) work
travailler to work
traverser to walk across, through, to cross
trempé jusqu'aux os soaked to the skin
trentaine (f) about thirty
très very
triangulaire triangular
trinquer to drink a toast
triste mournful, sad
se tromper to make a mistake
trop too (much)
trottoir (m) pavement
trou (m) hole
trouver to find, think
truite (f) trout
se tuer to get killed
tulipe (f) tulip
tutoyer to use the fam. form **'tu'**

U

un/e a, an
uni/e plain
unique only
université (f) university
un peu a bit, a little, slight
usine (f) works, factory
ustensile (m) utensil
utiliser to use, utilise

V

vacances (f)(pl) holidays
vache (f) cow
vague (f) wave
vaisselle (f) dishes
valet (m) Jack (card)
valise (f) suitcase
vanille (f) vanilla
vase (m) vase
veau (m) calf, veal
veilleur de nuit (m) night-watchman
vélo (m) bicycle
vendeuse (f) shop assistant

vendredi (m) Friday
venir to come
vent (m) wind
ventre (m) stomach
vérifier to check
véritable real, true
verre (m) glass
vers towards, to
verser to pour (out)
vert/e green
vestibule (m) hall
vêtement (m) garment
vêtements (pl) clothes
veuf/ve widowed, widow/er
viande (f) meat
vide empty
vie (f) life
vietnamien/ne Vietnamese
vieux (m), vieille (f) old
village (m) village
ville (f) town
vin (m) wine
vingtaine (f) about twenty
visage (m) face
visite (f) visit
visiter to visit
vite quick, fast
vitesse (f) speed
vitrine (f) shop window
vivement deeply, keenly, greatly
vivre to live
voici here is, are, this is, these are
voilà there is, are, there you are
voile (f) sail
voir to see
voisin (m) neighbour
voiture (f) car
voix (f) voice
vol (m) flight
vol de retour (m) return flight
volontiers gladly, readily
vouloir to want, wish
vous you (pl. and polite form)
votre, vos your (poss. adjective)
vouvoyer to use the polite form **'vous'**
voyage (m) voyage
voyageur/se (m & f) traveller
vrai true
vraiment really, truly
c'est vrai that's right

Y

yaourt (m) yoghurt
yeux (m) (pl) eyes

Z

zut gosh, dash it

ENGLISH - FRENCH
GLOSSARY

A

a, an **un/e**
about a hundred **centaine (f)**
about s.th., concerning **au sujet de qch.**
above, over **(au) dessus**
absence **absence (f)**
absolutely **absolument**
to accept **accepter**
accident **accident (m)**
to accompany **accompagner**
according to **d'après**
across, through **à travers**
to add (up) **additionner, ajouter**
to add pepper **poivrer**
to add salt **saler**
admiration **admiration (f)**
to admire **admirer**
to adorn **orner**
advance, start **avance (f)**
to advance, move forward **avancer**
advertisement, advertising **publicité (f)**
to advise **conseiller**
after all **après tout**
afternoon **après-midi (m & f)**
afterwards, then **après**
against, for **contre**
age **âge (m)**
agency, office **agence (f)**
airport **aéroport (m)**
alas **hélas**
alcoholic **alcoolisé/e**
all, everything **tout/e**
all right **d'accord, entendu**
all the same, nevertheless **quand même**
almost, nearly **presque**
along **le long de**
already **déjà**
also **aussi**
always **toujours**
ambulance **ambulance (f)**
American **américain/e**
to amuse **amuser**
amusing **amusant/e**
and **et**
animal **animal (m), bête (f)**
aniseed **anis (m)**
to announce, inform **annoncer**
to annoy, bother, worry **ennuyer**
to answer, respond, reply **répondre**
anyhow, in any case **de toute façon**
anyone, any **aucun/e, quelqu'un**
aperitif **apéritif (m)**
apparatus, appliance **appareil (m)**
to appear **paraître**
appearance **air (m)**
apple **pomme (f)**
to apply the brakes **freiner**
to appreciate **apprécier**
to approach, go up to **s'approcher**
arm **bras (m)**
around **autour**
to arrive, come **arriver**

art **art (m)**
as, because **car**
as, like, for **comme**
as far as, up to, until **jusque**
to ask **demander, interroger**
aspirin **aspirine (f)**
ass, donkey **âne (m)**
to assassinate, murder **assassiner**
to assure **assurer**
at, about **au**
at, in **chez**
at last **enfin**
at least **au moins**
at once, immediately **tout de suite**
at the end of, after **au bout de**
(pay) attention, care **attention (f)**
attic **grenier (m)**
aunt **tante (f)**
authorised, allowed **autorisé/e**
autumn **automne (m)**
avenue **boulevard (m)**
average, medium **moyen/ne**
to avoid **éviter**
awful, dreadful **affreux/se**
axe **hache (f)**

B

back **dos (m)**
bad **mal**
baker's shop **boulangerie (f)**
balcony **balcon (m)**
bald **chauve**
ball of string **peloton de ficelle (m)**
banknote, ticket **billet (m)**
bargain **affaire (f)**
baroque **baroque**
basket **panier (m)**
to bathe **se baigner**
bathroom **salle de bains (f)**
bathtub **baignoire (f)**
to be **être**
to be able, can, manage; to be
    allowed **pouvoir**
to be about to (do s.th.) **être en train de**
beach **plage (f)**
bean **haricot (m)**
to be angry with s.o. **en vouloir à**
beautiful, pretty, lovely **beau, belle**
to be born **naître**
to be called **s'appeler**
to be careful **faire attention**
because **parce que**
because of **à cause de**
to become **devenir**
to become anxious, to worry **s'inquiéter**
bed **lit (m)**
bedroom, hotel room **chambre (f)**
bedside table **table de nuit (f)**
to be delayed **être retardé/e**
to be fast, before time **être en avance**
to be late **être en retard**
before **avant**
to begin to **se mettre à**
to be good, nice (weather) **faire beau**
behind, beyond **derrière**
to be hungry **avoir faim**
to be ill **être malade**
to be in a hurry **être pressé/e**

below, under(neath) **(en)dessous**
to be lucky **avoir de la chance**
to be pleased **être content/e**
to be right **avoir raison**
to be sorry **être désolé/e**
to be thirsty **avoir soif**
beer **bière (f)**
beginner **débutant/e (m & f)**
to believe, think **croire**
to belong to **appartenir à**
belt **ceinture (f)**
bench **banc (m)**
to bequeath, hand down **léguer**
better (best) **meilleur/e, mieux**
between **entre**
bicycle **vélo (m)**
big **grand/e**
bilious attack **crise de foie (f)**
bill **addition (f)**
bird **oiseau (m)**
birth **naissance (f)**
a bit, a little, slight **un peu**
black **noir/e**
blouse **corsage (m)**
blue **bleu/e**
boarding **embarquement (m)**
boarding card **carte d'accès à bord (f)**
body **corps (m)**
to book **louer à l'avance**
to book, reserve **retenir**
bookcase **bibliothèque (f)**
book of tickets **carnet (m)**
bookseller **bouquiniste (m)**
bookshop **librairie (f)**
booth, phone box **cabine (f)**
booty, plunder **butin (m)**
bottle **bouteille (f)**
bottom **fesses (f)(pl)**
brand new **tout neuf (m), toute neuve (f)**
bread **pain (m)**
to break **se briser**
breakdown, mishap **panne (f)**
breakfast **petit déjeuner (m)**
bridge **pont (m)**
briefcase **porte-documents (m)**
to bring **apporter**
to bring, lead **amener**
brother **frère (m)**
brown **marron**
buckets (rain) **à seaux**
bunch **bouquet (m)**
to burst (out), explode **éclater**
bus **autobus, bus (m)**
business **affaires (f) (pl)**
business lunch **déjeuner d'affaires (m)**
busy, active **actif/ve**
butcher **boucher (m)**
butcher's shop **boucherie (f)**
butter **beurre (m)**
buttock **fesse (f)**
to buy **acheter**
by **au bord de**
by, through, for, with, in, on **par**
by mistake **par erreur**
by the way **au fait**

C

cabbage **chou (m), choux (pl)**
cake **gâteau (m)**
cake shop **pâtisserie (f)**
calculation **opération (f)**
calculator **calculatrice (f)**
calf, veal **veau (m)**
to call (for, in, up) **appeler**
candle **bougie (f)**
capable, able **capable**
car **voiture (f)**
car park **parking (m)**
card **carte (f)**
careful **prudent/e**
carpet **tapis (m)**
to carry on, continue **continuer**
to carry, wear **porter**
cash **en espèces**
cash-desk **caisse (f)**
cashier **caissier (m),caissière (f)**
castle, manor, palace **château (m)**
cat **chat (m)**
to catch **attraper**
cause, reason, object **sujet (m)**
ceiling **plafond (m)**
certain **certain/e**
chaffinch **pinson (m)**
chair **chaise (f), fauteuil (m)**
champagne **champagne (m)**
chance, luck **chance (f)**
to change **changer**
change **monnaie (f)**
changing room **salon d'essayage (m)**
chapel **chapelle (f)**
character **personnage (m)**
charming **charmant/e**
to check **vérifier**
checkpoint, control **contrôle (m)**
cheek **joue (f)**
cheers **à votre santé**
cheese **fromage (m)**
chemist **pharmacien/ne (m & f)**
chemist's **pharmacie (f)**
chess **échecs (m) (pl)**
chic, smart **chic**
chiffon **(en) mousseline (f)**
child **enfant (m)**
childhood **enfance (f)**
chips **frites (f) (pl)**
chocolate **chocolat (m)**
christening **baptême (m)**
Christian name **prénom (m)**
church **église (f)**
cigar **cigare (m)**
cinema **cinéma (m)**
circle **cercle (m)**
circumflex accent **accent circonflexe (m)**
class, division **classe (f)**
clean **propre**
cleaning lady **femme de ménage (f)**
'to clear', bargain price **en solde**
climbing **escalade (f)**
clock **horloge (f)**
to close **fermer**
closed **fermé/e**
clothes **vêtements (m) (pl)**
cloud **nuage (m)**
clue **indication (f)**

coach **car** (m)
coffee **café** (m)
coffee table **table basse** (f)
coin **pièce de monnaie** (f)
coincidence **coïncidence** (f)
cold **froid/e**
collaboration **collaboration** (f)
colour **couleur** (f)
comb **peigne** (m)
to come **venir**
to come back, return **revenir**
comfortable **confortable**
company **compagnie** (f)
compartment **compartiment** (m)
to complete **terminer**
composure **sang froid** (m)
compulsory **obligatoire**
to concern, be the matter **s'agir (de)**
concert **concert** (m)
to congratulate **féliciter**
to conjugate **conjuguer**
cooked, baked **cuit/e**
cooker **cuisinière** (f)
cork (of bottle) **bouchon** (m)
corner, spot **coin** (m)
to cost **coûter**
cough **toux** (f)
to cough **tousser**
to count **compter**
country **pays** (m), **campagne** (f)
countryside **paysage** (m)
couple **couple** (m)
course, dish **plat** (m)
a course of treatment **cure** (f)
to court **faire la cour**
courtyard **cour** (f)
cousin **cousin/e** (m & f)
to cover **(re)couvrir**
cover, blanket **couverture** (f)
cow **vache** (f)
to crash **s'écraser**
crayfish **écrevisse** (f)
cream **crème** (f)
credible **croyable**
crisis **crise** (f)
croissant **croissant** (m)
crossroads **carrefour** (m)
cry, shout **cri** (m)
to cry **pleurer**
cumbersome **encombrant/e**
cup **tasse** (f)
curly **frisé/e**
curtain **rideau** (m)
curve **arc (de cercle)** (m)
customer **client** (m)
customs **douane** (f)
customs officer **douanier** (m)
to cut **couper**

D

Daddy **papa** (m)
dairy **crémerie** (f)
dairy woman **crémière** (f)
to dance **danser**
dangerous **dangereux/se**
dark, deep **foncé/e**
date of birth **date de naissance** (f)
daughter **fille** (f)

daughter-in-law **bru** (f)
day **jour** (m), **journée** (f)
day after, next day **lendemain** (m)
day after tomorrow **après demain**
day before yesterday **avant-hier**
dead **mort/e**
deaf **sourd/e**
death **mort** (f)
to decide **décider**
decidedly, resolutely **décidément**
to declare **déclarer**
deeply, keenly, greatly **vivement**
delay **retard** (m)
delicately, gently **délicatement**
delicious **délicieux/se**
delighted, pleased **enchanté/e**
dentist **dentiste** (m)
departure lounge **salle d'embarquement**
(f)
departure, take-off **départ** (m)
desire, longing **envie** (f)
to desire, want **désirer**
desk **comptoir** (m)
(pay)desk **guichet** (m)
dessert **dessert** (m)
to dial, set, arrange **composer**
to die **mourir**
difference **différence** (f)
to dine, have dinner **dîner**
dining-room **salle à manger** (f)
direct, straight **direct**
direction **direction** (f)
to disappoint **décevoir**
dishes **vaisselle** (f)
to dislike, hate **détester**
distance **lointain** (m)
distant **éloigné/e**
to disturb, trouble **déranger**
diversion **déviation** (f)
to divide **diviser**
to divide, part, share **partager**
doctor **docteur, médecin** (m)
dog **chien** (m)
donkey **âne** (m)
door **porte** (f)
to doubt **douter**
down (below) **en bas**
dozen **douzaine** (f)
to drag **traîner**
drain, sewer **égout** (m)
drawer **tiroir** (m)
to dread **redouter**
to dream **rêver**
dream **rêve** (m)
to dress **s'habiller**
dress **robe** (f)
to drink **boire**
drink **boisson** (f)
to drink a toast **trinquer**
to drive **conduire**
to drive, speed **rouler**
driver **chauffeur** (m)
driving licence **permis de conduire** (m)
drowsiness, sleepiness **sommeil** (m)
drunk, tipsy **ivre**
dry **sec, sèche**
duck **canard** (m)

E

each, every **chaque**
ear **oreille (f)**
early **tôt**
easily **facilement**
easy **facile**
to eat **manger**
effect, result **effet (m)**
egg **oeuf (m)**
egg yolk **jaune d'oeuf (m)**
elder, eldest **aîné/e**
elegant **élégant/e**
embankment **quai (m)**
to embrace **embrasser**
employee **employé/e**
empty **vide**
end **bout (m)**
end, finish **fin (f)**
engaged **occupé/e**
engine **moteur (m)**
England **Angleterre (f)**
English **anglais/e**
engraving **gravure (f)**
enough, rather, fairly **assez**
to enrage **mettre en fureur**
to enter **entrer**
to entrust s.o. with s.th **confier à qn.**
equal, (all) the same **égal**
ermine (fur) **en hermine (f)**
especially **surtout**
Eurocheque **Eurochèque (m)**
even, same **même**
evening **soir (m), soirée (f)**
event **événement (m)**
everyone, everybody **tout le monde**
everywhere **partout**
evidence, testimony **témoignage (m)**
exactly **exactement, justement**
to examine **examiner**
example **exemple (m)**
excellent, lovely **excellent/e**
exchange rate **cours (m)**
exciting, thrilling **passionnant/e**
to exclaim **s'exclamer**
to excuse, pardon **excuser**
excuse me, sorry **pardon**
exit **sortie (f)**
expensive **cher, chère**
to explain **expliquer**
explanation **explication (f)**
to export **exporter**
eye **oeil (m)**
eyebrow **sourcil (m)**
eyes **yeux (m) (pl)**

F

face **visage (m)**
fair **blond/e**
to fall **tomber**
family **famille (f)**
family (life, ties) **familial/e**
famous **célèbre**
fan **éventail (m)**
far (back), distant **loin**
Far East **Extrême-Orient (m)**

father **père (m)**
fatigue, weariness **fatigue (f)**
fear, fright **peur (f)**
to feel, to smell **sentir**
to feel sleepy **avoir sommeil**
to feel well/ill **se sentir bien/mal**
about fifty **cinquantaine (f)**
figure, number **chiffre (m)**
to fill up, in **remplir**
film **film (m)**
to find, think **trouver**
fine **amende (f)**
to finish **finir**
firm **Maison (f)**
first **premier/ière**
first (of all) **d'abord**
fish **poisson (m)**
fishing harbour **port de pêche (m)**
fishmonger, (shop) **poissonnerie (f)**
to fix, attach **attacher**
to fix, make an appointment **donner rendez-vous**
fixed, permanent **fixe**
flat **plat/e**
flight **vol (m)**
floor **sol (m)**
floor, ground **terre (f)**
floor, storey **étage (m)**
florist ('s shop) **fleuriste (m & f)**
flour **farine (f)**
to flow **couler**
flower **fleur (f)**
fog, mist, haze **brouillard (m)**
to follow **suivre**
fondly **affectueusement**
foot **pied (m)**
for **pour**
to forbid **interdire**
forbidden **interdit**
forest **forêt (f)**
for example **par exemple**
to forget **oublier**
fork **fourchette (f)**
formerly, in the past **autrefois**
fortnight **quinze jours**
to found **fonder**
France **France (f)**
free **libre**
free, gratis **gratuit/e**
French **français/e**
French beans **haricots verts (m) (pl)**
French currency **centime (m)**
French stick **baguette (f)**
fresh **frais, fraîche**
Friday **vendredi (m)**
fridge **frigo (m)**
friend **ami/e**
friendly, nice, sympathetic **sympathique**
from far away **de loin**
from (a given time) **à partir de**
front door **porte d'entrée (f)**
fruit **fruit (m)**
full **plein/e**
funny, comic **comique, drôle**
funny, strange **bizarre**
to furrow, to travel **sillonner**
future **avenir (m)**
future, (life) to come **futur**

G

gaily, lively **gaiement**
gallant **galant/e**
to gallop **galoper**
game **partie (f)**
garage owner **garagiste (m)**
garden **jardin (m)**
garment **vêtement (m)**
Geneva **Genève**
to get back (to), walk back **remonter**
to get excited **s'énerver**
to get killed, kill o.s. **se tuer**
to get up **se lever**
to get washed **se laver**
giant **colosse (m)**
giraffe **girafe (f)**
to give **donner**
to give, hand back **redonner**
to give way **céder**
gladly, readily **volontiers**
glass **verre (m)**
to go away, leave **s'en aller**
to go up, climb, get in **monter**
to go, walk **aller**
to go, walk down, get off **descendre**
to (go for a) walk **se promener**
goal, aim **but (m)**
goat **chèvre (f)**
god **dieu (m)**
to go shopping **faire des courses**
to go swimming **faire de la natation**
to go to bed **se coucher**
good, fine, right **bon/ne**
good-bye **adieu, au revoir, salut**
good evening **bonsoir**
good heaven **mince, mon dieu**
good morning **bonjour**
goose **oie (f)**
gosh, dash it **zut**
grace, charm, gracefulness **grâce (f)**
granddaughter **petite-fille (f)**
grandfather **grand-père (m)**
grandmother **grand-mère (f)**
grandson **petit-fils (m)**
grasshopper **sauterelle (f)**
grated **râpé/e**
great, fantastic **chouette, formidable**
greengrocer **marchand de fruits
   et légumes (m)**
green peas **petits pois (m) (pl)**
grey **gris/e**
grizzly, iron-grey **poivre et sel**
grocers shop **épicerie (f)**
to guess **deviner**
guest **invité/e (m & f)**
guide **guide (m)**
guinea fowl **pintade (f)**
gymnastics **gymnastique (f)**

H

habit **habitude (f)**
hair **cheveu (m), cheveux (pl)**
hairdresser **coiffeur (m), coiffeuse (f)**
half **demi/e**
half-open, ajar **entrouvert/e**

hall, hotel lounge, foyer **hall (m)**
hall **vestibule (m)**
hammer **marteau (m)**
hand **main (f)**
to hang up **raccrocher**
happy **heureux/se**
hard **dur**
hat **chapeau (m)**
to have a headache **avoir mal à la tête**
to have a picnic **pique-niquer**
to have, possess **avoir**
to have to **devoir**
he, it **il**
head **tête (f)**
head, boss **chef (m)**
headache **mal de tête (m)**
health **santé (f)**
to hear, understand **entendre**
heart **coeur (m)**
heavens! **mon dieu (m)**
heavy **lourd/e**
hello **allô**
to help **aider**
hen **poule (f)**
Henry **Henri**
her, his, its, one's **sa, son, ses**
here **ici**
here is, are; this is, these are **voici**
to hesitate **hésiter**
hide and seek **cache-cache (m)**
high, tall **haut/e**
to hold, keep **tenir**
to hold one's tongue **se taire**
to hold up, jam **bloquer**
hole **trou (m)**
holidays **vacances (f) (pl)**
honour **honneur (m)**
to hoover **passer l'aspirateur (m)**
to hope **espérer**
horse **cheval (m)**
horse-riding **équitation (f)**
hostess **hôtesse (f)**
hotel **hôtel (m)**
hour, time **heure (f)**
house **maison (f)**
block of flats **immeuble (m)**
how much, many **combien**
how, what **comment**
hunger **faim (f)**
to hurry, hasten **se dépêcher**
husband **mari (m)**

I

I **je**
ice, ice-cream **glace (f)**
idea **idée (f)**
ideal **idéal/e**
identical **identique**
identity **identité (f)**
I don't mind **ça m'est égal**
if, yes **si**
igloo **igloo (m)**
ill **malade**
immediately **immédiatement**
impatient **impatient/e**
to import **importer**
importance **importance (f)**

important **important/e**
import-export **import-export (m)**
impressive **impressionnant/e**
in **dans**
in, at, to **à**
to include **incorporer**
included **compris/e**
incredible **incroyable**
indeed **effectivement**
in front of **devant**
inside, within **dedans**
to insist **insister**
inspector **contrôleur (m)**
installed **aménagé/e**
intelligent **intelligent/e**
interest **intérêt (m)**
to introduce, to show **présenter**
to invent, make up **inventer**
to invite **inviter**
in...way, manner **à la mode de...**
is **est**
island, isle **île (f)**
Italien **italien/ne**
Italy **Italie (f)**
it is, this is **c'est**

J

Jack (card) **valet (m)**
jam **confiture (f)**
jazz **jazz (m)**
job, profession, trade **métier (m)**
jogging **jogging (m)**
to join **rejoindre**
jolly **jovial/e**
jug **carafe (f)**
to jump **sauter**

K

keen, anxious **avide**
to keep, observe **garder**
to keep o.s. busy **s'occuper**
key **clé (f)**
kilo (2.2 lbs) **kilo (m)**
kilometre (1000 mtrs) **kilomètre (m)**
kind, sort, way **sorte (f)**
king **roi (m)**
kitchen **cuisine (f)**
knee **genou (m), genoux (pl)**
knife **couteau (m)**
to know **connaître, savoir**
to know, find out **savoir**
to know about s.th., to be informed **être dans le coup**
knowledge, acquaintance **connaissance (f)**

L

lace **dentelle (f)**
ladder **échelle (f)**
lady **dame (f)**
lady-apple **pomme d'api (f)**

lake **lac (m)**
lake Geneva **Lac Léman**
lamb **agneau (m)**
lamp **lampe (f)**
to land **atterrir**
lane **file (f)**
last night **hier soir**
late **tard**
later **plus tard**
latest **dernier/ière**
to laugh **rire**
lawyer **notaire (m)**
to lead **mener**
to lead, take some one away, out **emmener**
to leave **quitter**
to leave, go (off) **partir**
to leave, go, come out, take out **sortir**
to leave, to let, allow **laisser**
left **gauche (f)**
left-hand lane **file de gauche (f)**
leg **jambe (f)**
leg of lamb **gigot (m)**
leisure **loisirs (m) (pl)**
to lend **prêter**
less, minus **moins**
less than **moins de**
to let go **laisser aller**
letter **lettre (f)**
lettuce **laitue (f)**
to lie down **s'allonger**
life **vie (f)**
lift, **ascenseur (m)**
light **clair/e**
light **lumière (f)**
lightly, slightly **légèrement**
limit **limite (f)**
liqueur, brandy **digestif (m)**
to listen (to) **écouter**
lit **éclairé/e**
litre (1.75 pts) **litre (m)**
little, not much **peu**
a little, rather, just **un peu**
to live **habiter, vivre**
liver **foie (m)**
living-room **salon, séjour (m)**
to load, charge **charger**
London **Londres**
long **allongé/e, long/ue**
long, for a long time **longtemps**
to look after, be busy **s'occuper de**
to look (at), watch **regarder**
to look (for, up), fetch, get **chercher**
to loom (up), to appear **surgir**
lorry **camion, poids lourd (m)**
lotto **loto (m)**
loud, rough, big, large **gros/se**
to love, like **adorer, aimer**
lovely, gorgeous, great **superbe**
low, deep **bas**
luggage **bagages (m) (pl)**
lunch **déjeuner (m)**

M

magnificent **magnifique**
main **principal/e**
to make, do, get, be **faire**
to make a mistake **se tromper**

to make one's way, go up to, proceed **se diriger**
man **homme (m)**
manager, head teacher **directeur (m)**
managing director **président directeur général (m)**
many people, crowd **beaucoup de monde**
market **marché (m)**
marriage, wedding **mariage (m)**
married **marié/e**
to get married **se marier**
marvel wonder **merveille (f)**
mathematics **mathématiques f) (pl)**
meadow **pré (m)**
meal **repas (m)**
to measure **mesurer**
meat **viande (f)**
medicine **médicament (m)**
medium **à point**
medium length **mi-long**
to meet **rencontrer, se retrouver**
meeting, appointment **rendez-vous (m)**
melon **melon (m)**
menu, card **menu (m)**
merry, happy **gai/e**
message **message (m)**
metal **métal (m)**
midday **midi**
middle **milieu (m)**
middle lane **file du milieu (f)**
midnight **minuit**
mild, soft, sweet, gentle **doux/ce**
milk **lait (m)**
mind **esprit**
mineral water **eau minérale (f)**
minute **minute (f)**
to miss **manquer**
Miss **mademoiselle (f)**
mist, haze **brume (f)**
mistake, fault **faute (f)**
modern **moderne**
moist **moîte**
moment **moment, instant (m)**
Mona Lisa **La Joconde**
Monday **lundi (m)**
money **argent (m)**
monkey **singe (m)**
month **mois (m)**
monument **monument (m)**
moon **lune (f)**
moped **mobylette (f)**
more **davantage, plus**
more and more **de plus en plus**
more than **plus que**
morning **matin (m)**
most **la plupart de**
mother **mère (f)**
motor-bike **moto (f)**
motorway **autoroute (f)**
mould, tin **moule (m)**
mountain **mont (m), montagne (f)**
mournful, sad **triste**
mouse **souris (f)**
mousse, cream **mousse (f)**
moustache **moustache (f)**
mouth **bouche (f)**
mouthful, bite, morsel **bouchée (f)**
to move back **reculer**
Mr. **monsieur (m)**
Mrs., lady **madame (f)**

museum **musée (m)**
to multiply **multiplier**
mushroom **champignon (m)**
mushroom soufflé **soufflé aux champignons (m)**
music **musique (f)**
my **mon, ma, mes**
mysterious **mystérieux/se**
mystified **intrigué/e**

N

nail **clou (m)**
name **nom (m)**
name-day, festivity **fête (f)**
nature **nature (f)**
near(by) **près (de)**
necessarily, inevitably **forcément**
necessary **nécessaire**
neck **cou (m)**
to need **avoir besoin de**
neighbour **voisin (m)**
nephew **neveu (m)**
never **jamais**
nevertheless **tout de même**
new **neuf/ve**
new, another **nouveau/elle**
news **nouvelles (f) (pl)**
newspaper **journal (m)**
next **prochain/e**
next, following **suivant/e**
next one **suivant (m)**
next to, beside **à côté**
nice, pleasant **agréable**
nice, kind, friendly **gentil/le**
niece **nièce (f)**
night **nuit (f)**
nightclub, disco **boîte (f)**
nightwatchman **veilleur de nuit (m)**
no **non**
noise **bruit (m)**
non-smoker **non fumeur**
no-one, nobody **personne**
normal, standard **normal**
north **nord (m)**
nose **nez (m)**
not **pas (neg.)**
not at all **pas du tout**
nothing **rien**
nothing whatsoever **rien du tout**
to notice, to state **constater**
to notice, realise, perceive **apercevoir, remarquer**
now **maintenant**
now and then, again **de temps en temps**
nowhere **nulle part**
number, size **numéro (m)**
nurse **infirmière (f)**

O

to oblige **obliger**
obstinate, stubborn **têtu/e**
of, from **de**
of course **bien sûr**
to offer, give **offrir**
often **souvent**

oil huile (f)
old âgé/e, ancien/ne, vieux/vieille
on sur
on behalf of de la part de
one has to il faut + inf.
on foot, walk(ing) à pied
onion oignon (m)
only unique
open ouvert/e
to open ouvrir
to open the champagne (i.e. to
    celebrate) sabler le champagne
opinion, advice avis (m)
opposite en face de
opposite contraire (m)
or ou
orange juice jus d'orange (m)
order commande (f)
to organise, get organised s'organiser
other autre
otherwise, (or) else, if not sinon
outside dehors
oven four (m)
over, down there là-bas
to overtake doubler, dépasser
to overturn renverser
owner patron/ne, propriétaire (m & f)

P

package, packet paquet (m)
painting, picture peinture (f)
pair paire (f)
(under)pants, shorts caleçon (m) slip (m)
paper papier (m)
parents parents (m) (pl)
Parisian parisien/ne
to park garer, stationner
parking stationnement (m)
part, share part (f)
partner associé/e
passenger passager/ère
passer-by passante (f)
passport passeport (m)
pastry cook pâtissier (m)
paté pâté (m)
path chemin (m)
patience patience (f)
pavement trottoir (m)
to pay payer
peas petits pois (m) (pl)
peaceful, quiet calme
pear poire (f)
peasant paysan (m)
to peck (at) picoter
pedestrian piéton (m)
pencil crayon (m)
people gens (pl)
pepper poivre (m)
performance, session séance (f)
perfume parfum (m)
perfume shop parfumerie (f)
perhaps peut-être
to permit, allow permettre
permit, licence permis (m)
person personne (f)
personnel manager chef du personnel (m)
to persuade persuader
petrol essence (f)

petrol pump attendant pompiste (m)
petrol station station-service (f)
phantom fantôme (m)
to pick up, collect ramasser
to pick up, unhook décrocher
picnic pique-nique (m)
piece, bit, morsel morceau (m)
piece, part pièce (f)
pillow-case taie d'oreiller (f)
pinch pincée (f)
pipe pipe (f)
pity (what a...) dommage (m)
place, seat, ticket place (f)
plain uni/e
plain, simple simple
plane avion (m)
to plant planter
(name) plate plaque (f)
to play jouer
player joueur (m)
to please plaire
please s'il vous plaît, prière de...
please do, don't mention it je vous en
    prie
to be pleased, glad content/e
pleasure, delight plaisir (m)
pleasure boat bateau-mouche (m)
plot coup (m)
plug, stopper, block bouchon (m)
pocket poche (f)
point, dot point (m)
police police (f)
policeman agent de police (m)
police station commissariat de police
    (m)
poor pauvre
poor, bad, terrible moche
Pope pape (m)
populated peuplé/e
pork butcher charcutier (m)
Portugal Portugal (m)
possible possible
to post poster
postcard carte postale (f)
post office poste (f)
potato pomme de terre (f)
pound (Sterling) livre (f)
to pour (out) verser
precious, valuable précieux/se
to prefer préférer
to prepare préparer
present cadeau (m)
presentation présentation (f)
pressure pression (f)
pretty, fine, lovely, nice joli/e
principle principe (m)
probably probablement
problem problème (m)
to proceed se rendre
product produit (m)
to profit profiter
proof, evidence preuve (f)
provided, equipped with muni de
to pull tirer
pupil élève (m)
to push, prompt, utter pousser
to put, bring back (again) remettre
to put (down), place, set, lay, set mettre,
    poser
to put s.o. to the test mettre qn. à
    l'épreuve

Q

quarter **quart (m)**
quarter, area, district **quartier (m)**
question, query **question (f)**
queue **queue (f)**
to queue (up) **faire la queue**
quick, fast **vite**
quickly **à vive allure, rapidement**
quietly, silently **silencieusement**

R

rabbit **lapin (m)**
(sport) race **course (f)**
rain **pluie (f)**
to rain **pleuvoir, tomber de l'eau**
rare, raw **saignant/e**
razor **rasoir (m)**
to read **lire**
ready **prêt/e**
real, true **véritable**
to realise s.th. **se rendre compte de qch.**
really, truly **vraiment**
to reassure **rassurer**
reassuring **rassurant/e**
reception **réception (f)**
to recognise **reconnaître**
record **disque (m)**
red **rouge**
reddish-brown, red (hair) **roux/sse**
refrigerator **réfrigérateur (m)**
to refuse **refuser**
registration **enregistrement (m)**
to regret, be sorry **regretter**
relative **parent/e (m & f)**
relief **soulagement (m)**
to remove, take off (clothes) **ôter**
to replace **remplacer**
to request, ask, invite **prier**
resemblance **ressemblance (f)**
to resemble, look alike **ressembler**
reservation **réservation (f)**
to reserve, book **réserver**
to reserve, to rent **louer**
reserved **réservé/e**
to rest, stay (on) **rester**
restaurant **restaurant (m)**
to retire **prendre sa retraite**
retirement **retraite (f)**
return **aller-retour (m)**
to return, come back **rentrer, repartir, retourner**
return flight **vol de retour (m)**
return ticket **aller-retour (m)**
rich **riche**
riddle **devinette (f)**
right **droit (m)**
right (dir.) **droite (f)**
right, correct **exact/e**
right, just **juste**
to ring **sonner**
to ring again, to recall **rappeler**
ring road **boulevard périphérique (m)**
river **rivière (f)**
(large) river **fleuve (m)**
roast **rôti (m)**
roast beef **rosbif (m)**

roast veal **rôti de veau (m)**
rock **rocher (m)**
to do rock climbing **faire de l'escalade**
room **pièce (f)**
room, hall **salle (f)**
rose **rose (f)**
rosé (wine) **rosé**
route **trajet (m)**
to rub **frotter**
to run **courir**
to rush, dash, bolt **se précipiter**
rush hour **heure d'affluence (f)**

S

safety belt **ceinture de sécurité (f)**
sailing **faire de la voile (f)**
sailor **marin (m)**
Saint **Saint (m)**
sales manager **chef des ventes (m)**
salt **sel (m)**
sandwich **sandwich (m)**
satisfied **satisfait/e**
sausage **saucisse (f)**
to save **sauver**
to say **dire**
scarcely, hardly **à peine**
scarf **écharpe (f)**
school **école (f)**
second **deuxième**
second (class) **seconde**
to see **voir**
to see again **revoir**
see you again **à bientôt**
to seem, appear **sembler**
to send **envoyer**
serious **grave**
to serve **servir**
service **service (m)**
setting **cadre (m)**
to settle (down) **s'installer**
to settle, pay **régler**
set-up, staging **mise en scène (f)**
several **plusieurs**
to shake hands **serrer la main**
to shape, form **former**
share **action (f)**
sharp, pointed **pointu/e**
to shave **se raser**
she, it **elle**
sheep **mouton (m)**
sheet **drap (m)**
to shine **briller**
shirt **chemise (f)**
shoe **chaussure (f)**
shop **boutique (f), magasin (m)**
shop assistant **vendeuse (f)**
shopkeeper **commerçant/e, marchand/e (m & f)**
shop window **vitrine (f)**
short **court/e**
shoulder **épaule (f)**
to show **montrer**
to show up **se présenter**
shower **douche (f)**
shy **timide**
side **côté (m)**
side **bord (m)**
sign, board **panneau (m), pancarte (f)**

to sign **signer**
since **depuis**
since, as **puisque**
singer **chanteur (m)**
single **célibataire**
single, alone **seul/e**
single ticket **aller (m)**
sister **soeur (f)**
to sit down **s'asseoir**
situation **situation (f)**
(about) sixty **soixantaine (f)**
size **dimension, grandeur (f)**
size, figure **taille (f)**
skin **peau (f)**
skirt **jupe (f)**
sky **ciel (m)**
to sleep **dormir**
slice of bread and butter **tartine (f)**
sliding, slippery **glissant/e**
slim **mince**
slow **lent/e**
to slow down **ralentir**
slowly **lentement**
slowly, in slow motion **au ralenti**
sly, cheeky, cunning **coquin/e, malin/
igne**
small, little **petit/e**
small square **carreau (m)**
smell **odeur (f)**
smile, to smile **sourire (m)**
to smoke **fumer**
smoked herring **hareng saur (m)**
smoker **fumeur (m)**
snack bar, restaurant **bistro (m)**
snail **escargot (m)**
snake **serpent (m)**
to snow **neiger**
so, then, well **alors**
so, therefore, well, just **donc**
so, very **tellement**
soaked to the skin **trempé jusqu'aux os**
soap **savon (m)**
sock **chaussette (f)**
sofa **divan, canapé (m)**
sole, tread **semelle (f)**
solicitor, lawyer **notaire (m)**
some, any **quelque**
someone **quelq'un**
something **quelque chose**
something else **autre chose (f)**
sometimes **parfois**
so much **tant**
son-in-law **gendre (m)**
soon **bientôt**
to sound one's horn **klaxonner**
Spain **Espagne (f)**
Spanish **espagnol/e**
spare time **temps libre (m)**
sparkling **pétillant/e**
to speak, talk **parler**
spectacles **lunettes (f) (pl)**
speed **vitesse (f)**
to spell **épeler**
to spend, pass (on, over, by), go **passer**
splendid **splendide**
spoon **cuillère (f)**
spoonful **cuillerée (f)**
(soup) spoonful **cuillerée à soupe (f)**
to spot **repérer**
sporting **sportif/ve**
spring **printemps (m)**

square **carré/e**
square, park **square (m)**
staggering, astounding **étourdissant/e**
staircase, stairs **escalier (m)**
stamp **timbre (m)**
to stamp (ticket) **composter**
to start, begin **commencer**
to start, move off **démarrer**
starter, entry **entrée (f)**
station (rail) **gare (f)**
station (tube) **station (f)**
statue **statue (f)**
steak **bifteck (m), entrecôte (f)**
step, stair **marche (f)**
stereo unit **chaîne hi-fi (f)**
still, yet, again **encore**
to stink **puer**
stomach **ventre (m)**
to stop **s'arrêter**
(thunder)storm **orage (m)**
story, yarn, tale **conte (m)**
straight on **tout droit**
strange **curieux/se**
straw **paille (f)**
strawberry **fraise (f)**
street, road **rue (f)**
street map **plan (m)**
strike **grève (f)**
string **ficelle (f)**
striped **rayé/e**
strong **fort/e**
student **étudiant/e**
study **étude (f)**
study, desk **bureau (m)**
stupid **bête**
suddenly **soudain**
to suffice, be sufficient **suffire**
sugar **sucre (m)**
to suit **aller bien**
suitcase **valise (f)**
summer **été (m)**
sun **soleil (m)**
sunburn **coup de soleil (m)**
supermarket **supermarché (m)**
sure, certain **sûr**
surprise **surprise (f)**
surprised **surpris/e**
to surround, encircle **entourer**
survivor **survivant (m)**
to suspect **se douter de qch.**
suspense **suspense (m)**
swallow **hirondelle (f)**
to swear **jurer**
sweetbread **ris de veau (m)**
swift, fast **rapide**
swimming **natation (f)**
to switch on, light **allumer**

T

table **table (f)**
tablecloth **nappe (f)**
tablet **comprimé (m)**
to take again **reprendre**
to take away, subtract **enlever**
to (take a) walk **faire un tour**
to take care **faire attention**
to take, carry away **emporter**
to take, have **prendre**

to take leave **prendre congé de qn.**
take-off **décollage (m)**
to talk, discuss **discuter**
talkative **bavard/e**
tall, big **grand/e**
a tall yarn **histoire à dormir debout**
to tap **taper**
tap **robinet (m)**
tart **tarte (f)**
taste **goût (m)**
taxi **taxi (m)**
taxi driver **chauffeur de taxi (m)**
tea **thé (m)**
tea pot **théière (f)**
teacher (primary school) **instituteur (m)**
teacher **professeur (m)**
telegram **télégramme (m)**
telephone **téléphone (m)**
to telephone, ring **téléphoner**
television (set) **télévision, télé (f)**
temperature, fever **fièvre (f)**
tender **tendre**
tennis **tennis (m)**
terminal **aérogare (f)**
terminus, terminal **terminus (m)**
terrace **terrasse (f)**
to test **tester**
test, exam **épreuve (f)**
testimony, evidence **témoignage (m)**
to thank **remercier**
thanks to you **grâce à toi**
thank you **merci**
that, it, so; about that **cela, ça**
that is to say **c'est à dire**
that's right **c'est vrai**
that, which, what, than (comp.) **que**
theatre **théâtre (m)**
then, after that **ensuite, puis**
there is, are **il y a**
there is, are, here you are **voilà**
there, then, that **là**
thick **épais/se**
thing **chose (f)**
to think **penser**
to think, reflect **réfléchir**
thirst **soif (f)**
about thirty **trentaine (f)**
this **ceci**
this, that, such **ce, cet, cette**
to throw **jeter**
ticket **ticket (m)**
tie **cravate (f)**
to tighten, close (up) **serrer**
tights **collant (m)**
time **temps (m)**
tip, point **pointe (f)**
tip **pourboire (m)**
tired, exhausted **fatigué/e**
tobacconists's **bar tabac, bureau de tabac (m)**
today **aujourd'hui**
tomato **tomate (f)**
tomorrow **demain**
tone **ton (m)**
too (much) **trop**
toothbrush **brosse à dents (f)**
toothpaste **dentifrice (m)**
top **haut**
at top speed **à toute vitesse**
tourist **touriste (m & f)**

tourist info. office **syndicat d'initiative (m)**
towards, to **vers**
towel, napkin **serviette (f)**
town **ville (f)**
traffic **circulation (f)**
traffic jam, bottleneck **embouteillage (m)**
traffic lights (red) **feu rouge (m)**
train **train (m)**
(travel) expenses **frais de voyages (m) (pl)**
travel, journey **voyage (m)**
traveller **voyageur (m), voyageuse (f)**
traveller cheque **chèque de voyage (m)**
tray **plateau (m)**
tree **arbre (m)**
triangular **triangulaire**
trousers **pantalon (m)**
trout **truite (f)**
true **vrai**
to try **essayer**
T-shirt **maillot de corps (m)**
Tuesday **mardi (m)**
tulip **tulipe (f)**
to turn (round, towards, to) **se retourner**
to turn, spin **tourner**
about twenty **vingtaine (f)**
twins **jumeaux, jumelles (m & f) (pl)**
tyre pressure **pression des pneus (f)**

U

umbrella **parapluie (m)**
uncle **oncle (m)**
under **sous**
underground **métro (m)**
underlined **souligné/e**
underpants **slip, caleçon (m)**
to understand **comprendre**
undertaking, firm **entreprise (f)**
underwear **sous-vêtements (m) (pl)**
to undo, untie **défaire**
university **université (f)**
unpleasant **désagréable**
unusual, incredible **extraordinaire**
up (above) **en haut**
to use, utilise **utiliser**
to use the fam. form 'tu' **tutoyer**
to use the polite form 'vous' **vouvoyer**
usherette **ouvreuse (f)**
usually **en principe**

V

vanilla **vanille (f)**
vase **vase (m)**
vegetable **légume (m)**
very **très**
very much, a lot **beaucoup**
Vietnamese **vietnamien/ne**
village **village (m)**
visit **visite (f)**
to visit **visiter**
voice **voix (f)**
vol-au-vent **bouchée à la reine (f)**

W

to wait, expect **attendre**
waiter, boy **garçon (m)**
waiter **serveur (m)**
waitress **serveuse (f)**
to wake up **se réveiller**
to walk, go, run, work, get along **marcher**
to walk across, through, to
    cross **traverser**
walk, stroll **promenade (f)**
walk, tread **allure (f)**
wall **mur (m)**
wallet **porte-feuille (m)**
walnut **noix (f)**
to want, have a fancy for s.th. **avoir
    envie de qch.**
to want, wish **vouloir**
wardrobe **armoire (f)**
warm **chaud/e**
to wash, to get washed **se laver**
to wash dishes **faire la vaisselle**
washing-machine **machine à laver (f)**
watch **montre (f)**
water **eau (f)**
wave **vague (f)**
wavy **bouclé/e**
way, manner, mode **façon (f)**
way, road **route (f)**
way through **passage (m)**
weather **temps (m)**
weather forecast **météo (f)**
Wednesday **mercredi (m)**
week **semaine (f)**
to weigh **peser**
weight **poids (m)**
welcome **bienvenu/e**
well, fine **bien**
what **qu'est-ce que**
what a pity, too bad **tant pis**
wheel **roue (f)**
when **quand**
where **où**
which, what (a) **quel/le**
which one **laquelle, lequel**
while, during **pendant que**
white **blanc/he**
who, whom, which, that **qui**
why **pourquoi**
wicked, evil, mischievous **méchant/e**
widowed, widow/er **veuf/ve**
wild **sauvage**
will **testament (m)**
to win, earn **gagner**
wind **vent (m)**
window **fenêtre (f)**
wine **vin (m)**
winner **gagnant (m)**
winter **hiver (m)**
with **avec**
without **sans**
without success **sans succès (m)**
woman, lady **femme (f)**
to wonder **se demander**
wonder **merveille (f)**
wonderful, fantastic **merveilleux/se**
wool **laine (f)**
work **travail (m)**
to work **travailler**
works, factory **usine (f)**

world **monde (m)**
worried, anxious **inquiet/ète**
worry, trouble **ennui (m)**
wounded, injured **blessé/e**
to write **écrire**

Y

year **an (m), année (f)**
yes **oui, si**
yesterday **hier**
yoghurt **yaourt (m)**
you (pl. and pol.form) **vous**
young **jeune**
younger, junior **cadet/te**
your (poss. adjective) **votre, vos**
youth **jeunesse (f)**